THE

OXYRHYNCHUS PAPYRI

VOLUME LXXIII

THE
OXYRHYNCHUS PAPYRI
VOLUME LXXIII

EDITED WITH TRANSLATIONS AND NOTES

IN HONOUR OF

PETER PARSONS AND JOHN REA

BY D. OBBINK AND N. GONIS

WITH CONTRIBUTIONS BY

R. S. BAGNALL	A. BENAISSA	A. K. BOWMAN
A. BÜLOW-JACOBSEN	D.COLOMO	J. CHAPA
T. GAGOS	H.-C. GÜNTHER	E. W. HANDLEY
R. HATZILAMBROU	N. LITINAS	M. MALOUTA
A. NODAR	C. E. RÖMER	P. SCHUBERT
D. N. SEDLEY	J. D. THOMAS	Y. TRNKA-AMRHEIN
S. R. WEST	J. WHITEHORNE	

Graeco-Roman Memoirs, No. 94

PUBLISHED BY
THE EGYPT EXPLORATION SOCIETY
WITH THE SUPPORT OF
THE ARTS AND HUMANITIES RESEARCH COUNCIL
AND
THE BRITISH ACADEMY
2009

TYPESET BY
THE STINGRAY OFFICE, MANCHESTER
PRINTED IN GREAT BRITAIN BY
THE CHARLESWORTH GROUP, WAKEFIELD
AND PUBLISHED BY
THE EGYPT EXPLORATION SOCIETY
(REGISTERED CHARITY NO. 212384)
3 DOUGHTY MEWS, LONDON WC1N 2PG

Graeco-Roman Memoirs

ISSN 0306-9222

ISBN-13 978 0 85698 182 1

N. GONIS	A. K. BOWMAN
D. OBBINK	R. A. COLES
P. J. PARSONS	J. R. REA
General editors	J. D. THOMAS
	Advisory editors

PREFACE

This volume publishes a selection of texts prepared to highlight recent work on the Oxyrhynchus Collection: in Part I, papyri of the Old and New Testaments. Part II offers Comedy Old and New: Aristophanes, a sizeable chunk of Menander's *Epitrepontes* (**4936**), and another from his *Georgos*. Part III presents previously unknown Greek literature, including a new papyrus of Empedocles (**4938**); a work by Thrasyllus (Tiberius' court astrologer and philosopher in residence) on the classification of Plato's dialogues (**4941**)—together with Dictys of Crete's account of the Trojan War in unpretentious prose, complete with its 'author's' own subscription (**4943–4944**). These add two new papyri of the Greek original to the two already known. They show more clearly the relation of the Greek original to the Latin version, casting doubt on the status of the latter as a straightforward translation. In **4939**, a distraught lover laments his girlfriend's untimely passing at considerable length in hexameter verse. A glimpse of the sleek, dark underbelly of Greek culture is afforded by a slice of Lollianos' novel *Phoinikika* (**4945**); a fragment of Hellenistic history (**4940**) may be the earliest textual attestation of the histories of Timagenes. Part IV showcases texts of previously known Greek literature of the Roman period uncommon among the papyri, while Part V presents texts at the subliterary level. On the documentary side, in part VI we find themes of extortion in petitions (**4953–4954**); a military muster, in Latin (**4955**); a letter on recovery from illness in high-flown Greek; a certified copy of a petition to a prefect (**4961**), which besides its impressive format has interesting though enigmatic implications for the use of Roman Law. **4965** is a Manichaean letter. **4956** is a census declaration, written in a standard scribal book-hand; **4967** contains a new but unread notarial signature. In **4966** we get what is possibly the first Egyptian member of the senate at Constantinople; and in **4967** the terms of employment of a public herald.

In editorial matters, Dr Gonis took responsibility for co-ordinating and overseeing most of the documentary section, Dr Obbink most of the literary one—both assisted by those expert readers whose contributions are only occasionally indicated in the editions. A special note of gratitude is due to Professors Donald Mastronarde and Nicholas Horsfall. A number of items are the revised product of dissertation work undertaken by A. Benaissa, R. Hatzilambrou, N. Litinas, M. Malouta, and A. Nodar. No less than in previous volumes, special thanks are due for the discerning judgement of Dr Benaissa in revision of copy and compilation of indexes, and to Dr Daniela Colomo for checking of collations, deft conservation, and eagle-eyed proof-reading. As in past volumes, Dr Jeffrey Dean of Manchester kindly provided expert professional and artistic assistance in matters of typesetting and typography. Without the guidance and financial support of the British Academy and the Arts and Humanities Research Council the continuing publication of the Oxyrhynchus Papyri would not be possible.

Most of the contributions in this volume were produced in honour of Peter Parsons and John Rea by editors who worked with these two in various capacities, commemorating a time when, as one contributor put it, 'Oxford breathed papyrology' ('even Latinists were made to do it'). The contributors join the rest of the General and Advisory editors of the Graeco-Roman Memoirs in expressing their thanks to both these scholars for their personal and professional contributions to the effort of making sense of Oxyrhynchus. Their careers, spanning well over a half-century, have rung in changes in our ways of working on the papyri that include the binocular microscope, the computer database, and digital images.

May 2009   D. OBBINK

CONTENTS

TEXTS

INDEXES

TABLE OF PAPYRI

V. SUBLITERARY TEXTS

VI. DOCUMENTARY TEXTS

RSB = R. S. Bagnall   AB = A. Benaissa   AKB = A. K. Bowman
AB-J = A. Bülow-Jacobsen   DC = D. Colomo   JC = J. Chapa
TG = T. Gagos   NG = N. Gonis   HCG = H.-C. Günther
EWH = E. W. Handley   RH = R. Hatzilambrou   NL = N. Litinas
MM = M. Malouta   AN = A. Nodar   DO = D. Obbink
CER = C. E. Römer   PS = P. Schubert   DNS = D. N. Sedley
YT-A = Y. Trnka-Amrhein   JDT = J. D. Thomas   SRW = S. R. West
    JW = J. Whitehorne

LIST OF PLATES

NUMBERS AND PLATES

NOTE ON THE METHOD OF PUBLICATION AND ABBREVIATIONS

The basis of the method is the Leiden system of punctuation; see *CE* 7 (1932) 262–9. It may be summarized as follows:

αβγ	The letters are doubtful, either because of damage or because they are otherwise difficult to read
. . .	Approximately three letters remain unread by the editor
[αβγ]	The letters are lost, but restored from a parallel or by conjecture
[. . .]	Approximately three letters are lost
( )	Round brackets indicate the resolution of an abbreviation or a symbol, e.g. (ἀρτάβη) represents the symbol ⌐, cτρ(ατηγόc) represents the abbreviation cτρ∫
⟦αβγ⟧	The letters are deleted in the papyrus
'αβγ'	The letters are added above the line
⟨αβγ⟩	The letters are added by the editor
{αβγ}	The letters are regarded as mistaken and rejected by the editor

Bold arabic numerals refer to papyri printed in the volumes of *The Oxyrhynchus Papyri*.

The abbreviations used are in the main identical with those in J. F. Oates *et al.*, *Checklist of Editions of Greek Papyri and Ostraca* (*BASP* Suppl. no. 9, ⁵2001); for a more up-to-date version of the *Checklist*, see http://scriptorium.lib.duke.edu/papyrus/texts/clist.html.

I. THEOLOGICAL TEXTS

4931. LXX, Psalm xc 3–8

96/77(b)   5.8 × 8.5 cm   Fifth century

Leaf from a papyrus codex with 11 lines of writing on each side; margins survive in part on all sides, but nowhere to more than 0.5 cm. With a written area of 5.5 × 7.5 cm, it belongs in Turner, *Typology of the Early Codex* Group 11, 'Miniature' Codices (p. 22).

The surviving leaf as reconstructed has 140.5 letters (counting ι as half letter) on → and 136.5 letters on ↓. The portion of the psalm missing before this has 144 letters (without title), i.e. it could fit on one page. The portion missing after the surviving leaf has 494.5 letters, i.e. 3.5 pages at a rate of 140 letters per page (average between the number of letters known for the three pages above-mentioned). Therefore the whole psalm would occupy nearly seven pages. A likely arrangement would be: two bifolia folded to give four leaves, which makes eight pages:

Page 1: left blank as a cover (→?)

Page 2: verses 1–3 (↓?)

Pages 3–4: **4931** → ↓

Pages 5–6 (↓→?) and 7–8 (↓→?): rest of the psalm with some blank space at the foot of page 8.

This reconstruction is compatible with the fact that the psalm has been written with no regard to the verse-division (but see below).

The script is a middle-sized hand to be ascribed to the 'formal-mixed' type or Severe Style. The execution is rather rough and rapid, so that irregularities and inconsistencies in letter shape and size are not surprising. It is roughly bilinear, apart from the uprights of ρ and γ, which protrude below the baseline, and of φ, which protrudes above and below the writing-space, and sometimes ι. On the whole the script tends to slant to the right. Letter size is sometimes reduced at line-end. Among the characteristics of individual letters, it is worth noting the narrow wedge of α; the big central body of φ; the diagonals of κ, which are detached from the upright; the flat top of c, in most occurrences apparently drawn as a separate stroke, which often ends with a sort of hook; the right-hand diagonal and upright of γ, which combine in a single stroke, protruding above the baseline and slightly curving to the left. The shape of individual letters and general graphic impression may be compared to P. Laur. IV 141, Ps xc 1–6 (see Cavallo–Maehler, *GBEBP* no. 19b), dated to *c*.485 AD, although the latter shows a completely upright script written with much less competence and more evident effort.

With regard to the layout, individual lines of the text do not correspond to the division into *stichoi* of the *textus receptus*. However, some traces suggest the use of dicolon to mark the end of a *stichos* (in →8 and in ↓5 the end of a *stichos* coincides with the end of a verse, and a blank space was possibly left before the beginning of the new verse; see ↓5 n.); dicolon perhaps occurs also in ↓2, again corresponding to verse-end, but no space can be discerned. Examples of this use of dicolon are to be found in PUG I 1 and XI **1352** (in the last item somewhat erratic). Inorganic diaeresis occurs in →5.

Psalm xc is well represented in papyri and parchments from Egypt. Table 1 identifies them by their numbers in A. Rahlfs, *Verzeichnis der griechischen Handschriften des Alten Testaments*, rev. D. Fraenkel, I i (Göttingen 2004), abbreviated R–F, and also by their numbers in J. van Haelst, *Catalogue des papyrus littéraires juifs et chrétiens* (Paris 1976), abbreviated vH. In the table the column 'Type of Text' includes a summary of the contents, and a rough classification of the texts. Most of these are or may have been single sheets, which presumably served as amulets. This psalm was a favourite text for such a use because of its exorcistic content; it appears also on personal jewellery (see vH 184–91; T. J. Kraus, *XXIV Congr. Proc.* 497–514; id., *Biblische Notizen* 125 (2005) 39–73).

A number of these items show a free use of the text of Psalm xc in a remarkable variety of arrangements and layouts. Three principal categories can be distinguished. (1) Items that use the text of Psalm xc alone (R–F 2105, 2124, 2020, 2062) or with minor additions (2106, 2179). (2) Items that omit parts of the text (2048) or select a short section of it (2081), with a strong preference for the incipit. (3) Composite items, which contain individual lines of this psalm together with quotations from other sources, mainly from the New Testament (2115, oS-54, oS-25, 2075, 2074).

As it stands, **4931** can be ascribed to the first category, but since it is clearly not a single sheet but one leaf from a codex we cannot prove that it did not contain other materials. The closest parallel to our text in size and format is 2124, a miniature codex; cf. also 2105, a single bifolium or a miniature codex. Of course, the miniature format is not confined to amulets (P. Köln IV p. 37; M. J. Kruger, *JTS* 53 (2002) 81–94); but a miniature codex that presents a careless text in informal script may well have served this function.

For collation I have used the edition of A. Rahlfs, *Psalmi cum Odis* (Göttingen 1979^3). In the notes, several spelling mistakes and spelling variations in the other papyrological witnesses have intentionally been recorded to offer a more precise picture of the level of linguistic competence peculiar to amuletic texts.

4931 presents no significant deviation from the *textus receptus*, except for two idiosyncratic omissions (perhaps simply mechanical mistakes) in →4 and ↓2.

Table 1: Papyri containing Psalm xc

R–F	vH	Published	Date	Material	Format	Provenance	Text Type[a]
1219	83, 235	Smithsonian Institution Libraries, Freer Gallery of Art, inv. no. o6.273	v, vii/viii	parch.	codex	?	Psalter (?)
2015	153	L. Delaporte, *Revue de l'Orient Chrétien* 18 (1913) 87–8 (descr.; ined.)	v/vi (R–F)	parch.	codex	Panopolis, White Monastery	Part of a Greek/Coptic Psalter (codex fragmented in different collections)
2020	201	P. Ryl. I 3	v/vi	pap.	sheet	Oxyrhynchus	**Ps xc 5–16** (originally the whole Ps?).
2031	195	P. Vindob. G 2312	iv (Henrici) vi/vii (Wessely)	pap.	sheet	?	M: **Ps xc 1b–2b**, Rm xii 1, Io i–ii, invocations partially in Coptic
2043	197	BKT VIII 12	vii/viii	parch.	sheet	?	**Ps xc 1b–6a.** Amu.?
2048	198	P. Gen. 6	vi	wood	codex[b]	?	**Ps xc 1b–7b, 10a–13a.** Amu.?
2062	199	BKT VIII 13	vi/vii (Turner) vii/viii (R–F)	parch.	sheet	?	**Ps xc 1b–13b** (the whole Ps meant to be included?) Amu.?
2074	196	PSI VII 759v (ZAW 78 (1966) 224)	v/vi	pap.	sheet	?	M: **Ps xc 1b–4a**, unidentified Coptic text (recto: Lc xv 33, Ps vii 15b, Mt xix 29)
2075	423	PSI VI 719	vi (*Anal. Pap.* 2 (1990) 27)	pap.	sheet?	Oxyrhynchus	M: incipts of the 4 Gospels, **Ps xc 1b**, beginning of the Pater noster, doxology. Amu.
2081	202	P. Bodl. 4	v/vi	pap.	sheet?	?	**Ps xc 13b–16b**
2105	200	XVII **2065**	v/vi	parch.	bifolium (mini-codex?)	Oxyrhynchus	**Ps xc 5b–10b** (originally the whole Ps). Amu.
2106	183	XVI **1928**v	v/vi	pap.	reused sheet	Oxyrhynchus	M: **Ps xc 1b–16b**, list of the 4 Gospels. Amu.?

R–F	vH	Published	Date	Material	Format	Provenance	Text Type[a]
2110	118	P. Bodm. XXIV	iii/iv	pap.	codex	Panopolis?	Psalter
2115	345	P. Oslo inv. 1644 (*SO* 24 (1945) 141–7) + P. Schøyen I 16	iv/v	pap.	sheet	Oxyrhynchus?	Mt vi 9–13, 2 Cor xiii 13, **Ps xc 1b–13a**. Amu.
2124	—	P. Lugd.-Bat. XXV 10	v	parch.	mini-codex (2 bifolia)	?	**Ps xc 1b–4c, 7b–9b**; at the end rephrased v. 2 of the Ps. Amu.
2131	731	BKT VI vii 1	vi (see *Anal. Pap.* 7 (1995) 57 n. 49)	parch.	sheet	Fayum	M: **Ps xc 1b–c**, incipits of the Gospels, Ps cxvii 6–7, Ps xvii 3a, Mt iv 23, liturgical formulae. Amu.
2166	—	P. Laur. iv 141	v	pap.	sheet	?	**Ps xc 1–6** (remains of a documentary text, which was written as first text; to write the Ps the sheet has been rotated 90°)
2179	—	P. Vindob. G 348 (*Vig. Chr.* 37 (1983) 400–4)	vi/vii	pap.	sheet	?	M: incipits of the 4 Gospels, **Ps xc 1b–16b** (but 7c–8 left out). Amu.
2199	—	P. Duke inv. 778 (see *BASP* 41 (2004) 93–113)	vi/vii	pap.	sheet	?	M: Pater noster, **Ps xc**, incipit of Ps xci, doxology. Amu.
0S-2	203	Cambridge UL T-S 12.187 etc.	v/vi	parch.	codex palimpsest	Cairo, Genisa	M: Aquila's version of Pss **xc** (89LXX)17, xci (90LXX), xcii (91LXX)10c, xcvi (95LXX)7a–12a, xcviii (97LXX)3a; cii (101LXX), ciii (102LXX)
0S-16	—	P. Berlin 21917 (*Suppl. Mag* I 26)	v	pap.	sheet	?	M: prayer against eye disease; **Ps xc 1b–1c**. Amu.
0S-25	917	P. Iand. I 6 (P. A. Kuhlmann, *Die Giessener literarischen Papyri und die Caracalla-Erlasse*, 1994, no. 5)	v/vi	pap.	sheet	Hermopolis (purchased)	M: exorcism of Salomon against disease and daemons; Pater noster (mixed tradition); allusion to **Ps xc 5f**, Ps xci 13. Amu.

R–F	vH	Published	Date	Material	Format	Provenance	Text Type[a]
0S-54 967		P. Princ. 107 (*Suppl. Mag.* I 29)	iv/v	pap.	sheet	?	M: prayer to the Archangel Michael against fever; **Ps xc 1b–2a** (partially paraphrased), Mt vi 9–11, Liturgia Marci p. 132 Brightman. Amu.
—	193	PGM II T2a	?	wood	tablet	?	M: **Ps xc 1a** (verso), declension of βοῖς (recto)
—	194	PGM II T2b	?	wood	tablet	?	M: **Ps xc 1a** (uncorrected and mutilated, verso), declension of βοῖς (recto)
—		W. Pleyte, A. Boeser, *Manuscrits coptes du Musée d'antiquités des Pays-Bas à Leide* (Leyden 1897), 441–79; LDAB 100023	v/vi	pap.	codex	Djeme	M: Coptic/Greek magical handbook: prayers of Gregorius Naz., correspondence between Christ and Abgar, list of the 7 sleepers of Ephesos and the 40 martyrs of Sebaste, incipits of the 4 Gospels, **Ps xc**.
—		P. Duke inv. 448 (*BASP* 43 (2006) 59–61)	vi/viii	pap.	sheet	?	**Ps xc 6–14** (originally the whole Ps) in Coptic. Amu.?
—		P. Heid. Kopt. 184 (see *Festschrift Elmar Edel* (Bamberg 1979) 332–7)	vi	pap.	sheet	Fayum	**Ps xc 11–16**. Amu.
—		T. IFAO s.n. (see *BIFAO* 101 (2001) 160–62; *Eulimene* 3 (2002) 201)	v/vi	wood	tablet from a codex	?	M: school exercise: schoolboy name, date, incipit of **Ps xc** repeated 8 times; names of months (syllabary on the other side)

a M = Miscellany, Amu. = Amulet.

b Reused tablet, part of a codex (front used for accounts).

→   θηρευτων κ[αι απο   (3)
     λογου ταραχ[ωδους
     εν τοις μεταφρε   4
     νοις επιϲκιαϲι ϲοι
5   κ̣αι ϋπο τας π̣τ̣ερυ
     γας αυτου ελπιεις
     οπλ̣ω κυκ[λ]ωϲι ϲε
     η̣ α̣λ̣η̣θ̣ε̣ι̣α̣ α̣υτο̣υ :
     ου φοβηθηϲ[η]   5
10   απο φοβου [νυ
     κτερινου [

↓   [απο βε]λ̣ους πετομενου
     [c.5].. απο ϲυμ   5–6
     πτωμ̣α̣τος και δαι
     μονιου μεϲημβρι
5   νου [ ] π̣εϲειται   7
     εκ το[υ κ]λειτου ϲο̣υ̣
     χιλια[ϲ] : και μυ
     ριας εκ δεξιων
     [ϲο]υ̣ προς ϲε̣ δε
10   [ουκ] ε̣γγιει
     [πλην] τοις οφθαλ   8

2 ταραχ[ωδους: so Rahlfs and papyri (ταραχοδους P. Duke inv. 778), apart from BKT VIII 13, which has the form ταραχοτου.

3–4 εν τοις μεταφρενοις: the other witnesses unanimously transmit ἐν τοῖς μεταφρένοις αὐτοῦ (εν τες μεταφρονεις [influenced by μεταφρονέω?] BKT VIII 13, εν ταις μεταφρεναις P. Duke inv. 778), but our scribe omitted αὐτοῦ.

4 επιϲκιαϲι (l. επισκιασει) ϲοι: so Rahlfs, BKT VIII 13, P. Lugd.-Bat. xxv 10: επιϲ]κιαϲι ϲε P. Oslo inv. 1644, but doubtful in XVI **1928** (ϲιο for ϲοι edd.; επιϲκλειϲιν? RAC): ϋποϲκιαϲ̣[ει ϲ]α̣ι P. Laur. IV 141: ελπιϲ P. Gen. 6 (probably because of accidental omission of the last two words of 4.1 and the whole of 4.2 apart from the final verb. Moreover, note that in the *textus receptus* the penultimate word of 4.2 is the same pronoun αυτου that occurs in 4.1): επιϲκιαϲι ϲε P. Duke inv. 778.

6 ελπιεις: so Rahlfs, XVI **1928**, P. Lugd.-Bat. xxv 10, (ελπι̣[εις] P. Vindob. G 348, ελ[πιεις] BKT VIII 12): ελπεις BKT VIII 13, ελπιϲ P. Laur. IV 141, P. Gen. 6 (but see 4 n.) and P. Duke inv. 778 by haplography of the double *i*-sound.

7 κυκ[λ]ωϲι (l. κυκλωϲει): so Rahlfs and papyri (κηκλοϲει BKT VIII 13, κυκλωϲη P. Laur. IV 141, κεκλωϲι P. Duke inv. 778, κυκλωϲιν XVI **1928**). After ϲε accidental traces?

8 At line-end it is possible to observe the lower dot of a dicolon, coinciding with verse-end: possibly blank space left; verse-end coincides here with line-end.

9–10 ου φοβηθηϲ[η] | απο φοβου: so Rahlfs, P. Vindob. G 348, BKT VIII 13 (ο⟨υ⟩ φοβ.), P.

Gen. 6, P. Ryl. I 3 ([ου φοβηθ]ηcη): ου φοβηθηcαι οι απο φοβου XVI **1928** (οι meant as οὐ or ἤ? [*ed. pr.*]): ου φοβη[θη]cη και απο φο[β]ου P. Laur. IV 141: οὐ φ[ο]βηθηcομαι ἀπὸ φόβου P. Duke inv. 778.

↓

1–2 [απο βε]λους πετομενου |[*c.*5] .. Spacing shows that the papyrus omitted something. The full text as printed in Rahlfs runs ἀπὸ βέλους πετομένου ἡμέρας, ἀπὸ πράγματος διαπορευομένου ἐν cκότει, ἀπὸ cυμπτώματος κτλ. The space and traces at the beginning of 2 would allow us to restore either (1) [εν cκοτ]ει or, as Dr Coles suggests, (2) [ημερα]c :. If (1) is right, the scribe jumped from -μένου to -μένου; if (2), from ἀπό to ἀπό. For the possible dicolon at verse-end, see 5 n.

Rahlfs's text is that of a substantial group of MSS, with P. Vindob. G 348, BKT VIII 13 (but τιαπορευομενον), P. Gen. 6, P. Duke inv. 778 (and probably BKT VIII 12 also, since the text breaks off with the first two letters of the participle δι[απορευομενου]). Another group, with XVI **1928** (but διαφορευομενου), XVII **2065**, P. Laur. IV 141 (but εν cκοτια) and P. Ryl. I 3, reverse the word order at the end of verse 6a, ἐν cκότει διαπορευομένου, the word order found in the Massoretic Text, supported by a witness from Qumran, 4QPs^b (see E. Ullrich et al., *Qumran Cave 4*, DJD XVI (Oxford 2000) 27). Note also that a leather roll from Qumran, 11QPsAp^a, presents a transposition between 6.1 and 6.2; see P. W. Flint, *The Dead Sea Psalms Scrolls and the Book of Psalms* (Leiden 1997) 94.

If **4931** 2 is to be restored as [εν cκοτ]ει, we can assume that the scribe's exemplar had the word order διαπορευομένου ἐν cκότει; if [ημερα]c :, it provides no evidence.

Note the spelling πετομενους in P. Gen. 6 and P. Ryl. I 3.

2–3 cυμ|πτωματος: so Rahlfs, XVII **2065**, P. Ryl. I 3: cυμπομaτoc XVI **1928**. At the end of 2 after cυμ, an apparently accidental dot at mid-height occurs.

5 -νου. The space before [ ] πεcειται suggests that a blank was left to mark the beginning of a new verse; and some unexplained ink after -νου, in the upper and lower parts of the writing space respectively, may represent a dicolon to mark the end of the previous verse. Cf. 10 n.

πεcειται: so Rahlfs, XVI **1928**, P. Vindob. G 348 (but πεcιται), P. Gen. 6, and apparently P. Duke inv. 778 (πεcι[ται]): πεcειτ]ον P. Ryl. I 3.

6 κ]λειτου cου: so XVI **1928** (κλητου), P. Vindob. G 348 ([κ]λιτου), XVII **2065** (κλιτου), BKT VIII 13 (κλητου), P. Ryl. I 3 (κριτου), P. Duke inv. 778 (κλιτ[o]υ): the same form is recorded in the apparatus of the edition by R. Holmes and J. Parsons, *Vetus Testamentum graecum cum variis lectionibus*, iii (Oxford 1823), as a variant transmitted by nine twelfth/thirteenth-century MSS: κλιτουc cου Rahlfs and P. Gen. 6. Since κλιτου is so widely attested, we should not take it as a mechanical error of haplography but as an example of a general tendency to decline third-declension neuters in -oc as second-declension masculine; see Gignac, *Grammar* ii 43–4.

7–8 χιλια[c] : και μυ|ριας: so Rahlfs, P. Vindob. G 348, BKT VIII 13, P. Gen. 6, XVII **2065**, P. Duke inv. 778 (χελειας και μηρ[ια]c): χιλια και μυρια XVI 1928: μ]υριας και μυρια[c P. Ryl. I 3 (a slip).

9 co]υ. This reading takes a high trace of ink as the end of the right-hand prong of Υ. There are other apparent traces, and perhaps we should consider (as Dr Coles suggests) cου] : or co]υ :; the dicolon here would mark the end of a *stichos*; see 5 n.

προc cε: so Rahlfs, BKT VIII 13, P. Lugd.-Bat. xxv 10, XVII **2065**: προ cε P. Ryl. I 3 (haplography of sigma): ποc cε XVI **1928** (mechanical error).

10 This line ends short by two average letters. Perhaps a blank was left to mark the end of the verse. But there is also a practical consideration: the scribe could not have fitted the next word, πλην, into the remaining space without severe compression and could not divide it. This may also apply to the end of →11.

D. COLOMO

4932. AMULET: PSALM LXXII 21–3

63 6B.62/c(1–3)c   14.1 × 6 cm   Fifth century

On one side of this fragment there are line-ends from an account of goods, written along the fibres in a semi-cursive hand assignable to the fourth/fifth centuries (3] εἰc cυνπλήρ(ωcιν) τιμ(ῆc) κρέ[ωc, 6] ὀπτοῦ καὶ λαχάνων, 7 τι]μ( ) πίccηc, 10 θρυδρακ( ), l. θριδακ( )). A piece was then cut from the account, turned over and rotated ninety degrees to the left, so that the writing on the back also runs with the fibres. Here a different hand has copied three verses of Psalm lxxii, of which the line-beginnings survive, with a preserved left-hand margin of 1.3 cm, upper margin of 1 cm, and lower margin of 1.7 cm. Since the upper margin is approximately as wide as the interlinear space, we cannot rule out that other lines of writing preceded. More likely, however, these three verses were written out alone, as a self-contained unit. In that case, assuming that the text was copied in full, without omitting any half-verses, we can reconstruct the original dimensions as 30 × 6 cm, a long strip with unusually long lines. Such dimensions suggest that **4932** was made to be used as an amulet, rolled up and hung round the neck; in fact two folds can be distinguished on the preserved fragment, one roughly in the middle, the other about 2.5 cm further to the right. The format is paralleled by three other psalm amulets: see Rahlfs–Fraenkel nos. 2069 (vi c.), 2098 (vii c.), and 2200 (v/vi). Amulets of this type were often suspended in small capsules; for a picture of such containers, see W. M. Flinders Petrie, *Amulets* (Warminster repr. 1972), plate XIX no. 133. For frequent use of psalm texts in amulets see: G. Schmelz, *ZPE* 116 (1997) 61–5; C. La'da, A. Papathomas, *Aegyptus* 81 (2001) 37–46; P. Köln X 405; C. La'da, A. Papathomas, *BASP* 41 (2004) 93–113; A. Delattre, *BASP* 43 (2006) 59–61. Other psalm amulets made up from recycled writing material previously used to write documents are Rahlfs–Fraenkel 2106 (v/vi c.), which contains the entire Psalm xc written on the back of a Byzantine protocol, and Rahlfs–Fraenkel 2075 (vi c.; see *Anal. Pap.* 2 (1990) 27), including extracts from Gospels, Pater Noster, and Psalm xc written on the back of a dating protocol.

4932 is written in a not fully skilled hand of the 'sloping majuscule' type, probably to be assigned to the fifth century. Compare *GBEBP* 14b, assigned to the first half of the fifth century on the basis of its similarity with a document of AD 423 (*GBEBP* 14a). The scribe has difficulty in holding a consistent baseline (the last third of line 1 is written higher). Notable letter-forms include: ⲁ usually triangular, but an instance of round ⲁ with loop open on top is to be found in 3; ⲏ with central stroke consisting of an oblique ascending from left to right (but the last ⲏ in 2 has a central stroke approaching a horizontal); ⲟ rather small, lying sometimes in the upper part of the writing space, sometimes at mid-height, sometimes approaching the baseline.

The orthography shows common phonetic errors ($\eta/o\iota$ twice, δ/ζ as well as $\epsilon\iota/\iota$). All this suits an amulet homemade on recycled papyrus.

The scribe marks the division between two *stichoi* with an oblique stroke in the upper writing space (for such reading marks, see G. Bastianini, *WS* 97 (1984) 198, with examples).

The text has been collated with the standard edition by A. Rahlfs, *Psalmi cum Odis* (Göttingen 1979³), which takes into account three other papyrological witnesses (Rahlfs–Fraenkel nos. 2063, 2039, and 2149). A point of textual interest in **4932** is the agreement with a group of witnesses—among them Rahlfs–Fraenkel 2039—in transmitting a variant (**4932** has a minimal spelling difference; see 1 n.). In 3 the slight variation in the word order from the other witnesses seems to be a simple slip.

ευφρανθη οι καρδι͆α μου νεφρη μ[ου ηλλοιωθηςαν και εγω εξουδενωμενος   21–2

και ουκ ενων ′ κτηνωζης εγεν[ομην παρα ςοι και εγω δια παντος μετα ςου   22–3

ε̣κρατηςας της χιρ̣ο̣[ς μ]ο̣υ τη[ς δεξιας

1 Note that in the standard text *stichos* 21 begins with ὅτι, here omitted because the *stichos* has been excerpted for an amulet.

ευφρανθη: ηυφρανθη B''-2039 (= vH 171,]ανθη) Sa La^G Aug: εξεκανθη R' Ga L'' 1219'. Cf. the comment in Rahlfs's edition, Proleg. § 13 (under 'Bo'), pp. 16–17; and Rahlfs, *Septuaginta-Studien* ii 67. For the loss of the augment, see Gignac, *Grammar* ii 240 with n. 1.

After μου **4932** omits και.

οι: l. ή.

The μ added in the space above the second α of καρδια, apparently by the same hand in smaller size (perhaps later: the ink appears to be lighter), is difficult to explain. If it is meant as καρδιαμ μου, it should be interpreted as assimilation of ν before μ in word-junction from an original accusative καρδιαν (see Gignac, *Grammar* i 166–7); but in any case in this context the accusative would be wrong.

νεφρη: l. νεφροί.

2 ενων (l. ἔγνων). For the aorist indicative of the form γινώσκω, with loss of γ before ν, see Gignac, *Grammar* i 176.

κτηνωζης: l. κτηνώδης.

εγεν[ομην: with B'-2039 (= vH 171) R T 1219': εγενηθην 2039 ([εγεν]ηθην) 2149 S L' 1219. In restoring the text in lacuna I have followed Rahlfs, but only *exempli gratia*: in fact, the alternative reading—also supported by a papyrological witness (2039)—could alternatively be restored, since it is only a letter longer. On the two readings cf. A. Pietersma, *Two Manuscripts of the Greek Psalter in the Chester Beatty Library Dublin* (Rome 1978) 44–5.

3 χιρο̣[ς (l. χειρός) μ]ο̣υ τη[ς δεξιας: χειρὸς τῆς δεξιᾶς μου cett.

D. COLOMO

4933. COLLECTION OF BIBLICAL EXCERPTS

63 6B.71/H (1–5) (e)	5.1 × 10.1 cm	Third/fourth century

Portion of a leaf, probably from a papyrus codex, with the remains of 18 lines on the ↓ side and of 21 lines on the → side. The text contains excerpts from the Old Testament (*testimonia*), except for an unidentified text on the ↓ side: Jeremiah xxxviii 24–6, Amos ix 11–12 on the ↓ side, and Psalm xvii 1–112 on the → side. On the ↓ side a lateral margin is extant to a maximum of 1.2 cm.

If we take ↓ 8 as basis, we have 10 letters, which occupy 4.2 cm. Assuming an average of 33 letters per line, we would obtain 13.8 cm. Adding margins on a minimum assumption of 1.5 cm each, we would have a page width of 17.5 cm, which corresponds to many in Turner's Group 5 (*The Typology of the Early Codex* 16–18). These codices mostly have heights of 25–30 cm. If we assume 25 cm, and deduct a minimum of 3 cm for upper and lower margin, and given that the fragment gets 18–21 lines into a height of 11 cm, we could guess that originally the page had *c.*40 lines. In any case we cannot determine with absolute certainty if this is a single leaf or belongs to a codex. However, on the ↓ side the text is badly aligned on the left, which may suggest that the text was copied—with some difficulty—when the (assumed) codex was already bound; if so, this must be the inner edge, and the sequence of the two pages should be ↓ → (I adopt this sequence in the text).

The script is an upright semi-documentary hand, only roughly bilinear. On the ↓ side letters are sometimes slightly enlarged at line-beginning (6 and 7), while on the → side some final letters are prolonged in an attempt to even the right-hand margin (15, 16, and 17). On the one hand, features typical of book-hand script can be distinguished in short sequences of letters of which each is clear-cut and without ligatures with its neighbours (e.g. →12). On the other hand, the presence of ligatures and the shape of certain letters recall documentary scripts. Therefore, the same letter can occur in two different shapes: N, for example, presents both the standard book-hand shape (e.g. →10, in the standard abbreviation of the *nomen sacrum*, and 12), but also the documentary form in one movement with the central stroke approaching the horizontal (e.g. →11). A good documentary parallel is P. Flor. I 36, AD 312 (see *Scrivere libri e documenti*, tav. CXXVIII); cf. also the hand of P. Bodm. VII (plate in *ed. pr.* before p. 13), X (plate in *ed. pr.* before p. 7), and XI (plate in *ed. pr.* before p. 47), parts of the miscellaneous codex vH 138 (= Rahlfs–Fraenkel p. 57–8, LDAB 2565) to be ascribed to the fourth century (cf. E. Crisci, *Segno e testo* 2 (2004) 122–6, esp. 124 nn. 56–7); P. Palau Rib. Lit. 4 (*Aegyptus* 66 (1986) 106–7, plate after p. 128), third/fourth century. I am inclined to assign the script of **4933** to the late third/early fourth century.

Organic diaeresis, in a ligatured form approximating an acute accent, appears in ↓3 (first ϵ), 7 (first ϵ of $\epsilon\kappa\epsilon\iota\nu[\eta$, 11 ($\eta$ of $\eta\mu[\epsilon\rho\alpha$), 13 (on ϵ of $\epsilon\theta[\nu\eta$), →14 (first η).

A *nomen sacrum* in the standard abbreviated form occurs in →10. Phonetic writing of Δαυειδ occurs in ↓8. The section of Ps xvii in →1–21 is written continuously without division into *stichoi*.

Such a collection of scriptural excerpts is to be ascribed to the well-known genre of *testimonia*, i.e. collections of Old Testament quotations ordered by subject and introduced by short headings, very popular in Qumran literature and early Christianity. Their themes concern messianism, eschatology, the Law, Christ's passion, death, and resurrection, the downfall of Israel, and the vocation of the Gentiles; see N. Fernández Marcos, *The Septuagint in Context: Introduction to the Greek Versions of the Bible* (Leiden 2000) 269–71; A. Steudel, in *Encyclopedia of the Dead Sea Scrolls*, ii (Oxford 2000), s.v. 'Testimonia', 936–8; P. Prigent, *Les Testimonia dans le christianisme primitif: L'Épître de Barnabé I–XVI et ses sources* (Paris 1961); J.-P. Audet, *RB* 70 (1963) 380–405; M. C. Albl, *'And Scripture Cannot Be Broken': The Form and Function of the Early Christian Testimonia Collection* (Köln 1999) esp. 65–9, 286–90; A. Falcetta, *NT* 45/3 (2003) 280–99; M. C. Albl, *Pseudo-Gregory of Nyssa: Testimony against the Jews* (Atlanta 2004) pp. xiii–xxi, esp. pp. xiii–xvi. An instructive example of a Christian *testimonia* collection is a codex of the fourth century, vH 299 = P. Oslo II 11 + P. Ryl. iii 460 (Rahlfs–Fraenkel 242–4 and 269, LDAB 3177), which contains Is xlii 3–4, lxvi 18–19, lii 15 – liii 3, liii 6–7, liii 11–12, Gn xxvi 13–14, an unidentified text, 2 Chr i 12, and Dt xxviii 8–11. According to A. Falcetta, *BJRL* 83 (2001) 3–19, the excerpted passages focus on the theme of God's servant persecuted and eventually rewarded, to be interpreted as *praefiguratio* of Christ's life, which becomes a model for the believer.

For **4933** one can similarly identify a common theme. A remarkable feature is the presence of Am ix 11–12, focusing on the restoration of the fallen tent of David, a very popular passage interpreted in a messianic sense and often included in collections of *testimonia*. A similar interpretation, to judge from the exegesis of Church Fathers, could be applied to Jr xxxviii 26 and Ps xvii 10^2: in the Jeremiah passage, the figure of God as liberator of his people and guarantor of its prosperity, followed by the image of the divine fulfilment of the human soul, and the awakening and the sweet sleep are to be interpreted as a *praefiguratio* of the resurrection; in Ps xvii God's role as saviour of David from the enemies through his descent in the world is to be interpreted as *praefiguratio* of Christ's *katabasis* at the end of the world. Thus the three passages of **4933** share a messianic dimension and seem to be used to illustrate Christ's mission, focusing on three main aspects: the redemption of mankind through the resurrection (Jr xxxviii 25–6), the foundation of the Church as the restored tent of David (Am ix 11–12), and Christ's *katabasis* and victory over sin and death (Ps xvii). This is further supported by the fact that Pseudo-Epiphanius, *Testimonia ex divinis et sacris scripturis*, includes Jr xxxviii 26 in the section concerning the resurrection of Christ, and Am ix 11 and Ps xvii 10^1 in the section concerning the advent of the Messiah.

Testimonia often show notable deviations from the standard text of the LXX or its recensions and the Massoretic Text (cf. Albl, *Scripture* 100–101, and id., *Pseudo-Gregory* p. xiv; for the specific case of vH 299, see Falcetta, *BJRL* 83 (2001) 6, 8–10). Unfortunately the fragmentary state of **4933** does not allow us to assess it in detail. The extent of lacunas suggests in some cases the possibility of omissions (see ↓1, 4 nn., and →2–6, 11–12 nn.); an idiosyncratic reading seems to occur in ↓4; a banal omission in →10; a slightly different word order in →10–11; cf. also →18.

In the preserved part of the text there is no clear-cut separation between individual passages, whereas in vH 299 individual quotations are introduced by the title of their respective book (see ↓6 n.). This may suggest that **4933** is a private copy: the informality of the script, and perhaps also the fact that the section of Ps xvii is written without arrangement into *stichoi*, could support this view. To this one could add that the reconstructed width of the page (10 cm + missing lateral margins) suggests a rather small format, which makes the codex easy to handle and transport, in other words, very practical for travelling teachers and missionaries (see Falcetta, *BJRL* 83 (2001) 17–18). vH 299, written in a clear but somewhat untrained hand and quite easy to handle thanks to its very narrow format (cf. Falcetta, *BJRL* 83 (2001) 6), may also be a personal copy. Private copies are also found among Jewish testimony collections, for example 4Q175 and 4QTanḥumin (cf. Albl, *Scripture* 89–90, and A. Steudel, *Der Midrasch zur Eschatologie aus der Qumrangemeinde (4QMidrEschat^{a.b})* (Leiden 1994) 179–80).

4933 ↓1–6 is the only papyrological witness of Jr xxxviii 24–6. **4933** ↓6–14 is the only Christian papyrological witness for this section of Amos, to which Jewish collections of scriptural passages may be added (cf. ↓6 n.). **4933** → overlaps with vH 114 (= Rahlfs–Fraenkel p. 396, LDAB 3438), containing Pss xvi 15 and xvii 3, parchment codex, vii–viii AD; vH 731 (= Rahlfs–Fraenkel p. 21, LDAB 6091), an amulet on parchment containing Ps xvii 2 together with other biblical quotations, vi–vii AD; vH 115 (= Rahlfs–Fraenkel p. 406, LDAB 3383), containing Ps xvii 7–8, 9–11, parchment codex, vi–vii AD.

The text has been collated with the following editions: J. Ziegler, *Ieremias, Baruch, Threni, Epistula Ieremiae* (Göttingen 1976²); id., *Duodecim prophetae* (Göttingen 1967); A. Rahlfs, *Psalmi cum Odis* (Göttingen 1979³).

↓   .   .   .   .

κ̣α̣ι εν[οικουντες εν πολεcιν Ιουδα και εν παcη τη γη	Jr xxxviii 24
α̣υτου α̣[μα γεωργω και αρθηcεται εν ποιμνιω ο	24–5
τ̣ι εμεθυcα̣ π̣[αcαν ψυχην διψωcαν και παcαν	
ψυχην εψ̣.[c.12? ενεπληcα δια	25–6
5 τουτο εξεγ[ερ]θ[ην και ειδον και ο υπνοc μου η	
δυc μοι εγενε[το εν τη	26; Am ix 11
ημερα εκειν[η αναcτηcω την cκηνην	

Δαυειδ την π[επτωκυιαν και ανοικοδομησω

τα πεπτωκοτ[α αυτης και τα κατεσκαμμενα αυ

10   της αναστη[σω και ανοικοδομησω αυτην

καθως αι ημ[εραι του αιωνος οπως εκζητη   11–12

σωσιν οι κατ[αλοιποι των ανθρωπων και

παντα τα εθ[νη εφ ους επικεκληται το ονομα

μου επ αυ[τους   c.22   12; ?

15   νεστη[

πορευ[

]σου[

].[

·   ·   ·   ·

8 1. Δαυιδ

→   ·   ·   ·   ·   ·

αυτου και εκ χειρος Cαουλ και ειπεν κ̅ε̅ αγα[Ps xvii 1–2

πησω κ̅ε̅ η ισχυς μου κ̅ς̅ στερεωμα μου και] κατα φ[υ   2–3

γη μου και ρυστης μου ο θ̅ς̅ μου βοηθος μο]υ και ε[λ

πιω επ αυτον υπερασπιστης μου και κε]ρ[α]ς σωτη[ρι

5   ας μου αντιλημπτωρ μου αινων επι]καλεσωμαι

κ̅ν̅ και εκ των εχθρων μου σωθησο]μαι περιεσχον   4–5

με ωδινες θανατου χειμαρρ]ο[ι] ανομιας εξετ[α

ραξαν με ωδινες αδου περι]εκυκλωσαν με   5–6

προεφθασαν με παγιδες θαν]ατου και εν τ[ω   6–7

10   θλιβεσθαι με επεκαλεσα]μην κ̅ν̅ και εκ[ε

κραξα προς τον θ̅ν̅ μου ηκο]υσεν εκ ναου τη[ς

φωνης μου και η κραυγη] μου ενωπιον α[υ

του εισελευσεται εις τα ωτα] αυτο[υ] και εσα   7–8

λευθη και εντρομος εγενηθη] η γη και τα θεμε

15   λια των ορεων εταραχθη]σαν και εσαλευ

θησαν οτι ωργισθη αυτοις ο θ̅ς̅ α]νεβη καπνος   8–9

εν οργη αυτου και πυρ απο προσ]ωπου αυτου

κατεφλογισεν ανθρακες ανη]φθησαν

απ αυτου και εκλινεν ουρανον κα]ι κατεβη   9–10

20   και γνοφος υπο τους ποδας αυτου κ]αι επεβη   10–11

επι χερουβιν και επετασθη ε]πε[τασθη

·   ·   ·   ·

↓

1–6 It is worth investigating the relationship between this passage and the following. The latter, a typical testimonial excerpt, focuses on the restoration of the ruined tent of David, symbol of the alliance between God and Israel, to be interpreted in a messianic sense as *praefiguratio* of the new alliance between God and mankind established by Christ through the foundation of the Church. Jr xxxviii 24–6 belongs to a speech by God starting in 23 (which is very likely to have been included in the lost part of **4933**), where God appears as the liberator from the captivity (ἀποϲτρέψω τὴν αἰχμαλωϲίαν) and guarantor of the prosperity of his people in the land of Judah. Thus one could see a coherent thematic development between the two passages (and eventually a plausible connection with Ps xvii on the following page).

From a TLG search it emerges that 23 and 24 seem not to have had a great echo in scriptural and patristic literature (24 together with 26 is briefly explained by Joannes Chrysostomus, *Fragmenta in Jeremiam* PG 64, 980.12–26 in a rather literal sense). 25 and the second half of 26 are quoted by Didymus Caecus, *Commentarii in Zacchariam* 1.275–6 and interpreted, together with other quotations, in a messianic sense as *praefiguratio* of Christ's resurrection. Moreover, 26 is listed in Pseudo-Epiphanius, *Testimonia* 74.4, in the section containing the scriptural passages related to Christ's resurrection (ο̄δ̄ ὅτι ἀναϲτήϲεται). It is worth noting that 25 contains two popular scriptural metaphors: the thirsty soul (cf. for instance Ps xli 2–3 and Ps lxii 2) and the hungry soul (cf. for instance Ps cvi 92 and Is xlviii.10; but see the textual problem in **4933** ↓4 n.), both echoed in NT Mt v 6.

As said above, it is plausible to assume that the missing part of the text included at least Jr xxxviii 23, but we have no good reason to think that the excerpt from Jeremiah was much longer: on the basis of the evidence concerning *testimonia* collections, quotations from individual books usually include no more than a couple of verses (see the tables offered by Albl, *Scripture* 108, 129–31, 135–6, 143, 151, 180–81, 199, 281–3). In any case the section of Ps xvii in **4933** → is longer (11 verses) than the other excerpts.

1 The *textus receptus*, as printed by Ziegler, which I have restored only *exempli gratia*, would produce a line of 38.5 letters (counting iota as a half-letter), while the average is 33. One could assume that something has been left out. Since **4933** is an informal copy, we need not expect uniformity in the layout of the page.

4 ψυχην εψ̣[. After ψυχην the *textus receptus* has πεινωϲα ενεπληϲα· δια κτλ. There are two problems here. (1) The phrase is too short for the space, unless the scribe added αγαθων after ενεπληϲα, an addition attested by 88 (sub ※) *L'*: ex 14 Lc 1.53. (2) The last surviving letters cannot be reconciled with πει[νωϲαν. εψ seems certain; the last traces suggest that something has been overwritten, but they may suit the left-hand branch of γ. Yet I can find no parallel for e.g. εψυ[γμενην αγαθων ενεπληϲα or εψυ[ξα και αγαθων ενεπληϲα.

5 εξεγ[ερ]θ[ην. Grammatically, we expect εξηγερθην. The scribe wrote ε instead of η by mistake, or replaced εξηγερθην και with εξεγερθειϲ.

6 εγενε[το: with A (cf. li 22): ἐγενήθη cett. (Ziegler).

On the basis of the next line we have to assume that the passage from Am ix 11 begins in the part now lost. There would be space for the name of the book from which the new passage comes between two blank spaces, e.g. εξ Αμωϲ or simply Αμωϲ. The title of the book of individual quotations occurs in vH 299 on a fresh line and surrounded by short vertical strokes; see Falcetta, *BJRL* 83 (2001) 6–7 and 17 (parallels with comparable introductory phrases in Cyprian, *Ad Quirinum*, a work based on *testimonia*); on introductory formulas of quotations in *testimonia*, see Steudel, *Midrasch* 138–9, and Albl, *Scripture* 202.

6 ff. Am ix 11, containing the motif of the restoration of David's tent, is one of the most popular passages interpreted in a 'Messianic' sense, both in the Qumran scrolls (see P. W. Flint, in *Encyclopedia of the Sea Dead Scrolls*, i (Oxford 2000) 180 s.v. 'David: David in Eschatological and Messianic

Traditions'; cf. Albl, *Scripture* 45, and J. Lust, *Messianism and the Septuagint* (Leuven 2004) 30, 83, 125 n. 34) and in the Christian tradition. In particular, among Qumran texts, it occurs in a collection of *testimonia*, 4Q174, *c.*100 BC (= J. M. Allegro, *Qumran Cave 4.I (4Q158–4Q186)*, *DJD* V (Oxford 1968) no. 174; Steudel, *Midrasch* 138–9; Albl, *Scripture* 91) and CD VII 16 (the Damascus Document; see Steudel, *Midrasch* 174–8; cf. J. M. Baumgarten, *Qumran Cave 4.XIII: The Damascus Document (4Q266–273)*, *DJD* XVIII (Oxford 1996): Damascus Document[d], 4Q266 (late first century BC) Frg. 3 iii, 17, p. 43–5). In Act xv.16 it occurs with variants (μετὰ ταῦτα ἀναστρέψω καὶ ἀνοικοδομήσω τὴν σκηνὴν Δαυὶδ τὴν πεπτωκυῖαν, καὶ τὰ κατεσκαμμένα αὐτῆς ἀνοικοδομήσω καὶ ἀνορθώσω αὐτήν) and agrees with 4Q174, col. iii 12 and CD VII 16 against MT and LXX, as observed by J. de Waard, *A Comparative Study of the Old Testament Text in the Dead Sea Scrolls and in the New Testament* (Leiden 1965) 24–6. This suggests the possibility that all the three works go back to a collection of *testimonia*, also because 4Q174 and Act xv 16 contain a vague introductory formula (in the Greek form καθὼς γέγραπται) without indicating the source of the quotation, which is typical for testimonial collections; see A. Steudel, *Encyclopedia of the Dead Sea Scrolls* 938 s.v. 'Testimonia'; cf. ead., *Midrasch* 138–9, and Albl, *Scripture* 198 n. 145. For the interpretation of the passage in a messianic sense in Christian authors, cf. M. Black, 'The Christo-logical Use of the Old Testament in the New Testament', *NTS* 18 (1971–2) 2–4; C. H. Dodd, *According to the Scriptures: The Sub-Structure of New Testament Theology* (London 1952) 106, 108; Albl, *Scripture* 45. Among patristic literature, note especially that the passage appears in Pseudo-Epiphanius, *Testimonia* 5.4, in the section including the scriptural passages concerning the advent of the Messiah (ἒ ὅτι ἥξει; cf. →1–21 n.). Eus., *DE* Book 2, chap. 3, sections 5–6, a work evidently based on *testimonia* (see Albl, *Scripture* 141–2), quotes Am ix 11–12 in the LXX form (including also ix 9–10) within a series of passages concerning the downfall of Israel.

In **4933** the passage can basically be reconstructed in the LXX form.

10 αναϲτη[ϲω και ανοικοδομηϲω: ανοικοδομηϲω και ανορθωϲω 764 = Act xv 16 (cf. ↓6 ff. n.): αναϲτηϲω και οικοδομηϲω V.

11 I have reconstructed the lost part of the line e.g. according to Ziegler's text. Some of the witnesses (A′-49′′ 36 130′-239 = Act xv.17) add the particle αν after οπωϲ: the space available in lacuna would be enough to include it, although it is not necessary.

12 I have reconstructed the lost part of the line *exempli gratia* according to Ziegler's text. Some of the witnesses—A′′-49′-198-407-456-534 86^mg SyhArab = Act xv 17 (cf. ↓6 ff.)—add τον κυριον after των ανθρωπων. Here there would be space to add it in the form of the *nomen sacrum* τον κ̅ν̅.

14 ff. μου επ αυ[τουϲ. The letters surviving in 15 and 16 do not fit the quotation from Amos as transmitted. Therefore, unless there was a very substantial variant, the quotation must end some-where in the missing part of 14. Its next phrase, λεγει κ̅ϲ̅ ο ποιων ταυτα would just leave room for the next text to begin at the line-end, where a supplement like α]|νεϲτη seems probable. However, it is always possible that this phrase was omitted altogether or in part (dropping ο ποιων ταυτα), since such an omission would not alter the basic sense of the passage.

14–18 I have not been able to identify this text. In principle it might be a new excerpt, or an ex-egetical comment on the preceding text (for such comments see Albl, *Scripture* 66). If the latter, it may have followed directly after the text which it explains; if the former, we would expect at least a blank space, and perhaps also a book-title, before it (see 6 n.). In 15 νεϲτη[may be divided -νεϲ τη[, but if the letters belong together the most likely restoration would be α]|νεϲτη[, ε]|νεϲτη[, ϲυ]|νεϲτη[, or one of their compounds. Of these, α]|νεϲτη[could be combined with 16 (-)πορευ[. These two verbal forms often occur together in a LXX narrative, e.g. Jon iii 3 καὶ ἀνέστη Ιωνας καὶ ἐπορεύθη εἰς Νινευη; cf. Nu xvi 25, 3 Rg xviii 27, xxiii 16, 4 Rg vi 2, 2 Esr x 6. More interesting, however, is 2 Chr xxiv 20 (a reproach by the priest Azarias under God's inspiration): καὶ **ἀνέστη** ἐπάνω τοῦ λαοῦ καὶ εἶπεν τάδε λέγει κύριος. τί **παραπορεύεϲθε** τὰς ἐντολὰς κυρίου; καὶ οὐκ εὐοδήϲεϲθε, ὅτι ἐγκατελίπετε τὸν κύριον, καὶ ἐγκαταλείψει ὑμᾶς (here the sequence πορευ- is to be found in the compound **παραπορεύεϲθε** in the sense of 'to disobey'). Such a passage would be compatible with the preceding excerpt from Amos, since both focus on the relationship between God and men. However, the precise wording cannot be restored in **4933** (line 15 would have 43 letters, unless something (τάδε λέγει κ̄ς̄?) was omitted), and the sequence]ϲου[in 17 is not compatible with it.

18   ] . [, traces in the upper, middle, and lower part of the writing-space: possibly ϡ.

→

1–21 Psalm xvii was originally an ode by David to thank God for victory over his enemies. In the section preserved in **4933**, David represents God as the saviour and liberator from the danger of death, which is expressed through the metaphor of drowning: God hears his cry, his anger causes an earthquake, and he descends in a storm cloud. In a broad sense, this representation of God is compatible with the figure of the restorer and guarantor of the 'alliance' expressed with the metaphor of David's tent in the passage from Amos. As in the case of the Jeremiah and Amos passages, interpretations in Christological and eschatological senses can be traced back to patristic literature: the descent of God is understood as *praefiguratio* of the *katabasis* of Christ at the end of the world, the victory of David on his enemies as *praefiguratio* of the victory of Christ over sin and death. See Eusebius, *Commentaria in Psalmos* PG 23, 165.52–53, 168.1–50, 169.1–36; cf. also id., *DE* 6.1.1–4, where Ps xvii 9–12² is quoted and explained in the same Christological direction. Moreover, Eusebius (*DE* 10.8.33) inserts Ps xvii 2, where David addresses an invocation to God as his strength, foundation, refuge, saviour, helper, protector, horn of his refuge, and his succour, in a Christological context through a comparison with the invocation addressed by Christ to his Father at the moment of his death on the cross. Note also that Ps xvii 10¹ is included by Pseudo-Epiphanius, *Testimonia* 5.46, in the section concerning the coming of the Messiah (ε̄ ὅτι ἥξει). Probably **4933** also contained v. 12, where the image of the ϲκηνή occurs, to be interpreted as *praefiguratio* of the Church as in the Amos passage: this word would function as a 'catchword' connecting the two passages in the collection.

1 κ̄]ε̄. In **4933** the horizontal stroke of the *nomen sacrum* is not preserved.

2–6 I have reconstructed these sections *exempli gratia* according to the text printed by Rahlfs. It must be said that the number of letters per line is slightly higher (lines 2 and 3 would have 36 letters, line 4 37, line 6 *c.*35; line 5 with 34 letters is acceptable) in comparison with the rest of the text. This leads us to assume a different text, perhaps a simple omission: for example in 2, 3, and 4 a μου could easily be omitted. In fact, the textual tradition for v. 3 of Ps xvii records the omission of occurrences of μου in several places in some MSS.

5   επι]καλεϲωμαι: επικαλεϲομαι cett. Either a mere slip or a case of ω instead of ο (Gignac, *Grammar* i 275–7); the parallelism with ϲωθηϲομαι in v. 4² requires the future indicative.

8 περι]εκυκλωϲαν: περιεϲχον U: ex 5.

10 **4933** omits the article τον before the *nomen sacrum*, which is unanimously transmitted by the rest of the tradition: probably a mere slip.

10–11 **4933** apparently has a slightly different word order, not attested in the rest of the witnesses: the verb εκεκραξα precedes the phrase προϲ τον θ̄ν̄ μου instead of following it. In this case the *chiasmus* of the *textus receptus* in v. 7 (επεκαλεϲαμην τον κυριον και προϲ τον θεον μου εκεκραξα) is replaced by a parallel collocation of verbal forms and related object-phrase.

11–12 After εκ ναου the textual tradition is as follows: αγιου αυτου φωνηϲ μου B′ L′ A′′ (text printed by Rahlfs): αγιου αυτου τηϲ φωνηϲ μου U R. αγιου is obelized in Ga, omitted in La^G = MT. **4933** seems to contain an article in the genitive to be referred to φωνηϲ (as in U R), i.e. αγιου αυτου is apparently omitted. If so, line 12 would consists of 29 letters, under average but perhaps still acceptable.

13 και: om. U VulgGa^c.

14 και: om. Vulg.

15 και: om. U.

17 απο προc]ωπου: εναντιον B.

18 I have reconstructed this line e.g. according to Rahlfs's text: it would contain 28 letters, slightly fewer in comparison with the other lines. One could suppose that it contained a different text. At this point the textual tradition is as follows: κατεφλογιϲεν B'' U' Ga A: καταφλεγηϲεται *L''* 55: καταφλεχθηϲεται 1219: καταφλογιϲεται R(vid.), *exardescet* La (La^(G)Aug -*cit*, cf. proleg. § 23). ανθρακεϲ add. πυροϲ Bo ex 13.

20 επεβη: ανεβη U.

D. COLOMO

4934. First Letter of Peter i 23 – ii 5, 7–12

102/96(c)   9.5 × 15 cm   Late third or early fourth century
𝔓^125   Plates II–III

   I am both conscious of the honour of participating in this volume and at the same time sincerely grateful that thereby I may acknowledge my own immense debt to Professor Peter Parsons as a teacher and as a master of humane scholarship. In LX **4009**, P. J. Parsons, in collaboration with D. Lührmann, edited a fragment of a codex that they ascribed with some doubts to the Gospel of Peter. Whether it belongs to this gospel or not is still a subject of dispute (cf. T. Kraus, T. Nicklas, *Das Petrusevangelium und die Petrusapokalypse* (2004); D. Lührmann, *Die apokryph gewordenen Evangelien* (2003)), but in any case the text is an early witness to the non-canonical Petrine tradition in Oxyrhynchus, a tradition that is also attested by another fragment, perhaps from the same gospel (XLI **2949**, second–third century), and by other apocryphal texts related to the figure of Peter such as X **1224** (fourth century) and VI **849** (fourth century); see E. J. Epp, *JBL* 123 (2004) 14–18. Up to now, the canonical Petrine tradition in Oxyrhynchus has been restricted to a fragment on parchment of 1 Peter (XI **1353** = 0206), dated by the editors to the fourth century. **4934**, if it has been correctly dated, provides now the earliest evidence of the letters of Peter in this city and is contemporary with P. Bodm. VIII (third–fourth century) (𝔓^72), which contains an almost complete text of 1 and 2 Peter. The two other papyri of the letters of Peter published so far are Pap. Castr. II (fourth century) (𝔓^81) and P. Bodm. XVII (seventh century) (𝔓^74).

   4934 is a tattered, electric-guitar-shaped fragment, broken on all sides, which preserves the upper part of a leaf of a codex. The hand is a medium-sized, slightly right-sloping, rather informal version of the formal mixed group. On the whole it is bilinear, except for ρ, γ, φ, and ϯ. The letters are written separately with no ligatures. Although on some occasions ⲁ is written cursively in one stroke, most times it is written in two, the bow being either sharply angled or rounded and the oblique recurved. ω is rather wide with its curved sides meeting in the centre. γ is Y-shaped, with a high intersection. The descending diagonal of κ, and sometimes x, tends to finish with a little curve. Occasionally ʌ has a top curving to the left over the first stroke. The middle of м is deep, almost reaching the line. This type of hand is very difficult to date. It shows some similarities with P. Flor. II 108 (*GLH* 22a), a text of the *Iliad* that bears on the back a letter of the Heroninus archive (mid third century), and can also be compared with I **2** ($\mathfrak{P}^1$) and LXIV **4401** ($\mathfrak{P}^{101}$), both dated by the editors to the third century. However, **4934** shows few traits of the severe style and has some elements characteristic of P. Herm. 4 and 5 (*c.*325) (*GBEP* 2a and *GMAW*² 70) and other MSS of the early fourth century (*GBEP* 1–3); it can be also compared with VII **1008** ($\mathfrak{P}^{15}$), which has been dated to the fourth century by the editors and to the third century by Aland and Aland (*The Text of the New Testament* 97). A date in the late third or early fourth century for **4934** would be probable.

On the right-hand of ↓ there are remains of a margin of 0.7 cm. On → a margin of 1.5 cm on top and 0.5 on the left-hand side are visible. There are traces of 20 lines in → and 24 in ↓. The number of letters to the line varies from 19 to 23 in → and from 19 to 25 in ↓. The original length of the line was *c.*10 cm. This would give a written area of *c.*10 × 18 cm, which suits Turner's category 8. Assuming a standard text, there is a gap of 10 lines between the front and the back, which gives a page of *c.*30 lines, and *c.*90–92 lines missing from the beginning of the letter to the first line of **4934**, which means that about three pages of text have been lost. This suggests that the letter probably began on a verso page, and might have been part of a codex containing other books. Considering a Nestle–Aland text of 1,648 words, the whole letter would have occupied *c.*27.5 pages.

Inorganic trema over ι and υ is visible in lines →8, 13, and 17 and ↓21, 22, and 23. The *nomina sacra* attested are $\overline{χ[c}$ and $\overline{θω}$ in lines →15 and 19 and $\overline{θυ}$ in ↓14. No other lectional signs are preserved. The text presents some misspellings and phonetic mistakes (→13, 15, and 18, and probably →14). In ↓5 we might have to read κε for και. An apparent new reading in →11 should be probably considered a mistake by the scribe. ↓14 may also conceal a minor new reading (see ↓13–14 n.).

The verses attested in **4934** have previously appeared in $\mathfrak{P}^{72}$ and overlap with those in $\mathfrak{P}^{74}$.

The supplements in the transcriptions and the information in the apparatus are taken from Nestle–Aland, *Novum Testamentum graece* (1993²⁷). The text is collated with Nestle–Aland²⁷; B. Aland, K. Aland, G. Mink, K. Wachtel, *Novum Testamentum graecum: Editio critica maior* iv (2000); W. Grunewald, K. Junack, *Das Neue Testament auf Papyrus* i: *Die Katholischen Briefe* (1986); Tischendorf, *Editio octava critica maior*; and W. Thiele, *Epistulae Catholicae: Vetus Latina* (1958). All abbreviations and symbols are those of Nestle–Aland²⁷, except that Old Latin MS letters are prefixed by Lvt.

For the text of 1 Peter, see K. Aland, *Text und Textwert der griechischen Handschriften des Neuen Testaments*, Part I: *Die Katholischen Briefe*, 3 vols. (1987).

→　με]νοντος δ[ιοτι πασα σαρξ　　　　　　i 23–4
　　ως] χορτος κ[αι πασα δοξα
　　ω]ς ανθος χ[ορτου εξηραν
　　θη ο] χορτος κα[ι το ανθος εξε
5　πεσεν] το δε ρη[μα κ̄ῡ μενει εις　　　　25
　　τ]ον αιωνα [τουτο δε εστιν
　　το ρημα το ε[υαγγελισθεν
　　εις ϋμας απο[θεμενοι ουν πα　　　　ii 1
　　σ]αν κακιαν κ[αι παντα δολον
10　κα]ι υποκρις[ει]ς και φ[θονους
　　και συνκαταλαλια ως α[ρτιγεννη　　2
　　τα βρεφη τ[ο λ]ογικον α[δολον
　　γελα επιπ[οθ]ησατε ϊν[α
　　αυτων αυξ[η]θητε ει[ς σωτη
15　ριαν ει ευγεσασθε οτι χ[̄σ̄ ο κ̄σ̄　　3
　　προς ον προσε[ρ]χ[ομενοι λι　　　4
　　θον ζωντα ϋπο α[νθρωπων μεν
　　α[π]οδεδοκασμ[ενον παρα
　　δε θ̄ω̄ εκλεκτον [εντιμον
20　κ[α]ι αυτοι ω[ς.]....[　　　　　5

　　.　　.　　.　　.　　.　　.

↓　　　　　　].[
　　απ]ε[δ]οκιμ[ασαν　　　　　ii 7
　　οι οικοδομουντες] ουτος ε[γενη
　　θη εις κεφαλην γω]νιας κα[ι λι　　8
5　θος προσκομματος].ε πετρ[α
　　σκανδαλου οι π]ροσκοψου[σιν
　　τω λογω απειθουν]τες εις ο [και
　　ετεθησαν υμεις] δε γεν[ο]ς εκ[λεκ　　9
　　τον βασιλειον ι]ερατ[ε]υμ[α ε
10　θνος αγιον λαος] εις περιποιη
　　σιν οπω]ς τας [αρ]ετας εξ[.]γ..[
　　].[.].τ[. υ]μας καλεσαντος [ει]ς
　　το θ]αυ[μ]αστον φως οι ποτε.υ　　　10
　　....].ου νυν [δε] λαος θ̄ῡ ο[ι
15　ουκ ηλ]εημενο[ι ν]υν δε ελ[ε]η
　　θεντε]ς αγαπητ[οι] παρακαλω　　　11

ωϲ παροικου]ϲ κ[αι] παρεπιδη
μουϲ απε]χεϲ[θαι] των ϲαρκι
κων επιθυ]μιων αιτινεϲ
20   ϲτρατευο]νται κ[α]τα της ψυ[χηϲ
την αναϲτ]ροφην ϋμων εν   12
τοιϲ εθν]εϲιν καλην ϊνα
εν ω κατ]αλαλ[ουϲι]ν ϋμω[ν
                    ].[

            .   .   .   .   .

→

1 με]νοντοϲ δ[ιοτι: the traces after ϲ are very slight, but an oblique descending to the right is still visible. The papyrus did not add ειϲ τον αιωνα (1838 and few MSS ειϲ τουϲ αιωναϲ) after μενοντοϲ with K L P 𝔐 Lvt (l t) vg^{cl.ww} sy^p; Prisc. It is also omitted by 𝔓^{72} ℵ A B C Ψ 33. 81. 323. 945. 1241. 1505. 1739 *al* vg^{st} sy^h co; Hier.

Instead of διοτι, 𝔓^{72} reads οτι. Ψ and 1852 read διο.

1–2 παϲα ϲαρξ | [ωϲ χορτοϲ: spacing suggests that the papyrus read ωϲ with 𝔓^{72} ℵ^{*.(1)} B C P 049 𝔐 sy^{hmg} co. It is omitted by ℵ^2 A Ψ 33. 323. 614. 945. 1241. 1505. 1739 *al* Lvt (l) vg^{mss} sy; Aug.

2 κ[αι: there appears to be a horizontal mark above kappa.

Spacing after δοξα suggests that the papyrus did not read αυτηϲ (𝔓^{72} ℵ^2 A B C 33. 81. 614. 945. 1241. 1505. 1739 *al* lat sy bo), αυτου (ℵ^* bo^{ms}) or ανθρωπου (K L P Ψ M; Aug^{pt}), which are also omitted by 322 and 323.

3 χ[ορτου: omitted by 𝔓^{72}.

3–4 εξηρανθη ο] χορτοϲ: omitted by 1838 and a Syriac manuscript.

4 Spacing suggests that the papyrus did not read αυτου after ανθοϲ with 𝔓^{72} ℵ A B Ψ 33. 81. 1505. *al* vg^{st.ww} sy. It is added by C K L P 1739 𝔐, Lvt (l^{vid} t) vg^{cl} co.

7 το ρημα το: omitted by A.

7–8 ε[υαγγελιϲθεν] ειϲ ϋμαϲ: so most of MSS. 𝔓^{72} Lvt (l) vg^{mss} read ειϲ υμαϲ ευαγγελιϲθεν.

10 At this point MSS present the following variants:
υποκριϲειϲ και φθονουϲ: most MSS.
υποκριϲειϲ και φθονον: vg^{mss} Or^{lat}
υποκριϲιν και φθονουϲ: ℵ^1 B (και φονουϲ) L (και φθονον) Cl Ambr Aug.
υποκριϲιϲ και φθονον: Lvt (l t) sy^p; Cl (την υ.)

A curve before και indicates that the papyrus did not read υποκριϲιν and most probably read υποκριϲ[ει]ϲ.

11 και ϲυνκαταλαλια : most MSS read παϲαϲ καταλαλιαϲ. ℵ^* reads παϲαν καταλαλιαν and L παϲηϲ καταλαλιαϲ. A 1881 Lvt (l) read καταλαλιαϲ and Cl καταλαλιαν. ϲυν is clear, but unfortunately nothing can be traced with certainty after the last alpha of καταλαλια. The expression ϲυν καταλαλια is not attested elsewhere, nor the words ϲυγκαταλαλια/ϲυγκαταλαλω. εν καταλαλια occurs in *Ep. Barnab.* 20.2h; *Apothegm. Patr.* PG 65.429 (John Dam. PG 96.73). Note, however, the expression ϲυν παϲη κακια, which occurs in Eph iv 31 (see παϲαν κακιαν in lines 8–9).

11–12 α[ρτιγεννη]τα seems rather long for the spacing; there are no other variants at this point, even if the papyrus read αρτιγενητα (so A). γεννητα would suit the space, but γεννητα βρεφη is not attested elsewhere.

12 και omitted before αδολον with 33. 614. 630. 1505. 1881 *al* Lvt (l) vg^{ww} sy^h bo^{ms}; Or^{pt} Eus Cyr.

7

13 γελα: l. γαλα, with all other MSS. For the phonetic interchange of α and ε, see Gignac, *Grammar* i 278–82. Between γαλα and επιποθησατε, 919 includes και θειον cωμα και αιμα.

επιπ[οθ]ηcατε: so most MSS. επιποτιcθητε 378. ποθηcατε 621. Cyr. εποθηcατε 2718. εποτιcθητε 365.

13–14] αυτων: this may be a mistake. All MSS read ινα εν αυτω.

14 αυξ[η]θητε: 61. 69. 915 read αξιωθητε.

14–15 ει[c cωτη]ριαν: so 𝔓⁷² ℵ A B C K P Ψ 33. 69. 81. 323. 614. 630. 945. 1241. 1505. 1739 *al* latt sy co; Cl. ειc cωτηριαν τε: 0142. It is omitted by the majority text.

15 ει ευγεcαcθε (l. εγευcαcθε: for a similar phonetic phenomenon, see Gignac, *Grammar* i 229) οτι: so 𝔓⁷² ℵ* A B *pc* Lvt (t) vg^st co?; Cl. ειπερ ευγεcαcθε is the reading of ℵ² C K L P Ψ 1739 𝔐 Lvt (l) vg^cl.ww; Cyr. Before οτι 𝔓⁷² reads εγευcαcθαι επιcτευcατε, and a few manuscripts and sy^p add και ειδετε.

ει: three successive horizontal dots above epsilon suggest a diaeresis.

χ̅[c̅: χριcτοc is the reading of 𝔓⁷² K L 049. 33. 69. 614. 1241. 1243. 1852. 2298. 2464 *al*. χρηcτοc is read by ℵ A B C Ψ 1739 𝔐 sy.

17 ϋπο: so most MSS. C 323. 945. 1241. 1505. 1739 *al* read απο. 623 and a few MSS read υπερ.

18 α[π]οδεδοκαcμ[ενον: the papyrus is very damaged between the second δ and c, but the proposed reading suits the traces. It is probably a haplography for αποδεδοκιμαcμενον, which is the reading of all MSS.

20 .]....[: presumably λ]ιθοι [, but the traces are too exiguous for confirmation.

↓

1 A trace of a horizontal is visible; this may correspond to the page number (e.g. base of δ), but it would be rather far to the right of the column.

4–5 All MSS read λιθοc προcκομματοc και πετρα cκανδαλου. The traces here are very weak. The broken half of the first visible letter of line 5 suits κ, but μ cannot be excluded. It is possible that the scribe wrote κε for και (see Gignac, *Grammar* i 192).

6 π]ροcκοψου[cιν: this is also the reading of 1409 and the Bohairic tradition. Almost all MSS read προcκοπτουcιν. In OT Is viii 15, following the words of viii 14 και λιθοc προcκομματοc και πετρα cκανδαλου quoted before, Symmachos' version read προcκοψουcιν εν αυτοιc πολλοι, instead of αδυνατηcουcιν εν αυτοιc πολλοι (cf. Theod. Cyr., *In Isah.* ad loc.). *offendant* is the reading of a Latin MS (Ω^D).

7 απειθουν]τεc: so most MSS. απιcτουντεc is the reading of B, απειθουcιν of 1852, and απειθουντι of 1241.

ειc ο [: the papyrus did not read ειc ην παρεcκευαcαν εαυτουc ταξιν with 614. 630 *pc*.

11–12 εξ[.]χ..[|].[.].τ[: after the traces of ξ and in the beginning of line 12 the papyrus is very damaged. Most MSS read εξαγγειλητε (𝔓⁷² εξανγειλητε) and 0142 reads εξαγγελλητε. Spacing suggests that the papyrus omitted του εκ cκοτουc before υ]μαc, an omission not attested by other MSS.

12 υ]μαc καλεcαντοc: so most MSS, but καλεcαντοc υμαc is read by *l* 1575 (0203) and υμαc καλουντοc by Cyr.

13 θ]αυ[μ]αcτον φωc: so 𝔓⁷² bo^ms. All other MSS read θαυμαcτον αυτου φωc. 1890 reads αγαθον φωc.

13–14 οι ποτε υ | [....].ου: MSS read οι ποτε ου λαοc. The papyrus perhaps read οι ποτε ου [λαοc] μου.

15 ηλ]εημενο[ι: so most MSS. 049 reads ηγαπημενοι.

18 απε]χεc[θαι]: so ℵ B Ψ 049. 1739 𝔐 lat sa. The damage of the papyrus does not permit determining whether it read απεχεcθε, which is the reading of 𝔓⁷² A C L P 33. 81. 623. 1241. 1243. 1852. 1881 *al* vg^mss sy^h bo? Cyr.

19 The average number of letters, according to the following lines, suggests that we would have to supplement something else after $αιτινες$, but there are no known other variants at this point.

20–21 The supplemented text in line 20 is rather long, but the space in the following line does not allow for $ψυ|[χης την αναστ]ροφην$.

21–2 $αναστ]ροφην ϋμων$ . . . $καλην$: before $καλην$ most MSS read $εχοντες$, which **4934** omits (so B). $\aleph$ and Cyp read $υμιν$. $\mathfrak{P}^{72}$ reads $καλην εχοντες$. 614. 630 *pc* read $παρακαλω δε και τουτο την εν τοις εθνεσιν υμων αναστροφην εχειν καλην$.

23 $κατ]αλαλ[ουσι]ν$: although the traces are slight, they fit the expected reading (L P 69. 614. 623. 1243. 1505. 2464 *al* vg^{mss} Cl^{v.l.} read $καταλαλωσιν$). It is certain that the papyrus did not read $κακοποιουσιν$ with 1881.

J. CHAPA

II. COMEDY

4935. Aristophanes, *Thesmophoriazusae* 1043–51, 1202–10

88/287 part	Fr. 1 1.7 × 4.1 cm	Second century
	Fr. 2 1.2 × 6.4 cm	

Two scraps from a roll written along the fibres by the same scribe as a papyrus of Plato, *Crito*, reserved for publication in vol. LXXVI. Both fragments are from the last 200 lines of the play. Fr. 1 shows no margins. Fr. 2 is from the top of a column with an upper margin of at least 1.4 cm. The back is blank.

The text is written in a medium to small informal but professional-looking hand, non-bilinear, unornamented, and leaning slightly to the right. Letters generally have a flattened aspect and are sometimes written in ligature (e.g. ΓΑ, ΕΡ, ΜΕ). Letter shapes and spacing are sufficiently similar to those of the *Crito* papyrus (see above) to guarantee an identity of the two hands: especially noteworthy is ∊ with upper and middle strokes made separately from the lower one, н in the shape of h, and deep and rounded м arching backward. The greater extent of the *Crito* papyrus, however, shows that this informal hand sometimes forms identical letters in slightly different ways. I assign the hand to the second century on the basis of its general similarity to the hands represented in P. Turner 14 (assigned to the second half of the second century and on whose back is a letter assigned to the third century) and *GMAW*² 33, 61 (both assigned to the second century).

The scribe probably punctuates with a high stop at line 1208 (see n.), and reconstruction of line lengths shows lines 1048–9 to be set in *ekthesis*. The fragments do not exhibit other lectional signs. An upright is visible at the top right-hand edge of fr. 2 at 1 cm from the first line and positioned above what would have been approximately the middle of the column. It conceivably represents a column number (cf. *GMAW*² p. 16 and LXIV **4432** introd.).

The text of the *Thesmophoriazusae* has been transmitted to us only in two medieval manuscripts, the Ravennas 429 (= R) of the tenth century with corrections and scholia by a second hand, and its mostly faithful and therefore negligible apograph Monacensis Gr. 492 of the fifteenth century. For collation materials I have relied on A. von Velsen, *Aristophanis Thesmophoriazusae* (Lipsiae 1883), but recent editions of the play have also been consulted. The papyrus omits R's μοι in line 1047, which Hermann had also deleted, though perhaps for a different reason. It also confirms that R's βάρβαρον in line 1051, a word suspected by some scholars and editors, is an ancient reading.

Three papyri of the *Thesmophoriazusae*, none overlapping with **4935**, have been published so far: LVI **3839** = M–P³ 153.1; LVI **3840** = M–P³ 154.01; PSI XI

1194 + PSI XIV p. xv = M–P³ 154; in addition, IX **1176** fr. 39 col. xii 1–16 quotes some lines from the play.

Fr. 1

.   .   .

$[oc \; ε]μ \; α[πεξυρηcε$

$[o]ς \; εμε \; κ[ροκοεν-$

1045 $[ε]πι \; δε \; τ[οιcδε$

$[ι]ερον \; [$

$[ι]ω \; μοιρ[ac$

$[ω \; καταρατ]οc \; εγω \; [$

$[παθοc \; α]μεγαρ[τον$

1050 $[ει]θε \; με \; [$

$[τ]ον \; β[αρβαρον$

.   .   .

Fr. 2

$[Ερμ]η \; δολ[ιε$

$[cυ \; μ]εν \; ου[ν$

$[εγω] \; δε \; λυ[cω$

1205 $[οταν \; λ]υθ[ης$

$[ωc \; τη]ν \; γ[υναικα$

$[εμοι \; με]λη[cει$

$[\quad c.6 \quad] \; co[ν$

$[ηκοντα] \; κα[ταλαβειν$

1210 $[ω \; γραδι] \; ωc \; [$

.   .   .

Fr. 1

1047 ι]ω μοιρ[ac (ω and ρ are virtually certain): ἰώ μοι μοίραc R and most editors. It is unclear whether the papyrus anticipates G. Hermann's deletion of R's μοι. Hermann appears to have read the rest of the line as ἄτεγκτε δαῖμον (Biset, Ellebodius) instead of R's ἀνέτικτε δαίμων, and so excised μοι to analyse the line as *ba* + *ith* (cf. O. Schroeder, *Aristophanis cantica* (1930²) 66). If the more widely accepted emendation ἄν ἔτικτε δαίμων (Casaubon) is assumed to have stood in the papyrus (*ith*), metrical considerations do not significantly affect the choice of readings. Without μοι the phrase ἰώ μοίραc can still be considered a dochmiac, but of the 'syncopated' variety found occasionally in tragedy; cf. M. L. West, *Greek Metre* (1982) 111. Some scholars have defended the inclusion of μοι on the basis of some Euripidean parallels, e.g. *Alc.* 393 ἰώ μοι τύχαc, *Phoen.* 1290 ἰώ μοι πόνων (cf. F. Bubel, *Euripides: Andromeda* (1991) 114; P. Rau, *Paratragodia* (1967) 76), so the converse possibility of a haplography at this point in the papyrus should not be completely excluded.

1048–9 These two lines must have been set in *ekthesis* relative to the other lines, 1048 by seven letters and 1049 by five letters. For the common use of *ekthesis* in lyric passages of drama 'to mark the presence of a longer metrical unit among shorter verses', see *GMAW*² p. 8, and for an example of varying levels of indentation in a papyrus of Aristophanes, cf. LXVI **4510** fr. 14. The colometrical layout of verses is a common preoccupation of the *scholia vetera* of Aristophanes and probably goes back to the first-century metrician Heliodorus, if not to earlier Hellenistic scholars and editions (see L. P. Parker, *The Songs of Aristophanes* (1997) 95–7). Although there is no *ekthesis* in R at this point, the distribution of these verses agrees with R (cf. Parker, *Songs* 98–102, and N. Gonis, LXVI p. 121.), whereas most editors distribute the passage over three lines: ὦ κατάρατος ἐγώ· | τίς ἐμὸν οὐκ ἐπόψεται | πάθος ἀμέγαρτον ἐπὶ κακῶν παρουσίᾳ.

1051 τ]ὸν β[αρβαρον: so R and most recent editors. The papyrus does not support Brunck's conjecture τὸν δύσμορον on the basis of a scholion in R (διχῶς· τὸν ἄθλιον), much favoured by older editors (cf. also Parker, *Songs* 445). For a defense of τὸν βάρβαρον as an unsyntactical *aprosdoketon*, see E. Mitsdörfer, *Philologus* 98 (1954) 89, Rau, *Paratragodia* 77–8, B. Zimmermann, *Untersuchungen zur Form und dramatischen Technik der Aristophanischen Komödien* ii (1985) 12, and C. Austin, *Dodone* 19.2 (1990) 28–9.

Fr. 2

1208] cọ[ν: preceding còν ἔργον, R before correction had the meaningless form λέλυcον, the ending probably arising from the anticipation of the following cόν. A second hand in R canceled the ν, emending to λέλυco ('be freed'), a reading adopted by most editors. Bentley emended to λέλυcαι ('you have been freed'); cf. Eur. *Or.* 1525 ἀφεῖcαι, *Hcld.* 789 ἠλευθέρωcαι. Unfortunately, the trace before cọ[ν is insufficient for a certain reconstruction of the papyrus' reading. The high dot just before c cannot form any part of omicron, so that λέλυc]ọ is out of the question. Given the dot's proximity to c, it can hardly be taken as the upper tip of ι, i.e. λελυcα]ι cọ[ν, which is invariably upright in this hand. The trace admittedly could correspond to the extremity of the right-hand arm of ν, yielding λελ]υcọ[, but this would not allow proper alignment with the other lines. cọ[, in other words, is certainly part of còν ἔργον. The likeliest interpretation is that the trace is a high stop, which is appropriate at this point. If this is the case, the available space between the punctuation dot and the left margin (*c*.6 letters) could theoretically accommodate either λέλυco or λέλυcαι. A tracing suggests that Bentley's λέλυcαι would fit the space comfortably.

A. BENAISSA

4936. MENANDER, *EPITREPONTES*

A 2B4 (13 iii 75)/8 M   5.5 × 15.5 cm   Second century
                                                                          Plate I

On the side of the vertical fibres, this tattered scrap of a roll gives, in a compact format, ends and beginnings of comic iambic lines from two columns, apparently of 34–5 lines each. The handwriting, small and professional-looking if less than calligraphic, is upright with rounded curves, in a style that suggests mid-to-late second century AD; the cursive on the recto, though too scrappy to offer a clear impression, could well have been written earlier in the same century. Comparable, though rather neater, is the Archilochus of VI **854** + XXX **2507** + LXIX **4708**, again on the back of a cursive document, both assigned to the second century; not unlike in type, though larger and more generously laid out, is XLI **2943**, Menander, *Samia*, which Turner assigns to the later second century or early third.

Paragraphos marks change of speaker. Elision is effected, and marked by apostrophe in col. i 17, col. ii 7 and 18, but not in col. ii 32 (in col. ii 17 it is not possible to say whether the apostrophe was written because of the damage to the surface). Phonetic spelling occurs in col. i 21 and 22.

The identity of the play is given by the name of Charisios in the text at col. i 22, taken together with abbreviated marginal speakers' names in col. ii that expand to give the names of Chai(restratos), One(simos) and Kar(ion). It is true that the last name is damaged on both of its appearances; but the part-marking at lines 28–33 confirms that three speakers were involved, not two, and no acceptable alternative to the name Karion offers itself. The line-endings surviving from col. i may be part of the same three-cornered conversation—a long one, if so—but no part-markings or speakers' names (unless perhaps at i 16) are present to help clarify the obscure hints that the words give.

The fragmentary hypothesis given by **LX 4020** verifies the presumption that the play began with the entry of Karion the cook with Onesimos, speaking lines long known from quoting sources, and now presented as *Epitr.* 1–3. It has been recognized that a main function of this opening dialogue was to give the background of the situation, in which Charisios, Onesimos' master, has deserted his wife and installed himself in the house of neighbour Chairestratos with the harpist Habrotonon for company. A day's partying is in prospect. Gossiping about the clients, as well as about his culinary skills, is a familiar enough routine with comic cooks; but this particular dialogue was pointedly motivated by having the cook presented as a prime specimen of an inquisitive chatterbox and the slave as a busybody of kindred spirit. So much can be seen not only from the surviving words accredited to this scene, but from the recollection of Karion and his role in one of the quoting sources, Themistios (*Or.* 21.262c, quoted by Martina, *ed. Epitr.*, test. 11, and in part by other editors under fr. 2). In the present fragment, the references to a beautiful girl (i 16), to meat (i 21), to Charisios (i 22), to Thasian wine (ii 31) and to chattering (ii 33) are probably sufficient to place it by kinship of motif in Act 1, and to discourage any effort to find room anywhere later in the play. The conspicuously new elements are the presence of Chairestratos with Onesimos and Karion, and the indications that the parties are not only exchanging views about the situation, but forming a plan. Thus in ii 17–19, a possibility is assessed, and an objection raised (ὡς ἔοικε . . . ἀλλὰ . . .); ii 24–7 'watching', 'I'll shut . . .' (the street door presumably), 'wait'; ii 30 'I agree with you.' It will be asked how far all this relates to our other knowledge of the largely conjectural opening of the play.

Several considerations, the length of the present fragment among them, suggest that a figure of 170-odd lines for Act 1 is too low (see below on line numeration). Webster, *Studies in Menander* (1960²) 34–5, following Wilamowitz, calls attention to the considerable amount of background information that needs to be given in dialogue and supplemented by a deferred prologue speech by a divinity or a personified abstraction; such a speech is needed to tell the audience the essential fact that the baby at the centre of the plot is the child of Charisios and Pamphile. All this, and very likely more, is to come before the scene with Smikrines, Chairestratos and Habrotonon that we have from **P**, the St Petersburg leaf, as the end of the act. Webster, like Arnott, thinks in terms of a number of lines in the 200s. It is worth noting that *Aspis* Act I has 249 lines (not counting a few lost by minor damage): 96 in the opening dialogue, before the deferred prologue speech by Tyche, consisting of 52 lines, then just over 100 lines in two further scenes. On this basis, there seems no reason why new discoveries of text for Act I (as well as for the early part of Act II) in *Epitrepontes* should not be accommodated within a modified reconstruction of the Cairo codex, without the need to presume irregularities in its make-up. If we consider that a dozen or so fragmentary copies of this popular play are already known, there is a fair prospect that further accessions from papyri or identifiable quotations will one day allow a more definitive presentation of the text to be made. It is disappointing therefore that any overlap between the present text and the other known or suspected remains of the play has so far eluded notice.

Taking *Aspis* as a model, there could be about 100 lines of dialogue, including the present fragment, before the deferred prologue speech that critics postulate. Lines 1–3 are known (see above); they and the reference to Onesimos as a busy-body in fr. 2 (I keep the current numbers) are the motivation for an extended chat about the present situation of Charisios and some of the treats that Karion has in store for the diners. This may be what Themistios is recalling when he says that the cook failed to satisfy his interlocutor, but 'exasperated the guests by (or while) elaborating on his flavourings' (οἷα δὲ λέγει ὁ μάγειρος ὁ κωμῳδικὸς οὐδ' ἐκεῖνα πάνυ ἐλυσιτέλει τῷ πυνθανομένῳ, ἀλλ' ἐπέτριβε τοὺς δαιτυμόνας ἐξαλλάττων τὰ ἡδύσματα). What upset them was the delay; the culinary talk is better imagined as a part of the opening sequence than at some point later; and it may even be that the reference to salting the salt fish in fr. 5 (6 Martina) is part of it (ἐπέπασα | ἐπὶ τὸ τάριχος ἅλας, ἐὰν οὕτω τύχῃ). On this view, the aorist describes the cook's habitual action, as in ἐκάλεσ' ἱερέαν, *Dysk.* 496; the rest means that he goes to any lengths, 'if it comes to that' (in another context, the expression might refer figuratively to making a bad situation worse, as it is often taken). Karion and Onesimos were perhaps accompanied by slaves carrying materials and equipment for the feast, including the large open-necked jar, the ἐχῖνος, of fr. 4. These people could then be sent into the house to make advance preparations while the talk of cook and slave continues, and it may be that their arrival prompted someone to come out and ask the cook why he was not getting on with the lunch, 'and there's himself been in the dining room for ages, wasting his time' (fr. 3). Evidently the response was not instant. If the speaker was not the host Chairestratos in person, the intervention will have to have happened before he came on scene, or more than the canonical three speakers will have been needed.

Aspis has two opening characters accompanied by a much more elaborate procession; *Dyskolos* (393–426 with 439 ff.) is a parallel for the arrival of party materials (if less rustic, the setting of *Epitr.* is still outside Athens). In fr. 3, the reference to 'himself', ὁ δέ, as πάλαι κατακείμενος must surely come from someone inside, and not Onesimos, who has just arrived from town with the cook. It sounds like a servant, but might perhaps be Habrotonon, in advance of her entry at 142, in which case the others will be able to comment and so to identify her. But what then brings Chairestratos out? Another request to hurry?

The kind of background information to be provided by this part of the play, culinary matters apart, can be illustrated from the exposition scene in Terence, *Hecyra* 143 ff. There Parmeno tells Philotis that Pamphilus is a reluctant husband, who has in fact not slept with his wife, and would like to annul the marriage; but he is unwilling to contemplate returning her to her father without fault on her part, and takes up with Bacchis while hoping that she will recognize the situation as impossible and go of her own accord . . . and so on. In *Epitrepontes*, to avoid distracting puzzlement, the audience needs to know minimally how Charisios came to marry Pamphile; how it was that he went away for some time soon after the marriage, while she had her baby and sent it to be exposed—about a month ago as we later learn (243); and how it is now, as the cook has heard from city gossip, that he has taken up with Habrotonon and is at present with Chairestratos his neighbour, much as Polemon in *Perikeiromene* leaves home and takes up residence next door. To this early part of the scene should belong, if it belongs at all, the scrap of papyrus in Berlin (fr. 12 Arnott, 5 Martina) which has remains of the first half of eleven lines, including the name Charisios (it is not known from any other play), and the coarse old word-play on boozing and screwing (πίνειν/βινεῖν) that is apt in the mouths of such characters as Karion and Onesimos. (For obscenity between cook and slave, *Dysk.* 891–2, slave and hetaira, *Perik.* 482–5; for πίνειν/βινεῖν note the two slaves' talk about Dionysos in Ar. *Frogs* 738–40.) As for the rest, fr. 5 (6 Martina) is considered above; fr. 6 (7 Martina) is now safely located in Act II by coincidence with the new Oxyrhynchus lines published as LXVIII **4641**. Somehow our present fragment must develop the dialogue and look forward to moves to come. That cannot, of course, involve the arbitration, except in so far as any mention of the exposed baby here or earlier will have prepared for the sudden appearance in Act II of Syriskos with wife and child, pursued by Daos. The discussion, however it went, must have attempted to plan for the situation that the characters knew of already, not least the prospect of an intervention by Smikrines. That is what the latter part of the act will take further.

The deferred prologue speech is likely to have enhanced interest in the information already given by presenting it in a different perspective; it must, as we noted, have contributed the essential fact that the exposed baby was fathered on Pamphile by Charisios at the Tauropolia, for no character is in a position to do that. We have no clue to the identity of the speaker or to the content of the speech, unless one of the unplaced fragments belongs to it.

If our new fragment is rightly placed as we have it, motivation is needed for the entry of Chairestratos to join the cook and the slave, and for the exit at the end of the sequence of all three. If Chairestratos was not simply anxious to get the lunch under way, as was suggested above, he may have intended, whether prompted by Charisios or not, to look in at Charisios' house to see how things were with Pamphile (compare Sosias' behaviour as seen at *Perik.* 354–60). To end the sequence, it must be that the cook goes to Chairestratos' house (and that will presumably dispose of him for a while); Onesimos too (for that is the expected end of his errand to fetch the cook). It would be normal for one of the three (therefore presumably Chairestratos) to be left behind to deliver a short monologue before he either joins the others, or (if he is Chairestratos) visits Pamphile as we suggested he may have set out to do. This seems to me a more plausible placing than if one imagined the present fragment to come after, and not before, a deferred prologue: all else apart, the cook and slave would have to go off and then be brought on again (for what reason?) to resume their conversation.

The end of Act I, with line-beginnings from the start of Act II, is given by the second side of **P**. Judging the format of the codex from its fragments, one can say that something between 10 and 30 lines may have been lost between the first side and the second (Turner, *GRBS* 10 (1969) 311 f., as quoted by Arnott in the Loeb and by Parsons on LX **4021**). Of these, LX **4021** frr. 1 + 2 (**O25**) gives 9 line-beginnings before it coincides with **P** at 159. We are accordingly in touch with $22 + x + 9 + 13 = 44 + x$ lines, where the identified speakers are Chairestratos, Smikrines and Habrotonon. (If by some chance **O25** happens to bridge the gap between the two sides of **P**, x will be zero or a small minus number; physically there is no way to tell.) Both at the beginning of this run of lines and just before he goes off at 163, eight lines before the end of the act, Smikrines is represented, by the common dramatic convention, as thinking aloud or talking to himself as he comments on Charisios' behaviour before deciding to find out the facts from Pamphile; his words are intercut with comments first from Chairestratos, and then from Chairestratos and Habrotonon, when she comes to call him in at 142. To all appearances, there is no contact between them and the old man. All their words, including Chairestratos' interventions from 131 onwards and his curse at 160 are (as we should say) aside (see Parsons on LX **4021**, fr. 1, 160–61 n.; the speakers' names in frr. 1+2 are helpful, all else apart, in confirming Habrotonon's presence, as diagnosed by Webster from the vocative γλυκύτατε in 143, where I prefer [τί ποτ' ἐc]τὶ δ', [ὦ] γλυκύτατ', 'Whatever's the matter . . . ?', to the usual [τίc ὅδ' ἐc]τὶ δ[ή] 'Who's this . . . ?', continuing Chairestratos' reply into 144, [ὁ περιπατ]ῶν ὡc ἀθλιόc τιc [φιλόcοφοc, κτλ.). A useful parallel is given by a sequence in *Misoumenos*, 284–323 = 684–725 Arnott. There Getas is presented as reliving his experience of the quarrel he has just witnessed indoors, followed around by Kleinias, who comments unseen and unheard by Getas until at last contact is made. This run of 39 lines compares with 36 tangibly represented in our passage of *Epitrepontes*. A few more lines should be allowed for the beginning of the sequence (not many, for Chairestratos' words at 131–3 show that Smikrines has not been long on stage, but long enough to have provoked one bad word against him already: so much from πάλιν, 133). It is therefore likely that the value of *x*, representing lines untraceably lost, is low. For that reason, and because what can be seen of its content is so hard to reconcile with the context as given, the 21 lines of fr. 3 of **O25** cannot with any plausibility be supposed to belong here. It is still for consideration whether they belong in this act, or indeed in this play at all.

To that issue, so far as I can see, our new piece has no direct contribution to make. Rejecting the idea (as has just been done above) that *x* takes in **O25** fr. 3, Professor Parsons considers two other placings: (*a*) in the lacuna before **P** begins at 127, and (*b*) near the beginning of Act II after **P** ends at 177, where in fact Martina tentatively places it as his fr. 8. More recently, R. Nünlist, *ZPE* 144 (2003) 59–61, with a new reading of line 10 of the fragment (κλίνην ἐμο.[), gives further arguments for a placing in Act II. The lines are lively and expansive, to judge by what is left, with two versions of the 'so help me' / 'so help you' idiom that is used to underline emphatic statements and requests in 8 and 12 (as in οὕτω πολλά μοι / coι ἀγαθὰ γένοιτο—see Parsons' useful note on 7–8); at least two third person narrative tenses (11 ἀπώλεcεν, 13 ἐλάλει); a second singular imperative 'go to sleep', κάθευδ' 9 (if not also ἀ]παλλάγηθι, which 'could be read' in 7); and a second person plural, ὑμᾶc in 15, not to say more. 'Some suggestions of dialogue', remarks Parsons' note. But no *paragraphoi* can be seen where they could be expected to show, and 'we may have a continuous speech which quotes a conversation'. One can ask who, of the known characters, might have delivered such a speech. Surely not Smikrines at any point: it is too far from his style as we are shown it. In Act I, hardly anyone else but Onesimos (who has been much used in the exposition already); or Chairestratos; or the speaker of the assumed delayed prologue; maybe in any case it described the break-up of relations between Charisios and Pamphile. Any of the three in question might well have addressed the audience (if that is what ὑμᾶc in 15 indicates); one might not expect a prologue speaker to quote direct speech, but the unidentified prologue speaker of *Sikyonioi* actually does that (13 ff.). There is certainly plenty of room for more, and some expectation of more, before the sequence that we know of with Chairestratos, Smikrines, and Habrotonon. There are still other unplaced fragments of the play, including one from XXXVIII **2829** (**O14**, 11b Arnott, VI Martina), part of a dialogue with the word ἀπόκοιτοc, which must refer to Charisios *vis-à-vis* Pamphile. None of this eliminates the chance that the speech may be by yet another speaker (say the Sim[m]ias of 630, with whom some have flirted in the past), or from elsewhere in the play, or (after all) from another play entirely. The progress of rediscovery of Menander shows well, whatever else it shows, that one must not claim to know too much.

Note on line-numeration. The current line-numbering of *Epitrepontes* derives from the OCT of Sandbach (1972; 1990²), and is presented with minor variations in Arnott's Loeb (1979), and Martina's edition of 1997. It allots to Act I lines 1–171, but is unfortunately no true guide to the length of the act, depending as it does on a bibliographical reconstruction of the Cairo codex that in this matter is no more than conjectural; and indeed Arnott himself suggests a length for this act of somewhere between 230 and 290 lines. Sandbach inherited the new numeration from Gomme (OCT, pref. vii); an account of it is given in Gomme–Sandbach, *Commentary* . . . 43–5, and it can be followed through in detail from the London facsimile of the Cairo codex (Institute of Classical Studies, 1978) with its Concordance. Koerte I⁴ (1955), pref. xi n. 3, presents the presumed distribution of the plays in the codex with the justified caution, 'Hanc distributionem valde incertam esse haud ignoro.' It can be seen from there, without further elaboration, that the effect of assuming that *Epitr.* began on p. 58 and not p. 60 of the codex would make some 70 more lines available for the beginning of the play: that at the cost of assuming a length for *Heros* of just under 1,000 lines, comparable with *Dyskolos*, instead of the proposed 1,065; but other adjustments are also possible. *Epitr.* is on any account a long play, maybe up to 1,300 lines, as Arnott suggests; the broken number at the end of the Paris *Sikyonioi* shows that it too was over 1,000, and so *Perikeiromene* is assumed to have been.

I am grateful to Dr William D. Furley for corrections and clarifications.

Col. i

top (?)

]	]
]	]
]	]
]	]

5
```
       ].....ϲιον              ].....ϲιον
       ].ι..ο....              ].ι..ο....
       ]ακ[                    ]ακ[
       ]...εϲε                 ]...εϲε
       ]..[                    ]..[
```
10
```
       ]..[...]ο..             ]..[...]ο..
       ].....ο[                ].....ο[
   ].ϲυν[.]...[              ].ϲυν[...]...[
   ]γενομε.[                 ]γενομεν[-
   ].....αϲι                 ].....αϲι
```
15
```
   ].....ιϲοληυ            ].....ιϲ ὅλην
                  ]ον.                      ]ον.
   ].λη[.]κορη.           κ]αλη[.] κόρη.
   ].φοδ.'οιϲθ'οτι         ] ϲφόδρ' οἶϲθ' ὅτι
   ].τι                    ].τι
   ]....μειϲιϲα            ]....μειϲ ἴϲα
```
20
```
   ]νουδε..                -]ν οὐδέπω
   ]ρ.αδειον               κ]ρεάδιον
   ]χαρειϲιο[              ] Χαριϲιο[-
   ]εν[.]..[               ]εν[.]..[
       ]ρ...[.]ϲι              ]ρ...[.]ϲι
```
25
```
       ]ομα.[.].           ὀν]όματ[ο]ϲ
       ].ειϲφρ.[.]ων       -].ειϲ φρε[ν]ῶν
       ]κειν                   ]κειν
       ]ϲιον                   ]ϲιον
       ]ϲτε..[                 ]ϲτε..[
```
30
```
       ]οπερ[...]υ             ]οπερ[...]υ
       ]νυν[                   ]νυν[
       ]αμαϲυ              -]αμα ϲύ
       ]δετου[                 ]δετου[
       ].επ[.]μ..[            ].επ[.]μ..[
```

foot (?)

16]. λη, remains of right-hand half of triangular letter   17]., trace in upper part of writing space   φοδ., remains of upright; traces on the right of its tip   20 ουδε..., first, two traces in horizontal alignment at line-level and at mid-height respectively; *c*.2.5 cm farther to the right, trace at mid-height: square letter? second, left-hand arc   21 ρ., blurred trace in lower part of writing space   25 ομα., very tiny dot slightly below line-level   26 φρ.[, very reduced trace at line-level   29 τε, vertical with possible trace of horizontal joining ε; less likely Γε, ιε

Col. i

It is likely, but not certain because of the damaged condition of the papyrus, that the 35 lines that can be made out from col. ii represent the full height of the original written area, that is about 14 cm. No doubt originally there will have been more margin at top and foot. The recto side suggests so at the top, where the writing is right at the present edge; towards the foot it is blank, and therefore indecisive.

5 *Xαρ(ε)ίϲιον* looks as if it might fit (cf. 22, 28–9 below), but cannot be trusted. Until 13, and to some extent later, the surface is badly rubbed and disturbed.

15 It is a shame the noun is lost: ἡμέραν, οἰκίαν, πόλιν or whatever; for the last, see 584 f., incorporating, after Robert, the quotation ἡ πόλις | ὅλη γὰρ ᾄδει τὸ κακόν. ?κᾳλ[ε]ῖϲ (WDF).

16 Spacing suggests κ]ᾳλῆ[ϲ] κόρης (or -ῆ[ν] -ην) rather than the dative. The letters ον., doubtfully read, may be a correction written over the line, or possibly a mid-line *nota personae* for Onesimos: the ink after the presumed ΟΝ might represent Η, if indeed it does not come from the line above.

17 ϲφόδρ' οἶϲθ' ὅτι, also at line end, *Epitr.* 1127, spoken by Smikrines.

19 Perhaps a verb like οἰκονομεῖϲ, but the articulation is unclear, -μ' εἰϲ ἴϲα being equally possible if the diastole is either absent or abraded.

20 οὐκ ἀγανακτῶν **οὐδέπω** at line end, *Sam.* 271.

21 κρεᾴδια in a cook scene, *Pseudherakles* 451.13 Koe/409.13 KA. For the singular κρεᾴδιον as a joint of meat, see Ar. *Plut.* 227 f. τουτοδὶ τὸ κρεᾴδιον | τῶν ἔνδοθέν τις εἰϲενεγκάτω λαβών; for the spelling κρεᾱι-, with iota, see Arnott on Alexis, *Atthis* 27.5.

22 The spelling *Xαρειϲ*- appears also in P. Berol. inv. 21142, line 3 = fr. 12 Arnott, 5 Martina.

26 φρενῶν seems likely, rather than φρονῶν or εἰϲφρέων. It suggests, though we lack a construction, that someone is being accused of having taken leave of his senses, as perhaps with ἀφειϲτή]κειϲ (ἀφεϲτάναι φρενῶν, S. *Phil.* 865); but not necessarily a second person, if -]θεὶϲ can be read and taken as a passive participle ending. The traces of ink before -ειϲ are indecisive.

27 E.g. ἐμοὶ δο]κεῖν, or τε]κεῖν; less likely ἔ]χειν.

28–9 Either or both lines might take the name of Charisios (see 22); there are several alternatives, including 28 πληϲίον and 29, ἀνόϲιε (at line end, as at *Dysk.* 108 and 469).

30 ὅπερ [ἐμο]ῦ would fit (at line end, like ὅπερ ἐμοί at *Dysk.* 157), but it is not inevitable: e.g. τ]ὸ περ[ὶ ϲο]ῦ.

32 E.g. τ]ἀμὰ ϲύ.

Col. ii

Top (?)

	] μͅε̣ . . [		μͅε̣ . . [
	λεγ . . . . [		λεγ . . . . [
.αρ	. . . . χα . [	Κ̣αρ.	. . . . χα . [
	[.]ν . . . . . . [		[.]ν . . . . . . [
	. . . . πακο̣ . . . [		. . . . πακο̣ . . . [
καρ	.ο̣ . λ . . [	Καρ.	.ο̣ . λ . . [
	ειρηκ'εγ . [		εἴρηκ' ἐγω[
χαι	. . φυκα[	Χαι.	πέφυκα[
	. υ . [		. υ . [
ον̣η̣	. . αν . [.] . [	Ονη.	. . αν . [.] . [
	[. . .] . . . θ . [		[. . .] . . . θ . [
	. . καν . [		. . καν . . [
	. . ωcθ . . [		ὅπωc θ . . [
	ταυτηνο[		ταύτην ο[
	ενγειτον[		ἐν γειτόν[ων
	αυτηνδι[		αὐτὴν δι[-
	α . αν . υ[		ἅ γ' ἂν τύ[χη
	εcθ'ωcεο̣[		ἔcθ', ὡc ἔο[ικε
	αλλαπα̣τ̣[		ἀλλὰ πατ[-
	αυτονπι[		αὐτὸν πι[-
	κ̣ . εμαν . [		κρ̣εμαν . [
	αλλ̣ . . [		αλλ̣ . . [
	coιδειπο[		coὶ δεῖ πο[-
	τηρ[.]νγαρ[		τηρ[ῶ]ν γὰρ[
	κλειcωπ[		κλείcω π[
	περιμε . [		περίμεν[ε
	τηνμια[		τὴν μία[ν
	αυτοcκα . [		αὐτὸc κα . [
ον̣η	καιθαcι[	Ονη.	καὶ Θαcι[-
χαι	coι̣πειθ[	Χαι.	coὶ πειθ[-
	οινονθα[		οἶνον Θά[cιον
	αλλουτιχ[		ἀλλ' οὔ τι χ[αίρων
ον̣η	ανετιλα[	Ονη.	ἂν ἔτι λα[λ-
	ποινυν[		ποῖ νῦν[
	. [.] . . . [		. [.] . . . [

Foot (?)

5 ͺπα, trace at line level; above, farther to the right, two reduced traces in upper part of writing space ͺκοͺ ͺ ͺ, first, remains of upright; second, three dots in diagonal alignment ascending from left to right, slightly below line-level; third, very tiny traces at mid-height and in upper part of writing space 7 εγ ͺ[, only join with the extremity of crossbar of previous ⌐ has survived 8 ͺφυ, first, scanty remains of square letter; second, left-hand arc 13 ͺωϲθ, first, remains of left-hand arc; second, remains of two uprights belonging to square letter 17 α ͺ, traces in horizontal alignment in upper part of writing space αυ ͺ, remains of crossbar joining vertical trace 21 κ ͺ ε, remains of upright 28 perhaps a dot of ink after α, καλ[(WDF)

Col. ii

Above line 1, as numbered here, there is about 0.5 cm of rubbed surface on which some trace of ink would be likely to show if this were not in fact the first line of the column. The situation is similar at the foot of both columns, where there is some blank but rubbed surface and no traces of ink. Accordingly, the reckoning of 35 lines, while probable, is not wholly beyond doubt.

3 What seems to distinguish the abbreviation of Karion's name from that of Chairestratos, given the damage here and in 6, is essentially the way in which the final stroke of ⋏ rises to form a loop for ρ instead of curving down to represent ι. Karion's presence is supported by the consideration that the labelling of the parts at 29–33 implies three speakers, and (marginally), by the mention of food and drink there and at i 21.

5 Puzzling: ὑπακουομ[- or ἐπακουομ[- is suggested: -ομ[εν, -ο[μαι, -όμ[εθα, or a form of the present middle/passive participle; before that, three letters rather than four, as for (e.g.) ἴϲωϲ: even ἴϲωϲ would be a squeeze.

8 The high tone of πέφυκα, from Chairestratos, lacks explanation without a context, unless one can see it as a retort to the firmness of εἴρηκα from the cook; as at 13 ff., it seems that more than culinary backchat is afoot.

10–18 With no signs of change of speaker (though we cannot be sure of 11–13) this looks like Onesimos suggesting a course of action. It is consistent with that notion that in 30 Chairestratos appears to say 'I agree', ϲοὶ πείθ[ομαι. If, from the talk in town, Smikrines is expected to intervene (θυγ[ατέρα cannot be verified in 13, but is not ruled out), it may be that the idea is to keep him away from Chairestratos' house where Charisios is with Habrotonon. For 15 ἐν γειτόνων 'next door' as at *Perik.* 147 and elsewhere, cf. fr. 777 Koe/657 KA. 17: presumably ἅ γ'ἂν τύ[χῃ, either 'at all events' with ἄν, or 'if this happens' with ἆν.

19–28 One supposes that the identity of the speakers must have been clear when the lines were complete, for there are no speakers' names until 29, in spite of the frequent *paragraphoi*. 19–21, with possible references to 'father' (19 ἀλλὰ πατ[έρ᾽ or another case) and punishment (21 κρεμᾶν or another part of the verb), may perhaps be the reaction of the cook rather than Chairestratos.

23 The surface is damaged: one cannot be sure that ϲοιδ᾽ειπο[was not written: ϲοὶ δ᾽ εἰ πο[- might lead to a question to be answered by the γάρ of 24. ϲοὶ (? ϲού) δεῦρο (WDF).

24–5 τηρῶν might suggest that Chairestratos is to be on the look-out for Smikrines, κλείϲω that Onesimos will shut the street door of the house where the party is taking place, somewhat as is done in Plautus, *Mostellaria* (400 ff.); there Theopropides is surprised to find the house shut up in the daytime (444), and Tranio has been waiting to fob him off with the false story that it is haunted.

26–8 Conjecturally, if κλείϲω (25) is said by Onesimos, περίμενε 'Wait' (if it is that and not περὶ μὲν) should be from Chairestratos; perhaps the word echoes an imperative at 25 end: 'Wait, you say?', as at adesp. 1017 KA, 60 f. 28 must then be Karion; he speaks once more, 31–2, in unlabelled lines between Chairestratos in 30 and Onesimos in 33–4. περιμει[ν (WDF) or -μει[ναι᾽?

29–33 If Onesimos is suggesting that (special) Thasian wine should be served, the idea must presumably be to keep the party happy and out of Smikrines' way in the house; Chairestratos apparently agrees (30), and so does Karion, in echoing the suggestion; but he seems to go on with 'You won't get away with it . . .' or 'It won't do him any good . . .' (32). That was perhaps his exit line, followed by Onesimos 'Any more talk from you . . .', ἂν ἔτι λα[λῇc (33), and 'Where now . . . ?', 34, looking towards the next move. For Thasian wine-jars (Θάcια) and wine, see Sandbach on *Kolax* 48 and Arnott on Alexis, *Tokistes* fr. 232.4; for ἄν . . . λαλῇc *Epitr.* 248 and 1069 (Smikrines, both times), though λά[βῃc is also possible. The cook's built-in tendency to talk too much is the basis of a stock joke at *Samia* 283–5; it would be a fitting motif to end the long sequence of dialogue from which the play begins. It need hardly be stressed how much of this reconstruction is tentative.

E. W. HANDLEY

4937. New Comedy (? Menander, *Georgos*)

58/A(21)b   7.6 × 2.6 cm   Sixth/seventh century
Plates II–III

A scrap from a vellum codex in a small sloping pointed majuscule (Cavallo–Maehler, *GBEBP* p. 4). The hair side (here side A) has 2.5 cm of margin and 5.1 cm of text, with remains of the earlier part of five iambic lines; the flesh side (Side B), has, correspondingly, five line endings in 5.1 cm. and 2.5 cm of margin, in which the abbreviated character-name ΧΑΙΡ(ΕΑC) appears. Lines for the writing are ruled with a sharp point some 4–5 mm apart, and there is vertical ruling both for the inner and for the outer margin of the column (B 4 runs right up to it). The original breadth can be calculated at about 15–16 cm, with a writing space between the vertical rules of 10–11 cm. The original height is a matter for guesswork, for which some guidance may be given by the tabulation given in Sir Eric Turner's *Typology of the Early Codex* (1977) 28. With a 'square' format, as in Turner's Groups VIII and X, the vertical dimension should be some 16–17 cm; with a 'not square' format, as in Groups VII and IX, it might be up to somewhere between 22 and 24 cm. If we allow 5 cm for the upper and lower margins, the number of lines per page should be somewhere between 22 and 32: that is to say, some 17 to 27 lines intervene between the two sides. Since the content of the two sides appears to be closely related, as the discussion below will suggest, something near to the lower estimate may be thought likelier than something near to the higher one.

The script is quite well spaced and sits firmly on the line, with descending strokes, as in Ρ, Υ, Φ, minimally, if at all, below it, while the upright of φ is so tall as to touch the line above (A 4, B 4). Λ is made with a fine narrow loop, Δ is a similarly flattened triangle, particularly so in cφοδρ' (A 4); ε and c tend to have straight backs (not always so), with a small base and the upper part overhanging the lower; ο is small and variable, the one clear specimen of θ (A 3) is more generously formed; κ is made as an upright with arms that are characteristically written together and a little out of contact with it. There are occasional variations in letter shape, e.g., κ, where its arms are detached from the vertical (A 5), or lower arm branches off the upper arm joining the vertical at the centre-point (B 2). These features, taken with the general impression made by the small specimen we have, suggest a date hardly earlier than, and possibly somewhat later than, the handwriting of Dioskoros, which is taken as a key point in the palaeography of the early Byzantine period, as by Cavallo and Maehler, *GBEBP* 32a, giving a date for it of AD *c.*560–75. It is notable that the contrast between thick and thin strokes, while strong, is less exaggerated than in some literary hands of this period. Compare also P. Berol. inv. 9722 (*GBEBP* 39b, Sappho, assigned to the second half of the sixth century). There is punctuation by single point, with changes of speaker marked by dicolon (no *paragraphoi* survive), there are two examples of elision marked by diastole (A 3, A 4), one of crasis (unmarked, A 5); there are no accents.

The text is probably to be counted among the latest surviving copies of Menander, a brief account of which is given in Handley–Hurst, *Relire Ménandre* (1990) 146–8. Though there is at present no external confirmation, there is strong circumstantial evidence of the identity of the play. For (i) Menander is to be presumed as the author of any New Comedy that survives in a copy datable by its handwriting to so late a period; (ii) the content is that of a scene of betrothal involving two characters named as Gorgias and Chaireas, the former, a young countryman known among the dramatis personae of the play *Georgos*, the latter suitable to the role of the rich young man who is there as a contrasting leading character, though not so far identified by name; and (iii) *Georgos* is known to be among the persistent survivors of Menander's plays from the remains of four previously known copies, namely P. Berol. inv. 21106, from a roll assigned to the first century BC (B4); PSI 100, a strip from a codex assigned to the fourth century AD (F); P. Lond. 2823, three scraps from another codex assigned to the fourth century (M); and P. Gen. 155, possibly to be assigned to the fifth century (G), the first leaf of a codex of Menander to be discovered, and at present our principal source of the text. A new critical edition of lines 1–98 is given by Colin Austin in G. Bastianini – A. Casanova (eds.), *Menandro: Cent'anni di papiri* (Florence 2001) 79–94.

If accepted as Menander, the fragment is to be added to the list of vellum codices of the author given by F. d'Aiuto, 'Graeca in codici orientali della Biblioteca Vaticana', in L. Perria (ed.), *Tra Oriente e Occidente* (Testi e Studi Bizantino-Neoellenici 14, 2004), 227–96 at 278–82.

Scenes of betrothal, such as are represented by these two scraps of text, are recurrent in plays of New Comedy. They can be recognized even in small fragments from the set forms of words that are used. Here one notes the reference to the dowry in A 2, and λαμβάνειν, B 4, of taking a woman in marriage from her κύριος: here a brother. A recently published fragment of this kind is LXVIII **4646**, discussed by me there with further references: see especially on Menander, *Dyskolos* 842–4, with Sandbach on *Perik.* 1010 ff., noting XV **1824** in PCG VIII 1045, where in 12 λα]μβάν[ω, δέ]χομα[ι, seems likely.

No overlap with any other surviving text has so far been seen. The reason for thinking specifically of Menander's *Georgos* is not of itself the common motif of betrothal, but the proper name of one of the parties, Gorgias, and the indications of reconciliation between that character and a richer interlocutor in a manner reminiscent of the rich/poor, town/country antithesis of *Dyskolos*, here with a hint of a more complicated and contentious background to the transaction such as has emerged from study of the Geneva leaf, as for example in T. B. L. Webster, *An Introduction to Menander* (1974) 141–4, with briefer accounts in Gomme/Sandbach, *Menander: A Commentary* (1973), and in vol. i of Arnott's Loeb edition (1979). The names of the two participating characters, Chaireas and Gorgias (there is nothing to show that anyone else is present), appear together as those of two friends in Achilles Tatius, *Leucippe and Clitophon* 4.15, where Gorgias is an Egyptian soldier, not an Attic countryman as he is in *Georgos*, *Dyskolos*, and elsewhere. This could be a random choice, for both the names are quite common; but they were perhaps thought of together from the two characters' prominence in this play. If the identification of the present fragment is valid, Chaireas will take his place as the speaker of the first lines of the Geneva fragment, so far unidentified by name.

Here, from B 4 f., we should suppose that it is Chaireas who accepts Gorgias' sister in marriage. Gorgias should therefore speak at the end of 3 and the beginning of 4, 'Absolutely nothing . . .' (one would assume he said something like 'stands in the way'); Chaireas, at the beginning of 3, refers in some sense to Gorgias' state of mind; Gorgias refers in 2 to something that is fitting treatment for, or behaviour by, the prospective bridegroom. Apart from the reference to justice or a lawsuit in 1, it is clear that, as in other scenes of this kind, the betrothal represents a reconciliation of conflict. So much is suggested by side A.

There is no way to determine physically whether A or B came first. Parallels indicate that a dowry may be referred to either before or after the formal words of betrothal. Perhaps one can say that, with the two snippets of text on opposite sides of a leaf, the interval between them may be something between 17 and 27 lines, depending on what we make of the format of the codex (see the discussion above); and that therefore the content of A, which suggests wealth (1), a concrete proposal (2), and a favourable measure of agreement (4), would be a suitable lead-in to B, and an anticlimax after it. *Georgos* apart, if we take a cue from Sostratos and Gorgias in *Dyskolos*, it should be Chaireas who is the wealthy party, and Gorgias the worthy and proud poorer man with something more than a cash dowry to offer or (as it might be) land (2).

The text was briefly presented by me in 'The Rediscovery of Menander', a paper given at the conference *Culture in Pieces*, for Peter Parsons, Oxford, 20–23 September 2006: it is to appear in the volume of the same title, edited by Dirk Obbink and Richard Rutherford.

Side A (hair side)

```
.....].:ευπορ.[                    .....]ς: εὐπορε[ι
.ερωμεταπροικο[                    φέρω μετὰ προικὸ[ς
ακηκοασμου·ταυθ’.[                 ἀκήκοάς μου· ταῦθ’ ἃ; [
cφοδρ’εcτινευδο.[                  cφόδρ’ ἐcτὶν εὖ δοχ[θέντα
καμοιδοκω...[                      κἀμοὶ δοκῶ...[
```
(5)

Side B (flesh side)

```
]..ιδικ.[                          π]ερὶ δίκη[c
]μειcηκετε:                        ὑ]μεῖc ἥκετε:
]νοειc: ουδεεν                     ]νοεῖc: οὐδὲ ἕν
]δελφηνλαμβανειν χαιρ     Χα.      ἀ]δελφὴν λαμβάνειν
]...cγοργια·                       ]...c, Γοργία.
```
(5)

Side A

1 first, foot of a letter, suits c, and lower dot of a dicolon; last, ε rather than ι: i.e. -εῖ, -εῖν, -εῖc, -εῖτε; or εὐπόρε[ι   2 trace of an upright on the line; for broad φ with vestigial descender, note cφοδρ’ in 4   3 .[, trace of low ink, perhaps tip of slanting stroke, on the line, thereby ruling out ι?   4 .[, trace of down-sloping upright   5 perhaps ạ followed by indistinguishable traces of two letters

Side B

1 lower parts of uprights for ε and ρ̣; end, traces of two verticals: i.e. possibly н, hardly ạ   2].̣, probably м, less likely ạι, then possibly ε with its middle stroke lost due to abrasion, c not excluded   5 before γοργια, perhaps top of c; before it, top of an upright

Side A

1–2 Perhaps εὐπορε[ῖc. Compare *Dyskolos* 284–6, μήτ’ αὐτός, εἰ cφόδρ’ εὐπορεῖc, πίcτευε τούτῳ, μήτε τῶν πτωχῶν πάλιν ἡμῶν καταφρόνει, spoken by Gorgias to the rich man's son Sostratos, on the theme of wealth and poverty; *Georgos* 1KT/2 Arnott, line 4, εἰ καὶ cφόδρ’ εὐπορεῖ γάρ . . . . Gorgias, who should be the speaker here, presumably continues (although the beginning of 2 is damaged, there is no sign of a *paragraphos*). At *Dyskolos* 844–47, Gorgias offers a dowry of one talent, which represents the value of half of the estate that Knemon has made over to him, but is told by the wealthy Kallippides to keep it all together: here too he seems, with something of the poorer man's pride, to be putting forward the best offer he can.

4 Aorist ἐδόχθην is first quoted by LSJ from Polybius; δοκοῦντα, which one might have expected, seems to be ruled out by the trace of an oblique stroke surviving after δο.

5 Possibly καί μοι, as at *Dysk.* 266 (corrected from καμοι by Winnington-Ingram), but without more context it is hard to be sure of the sense.

Side B

1–3 Nothing can be determined from here about the nature of the dispute; the mention of ὁ ἀδικῶν in line 149 KT (fr. 9c, 3 Arnott) of *Georgos*, together with other references to wealth, poverty and injustice in the quoted fragments, indicate that these themes were prominent in that play, and may account in part for the popularity that its long survival suggests. The young man we may now wish to think of as Chaireas had, it seems, had a surreptitious affair with Gorgias' sister, whom he eventually marries in spite of the other plans for his marriage that his father had for him; in this affair, no doubt, whatever its precise nature, lay the cause of the friction with Gorgias, whose anger at the dishonour to his family is paralleled in the reaction of the Gorgias of *Dyskolos* to Sostratos' approaches to his half-sister there (289–93). There are several ways to imagine words of reconciliation being spoken: for example, with Gorgias saying μετανοοῦντες ὑ]μεῖς ἥκετε or μετανοήςαντες ὑ]μεῖς ἥκετε 'so you have come to me out of regret', echoed by Chaireas in 3 with something like (cὺ) . . . μήδ᾽ αὖ μετα]νοεῖς; 'Nor you?'.

2 An infinitive accompanying cε presumably came earlier.

3–5 E.g. (**Γο.**) οὐδὲ ἕν | ἔςτ᾽ ἐμποδών, continuing with **Χα.** τὴν cὴν ἀ]δελφὴν λαμβάνειν | ἕτοιμός εἰμι πίςτιν ἐπι]θείς, Γοργία; for πίςτιν ἐπιθείς, see *Dysk.* 308. Variants can be devised, but if the sense is as indicated, and subject to what is said above about the order of Sides A and B, the formal betrothal (ἀλλ᾽ ἐγγύω, κτλ.) will be expected to follow.

3 Metre demands a short syllable before νοεῖς, e.g. ἃ νοεῖς; or a compound, μετανοεῖς, κατανοεῖς ('have you come to your senses?'), προνοεῖς; or possibly a word-group like οὐκ οἶδ᾽ ὅτι νοεῖς: see my *Dyskolos of Menander*, 66–8.

4 The *nota personae* to the right of the column presumably relates to a mid-line speaker change.

E. W. HANDLEY

III. NEW LITERARY TEXTS

4938. Empedocles, *Physica*

88/295(a)   4.1 × 6.1 cm   First half of second century
Plate I

A scrap bearing the remains of nine lines written along the fibres of a papyrus roll. The back is blank. No margin is visible, nor any other sign that the writing is near the beginning or end of the line. The reading in line 1 is abraded almost beyond recognition; the text disintegrates toward the bottom. Elsewhere the writing is clear enough.

The hand is an informal round capital, the work of a competent professional scribe, written with a fair amount of fluidity and connection between letters, especially at the top (e.g. 3 νπεπ, where the scribe has lifted his pen only between ε and π). Roberts, *GLH* 13a (document dated 120–24) and 13b (Hyperides, *Orations*, assigned to the first half of the second century, with later cursive scholia) provide reasonable comparisons. There is no evidence of correction, collation, or variants, and no opportunity to observe *paragraphoi* or marginalia, but the scribe seems to have employed a common form of punctuation (by blank space in 6) familiar from professional book production of the day. The scribe sometimes leaves a small space between words (3, perhaps 2).

In line 2 the sequence of letters is compatible with part of a verse from Empedocles (B 88 Diels–Kranz) quoted by Aristotle and Strabo (see 2 n.), to which the papyrus adds small portions of several of the preceding and following verses. The spaces employed (inconsistently) by the scribe confirm (at least as far as μία γείνεται), while the poetic form of the verb in 5 strongly argues for the text of a poem in hexameters, and is additionally attested for Empedocles. The sequences of letters in lines 2–7 are compatible with the middles of hexameters with corresponding caesurae. We thus seem to have stichic verses, and therefore a book-copy of Empedocles' poem, rather than quoted verse in wrapping format, such as might have been expected if we were dealing with the text of a prose author or commentary quoting the passage. Cf. P. Hamb. I appendix p. 129 = 'P. Ibscher 2', 9–11, containing Empedocles B 115.6 quoted as prose to illustrate prosodic shortening (identified by M. L. West, *CR* 12 (1962) 120). The poetic diction, such as can be glimpsed, may be assigned a plausible place in Empedocles' poetry. Of this context we can only offer a guess based on the preserved traces and the presumed place of B 88 in the poem as known in the secondary tradition, which the papyrus offers small scope for expanding. The fragment offers no evidence as to whether the papyrus consisted of a fully continuous text of the poem (in one or more books), or rather (for example) a series of extracts.

The reappearance of a papyrus of Empedocles may seem the less remarkable in the wake of the Strasbourg Empedocles: A. Martin and O. Primavesi, *L'Empedocle de Strasbourg (P. Strasb. gr. Inv. 1665–1666)* (1999), with which our fragment shows no overlap. Dating from the late first century AD, the Strasbourg copy precedes by a generation or two. It is striking to have two professionally produced copies produced within a half-century of each other, quite apart from the relatively minor footprint that the Presocratics have left in literary papyri from Egypt. Apart from Empedocles, the only Presocratic works to have survived on a papyrus to date are Antiphon's Περὶ ἀληθείας (P. Oxy. **1364 + 3647**, P. Oxy. **1797**) and Pherecydes Syrius' Θεολογία (P. Grenf. II 11). Empedocles remains the only Presocratic who composed in verse to have been preserved on papyrus. For the survival of a copy of Empedocles' Καθαρμοί (now lost) until well into the Renaissance (1494), see J. Mansfeld, 'A Lost Manuscript of Empedocles' Katharmoi,' *Mnemosyne* 47 (1994) 79–82. For the title of Empedocles' poem, alternatively cited by ancient authors as Περί φύσεως and (Τὰ) φυσικά, see the discussion of Martin and Primavesi (op. cit.) 243–51; D. Sedley, *Lucretius and the Transformation of Greek Wisdom* (1998) 2–3. The existence of Empedocles' Καθαρμοί as a separate work is controversial; the location of the present papyrus text in the physical poem is secured by the identification (widely accepted since Karsten) of B 88 as part of the poet's account of the creation by Aphrodite of animals and their body-parts known to have been narrated in that poem (see 2 n.).

```
        ·    ·   ·              ·    ·    ·    ·
   ]....[                  ].....[
   ].μια γεινετ.[     ............].. μία γείνεται ἀμφοτέρων ὄψ  B 88
  ]ωρονπεπ.[         ............]ωρον πεπ.[– ‿‿ – ‿‿ – ⏑
  ]εινοσακαιρ..[     ............]ειν ὅσα καιρ.[‿‿ – ‿‿ – ⏑
 5 ]χ..ϲ γελααν[  5  ............]χωϲ γελααν[‿‿ – ‿‿ – ⏑
   ]ιου.[.].επ[       ............]ιου.[.]ο επ[...........
   ].ε..[...]εκει.[   ............].ευϲ[..]εκειν[..........
    ].[..]υ..[        ].[..]υ..[
     ]κια[             ]κια[
        ·    ·   ·              ·    ·    ·    ·
```

1 ....., descender with diagonal trace to upper right as though right arm of γ, but ρ not excluded; round letter, ε θ ο ϲ ω; horizontal trace in lower part of writing-space, compatible with a round letter (ε θ ο ϲ); diagonal rising from below the line to right (as of γ in 6)   2]., tiny hairline diagonal at about mid-level, part of the tongue of ε or raised tail of λ, not ν   .[, dot on the line with trace of diagonal descending to right above it, together compatible with λ   3 .[, dot at the top line   4 .., circle not quite closed at upper right, where there is a dot at mid-level: not λ, but ω not excluded   5 .., loop of λ or right side of ω, then back-curving ι or right side of ω, thus λι or ω   6 .[, horizontal stroke in upper part connecting and continuing across an

upright, as of τ, less likely π, ν; on edge, a dot at mid-level   ]., round letter (imperfectly joined at bottom) as of ο, ω   7]., horizontal stroke in upper part, with a much shorter horizontal centred beneath it, just below mid-level: perhaps z, ξ, but π, τ not excluded   .., hook in upper part of writing-space connecting out of preceeding and another, similary hook connecting into following lunate letter (c, ε), taken together as of γ or x   .[, upright as of ν, н   8].[, round letter (ε θ ο c ω) or ι   .., horizontal stroke connecting from preceding γ to descender from which a diagonal descends to the right, ν м λ suggested; left side of a round letter, ε θ ο c ω

2 γείνετα[ι, l. γίνεται = γίγνεται

2 μία γείνεται ἀμφοτέρων ὄψ. The verse-fragment (ostensibly a line-end) is quoted by Aristotle, *Poet.* 21 1458a4 and Strabo VIII p. 364 (the latter explicitly from Apollodorus of Athens); lines 1 and 3–7 here are previously unattested. The point and context of the quoted fragment are unknown, apart from citation by grammarians for the illustration of poetically shortened words in apocope (here ὄψ for ὄψις). Editors of Empedocles have been led by the term ὄψ, together with the pairing implied in ἀμφοτέρων, to locate the verse-fragment in Empedocles' exposition of his theory of vision, following on from the detailed description of the structure of the eye, and its invention in the zoogony, as recounted in B 84. ὄψ is glossed by authorities as both ὄψις and ὀφθαλμός, as well as φωνή (Hesychius s.v. ὄψ· ὄψις. ὀφθαλμός. ἢ φωνή). ὄψ can thus mean 'appearance', 'face', 'eye', 'vision', or 'voice'. In addition, ancient commentators regularly use ὄψις to designate the ray-theory of vision and Empedocles' particular version of it. As quoted and in the papyrus, the sense is ambiguous, although the expression is obviously poetic; cf. ὄψ also in Antimachus (fr. 56 Schellenberg–Giles = 96 Wyss Δήμητρός τοι Ἐλευσινίης ἱερὴ ὄψ, similarly quoted by Strabo from Apollodorus), and in *SH* 65.7. Here it may be that either of the two eyes focuses on a single subject, or that one vision results from the impression on two eyes. The former is in agreement with the theories of vision attributed to Pythagoras and Parmenides (where the rays from each eye embrace the object like outstretched hands: Aet. 4.13.9–10), so that 'a "path" from each eye joins at the point where the two impressions are combined'; M. R. Wright, *Empedocles: The Extant Fragments* (1981) 243. However, Alexander of Aphrodisias, *Comm. de Aristot. De sensu* CIAG 3.1, 24, in quoting B 84, says that at one time Empedocles explains vision by fire coming from the eye, and at another by effluences from what is seen. Together they could be said to produce a single vision. This latter sense might be supported by the papyrus text, if we read in ῥόο[c (sc. e.g. φωτός) in 4, and if [τόccα] . . . ὅcα in that line refer to the emanation of effluences from objects (see 4 n.).

]. μία. The proposal of S. Karsten (*Philosophorum Graecorum veterum . . . operum reliquiae* (Amsterdam 1838) ii 130 (fr. 311) to restore ὀφθαλμῶν (taken with ἀμφοτέρων) before μία in Empedocles B 88, accepted by some subsequent editors, is ruled out by the position of a tiny horizontal speck in the papyrus at mid-level, seemingly excluding -ν. That is not to say that we should not understand ὀφθαλμῶν with ἀμφοτέρων, or posit it even earlier in the verse (Karsten actually prints '(ὀφθαλμῶν) μία' κτλ.); but alternatives are also available, e.g. ὁδῶν] or τρόπων]. As for the individuation of μία—essential for the identification of this sequence of letters as Empedocles B 88—lack of connection with the following μ suggests the kind of spacing between words that appears inconsistently in this papyrus, e.g. after μία (2), ὅcα (4), and before επ[(5, where it may also mark punctuation), though the trace is too exiguous to be certain that the scribe has left a space between words here. The possibility of a word ending in -μια cannot definitively be ruled out: e.g. ζη-μία, ἐπιθυ-μία, εὐρυθ-μία, μηδε-μία, ἀδυνα-μία, ὀφθαλ-μία—all construable with γίνεται (only the last three are compatible with the trace before μια). However, the expression μία γίνεται on its own is so common as to be practically idiomatic, while the poetic form in 5 presupposes verse, thus reinforcing the identification with Empedocles B 88.

3]ωρον. ζείδ]ωρον would be fitting, especially if used of the creator-goddess Aphrodite, to

whom we know it was applied by Empedocles in B 151 (her name to be restored here?). Other possible completions include χ]ῶρον, suggested by Professor Pontani (as in B 118.1, 121.1), which would be appropriate in a description of the movement of light or rays from one place to another, or the position of objects within the field of vision); ταλαίπ]ωρον or μετέ]ωρον might also be considered, although in these cases it would be less clear what entity is designated.

πεπ . [. The likeliest possible completion is perhaps πεπο[(ι)η- (suggested to us by Professor A. A. Long), probably with Aphrodite as subject. It is she who Empedocles describes as inventing and constructing the eye in the elaborate simile in B 84 comparing the eye to a man-made lamp. (πεπαρμέν- (B 112.12) is ruled out by the surviving trace after πεπ.)

4]ειν ὅσα καιρ . . [. A number of articulations are possible at the start, allowing for several different strategies for supplementation at the beginning. Completions such as ἐκ]εῖνος or φα]εινός (Pontani) are certainly possible. But]ειν ὅσα seems the most plausible articulation, effecting a correlation of particles as at B 71.5 τόσσ', ὅσα. We might therefore envisage a line beginning something like τόσσα . . . ἀπορρ]εῖν, enumerating in this case the quantity of effluences from the eye. Correspondingly, we might have a verse ending (see next note) e.g. ῥόο[ς αὐτὸς ἔλαμψεν (sc. φωτός or πυρός): see B 100.14 πυκινὸν ῥόον. Of course, in addition to ὅσα καὶ plus a word beginning with ῥ-, we could also divide ἃ καιρ- (cf. B 111.6 καίριον αὐχμόν). Spaces for word division (or the lack of them) unfortunately provide little indication here, since the scribe's practice is inconsistent in this respect.

5 συνε]χῶς seems a plausible supplement, especially in a description of continually flowing effluences either from the eye or the object of vision.

γελααν[. For the distracted form in -αα- in Empedocles see e.g. B 71.5 τόσσ', ὅσα νῦν γεγάασι συναρμοσθέντ' Ἀφροδίτηι; W. Veitch, Greek Verbs Irregular and Defective (1879) 148; more generally: D. B. Monro, A Grammar of the Homeric Dialect (1891) 50–54 (no. 56); Again, a number of articulations are possible, allowing for either the third person singular or the infinitive: (1) of γελάω: such an image might well be visual, connoting brightness (perhaps here of the swift-darting movement of light or rays from the eyes), as it does at Hes. Theog. 40, h. Cer. 14, Aesch. P.V. 90 ἀνήριθμον γέλασμα; cf. Lucr. 1.8 rident 'are bright' (Bailey), 2.559, 3.22, 5.1105; or (2) γ' plus a form of λάω, or, more likely, ἐλαύνω, as Professor Pontani suggests. It is true that the distracted form of the infinitive γελααν is never actually attested, while ἐλάαν is fully Homeric, as at Od. 12.124 ἀλλὰ μάλα σφοδρῶς ἐλάαν in the same metrical position. Here ἐλάαν could describe the motion of the light or rays (perhaps with συνε]χῶς) as they strike objects or the eye. This leaves γ' as somewhat rhetorically odd, though its occurrence in Empedocles is not lacking (B 3.1, 9.3, 23.10, 28.3, 129.5, 110.6, 114.2, 128.4). 3rd singular γελαᾶ in the distracted form is paralleled in Nonnus (33.151, 42.302).

6 το]ιοῦτ[ ]ο? (less suitable for the trace: πο]ιοῦν[τ]ο).

7 Ζεύς? (perhaps as a counterpart to Aphrodite in Empedocles' account of divine formation of human faculties and body-parts?).

]εκειν[. A form of the pronoun ἐκεῖνος is an obvious possibility; but we could also have]ε κειν- i.e. κιν- (an iotacistic spelling like 2 γείνετα[ι), presumably in this case a verb or noun indicating the movement of light or images.

D. OBBINK

4939. Imperial Hexameters: *Ethopoea?*

42 5B.75/G(1)   Fr. 1 12.2 × 25.5 cm   First half of second century
Plate IV

One large fragment together with some smaller unplaceable scraps and debris belonging to a papyrus roll written along the fibres. The verso is blank. The largest piece, fr. 1, contains the remains of two columns, 8 line-ends from col. i and 35 lines and foot of col. ii. Fr. 2 has a wide upper margin of 4.6 cm and remains of one line. It is possible that it belongs at the top of fr. 1 (col. i or col. ii), but the back fibres do not prove it. Col. ii in fr. 1, as it stands, is 21.2 cm high, with lower margin preserved to 4.3 cm. A different, cursive hand has used the intercolumnium to the left of col. ii 1–10 for a calculation in drachmae.

The literary hand, presenting medium-sized flattened capitals, is bilinear (exception made of φ, ρ and occasionally x and ʒ), but there are no well-defined upper and lower limits for the line, and letters are larger at the beginning of each line. Letters are fairly spaced, although some high horizontals (especially the broken one of τ) and obliques (e.g. the right one of ʌ) may touch the following character. Lines are also regularly spaced. The writing is uniform in width (although o is sometimes smaller than the rest of letters), tending to circular forms, even in square letters, which tend to soften their forms by curving their uprights. When drawn in a single sequence, strokes may present occasional loops at the junctions. The free ends of certain strokes are decorated regularly; the ornamentation normally takes the form of a hook to the right or to the left, although sometimes it can be reduced to a quick tick or just a small blob.

The hand may be classified as Informal Round (*GMAW*² p. 21). It shares some features with that of P. Berol. 6926, dated in the second half of the first century AD (Roberts, *GLH* 11a and Schubart, *PGB* 14), though its general appearance is more like that of XXVI **2441** (*GMAW*² 22), assigned to the second century AD, with flattened, round letters. Our hand is strikingly similar to that of XVIII **2161** (*GMAW*² 24), similarly assigned to the second century AD. We have the same general flattening and lack of well-defined upper and lower limits, occasional looping at junctions and general curvature of uprights. Thus I should be inclined to suggest the first half of the second century AD as a probable date for **4939**.

The text presents no accents, but it has one rough breathing (27) and a mark for long quantitiy (3), two cases of organic use of diaeresis (4 and 25), and low, middle, and high points, apparently arranged according to a system: low points (13 and 31) seem to mark a very short pause, so short that it might not even be marked in modern editions. Middle points (6, 9, 20, 26) seem to mark pauses equivalent to a modern comma (in 9, 20, and 26, they appear between two co-ordinate phrases). High points (19, 21, 22, 24, 27, 28, 29, 30) seem to mark full stops. Elision is always effected, but marked in only three cases out of ten. Iota adscript is written, but as a superscription; this is obvious in 24 and possible for 19 (see n.). The superscript iota, and the superscript lambda in 21 (correcting θεων into θέλων), raise the question of a possible second hand. It seems clear that the same ink used for the main text has also been used not only for lectional signs, but also for the superscripts. Furthermore, although it is very difficult to appreciate any similarities with the handwriting of the main text in the drawing of such small signs, the superscripts generally present comparable shapes. Thus it seems that the same scribe was responsible for all the writing; and the use of the same ink suggests that he wrote the lectional signs and the superscripts at the same time as the main text, or at a second pass when he was still using the same ink. We might therefore have here a professional production, if not an author's manuscript in which he has provided variants (cf. P. J. Parsons on L **3537** p. 59). However, readings that do not make sense or do not fit the metre (cf. 19 n.) can hardly be interpreted as alternatives offered by the author himself, since elsewhere he seems to have been a competent versifier. Thus, if we accept such cases as corrections, we might be forced to think of an independent scribe who, however skilled as a copyist, altered the text wherever he did not understand it or thought it incorrect.

Fr. 1 col. ii offers 35 lines of hexameters; presumably col. i also contained verse, since the line-ends were so irregular, but we cannot tell whether it was the same work. Col. ii seems to represent a single poem, in which a despairing lover reacts to the death of his beloved: 1–7 'Her beauty was exceptional'; 8–12 'Nothing could assuage my grief, except death itself'; 13–22 'And yet suicide is dishonourable'; 22–31 'Therefore life must be endured: even the gods could not save her from Fate'; 32–5 'May she rest in peace, as all living things must die'. Perhaps the poem ended here, with the conventional consolation. The structure is thus that of a first person monologue down to line 12, followed by what seems to be a self-addressing speech, and finishing with a more general statement, where a more detached speaker becomes apparent. The composition is highly rhetorical, using devices such as the impersonal second person singular, exempla, and maxims.

Perhaps the poem should be classified as an *ethopoea*. If this is so, it would be the earliest instance of hexametric *ethopoea* on papyrus known to us, either as a literary production or a school exercise; cf. J.-L. Fournet, *ZPE* 92 (1992) 253–66, J.-A. Fernández Delgado, *Pap. Congr. XX* 299–305, and see recently G. Agosti, in E. Amato and J. Schamp (eds.), *HΘOΠOIIA: La représentation de caractères entre fiction scolaire et réalité vivante à l'époque impériale et tardive* (2005) 34–60 (cf. also E. Amato and G. Ventrella's catalogue of *ethopoeae* in the second appendix of the same volume, pp. 213–31). However, the subject matter in our piece does not seem to agree with the rest of the examples of this genre found on papyrus: whereas there themes are drawn from Homeric and Hesiodic poetry, here we find one of the major motifs of the Greek novel as the subject-matter (see S. MacAlister, *Dreams and Suicides:*

The Greek Novel from Antiquity to the Byzantine Empire (1996)). On the other hand, the antilogical character of the composition seems to match one (much later) instance in Amato and Ventrella's repertoire: τίνας εἴποι λόγους ἡ Ἀφροδίτη ζητοῦσα τὸν Ἄδωνιν· ἀντιφθέγγεται δὲ πρὸς ταύτην ὁ Ζεὺς ἔπος πρὸς ἔπος ἀμειβόμενος. It seems therefore that in our case an individual with some literary interests and training might have practised themes from the novel and erotic poetry in the form of the *ethopoea*, thus further revealing a life for the genre outside the school. In this respect, this kind of paraliterary product itself may have had some effect on later Greek narrative poetry like that of Nonnus, who is also generally agreed to have been influenced by the novel (see F. Vian, *Nonnos de Panopolis: Les Dionysiaques* i (1976) pp. xlviii–xlix).

Various features show that this is a late and amateur composition. Note especially the form ζῶθι (23) and the combination τοίνυν γάρ (22); δαίσας (12) was understood as coming from δαίειν 'burn'; ὄρειος (35) was scanned as an anapaest. The dialect is basically Homeric, and here and there phrases or images are directly borrowed. But the piece is not just a patchwork, and elsewhere the language is paralleled in late hexameter poetry, including the *Anthologia Graeca* and Nonnus. The versification is generally competent (no breaches of Hermann's Bridge or Meyer's Second Law; no word-end after contracted second biceps), though the poet does not observe all the refinements of the Callimachean hexameter (Naeke's Law is infringed in 16). Meyer's First Law is generally respected, unless one includes the word-groups ending with the 'second trochee' in 16, 21, 33. Of 32 lines where the main caesura is preserved, 24 have feminine caesura = 75%. The bucolic diaeresis is observable in 14 out of 28 lines. Contraction of bicipitia occurs in 26 out of 33 lines, as follows: 13 in the first biceps (39%), 14 in the second (42%), 2 (lines 9, 22) in the third (6%), 9 in the fourth (27%), none in the fifth; there are two lines with three contractions (9, 22). These percentages are closely comparable with the figures for poets of the first three centuries AD (see M. L. West, *Greek Metre* (1982) 177–8). Line 20 has a hiatus at the masculine caesura and sentence-end.

Fr. 1

col. i

col. ii

       ·   ·   ·

            ].[

      [.]..ειϲρειακετηνδε.[

      ]αλλᾱωνπεριαλλον.[

· · ·   ] ρηϊδιωϲφραϲϲαιοδ.[

]   5] ωϲκτιλονενποιμ[

]   ] αιετον[..]ωνων·κ.[......]...[

]   ωϲκαλονενλειμων.[.....].ροφε.[

]ι·   τιϲθεοϲευνηϲειενε..ιτοϲονα.[

]   ουμηνπαιηων·αϲκληπιοϲουδεκ.[

]   10 ηπιαπαντ᾽αμυδιϲπιεεινχθονο..ν[

]   μουνοϲκενθανατοϲμεκακωνεκτ[

]ντων·   μουνοϲοκαιδαιϲαϲενεμοιφ[λ]ογατη.[

].ων·   τιϲπευδ...δειλαιε.κακαϲδε.[..]ηρα[

].   ο...αγαρ.[ ]καιτου.[..].[..]ων.[

]ϲϲαϲ·   15 ανδρε...[.]κεϲθ.ουθαν[.].[

]   καιγαρδη.ιϲανακτοϲαεικηϲδμ.[

]ν·   παυριδιονδ[.].πημαδερ...ρτηϲεμ.[

]   τυτθονα.[.].λητηροϲα[.].υαμενοϲχ.[

]   ουδενορα.[.]εγαπαιδι.[..]ιζεαι·ουγα..[

]   20 .μειρειϲθα.ατου·αχεωνδαφαροφρα.[

].·   εκφυγεειν.επελωραθεϣνκακα·πημ[

]   εκθυμουβα.εειν·ζωειντ.ινυνγαραν.[

]   τ.ληθιταλα[.].αιζωθικακ.ϲμηδ᾽αλγεα[

]   [.].κρυαμη.ευναζε·κορήγεμενουδεν[

]   25 [.].υτα·κακαι.ακαρωνμενοϊομαιουποτ.[

].·   .λαθεωνα.κητι·διοϲδαεκητιτετυκτ[

]   παϲιγαραθα..τοιϲινε᷈ηνδανεν·ουδετιϲη[

]   ονμακαρωναθεριζε·θυηδ᾽ωφελλενεκα.[

]   παρδυναμινπαντεϲϲι·ταδ.υκωνηϲεμιν[

]   30 ουχοτιοικοτ.οντοθεοι·μελεγαρϲφιϲικο[

]   αιϲηϲαλλαπανευθε.θεωνκεναμερμερα.[

]   ηδιϲτηϲυδεκουραφεροιϲρεακηραϲαφυκτ.[

]   ευθυμοϲδεγ.νοιοκαιεννεκυεϲϲιγεγηθ.[

]   παντωνουδετ[.]ϲεϲτινοϲουτ.θνηξεταιεμ[

]   35 ο.μενανηρου.ορνιϲαηϲυρο.ουδορειοϲθ.[

col. ii

.   .   .   .

].[
[.].. εις ῥεῖα κε τήνδε.[
ἀλλάων περίαλλον.[
ῥηϊδίως φράccαιο δι[
5   ὡς κτίλον ἐν ποίμ[νη
αἰετὸν [οἰ]ωνῶν, κα[...ἐν θή]ρεc[cι ⏑ – ⏓
ὡς καλὸν ἐν λειμῶνι [.....] προφερ[έcτατον – ⏓
τίς θεὸς εὐνήcειεν ἐμοὶ τόcον α.[⏖ – ⏓
οὐ μὴν Παιήων, Ἀcκληπιὸς οὐδέ κε [– ⏓
10 ἤπια πάντ' ἄμυδιc πιέειν χθονὸς αν[⏖ – ⏓
μοῦνός κεν θάνατός με κακῶν εκτ[– ⏖ – ⏓
μοῦνος ὁ καὶ δαίcας ἐν ἐμοὶ φ[λ]όγα τὴν[δ(ε) (⏑) ⏑ – ⏓
τί cπεύδεις, δείλαιε, κακὰς δ' ἐπ[ὶ κ]ῆρα[c (⏑) – ⏓
ο...αγαρ.[ ]καιτου.[..].[..]ων.[
15 ἄνδρες γ' ο[ὐ]κ ἐcθλοῦ θαν[ά]τ[ου ⏖ – ⏖ – ⏓
καὶ γὰρ δή τις ἄνακτος ἀεικὴς δμὼ[c ⏖ – ⏓
παυρίδιον δ[ι]ὰ πῆμα δέρην ἤρτηcε μ.[⏑ – ⏓
τυτθὸν ἀπ[ε]ιλητῆρος ἀ[λ]ευάμενος χό[λον – ⏓
ς[θαι]
οὐδὲν ὁρᾶν [μ]έγα παιδὶ λ[ογ]ίζεαι· οὐ γὰρ.[(⏑) – ⏓
20 ἱμείρεις θανάτου, ἀχέων δ' ἄφαρ ὄφρα κ[(ε) (⏑) – ⏓
ἐκφυγέειν τε πέλωρα θέλων κακά, πῆμ[α ⏑ – ⏓
ἐκ θυμοῦ βαλέειν. ζώειν τοίνυν γὰρ ἀνά[γκη
τλῆθι τάλα[c] καὶ ζῶθι κακῶς, μηδ' ἄλγεα [– ⏓
[δ]άκρυα μηδ' εὔναζε· κόρηϊ γε μὲν οὐδὲν [⏑ – ⏓
25 [τ]αῦτα. κακαὶ μακάρων μὲν ὀίομαι οὔποτε [– ⏓
ἀλλὰ θεῶν ἀέκητι, Διὸς δ' ἀέκητι τέτυκτ[ο.
πᾶcι γὰρ ἀθανάτοιcιν ἑήνδανεν. οὐδέ τις ἦ[εν
ὃν μακάρων ἀθέριζε, θύη δ' ὤφελλεν ἑκάc[τῳ
πὰρ δύναμιν πάντεccι· τὰ δ' οὐκ ὤνηcέ μιν [– ⏓
30 οὐχ ὅτι οἱ κοτέοντο θεοί—μέλε γάρ cφιcι κο[ύρη—,
αἴcης ἀλλ' ἀπάνευθε θεῶν κενὰ μέρμερα π[– ⏓
ἡδίcτη cὺ δὲ κούρα φέροις ῥέα κῆρας ἀφύκτο[υс,
εὔθυμος δὲ γένοιο καὶ ἐν νεκύεccι γέγηθι.
πάντων οὐδέ τ[ί]c ἐcτιν ὃc οὐ τεθνήξεται ἔμ[πης,
35 οὐ μὲν ἀνὴρ οὐδ' ὄρνις ἀήcυρος οὐδ' ὄρειος θή[ρ.

col. i

Lines in col i are not exactly parallel with those in col. ii.   14] ., apparently remains of arc facing right; to right low remains as of junction of two loops of ω; faint fleck above   17]ν·, fleck below ν , too high to belong to next line   21] ., faint, low(?) fleck

col. ii

1] .[, very low remains of ink indicate that we are not before the beginning of the column 2] .. ειϲ, first, low remains; second, low arc facing upwards, as if lower end of vertical or oblique descending sharply to the right   .[, lower half of vertical or oblique sharply rising to right; remains of middle horizontal or oblique descending to right from the remains of the vertical, and, above these, further traces; κ?   3 .[, ε or θ   4 .[, lower end of vertical or oblique ascending sharply to right   6 .[, high flecks of ink   ] ..., first, foot of long descender; second, middle to low remains of ink; third, low arc facing upwards like bottom of circular letter   7 .[, low flecks (or just burnt surface?)   ] ., н or π   .[, high remains of ink   8 ε . ι, first, left-hand end of low horizontal, then above to the right remains of vertical (м?); second, lower right quadrant of circular letter   .[, middle and high remains of ink   9 .[, faint low traces of ink   10 .. ν, first, remains of circular letter; second, long oblique descending flat to the right   12 .[, high fleck   13 δ ... δ, first, left semicircle; second, high spot; third, middle to high remains   .[, г or π   14 о ... α, first, lower end of upright; second, low arc facing upwards; third, low remains, as of arc facing upwards; above, to right, high remains   .[, low remains   .[, high fleck; below, faint traces?   ] .[, high dot   .[, high spot, as if junction of two strokes   15 ... [, first, о or c; second, remains of upright and high horizontal (г π τ); third, high remains   θ .ο, top of oblique descending to right; below, middle to low remains   .[, π or τ   16 η . ι, the right-hand end of a high horizontal touches the presumed ι at more than two-thirds of its height. This horizontal could belong to the same letter or to a different one from that presenting the upright   .[, remains of low arc facing upwards   17] ., middle to low traces, as if of end of oblique descending to right   ρ ... ρ, first, remains of upright; to the right, medial traces; second, high spot; third, high remains; to the right, remains of curved stroke facing right, like the right-hand one of н, π   .[, low and middle to high remains   18 .[, middle fleck   ] ., upright on edge   ] ., right-hand end of middle horizontal; traces below and above   .[, lower half of circular letter (ω also possible) 19 (interlinear space) .[, short upright or left-hand elements of a circular letter   19 .[, high spot   .[, top of descending oblique; below, fleck at line level   .. [, first, small high arc facing downwards; second, fleck at line level   20 .μ, Traces seemingly belonging to a tall upright; to the right, above the line, traces seem to reveal the presence of a lectional sign   ɑ .ɑ, upright   .[, upright, with a high horizontal going to the right from its top, slightly projecting to the left   21 ν .ε, lower part of upright   22 ɑ .ε, λ or χ   τ .ι, о or c   .[, low fleck; above, to the right, apparent end of oblique descending to right: λ, λ?   23] ., lower end of oblique descending to right; flecks above   κ .c, low to middle remains; to the right, curved stroke facing left   24] ., oblique descending to right; traces touching it from below at what must have been its mid-height   η .ε, long low horizontal   25] ., λ or λ   ι .ɑ, upright finishing with a lower long curved stroke to the right: м?   .[, middle spot; above, to the right, high spot   26 .λ, first, lower part of oblique ascending to right; second, lower end of oblique descending to right   ɑ .κ, low arc facing upwards; above, to right, middle fleck   27 ɑ .. τ, first, two high spots; second, remains of long oblique descending to right   28 .[, middle spot   29 δ .υ, small spot at line-level   30 τ .ο, remains of left-hand and upper parts of circular letter, with middle cross-bar   31 .[, π or (less likely) τ   32 .[, left-hand part of circular letter   33 γ .υ, left-hand part of circular letter (with middle cross-bar?)   .[, middle and low flecks of ink   34 τ .θ, ε or c   35 о .μ, κ or γ   υ .ο, lower extremity of oblique descending to right   о .ο, high remains; middle and low tiny flecks   .[, high and middle flecks

Fr. 2

]εωνπλ[ ]ηϲ.[
.   .   .

1 .[, faint medial traces

Fr. 3

.   .
]η[
].oϲ[
.   .

2]., left-facing semicircle

Fr. 4

.   .
].coυ[
.   .

1]., right-hand end of upward-facing arc at line level; remains of ink level with letter tops

Fr. 5

.   .
].ρ.[
]...[
.   .

1]., lower part of two parallel uprights   .[, lower half of right-facing semicircle   2 First, upper tip of ascending oblique; second, small loop (ρ?); third, high spot

Fr. 1 col. ii

'. . . easily her . . . above all other women . . . Easily you would notice her [standing out] like the ram in the flock [, that great leader of the sheep], the eagle of birds, [the lion among beasts], like the fair [rose] in the meadow, most excellent [of flowers]. What god could put to sleep for me so great an [insufferable grief]? Not Paean, nor Asclepius, [even if they gave me] to drink all the gentle [medicines?] of earth together. Only death could [take] me outside these evils, only the one who also kindled in me this [painful] fire.—Why do you hasten, miserable man, and [advance into] an evil destiny . . .? (15) Men [do not seek] a dishonourable death . . . Thus a mean slave [in fear] of his master, for a small pain, hangs himself [in vain], avoiding by a little the anger of the one who threatens him . . . (19) You reckon that life means nothing great to the slave. For you do not desire [. . .] death, but so that you may at once [be relieved] of suffering, and wishing to escape enormous evils, and to expel [so great] a pain from your heart. So (for it is necessary to live) endure, wretched man, and live miserably, and do not put to sleep [in your heart] your griefs nor your tears. The girl [will get no help] from this. [The destinies] of the blessed gods, I think, are never evil—but it was done against the will of the gods, against the will of Zeus. For she pleased all the immortals, nor was there any of the blessed whom she neglected. She increased sacrifices to all of them, each in turn, beyond her power. But that helped her not [at all], not because the gods were angry with her, for the girl was their care, but without Fate the deeds of [all] the gods are void. But you, sweetest girl, may you bear easily the inevitable destiny, may you be of good cheer and rejoice among the dead. Of all (creatures) there is none at all who will not die, not man, nor bird in the air, nor mountain beast.'

Fr. 1 col. ii

2 [.] . . εις: we probably have here a verb in the second person singular (the traces seem to exclude [ο]ὐδείς), yet the ending does not suit any form likely to combine with κε, like the optative in 4. Was it a separate utterance, e.g. 'Do you doubt? You would easily recognize her . . .'?

3 ἀλλάων (pap. αλλᾱων): the scribe has written a long mark over α to make it clear that this is the uncontracted form of the genitive feminine plural, and not the conjunction ἀλλά, which very frequently opens the line. Together with τήνδε, in the previous line, and following περίαλλον, this genitive helps to reveal the subject matter: we are dealing with a female figure who is being distinguished from all others of her kind (cf. *Od.* 19.326, where Penelope says of herself: ἀλλάων περίειμι νόον καὶ ἐπίφρονα μῆτιν).

περίαλλον: περίαλλα as an adverb occurs first in Pindar and *H. Hom.* 19.46, and often enough in Hellenistic and Roman hexameters. But the adjective itself is used only by Philodemus, *AP* 5.132.5 (another erotic context), and is plausibly restored in the same author's *De pietate* 1773–4 (see D. Obbink (ed.), *Philodemus: On Piety* (1996)). Here it might agree with a word like εἶδος, e.g. 'a beauty exceptional above all other women'. The adjective, like the adverb, might govern a genitive; cf. e.g. Opp. *Hal.* 1.144 πάντων περίαλλα.

4 φράccαιο: in the middle and passive voice, φράζω with a participle adopts the construction common to verbs related to any kind of sensory perception, thus meaning 'perceive, observe'. That we need an accusative as the object of the verb is also clear from the words which begin the following lines (κτίλον, αἰετόν), since ὡς introducing them indicates that they are part of two similes which should refer back to a previous accusative.

δι[: the similes express the idea of superiority; I therefore suggest e.g. δι[απρεπέα προφανεῖcαν, 'you could easily recognize her as she appeared standing out from the rest'. So Mosch. *Eur.* 71 (see below on 7) ἐν Χαρίτεccι διέπρεπεν Ἀφρογένεια.

5 ὡς κτίλον: the image occurs twice in the *Iliad*, of military commanders: 3.196 αὐτὸс δὲ κτίλοс ὣс ἐπιπωλεῖται στίχαс ἀνδρῶν (Odysseus), 13.492 λαοὶ ἕπονθ' ὡс εἴ τε μετὰ κτίλον ἕσπετο μῆλα (Aeneas); cf. also Alcm. fr. 1.45**. In 6 αἰετόν is followed by the genitive [οἰ]ωνῶν, which probably distinguishes it as the mightiest among birds, and thus the ram must have been chosen as the most conspicuous among the sheep. The object of the comparison is very probably the girl (2 τήνδε) whose death the speaker is lamenting; this dwelling on her excellence leads up to the outburst of grief in 8–12 and heightens it inasmuch as the lost love is seen as unique and outstanding. For the whole passage, compare particularly Opp. *Hal.* 2.539–42.

ἐν ποίμ[νῃ (or ποίμ[νηс(ι)?): the rest of the verse might extend the description of the ram, e.g. προβάτων μέγαν ἡγεμονῆα.

6 αἰετὸν [οἰ]ωνῶν: middle stop follows, which means that the syntactic relationship between the genitive and its governing noun has been established beforehand (by means of a construction similar to the one suggested in 5 n., or perhaps it will be established in the next phrase). In 35 the author divides non-human creatures into two categories, birds and beasts. We already have the birds; the beasts might occupy the second part of the line. Of beasts, the lion is the mightiest; so for example Opp. *Hal.* 2.540, or in the fabulistic tradition and the novel (Ach. Tat. 2.21.1, 22.1). Therefore something like ἐν θή]ρεc[cι λέοντα, with perhaps κα[ὶ ὡс or κα[λόν before, would be possible for the rest of the line.

7 [. . . . .] προφερ[έϲτατον – ⏑: I suggest the superlative form of the adjective, which would allow a plural genitive of the same kind as those found in 3 and 6, e.g. προφερ[έϲτατον ἀνθῶν. We expect here the pre-eminent feature of the meadow; if προφερ[έϲτατον ἀνθῶν is right, its name should occupy an iambic space (ῥόδον, ἴον, κρόκον etc.). I should be inclined to choose the rose as the most conspicuous flower. Compare for example the meadow scene in Mosch. *Eur.* 69–71, where the rose is associated with Europa, who is ἄναϲϲα among her companions, and so it becomes the leader among the other flowers. Similarly in Ach. Tat. 2.1.2: εἰ τοῖϲ ἄνθεϲιν ἤθελεν ὁ Ζεὺϲ ἐπιθεῖναι βαϲιλέα, τὸ ῥόδον ἂν τῶν ἀνθέων ἐβαϲίλευε.

8 εὐνήϲειεν: the metaphor goes back to *Od.* 4.758 εὔνηϲε γόον; frequently in Nonnus, e.g. *D.* 19.14 πένθοϲ, 96 ἀνίην.

a ̣[⏗ – ⏑: it seems clear that the object of εὐνήϲειεν must come here, and ἄλγοϲ looks very suitable as the object of a verb meaning 'to soothe'. Perhaps restore ἄλ[γοϲ ἄλαϲτον, as in Q.S. 3.595 (from Homeric πένθοϲ ἄλαϲτον).

9–10 The speaker answers his rhetorical question: 10 must be concessive, since it has been implied just before that no remedy is possible. There is a close parallel for the sense in Solon fr. 13.59–60 W: πολλάκι δ' ἐξ ὀλίγηϲ ὀδύνηϲ μέγα γίγνεται ἄλγοϲ | κοὐκ ἄν τιϲ λύϲαιτ' ἤπια φάρμακα δούϲ. In 10 I doubtfully read αν[, but αλ[may be possible. We could consider ἄλ[γεα in reference to the situation, or ἄν[θεα to agree with ἤπια (assuming that ἄνθεα could refer to herbal medicines). If the answer has a main verb, perhaps we could suggest e.g.:

οὐ μὴν Παιήων, Ἀϲκληπιὸϲ οὐδέ κε [δούϲ περ
ἤπια πάντ' ἄμυδιϲ πιέειν χθονὸϲ ἄλ[γεα λῦϲαι.

or

οὐ μὴν Παιήων, Ἀϲκληπιὸϲ οὐδέ κ' ἐ[ρύκοι
ἤπια πάντ' ἄμυδιϲ πιέειν χθονὸϲ ἄν[θεα δόντεϲ.

10 πάντ' ἄμυδιϲ (pap. παντ'αμυδιϲ): it might be expected that there was special reason to single out the marked cases of elision. However, the scribe in fact fails to use the elision-mark in similar circumstances. In this line the mark makes it clear that the second a belongs to the adverb, not to πάντα; but why then has he not marked the elision in αλλαπανευθε (31), where again the second a belongs to the adverb? On the other hand, the elision-mark would seem more useful in 24 μηδευναζε, where it is absent, than in 23 and 28, where the context is clearer.

11 εκτ[: cf. Hes. *WD* 115, which shows the words in the same position as they would occupy in our papyrus: τέρποντ' ἐν θαλίῃϲι, κακῶν ἔκτοϲθεν ἁπάντων. But in our case, we would need a transitive verb to govern με. In epic hexameter, ἔκτοϲ + transitive verb occurs always in a literal sense, but the transference seems easy, so that we could write e.g. ἔκτ[οϲθεν ἐέργοι. Alternatively, we could try something like κακῶν ἐκ τ[ῶνδε ϲαώϲαι.

12 δαίϲαϲ: clearly the poet understood this to mean 'kindling'.

φ[λ]όγα τήν[δ(ε) (⏑) ⏑ – ⏑: the flame is not the fire of passion (as φλόξ often is in *AP*) but the pain of bereavement; cf. Soph. *OT* 166: εἴ ποτε καὶ προτέραϲ ἄταϲ ὑπερορνυμέναϲ πόλει ἠνύϲατ' ἐκτοπίαν φλόγα πήματοϲ, ἔλθετε καὶ νῦν. It specifically refers to death in an inscriptional epitaph: φλόγα βαλὼν ἄϲβεϲτον ἐν τῇ καρδίᾳ (*App. Anth.*, *Ep. Sep.*, 746.18). At the end, a verb is not absolutely needed; we can think of an adjective qualifying φ[λ]όγα, e.g. the common epic epithet ἀλεγεινήν, often found at line-end (*Il.* 18.17 etc.).

13 ἐπ[ὶ κ]ῆρα[ϲ (⏑) – ⏑: e.g. κακὰϲ δ' ἐπ[ὶ κ]ῆραϲ ἐπέρχῃ, 'You advance upon an evil fate'.

14 The line has been very badly damaged and only provides syntactical information (γάρ). Apart from those before the first a, the unread traces are so insubstantial that they could fit any letter.

15 ἄνδρεϲ χ' ο[ὐ]κ ἐϲθλοῦ: εϲ might be read as οϲ, if the apparent cross-bar of epsilon is simply displaced ink. Since the preceding line is almost totally lost, we can have only a general idea of the

context: 'Men [should not desire] an ignoble death'. Alternatively, we could read ἀνδρὸς . . . θάν[α]-τ[ον, 'it is for an ignoble man [to seek his own] death'. I have assumed that the speaker is more likely to talk about honourable death than honourable men, but there is no way to be certain.

16 καὶ γὰρ δή: lines 16–18 seem to develop an exemplum, and the particles emphasize this point; cf. *Il.* 19.95, where the general account of Ate is illustrated by the story of her deception of Zeus.

ἄνακτος ἀεικὴς δμῲ[ς ⏑⏑ – ⏓: δμῲ[ς seems more likely than δμῳ[ός (Hes. *WD* 430 and West's note). If the slave committed suicide for a trivial reason, it must have been fear that decided him. Thus a word or phrase meaning 'in fear' and governing the genitive, otherwise semantically redundant, would be ideal. περιδείςας would be suitable (but note that in Homer the first iota is long), or ἐπὶ τάρβει.

17 δέρην ἤρτηςε: cf. Eur. *Andr.* 412 (with the compound ἀπαρτάω, however) and 811.

μ.[⏑ – ⏓: from the point of view of the narrator of this story, the slave committed suicide unnecessarily, carried away by his own anxiety, so that one can restore e.g. μα[ταίως. The form itself is not found in epic, where μάτην is preferred, but it occurs in other kinds of poetry, sometimes at the end of a hexameter (e.g. Scythinus, *AP* 12.232.5). For differences in the perception of self-killing in classical antiquity according to the causes and methods chosen to perform it, see MacAlister, *Dreams and Suicides* 55 ff. Hanging was regarded as a method of self-killing out of desperation and, therefore, a non-honourable one.

18 τυτθόν: this could be an adjective with χό[λον, 'trivial anger', or an adverb with ἀ[λ]ευά-μενος, 'just escaping' (cf. *Il.* 13.184–5 ἠλεύατο . . . | τυτθόν). χό[λον fits the trace, sense and metre. At line-end, since there is no connective in this line, I should think of an epithet of χό[λον (assuming that τυτθόν is an adverb), e.g. αἰνόν, or of ἀπ[ε]ιλητῆρος, e.g. ὠμοῦ, or a noun attached to it, e.g. ἀνδρός (cf. Nonnus, who frequently uses ἀπειλητήρ adjectivally).

19 οὐδὲν ὁρᾶν [μ]έγα παιδὶ λ[ογ]ίζεαι (superscript ς[θαι]): palaeographic doubts are ν (the trace is high ink, perhaps the top of an oblique descending to the right; above it is a clear upright trace on the edge) and λ (ink near the top of the line and at line-level, which I have taken as the apex and left foot of λ). There is also the question whether παιδί refers to the slave or to the dead girl (called κούρη in 24, 30, 32), and whether the second person verb addresses someone else, or even the reader, or the speaker himself (as in 13).

Grammatically, we must assume that the infinitive ὁρᾶν depends on λ[ογ]ίζεαι, which would imply taking the infinitive absolutely, meaning 'to live', 'carry on living'. Assuming that παιδί refers to the slave, I would interpret the clause as drawing the moral of the story just told: 'You see that life means nothing important to the slave'. The construction must have struck the scribe as odd, since he seems to have added a superscript above the last letter of ὁρᾶν. I suggest that he corrected ὁρᾶν to ὁράςθαι, which would give the verb a more usual meaning and clarify the syntax of παιδί ('You see how nothing seems important to the slave'). Of course, the correction would not fit the metre. On the other hand, if παιδί refers to the girl, we might look for the idea 'Nothing you can do will help her', even though that would anticipate 24. Professor Parsons has doubtfully suggested οὐδὲν ὁρᾶν [μ]έγα παιδὶ χ[αρ]ίζεαι, 'Are you offering (your) death as a great favour to the girl?', or writing ὁρᾶϊς (with iota adscript written above the line) parenthetically: 'You do the girl—do you see?—no great favour'.

οὐ γὰρ .[: after ρ there are only small remains of ink at line-level. Perhaps the connection was: 'Do not think of suicide. For you desire death [not from the right motive] but so that you can be free of misery, and wishing. . .'.

20 ἱμείρεις: to the top right of ι there is a trace that is too small to be superscript text. If it belongs to a lectional sign, it might be the right-hand dot of a trema or part of a rough breathing.

ὄφρα κ[(ε) (⏑) – ⏓: the genitive ἀχέων suggests a verb meaning 'be relieved, liberated from', e.g. λώφῃς; cf. A.R. 3.616 ἐξ ἀχέων . . . κατελώφεεν, 784 λωφήςειν ἀχέων.

21 θέλων: the lambda was added above the line, apparently by the same hand that wrote the main text. The original θεῶν could fit the grammar, if the infinitives ἐκφυγέειν and βαλέειν are governed by ἱμείρεις. The correction probably reflects the puzzlement of the scribe at the apparent contradiction implied by 'the monstrous evils of the gods', since it is said later that the gods were not at all responsible for these sufferings. However, this does not take into account the fact that the second voice is here presenting the first voice's presumed arguments in order to refute them afterwards, which makes 25 ff. more organic within the speech. Thus the 'correction' may be wrong.

πῆμ[α ⏑ – ⏓: we expect an object for βαλέειν and a connective to join this new infinitive phrase. This suggests πῆμ[α δέ or πήμ[ατα δ' (τε, in correlation with the one after the first infinitive, seems to be prevented by the strong punctuation after κακά). The end could be another noun, e.g. πῆμα κακοῖο (*Od.* 3.152) or πήματος ἄλγος (Q.S. 1.81), but these do not allow for δέ. An adjective seems most likely, e.g. πῆμ[α δ' ἄλαστον or πῆμ[α δὲ τόσσον (Q.S. 3.561 τόσσον . . . πῆμα).

22 τοίνυν γάρ: this combination of particles is not otherwise attested in Greek literature, but their presence can be accounted for separately. τοίνυν, according to Denniston, *GP* 569–74, may be used to introduce an answer as 'springing from the actual words, or general attitude, of a previous speaker. The logical force is often not very strong. . .'. In fact, as he points out, the answer may convey a criticism of the previous speaker's words, and can even be used at the opening of δευτερολογίαι. That is what we have here: a completely different reaction to the girl's death is set out. At the same time, it is quite common to find a γάρ-clause immediately after that introduced by τοίνυν, to explain the inference which in the mind of the (new) speaker has determined his answer (e.g. Pollianus, *AP* 11.127.3–4; *App. Anth., Ep. Exhort.* 83.17). Thus I believe that τοίνυν here belongs with τλῆθι, while γάρ introduces the reason behind the exhortation: τλῆθι τοίνυν· ζώειν γὰρ ἀνάγκη.

23 ζῶθι is not an attested form, but Gignac, *Grammar* ii 370 quotes 'an anomalous imperative ζώτω' from a private letter of the earlier third century AD (P. Meyer 20.21). Conversely, ἔζην replaces ἔζων as the first person singular of the imperfect, e.g. in the LXX (Blass–Debrunner–Rehkopf, *Grammatik des NT Griechisch*[17] § 882). It seems likely that the alternation of -ω- with -η- in the contracted forms, and the presence of ζώειν alongside ζάειν (ζῆν), might have led to taking ζω- as the radical of the verb and adding endings directly to it.

ἄλγεα [– ⏓: assuming that εὔναζε governs both ἄλγεα and [δ]άκρυα, we might suggest the very frequent formulaic ending ἄλγεα θυμῷ (*Il.* 9.321 etc.; Q.S. 5.470, 14.166). Q.S. 10.293 is especially relevant to our piece, since Paris there asks his wife to relieve him from his terrible (there physical) pain, and elements such as the administering of medicine (cf. 8–10) are also present.

24 μηδ': for the postponement of the conjunction, cf. *Il.* 9.31.

εὔναζε: cf. Nonn. *D.* 44.207 δάκρυον εὐνήσειε (line-beginning).

κόρηˌι: the added iota is written in the same ink as the main text. Since the end of the line is missing, it is not possible to determine whether the correction should be accepted or not, or indeed how far it is a correction, for it may well be that the original κόρη was intended as a dative, and that the superscript was made at a second pass through the text (we have no certain evidence about the normal practice of the scribe as regards iota adscript). In any case, the sense seems to be: 'To the girl these things will be of no use at all', or 'The girl will not care about these things at all'. I do not see how to fit in a form of μέλειν, but [ἀρήγει or [ἀρήξει seems to fit the meaning, and I should suggest the future as fitting the context better. These forms often occur at hexameter-end, with dative preceding (ἀρήγει *Il.* 15.42 etc.; ἀρήξει Nic. *Alex.* 141, Nonn. *D.* 27.182, 39.203).

25 It is obvious that [τ]αῦτα and κακαί do not belong to the same phrase. We do not find a single instance of the nominative plural form of the noun κάκη in the whole of extant epic poetry; therefore I take κακαί as an adjective. It occurs eight times in extant Greek epic, and in three cases it modifies κῆρες (Q.S. 5.536, 8.152, 11.39), which I suggest restoring at line-end. The nominatives imply that οἴομαι is here used parenthetically, as in e.g. *Od.* 14.363, 22.140 and A.R. 3.479, 4.197. The meaning would be: 'Bad destiny is never, I think, anything to do with the gods'.

26 τέτυκτ[ο: given that the following verbs are all imperfects (secondary sequence), I have preferred τέτυκτ[ο to τέτυκτ[αι as a supplement.

27 ἐήνδανεν (pap. ἑηνδανεν): rough breathing added perhaps to prevent confusion with the imperfect ἔην, particularly in the proximity of a dative.

οὐδέ τις ἦ[εν: for the same phrase at line-end cf. *Il.* 24.610, A.R. 4.976, Q.S. 2.529, 11.437; in A.R. 3.273–4 and Q.S. 13.130–31 it is continued as here by a relative clause referring to the indefinite τις.

28 ἑκάς[τῳ: ἑκάς[τοις would also be possible, but the plural would be a rarity (in hexameter literature only Ps.-Opp. *Cyn.* 3.20, 4.41).

29 τὰ δ' οὐκ ὤνησέ μιν [– ⏓: this new clause must finish at line-end, since the next line begins a new one. Thus I print τὰ δ', not τάδ', to provide a connective. For the line-end an adverb or a secondary accusative relating to ὤνησε (cf. *Od.* 23.24 cὲ δὲ τοῦτό γε γῆρας ὀνήcει; 14.67 πόλλ' ὤνηcεν etc.) would be suitable: οὐδέν would combine with the preceding simple negative to produce an emphatic negation; for the phrase, cf. Nonn. *Paraphr.* 6.193–4 οὐδὲν ὀνήcει (similarly 8.171, 12.83). An alternative, despite the repetition in 34, would be ἔμπηc, but I have not found it in combination with ὀνίνημι elsewhere in verse.

30 κο[ύρη: κο[ύρηc would be another possibility, with μέλε impersonal. In surviving hexameter literature we find 24 instances of μέλει, 15 with the nominative construction and 7 impersonal. In fact, authors may have their own preference: Homer, for example, uses only the personal construction, whereas Quintus never uses it. I only propose κο[ύρη because this is the more poetic construction.

31 θεῶν κενὰ μέρμερα: the genitive θεῶν is not likely to depend on κενά, since this adjective, in the epic language, when accompanied by a genitive, has a quite physical meaning. As for the meaning of the resulting θεῶν μέρμερα, the ancient commentators do not necessarily attribute a negative meaning to the adjective; cf. e.g. the scholion to *Il.* 10.48: μέρμερ' ἐπ' ἤματι· μερίμνηc καὶ φροντίδοc ἄξια. καταcτρέφεται εἰc τὸ κακά A A^int. Similarly, in Timaeus' *Lexicon Vocum Platonicarum* s.v. μέρμεροc· ὁ διὰ πανουργιῶν φροντίδα τιcὶν ἐμποιῶν. Thus the meaning should be 'without (the consent of) Fate, the mighty (devices) of the gods are void'.

π[– ⏓: for the line-end the traditional ἔργα accompanying μέρμερα is excluded for palaeographical reasons. A copula or a passive verb serving this function would suit the meaning of the line, but traces and metre exclude the commonest such verbs. I suggest θεῶν . . . π[άντων; cf. e.g. *Il.* 17.568, 22.15, *Scut.* 56; *Il.* 8.17, 9.159; *Theog.* 813, where we find the same words in the same sedes. π[άντων seems preferable to π[άντα (agreeing with μέρμερα), since it opposes more vividly the power of all the gods against the single authority of αἶcα.

32 κοῦρᾰ: Homer has only κούρη. The form with short α occurs in Callimachus, *Hymn* 3.72 (κοῦρα, cὺ δέ . . .) and Naumachius in Heitsch, *GDRK* 29.70.

ἀφύκτο[υc seems to be granted both palaeographically and from the point of view of the meaning; the adjective is not present in Homer or Hesiod, but there are parallels elsewhere (Opp. *Hal.* 3.111, Q.S. 10.286).

33–5 Professor Parsons notes that these lines elaborate a consolation formula found on gravestones (εὐθύμει· οὐδεὶc ἀθάνατοc); see J. Chapa, *Letters of Condolence in Greek Papyri* (1988) 36 f.

33 γέγηθι: the final trace is so small that it would be consistent with any letter. After γένοιο, we might expect an optative, i.e. γεγήθο[ιc, but I have not found this perfect optative attested anywhere in literature or documentary papyri. Only the imperative can be found, and that only in a single composition (in Doric dialect), *Hymnus Curetum* 5–6 γέγᾱθι.

34 τεθνήξεται: this is the form of the future commonly found in prose-writers of the Roman period.

ἔμ[πηc: widely attested at line-end in epic hexameter, although often, unlike here, as part of ἀλλὰ καὶ ἔμπηc or περ ἔμπηc.

35 ὄρειος: the metre requires this to be scanned as an anapaest. Perhaps the poet intended a hypothetical adjective ὄρεος; the scribe then wrote the much commoner ὄρειος. I have not been able to find evidence for such a form, except in an inscription from Amorgos quoted by LSJ, IG 12(7).75. However, it is possible that the poet had in mind alternations of the type χάλκειος/χάλκεος, which are common in Homeric diction (Chantraine, *Gr. Hom.* i 168). Alternatively, we could envisage a correption of ει, although West, *Greek Metre* 11–12, states that ει is one of the least frequently shortened diphthongs.

A. NODAR

4940. HISTORICAL FRAGMENT (TIMAGENES?)

5B.54/G(2)   14.8 × 13.4 cm   First century AD?
                                                                  Plate V

A medium brown papyrus, complete only at the top and containing remains of three columns. Of these, only col. ii is complete at both left and right, with a width of 6.5–7 cm and accommodating 16–20 letters. The intercolumnium is *c.*1.8 cm wide. The height of the incomplete column is 11.3 cm, and the data collected by W. A. Johnson, *Bookrolls and Scribes in Oxyrhynchus* (2004) 110–13, 203 ff., show that columns of this width might be *c.*13–15 cm in height (but could be more). There are thus 3 or 4 lines missing at the foot, possibly more. The back is blank.

The hand is a rounded bookhand of the early Roman (or possibly late Hellenistic) period. There are no diacritical marks or lectional signs. Bilinearity is significantly broken only by φ. The scribe employs the split-top τ characteristic of the Ptolemaic period. Also notable are the angular λ (though the more rounded form also appears), ε occasionally with a closed loop at the top, and ω made in three distinct strokes. These characteristics suggest a date within the range bounded by P. Fay. 6 (= Roberts, *GLH* 9c, Homer, late I BC) and P. Lond. II 141 [p.181] (= Roberts, *GLH* 12a, AD 88). Also worth comparing are XIX **2221** ('rounded informal', mid I AD) and IX **1182** (= *GMAW*² 67, I/II AD). This all points to a date certainly not later than the first century AD and possibly even a little earlier.

The content is historical, located firmly in the context of the early 50s BC, the events surrounding the departure of Ptolemy Auletes from Alexandria and the negotiations over his restoration. Evidence for this episode is provided by several sources, notably Plutarch (especially *C. min.* 34 ff., see below), Dio and Cicero; for modern summary accounts, see M. Siani-Davies, 'Ptolemy XII Auletes and the Romans', *Historia* 46 (1997) 306–40 (list of main sources at 318 n. 42), W. Huss, *Ägypten in hellenistischer Zeit* (2001) 686 ff. The events referred to in the present text fall in 58 BC. Ptolemy Auletes has left Alexandria, whether voluntarily or under duress, and is on his way to Rome hoping to persuade leading Romans to restore him by force of arms. Cato is in Rhodes and summons (or invites) Ptolemy to come and see him. They have an interview, and Cato persuades Ptolemy to return to Alexandria, but the latter is in turn dissuaded by his φίλοι and resumes his journey to Rome. This is the framework within which the exegesis of details in this papyrus must fit, but it is not entirely straightforward. The first important point is that its proposed syntactical structure rests on what seems to be the inescapable restoration of [ἔ]χεις in i 18. Therefore *oratio recta* at this point. It is uncertain how many lines are lost at the foot of col. i (see above) and where the *oratio recta* ends, but my hypothesis is that this falls immediately before ταῦτα in ii 1. Who is the speaker? Why not Cato himself, in the context of the interview in Rhodes, telling Ptolemy that he should pay off his debts to someone and perhaps advising him that if he places his hopes for restoration in Pompey, he should think better of it *vel sim.* (i 15–18)? Having been treated with contempt by the Rhodians, Ptolemy now regrets having fled Alexandria, and Cato's offer to go on an embassy persuades him to think of going back, since he takes Cato's advice and standing seriously; but he is then dissuaded or held back by a certain Tryphon . . . (after which point the text fails us). This exegesis is not unproblematical, and Professor C. B. R. Pelling suggests in Note B below an alternative understanding of this passage.

Except at the end of col. ii (where I am much indebted to Dr R. A. Coles for his attempts to realign the damaged fibres), the readings are reasonably secure; the more speculative restorations are confined to the notes. A few points of language and syntax deserve notice. If I have correctly located the end of the *oratio recta*, the narrative following the speech consistently employs the historic present. It is notable that the μέν in ii 2 is not balanced by a following δέ, but μὲν οὖν in ii 9 will be picked up by δέ in ii 17, if my understanding of the articulation of the text is correct. If there is a break in the sense after φυγῆς, as is proposed, we then have a genitive absolute (Κάτωνος ὑπεχομένου), followed by ἐκεῖνον (as the object of λαμβάνει) which must refer to Cato; thus the subject of the genitive absolute is identical with the object of the main verb (see Pelling on Plut. *Ant.* 53.1, citing *Nicias* 16.7 and *Ant.* 16.5, 22.4, 34.5, sometimes in order to avoid hiatus, as perhaps here—Κάτωνα ὑπεχόμενον).

The information in the text does not alter or add to our knowledge of the main sequence of events, but there are several minor points of historical interest. The reference to Ptolemy's debts may point to the name Canidius as the creditor, a friend of Cato sent to persuade Ptolemy of Cyprus to abdicate (Plut. *C. min.* 35.2; see i 16 n.). I find no direct reference in the existing sources to Ptolemy Auletes having been treated with contempt or arrogance by the Rhodians (ii 2–3, if the restoration stands), but this is not intrinsically implausible; note, however, that Plutarch refers to Ptolemy's being taken aback by Cato's treating him as an ordinary commoner. If the reference to Tryphon as the one responsible for holding Ptolemy back from the proposed return to Alexandria is correct, it will connect neatly with an inscription from Philae, SB V 8424: Τρύφων Διο[νύ|c]ου [τ]οῦ νέου | κίναιδος ἥκ[ω] | παρὰ τὴν Ἴσιν τὴν ἐ[ν | Φ]ί[λαις].

Finally, authorship. The palaeographical considerations firmly preclude attribution to the lost *Aegyptiaca* of Appian, which might have been an attractive hypothesis. A likely candidate, on various counts, would appear to be Timagenes (Fraser, *Ptol. Alex.* i 518–19). The hypothesis of an Alexandrian writer turning up on a papyrus at Oxyrhynchus has an obvious attraction. Further, Timagenes must have been thoroughly familiar with these matters, having been forcibly taken to Rome by Gabinius in 55 BC, only a few years after the events described in our fragment. He wrote βίβλια πολλά of which we know the title of only one (Περὶ Βασιλέων); see FGrH 88 T1 and cf. LXXI **4809**. He is cited by Plutarch, *Pomp.* 49, as the source for the fact that Ptolemy left Alexandria under pressure from Theophanes of Mitylene, who was scheming to get Pompey a new command. Finally, with all due attention to the dangers of circular argument, it is striking how close are the details in this fragment to the material in Plutarch, *C. min.* 35—the hopes placed in Pompey, Cato's wisdom and βαρύτης, Cato's offer to help restore him, the conflicting advice of Ptolemy's φίλοι. Timagenes could then well be imagined as the (or a) main source for Plutarch's account of this episode (and references to the corruption and rapacity of the Roman δύνατοι would also fit, given what else we know of Timagenes' later outspokenness on this subject). The present fragment might, then, belong to Περὶ Βασιλέων or one of the other books of Timagenes. If so, it may be our first direct testimony for this author. It is, however, also worth noticing P. Med. inv. 68.53 (C. Balconi, 'Rabirio Postumo dioiketes d'Egitto in P. Med. inv. 68.53?' *Aegyptus* 73 (1993) 3–20), of unknown provenance (perhaps Oxyrhynchus or the Arsinoite) and assigned to mid I BC to mid I AD on palaeographical grounds. This has a description of the rapacious behaviour of a certain Πόστομος, who might well be Rabirius Postumus. There are no grounds for connecting the Milan fragment closely with the Oxyrhynchus text (and the hand is certainly different), but the content of the latter might provide general support for locating the content of the former in the 50s BC rather than the postulated alternative (Postumus the prefect of AD 45–7; see Bastianini, *ZPE* 17 (1975) 272, *ANRW* II.10.1 (1988) 505), and an anti-Roman tone is congruent with Timagenes' reputation (FGrH 88 T3 = Seneca, *De ira* 23.4–8). This is hypothesis. In Note A below, Professor Pelling suggests that Plutarch likely drew on Munatius Rufus, as Timagenes might also have done, and makes the case for Munatius as the putative author of the present fragment.

In addition to the suggestions of Christopher Pelling, which are appended below, I am indebted to Dominic Rathbone, Nikolaos Gonis, and above all Peter Parsons, who has greatly enhanced my understanding of the text on several key points of palaeography, reading, and interpretation.

Col. i   Col. ii   Col. iii

```
         ]ωναπε              βεινυ̣.ομ̣.[ . . . . ]ταυ[
         ]υγχανοι            ταμενταμετ[ . . . ] . . . . ν . .
         ]ει̣[.]α             διωνυβρινπλειϲτον
         ] . . λλα           πτολε[.]αιωιμεταμε
5        ]ρχοντων       5    λονεργαζεταιτηϲφυ
         ]ληθηδε̣             γηϲκαι̣τ̣.υκατωνοϲυπε
         ]ωτ̣.ϲ              χομενουπρεϲβευϲειν
         ] . ην̣ .           ειϲτηναλεξανδρειαν
         ]ιουϲιαν            εκεινονμενουνλαμβα
10       ]αλλο         10    νειταχαμεντικαιβαρυ
         ]μενη̣ι             τερονπροϲταϲτοιαυταϲ
         ] . κατ̣[.].        λε̣.[.]ουργιαϲυπολαβων̣
         ] . . [ . . . . ]τον  παρεϲ.ιχ̣αραυτωιμηθ[
         ]ωνο[ . . . ]ων     νιμη̣ . . . . ρ̣ονεϲτερω[
15       ] . δ̣.αλυϲαιτ̣απροϲ  15  μητεκρε[.]ττονιτωνκα
         ] . . . νοφειλη      .αυ.ο̣ν̣η . . . [.] . . [.] . ει̣[
         ]αϲτεελπ̣[.]δαϲ      . . . χειν̣π̣.[.]α̣. ινειδε̣.[
         ]πηιον[.]χειϲ       τρυφωνε[.]. υ̣[.] . . υλομεν̣οϲ
                                              ] . ν̣[
```

Col. i

    4] . ., first, dot at line level and foot of upright curving to the right; second, right arc   7 τ.ϲ, left-hand part of oval letter, then horizontal at two-thirds height (ε?)   8] . ., foot of descending oblique with ligature to the foot of н   ν . ., trace at line level touching ν   12] . ., top of ascending oblique   ] . , ε or ϲ   13] . ., first, bottom of oval letter or join of descending oblique and upright (e.g. N); second, foot of ascending oblique   15] . ., horizontal speck at line level   δ . a, scattered traces   16] . . ., first, short vertical trace level with letter tops; second, traces of high descending oblique and scattered traces at line level (λ?); third, short upright or right arc

Col. ii

    1 ν . o, foot of upright or descending oblique with right serif   .[, ε or ɵ   2] . . . ., first, speck at mid-height then short ascending oblique at line level; second, upright curving to the left at bottom; third, vertical trace at mid-height, then dot at line level; fourth, upright with joins from the left at top and bottom   ν . ., first, upright with join at top (ρ?); second, ε ɵ o or ϲ   6 τ . ν, after lacuna scattered traces on edge   12 .[, join of mid-stroke of preceding ε with a letter (upright?) 13 ϲ . ι, horizontal speck at two-thirds height   14 η . . . . ρ, first, high horizontal trace; second, right end of upper arc; third, top of upright or steeply descending oblique; fourth, φ or ψ   16 . a, scattered traces at mid-height   ν . o, upright   . . .[, first, speck at mid-height (part of upright?); second, scattered traces on edge; third, short ascending oblique at one-third height then descending oblique (bottom left of м?)   ] . ., first, displaced horizontal or oblique trace; second, two specks of ink, one high, the other at mid-height   ] . , traces of high horizontal and confused traces below

Col. i

```
                    ]ων απε
               τ]υγχάνοι
                    ]ει[.]α
               ] πόλλα
5          ἀ]ρχόντων
           ἀ]ληθῆ δὲ
               ]ωτες
               ].ην.
               ]ιουσιαν
10             ] ἀλλο
           -]μένηι
               ]υ κατ[.].
           ]..[....]τον
               ]ωνο[...]ων
15         ]. διαλῦσαι τὰ πρὸς
     c.5  ].δ.ν ὀφειλή-
     ματα τ]άς τε ἐλπ[ί]δας
     πρὸς Πομ]πήιον [.]χεις
        .      .      .      .
```

Col. ii

```
     βειν ὑπομε[.....] ταῦ-
     τα μὲν τὰ μετ[...]....ν..
     διων ὕβριν πλεῖστον
     Πτολε[μ]αίωι μετάμε-
5    λον ἐργάζεται τῆς φυ-
     γῆς καὶ τοῦ Κάτωνος ὑπε-
     χομένου πρεσβεύειν
     εἰς τὴν Ἀλεξάνδρειαν
     ἐκεῖνον μὲν οὖν λαμβά-
10   νει τάχα μέν τι καὶ βαρύ-
     τερον πρὸς τὰς τοιαύτας
     λει[τ]ουργίας ὑπολαβών·
     πάρεστι γὰρ αὐτῶι μηθ[ε-
     νὶ μητ.. φρονεστέρω[ι
15   μήτε κρε[ί]ττονι τῶν κα-
     τ' αὐτὸν ἡγεμ[ό]νω[ν] πει-
     θαρχεῖν π.[.]α.εινει δε κ[
     Τρύφων ε[.]ου[.]..υλομενος
                         ].ν[
         .      .      .      .
```

17 ...χ, first, horizontal at mid-height; second, thick top of descending oblique; third, small upper arc   π.[, the foot of the right leg of π extends horizontally to join the foot of an ascending oblique   α..ι, first, foot of upright and high horizontal (τ or τ); second, horizontal touching ι at two-thirds height   .[, upright with horizontal join from the right at one-third height (κ?)   18]., part of right arc at mid-height   ].., first, traces of upright then thick ascending oblique just below line level; second, thick dot at one-third height   19]., speck at mid-height

' "... to repay debts owed to Canidius(?) ... and the hopes (that?) you place on Pompey ... tolerate(?)." And these things then, after the arrogant behaviour of the Rhodians(?), caused Ptolemy to repent greatly of his flight even as (?) Cato was promising to go on an embassy to Alexandria. So he (sc. Ptolemy) was anyway for taking him (sc. Cato) up on it, understanding that he was perhaps somewhat more weighty for such public duties. For he had the opportunity to obey no-one better disposed (*or* wiser) or better among the contemporary leaders(?). But Tryphon in turn was for delaying(?), ... not(?) wishing ...'

Col. i

Assuming that the column width is uniform, there will be up to 12 letters missing at the left of lines 1–12 and 10–11 letters missing at the left of lines 13–14, which precludes any attempt to extract continuous sense.

5 ἀ]ρχόντων: perhaps a reference to leading Romans whom Plutarch terms δυνατοί (*C. min.* 35.6; ἄρχοντος also occurs in 35.7).

15–18　About 5 or 6 letters missing at the left.

15–16　Reference to the repayment of debts seems very plausible, given the evidence for Ptolemy's borrowing from prominent Romans, of whom the best known, a little later, was Rabirius Postumus (Cicero, *Rab. Post.* 4).

16　*c.*5] ˳δˏ˳ν: perhaps τὸν Καν]ίˏδˏιˏον. The restoration is proposed with some reservations. The second trace after the lacuna very well suits the top of ⲁ (the only other possibility is ⲁ), but the space between that and ν is barely adequate for ιο. Six letters in the lacuna at the left is certainly a maximum (giving a total of 18) but three seems minimal. The historical evidence, circumstantial though it is, is attractive. Ptolemy contracted debts to leading Romans. Canidius was a friend of Cato who figures prominently in the negotiations with Ptolemy of Cyprus (*C. min.* 35.2, 37) and could perhaps have been a creditor of Auletes. The arguments for identifying him with P. Canidius Crassus, partisan of Antonius and consul in 40 BC, are set out at length in M.-C. Ferriès, 'La Légende noire de P. Canidius Crassus', *Athenaeum* n.s. 88 (2000) 413–30; additional documentary evidence for a later and substantial financial stake in Egypt on his part would be a welcome accretion to this hypothesis, but certainty cannot be claimed; see P. van Minnen, *Anc. Soc.* 30 (2000) 29–34, *APF* 47 (2001) 74–80; K. Zimmermann, *ZPE* 138 (2002) 133–9.

17–18　The restorations proposed yield lines of 16 and 17 letters respectively. ἆϲ at the beginning of 18 is perhaps not out of the question. Despite the loss of the bottoms of letters,]πηιον is certain and compels Πομ]πήιον.

[ἔ]χειϲ seems the only plausible restoration and forces the presumption of *oratio recta* (see introd.).

Col. ii

1　βειν is perhaps the end of an infinitive, followed by an imperative (ὑπόμε[νε; cf. LSJ s.v. ὑπομένω II.4), but something more is required: if this is the end of the speech (see introd.), καὶ ταῦτα μέν κτλ.?

2　μέν is not balanced by δέ if my articulation of the text is correct; a usage most commonly but not always with πρῶτον or πρότερον (J. D. Denniston, *The Greek Particles* (1954) 376).

2–3　Restore μετ[ὰ τὴ]ν τῶν Ῥοδίων ὕβριν? ρο is attractive and is permitted though hardly compelled by the traces at the end of line 2; τῶν is more difficult but perhaps just possible if ω was written in three strokes as it is elsewhere. The context is good, for Cato is in Rhodes (*C. min.* 35.3). Plutarch does not record Ptolemy being arrogantly treated by the Rhodians, but as a new detail it would not be implausible. An obvious alternative in this historical context would be the name of the Alexandrian ambassador Dion (*Pros. Ptol.* 16749, 16797; cf. Huss, *Ägypten in hellenistischer Zeit* 687–8), but I can think of no syntactical restoration that would support this.

4–6　μετάμελον ἐργάζεται τῆς φυγῆϲ: cf. Isocrates, XVIII.21.5 (*in Callimachum*), καὶ εἰ μὲν ἑώρα μετάμελον τῇ πόλει τῶν πεπραγμένων, Dem. 61.11, ἀθάνατον τοῖϲ ἰδοῦϲιν ἐργάζεται πόθον.

6–9　One hypothesis is that there is a break in the sense between φυγῆϲ and καί. The alternative is that it comes at the end of line 8: 'these things . . . caused Ptolemy to repent of his flight and [or even as] Cato was promising . . .'. Against this is the awkward placing of the genitive absolute at the end of the period. In favour of it are the facts that μὲν οὖν in ii 9 should stand at the beginning of a new period (Denniston, *GP* 470) and that ἐκεῖνον must refer to Cato (see introd.).

9–11　λαμβάνει: or perhaps 'took him on', but see Pelling's Note B below.

τάχα μέν τι καί: cf. e.g. Thuc. 8.94.2 and many post-classical authors, e.g. Jos. *BJ* 5.534.3.

βαρύτερον: here perhaps 'weighty' in a positive sense (LSJ s.v. βαρύϲ 4), rather than 'severe' in a pejorative sense (as in *C. min.* 35.5). For the latter we would need something to indicate that Ptolemy wanted to take Cato along even though he understood that he was rather heavy-handed, and that is not the force of τάχα μέν τι καί.

14 ..φρονεϲτέρω[ι: the first two traces are inconclusive, but perhaps favour ἐμφρονεϲτέρω[ι (cf. *C. min.* 35.7) or εὐφρονεϲτέρω[ι rather than ϲωφρονεϲτέρω[ι.

16–17 αρχειν is reasonably secure. The suggestion for what precedes I owe to Peter Parsons. The restoration of ἡγεμ[ό]νω[ν] is extremely tentative; it gives very good sense but can only be said to be compatible with the exiguous surviving traces.

17–18 π.[.]α. εινει δε κ[: I suggest πα[ρ]ατείνει δὲ κ[αὶ (ὁ)] | *Τρύφων*: the reading of πα[ρ]ατείνει is not difficult apart from the τ, which will have lost the left-hand part of the top-stroke; but πα[ρ]αγείνει seems to lead nowhere. For the force of δὲ καί (= αὖ), perhaps see Denniston, *GP* 305.

18 For Tryphon, see introd. The sense, if correctly understood, would suggest βουλόμενος (compatible with traces?), preceded by a negative of some sort. *C. min.* 35.7 has Ptolemy dissuaded by his friends from following Cato's advice.

A. K. BOWMAN

Two notes added by Professor C. B. R. Pelling

Note A

It is highly likely that Plutarch draws the material for this section not from Timagenes but from Munatius Rufus, probably via Thrasea Paetus (so J. Geiger, *Athen.* 57 (1979) 48–72 at 50–52). Munatius was an eye-witness of these events, figuring several times in Plutarch's narrative of Cato's Cypriot expedition (36.5, 37.1–9). Plutarch indeed quotes his work at 37.1, noting that 'Munatius published his own book on Cato, which Thrasea took and followed as his main authority' and continuing λέγει . . . : the syntax makes it clear that the 'he' is there Munatius rather than Thrasea, though it need not follow that Plutarch knows the work at first hand rather than through a citation in Thrasea. At 25.2 he has similarly quoted as his source for an anecdote of Cato's private life 'Thrasea, who gives as his authority Munatius, Cato's friend and close companion'. Valerius Maximus also quotes Munatius for Cato's impeccable treatment of Cyprus' royal wealth: *id Munatius Rufus Cypriacae expeditionis fidus comes scriptis suis significat* (4.3.2).

The Cypriot section is one of several passages in Plutarch's *Life* that are peculiarly rich in narrative colour, and where Munatius is named as a source or it is noted that he was present (9, 25, 27, 30; Geiger, loc. cit.; Pelling, *JHS* 99 (1979) 82, 85 = *Plutarch and History* (2002) 10, 13). If Munatius is Plutarch's source, our fragment too may well be Munatius. Nothing precludes Munatius from having written in Greek; his philosophical interests and emphasis would have made this appropriate. Compare the works on Brutus a little later: Jacoby assumes that Empylus wrote in Greek (FGrH 191), and for all we know Bibulus may have written in Greek as well (Plut. *Brut.* 13.3, 23.7). The use of dramatic dialogue would fit Munatius' manner, if he lies behind *C. min.* 9.2, 25.4–11, 30.5, and 37.4–9.

Equally, Timagenes—a much better-known author—certainly remains a strong possibility, for the reasons given in the introduction above. It is possible that Timagenes himself was drawing on Munatius, and that could explain the closeness of this account to Plutarch.

Note B

The present tenses in col. ii might indeed be historic presents, as suggested above, but:

(*a*) that interpretation of πάρεϲτι in particular seems strained: historic presents more naturally recreate a past event as it would have seemed to onlookers or participants at the time, less naturally describe a continuing state of affairs in the past.

(*b*) λαμβάνει seems hard to interpret as 'was . . . for taking him (sc. Cato) up on it' (the translation suggested above), or as 'took him on' (the alternative suggested in the commentary): it is easier to interpret as 'took Cato with him', especially just after Cato's offer to serve on an embassy. Yet it is clear from Plutarch's account that the journey never took place.

(*c*) βαρύτερον 'in a positive sense' is rare, and the instances quoted in LSJ s.v. I.iv do not include any where it is used of persons. As the comm. above notes, that interpretation also requires taking the word in a different way from its use of Cato at *C. min.* 35.5, where it is coupled with 'arrogance'. The rest of the sentence is also in that case odd: 'more' weighty than what? Presumably than Ptolemy himself, but if so πρὸς τὰς τοίαυτας λειτουργίας is an awkward way of continuing the comparison of the two. λειτουργία is the appropriate word for a magistrate's duty or for a task performed by a citizen for his state: Cato would be returning to reconcile Ptolemy with his enemies, which might be a 'public duty' for Cato but would be strangely described as such for Ptolemy himself. In the negative sense, 'more heavy-handed (than he should be)' is easy, and there is then no comparison with Ptolemy; but then the combination is difficult both with λαμβάνει, as noted in the commentary above, and with the following positive remarks on Cato's wisdom (or good will) and virtue.

These difficulties can be met if we follow the hint given by ἔχεις and assume that this column too represents *oratio recta*—but in this case *oratio recta* of Ptolemy's nefarious 'friends', the φίλοι of *C. min.* 35.7, who will go on to persuade Ptolemy not to abandon his flight but to go on to Rome. We would have to assume that this *mise-en-scène* would have been made clear in the gap of perhaps 4 lines or more at the bottom of col. i. These worried friends would first be noting that Ptolemy 'is' regretting his decision and changing his mind: the present tenses are on this reading wholly explicable. A particular extra concern, however ii 6–8 are punctuated, is that Cato is offering to accompany him to Alexandria, and Ptolemy 'is' taking him along. The λαμβάνει is now unproblematic, as the journey has not yet been abandoned. These friends have every reason to worry that Cato will be more heavy-handed than they think appropriate or desirable, as the sequel in Plutarch's narrative goes on to demonstrate. Yet the reason for their alarm is precisely the combination of positive qualities that a Roman, or even a less self-interested observer, would acknowledge, his wisdom (ἐμφρονεστέρωι on this interpretation is to be preferred to εὐφρονεστέρωι) and moral superiority. The implication is that the friends should urge Ptolemy to abandon his change of heart, and to go on to Rome. Possibly the *oratio recta* ends at this point, and if so Tryphon, presumably another 'friend', will then be about to put the alternative case for (?) 'delaying' any approach to Ptolemy—unavailingly, as Plutarch's account makes clear. Or possibly the *oratio recta* is continuing, and the speaker is addressing Tryphon's reluctance. This all fits well into the context explained by Plutarch.

4941. A Thrasyllan Interpretation of Plato's *Theaetetus*

114/44(d)   Fr. 1 9.3 × 10.1 cm   Second half of second century
                                                                        Plate VI

A single principal fragment containing the final fourteen lines of one column and the final six line-beginnings of a second column to its right, with an inter-columnium of 1.5 cm.; two further small fragments of uncertain location, only one of them with any legible traces of writing. A column width of around 30 letters = *c.*8 cm. Back blank.

The script consists of upright, oval capitals (i.e. exhibiting some vertical extension) related to the Formal Mixed style, but basically bilinear (top and bottom line violated only by ι, φ, and χ); in this respect it bears a resemblance to some of the better-known earlier examples of the mixed style: e.g. I **26** = P. Lond. Lit. 129 (Roberts, *GLH* 19a; Demosthenes, *Prooemia*), X **1234** (Plate IV; Alcaeus), and IV **665** (Plate I; History of Sicily)—all assigned to the second century. Our specimen is penned more rapidly than these, and so exhibits more connection of letters and other cursive features, in addition to the supra-linear stroke to represent nu at the ends of lines (inception datable to the second half of the second century, according to Turner, *GMAW*^{2} introd. p. 17). For an objectively dated comparison, see P. Mich. 3 (Roberts, *GLH* 15c; Dioscorides, *De materia medica*), which bears a date of AD 190 on the verso.

It is impossible to be sure that the raised point and following space in i 10 were accompanied by a *diple* or *paragraphos* at the lost line-beginning, but in view of the *diplai* at the line beginnings of ii 5 and 6, the former seems probable (cf. XLVII pp. 38–9). At line endings a wedge-shaped line-filler is occasionally used. Iota adscript is consistently written. The same applies to the raised point in i 7, if this has been correctly deciphered (possible doubt arising from the weak break in the syntax to which it would have to correspond).

The suggestions of Professor Harold Tarrant, Professor Apostolos Pierris, Professor Antonio Carlini, and the General Editors in correspondence are gratefully acknowledged, as are the comments of discussion groups at the Scuola Normale Superiore, Pisa, and the Université de Paris 1. It is a great pleasure to be able to join other contributors to this volume in honouring Peter Parsons and John Rea. They gave me my first introduction to the Oxyrhynchus Papyri decades ago, and have set a standard for papyrological research that continues to serve as an inspiration.

Fr. 1

Col. i   Col. ii

```
 .    .    .    .    .    .                       .    .
[ . . . . . ]ηδους[ . . . . . ]θοδικ[ 4–5 ]μα>           . [
[ . . . . . ].μενο.[ . . . . ]μοστηνπεριτω̄              τ.[
[ . . . . . ]ατων[ . . . . . ].τειανπαρεχομε            χ[
[ . . . . . ].ιδετο[ . . . . . ]ατυλοστηνπεριο           τ[
[ . . . . . ].ν[.]ρθοτητο..[ . . . . . ]αλιανπερι         > τ[
[ . . . . . ]εξηςδετουτω.[ 6–7 ].τ.ςουτος.               > ..[
[ 2–3 ].μ..δηεπιτωιθε[.].[.].τωι· [ 2–3 ]φιςτης
[.]εκαιπο.[.]τικοςτηνοριςτικηντεκ[ 2–6
[.].[.].ρετικηνμεθοδονδιδαςκοντες>
[..]αμφιλογωςμενεκεινοι· οδεθεαιτη
[.].ςαμφιδοξ[ . . . . . . ]καιβουλεταιπερι
[.].ιςτημης.[ . . . . . . ].αςαναςκευαζω̄
[..]..αιτ.[ . . . . . . ].δριτωντρ.[.]νδια
[ . . . ].ντη[ . . . . . . ].νημονευςεωςανα
```

Fr. 2

```
     .    .
]....
]πομε
]μενου
]υγαρ
     .    .
```

Fr. 1 col. i

2]., vertical trace   .[, prob. ϲ   3 .τ: right end of horizontal or descending stroke, suggesting ʌ, ε or λ   π corrected from ε by overwriting, probably *scribendo*   4 н, м, or π, or possibly ι or N   5 ν: θ, ο or ω   ο .[: ε, θ, ο, or ϲ, followed by left end of low horizontal, suggesting ʌ, z, or ᴣ   6 υτ: the vertical stroke of γ is too far to the right, but this seems to be due to distortion of the papyrus; without such rectification, the sequence of traces would have suggested rather γπ   .τ: top of final vertical   τ.: right arc of curved letter, almost certainly ο   ϲ.: part of a vertical stroke, followed after a break in the papyrus by a raised dot or the right-hand end of a vertical stroke; possibly г, ε, н, or ι followed by a raised point   7 μ: top of final vertical, matching н, ι, м, N, or π   μ..δ: bottom of oval or circular letter (ε, θ, ο, or ϲ) and foot of upright].: minimal low trace of ink   .τ: base of vertical, suggesting н, ι, м, N, or π   The apparent raised point may be followed by a space, as in 10   8 .[: beginning of ʌ, λ, or χ   9 Two bases of verticals   10 After νοι raised point followed by space   11].: ʌ, ο, or ω   12].: high perpendicular junction   .[: ε or θ   ].: upright with join from left at the bottom (N?)   13]..: top half of high vertical, almost certainly ι, followed by low horizontal, compatible with ʌ, z, or ᴣ   .[: thick traces of rising oblique, compatible with ʌ, ω   ]., bottom of upright with hook

Fr. 1

Col. i

·   ·   ·   ·   ·   ·

[. . . . . .]ηδους[. . . .με]θοδικ[. . . .]μα
[. . . . .].μενος[. .ἀρ]μοστὴν περὶ τῶ(ν)
[. . . . .]ατων [πραγμ]ατείαν παρεχομέ-
[. . προ]ήιδετο [γὰρ ὁ Κρ]άτυλος, τὴν περὶ ὀ-
5 [νομάτ]ων [ὀ]ρθότητος δ[ιδασκ]αλίαν περι-
[. . . . .]· ἑξῆϲ δὲ τούτωι [ὁ Θεαίτ]ητοϲ οὑτοϲί,
[κα]ὶ μὲν δὴ ἐπὶ τῶι Θε[α]ι[τ]ήτωι [ὁ Ϲο]φίϲτηϲ
[τ]ε καὶ Πολ[ι]τικὸϲ, τὴν ὁριϲτικήν τε κ[αὶ τὴν
[δ]ι[α]ιρετικὴν μέθοδον διδάϲκοντεϲ,
10 [ἀν]αμφιλόγωϲ μὲν ἐκεῖνοι, ὁ δὲ Θεαίτη-
[τ]οϲ ἀμφιδόξ[ωϲ, ἐπεὶ] καὶ βούλεται περὶ
[ἐ]πιϲτήμηϲ ἐ[κεῖ πλά]ναϲ ἀναϲκευάζω(ν)
[δε]ῖξαι τὰ [ἐπὶ τῶι ἀ]νδρί, τῶν τρι[ῶ]ν δια-
[λόγ]ων τὴ[ν ἐκ τῆϲ] μνημονεύϲεωϲ ἀνά[πτυξιν

Fr. 2

·   ·

]. . . .
]πομε-
]μενου
]υ γὰρ

·   ·

to right, as of N   .[: top of upright on edge   14]. : scattered traces on broken surface   ]. :
dot at line level on edge

Fr. 1 col. ii
   1 Base of curved letter, probably first of line   2 Upright, probably н or ι   6 Two
low traces of verticals, the second descending further than the first

Fr. 2
   1 Minimal and indecipherable traces (letter feet)

   '. . . methodical . . . provide a harmonized study about . . . . For the *Cratylus* used to be sung as
a prelude, [bringing in] (his) teaching on correctness of names. Directly after it comes this (dialogue),
the *Theaetetus*, and, following upon the *Theaetetus*, the *Sophist* and *Statesman*, which teach the methods of
definition and division. They do this transparently, whereas the *Theaetetus* does so ambiguously, since
he also aims there, in eliminating errors about knowledge, to demonstrate those points that bear upon
the individual man (Theaetetus), with the three dialogues [showing that] the unfolding, as a result of
a memory process, [of innate concepts . . .]'

In our modern editions of Plato the dialogues are ordered in tetralogies. Thus volume 1 of the OCT contains the first tetralogy, consisting of *Euthyphro, Apology, Crito,* and *Phaedo,* followed by the second, consisting of *Cratylus, Theaetetus, Sophist, Statesman.* This canonical arrangement is due to Thrasyllus, who in addition to his philosophical scholarship is also notable for having served as court astrologer to the emperor Tiberius (died AD 36). Despite being generally rejected or ignored by the other Platonist thinkers of later antiquity, his tetralogical ordering had a decisive effect on the codex tradition. Comparisons have been made to Andronicus' reported role, in the mid to late first century BC, in establishing the canonical ordering of Aristotle's works.

There can be little doubt that, in explaining the purpose of the *Theaetetus,* the present fragment locates it in Thrasyllus' second tetralogy, for which cf. DL 3.58: δευτέρα τετραλογία, ἧς ἡγεῖται Κράτυλος ἢ περὶ ὀρθότητος ὀνομάτων, λογικός· Θεαίτητος ἢ περὶ ἐπιστήμης, πειραστικός· Σοφίστης ἢ περὶ τοῦ ὄντος, λογικός· Πολιτικὸς ἢ περὶ βασιλείας, λογικός.

It is impossible to say with confidence that Thrasyllus is the fragment's author, but the following considerations favour the possibility:

1) Although there were other tetralogists, we know of no other writer on Plato who adopted Thrasyllus' ordering (beyond the bare report of DL 3.61 that Thrasyllus 'and some (others)' follow it), and of many who adopted alternative orderings. These start with Thrasyllus' predecessor Aristophanes of Byzantium, who had in fact organized Plato's works into trilogies, placing *Sophist, Statesman,* and *Cratylus* in his second trilogy but *Theaetetus* in his fourth (DL 3.61–2). Thrasyllus, who also organized Democritus' works into tetralogies, was almost certainly the originator of tetralogical arrangements of the Platonic corpus, as is fully argued by H. Tarrant, *Thrasyllan Platonism* (Ithaca, N.Y., 1993). A certain Dercyllides, of unknown date, is reported to have advocated the same first tetralogy as Thrasyllus (Albinus, *Intr.* 4), but there is little reason to think that he adopted the whole Thrasyllan ordering, and still less to think that he anticipated it (cf. also J. Mansfeld, *Prolegomena: Questions to be Settled before the Study of an Author, or a Text* (1994) 64). Even Theon of Smyrna, who was heavily influenced by Thrasyllus and quoted him extensively, adopted his own tetralogical ordering of the corpus rather than replicate the Thrasyllan one (Tarrant, *Thrasyllan Platonism* 58–72).

2) Thrasyllus proposed the tetralogical scheme, not as his own editorial device, but as representing Plato's original ordering: according to him, Plato actually 'published', or 'edited', the dialogues in tetralogies (DL 3.56). The present fragment says nothing about publication, but does likewise apparently purport to recount the original educational use of the dialogues in the early Academy: hence in line 4 the imperfect προ]ῄδετο.

3) Two terminological details match our evidence for Thrasyllus' usage. (*a*) At 7, the unusual ἐπί + dative to describe one dialogue as continuing another in a tetralogy seems to be Thrasyllan (see 7 n. below); (*b*) in 11 ff., the use of ἐπεί] καὶ βούλεται . . . [δε]ῖξαι κτλ. to convey Plato's authorial intentions (see further below, 11–14 n.) mirrors what Thrasyllus, as reported at DL 3.57, says about Plato's intentions in the first tetralogy: παραδεῖξαι γὰρ βούλεται κτλ.

In constructing his tetralogical schema, Thrasyllus labelled each dialogue generically: λογικός, πειραστικός, ἠθικός, etc. For example the first tetralogy, which displays in the person of Socrates a paradigm of the philosophical life, consists of one 'peirastic' dialogue (*Euthyphro*) and three 'ethical' (*Apology, Crito, Phaedo*), following a favoured pattern according to which a tetralogy typically consisted of three dialogues of a single generic type appropriate to the group's overall function, plus one odd man out, analogous to the satyr play that was combined with a tragic trilogy to make up a full dramatic tetralogy (DL 3.56; see Tarrant, *Thrasyllan Platonism* 70–72). Along these same lines, the second tetralogy (see DL 3.58, quoted above) consisted of one 'peirastic' dialogue, namely the *Theaetetus,* and three 'logical' ones.

The new fragment for the first time elucidates what this particular 3 + 1 arrangement amounted to. (For past suggestions, which find some measure of support in the new papyrus, cf. M. Dunn,

'Iamblichus, Thrasyllus and the Reading Order of the Platonic Dialogues', in R. B. Harris (ed.), *The Significance of Neoplatonism* (1976) 59–80, esp. 63–4; Mansfeld, *Prolegomena*, esp. 70; and A. Dunshirn, 'In welcher Reihenfolge die Dialoge Platons lesen?', *Gymnasium* 115 (2008) 103–22, esp. 110–12.) The tetralogy's overarching theme is, it seems, the methodology for acquiring the ideal philosophical knowledge that the first tetralogy has already advertised. The second tetralogy's main thrust is thus 'logical', in the broad sense of this term which includes both inferential method and epistemology. Its solitary peirastic dialogue, i.e. the one that tests and finds wanting the views of others, is the *Theaetetus*, whose main task is to clear away a series of misconceptions about what knowledge is (perception, true belief, true belief plus an account), thereby indirectly pointing to the term's correct Platonic definition. As a result this dialogue's more far-reaching task, to teach philosophical method, remains somewhat hidden (10–11). The other three members of the tetralogy are straightforwardly 'logical'. The first is the *Cratylus*, devoted to 'correctness of names'. The other two are the *Sophist* and *Statesman*, which serve as paradigms of methodology, consolidating and amplifying the hints already given by the *Theaetetus* as to how knowledge is really constituted.

The work from which the fragment derives was either closely dependent on Thrasyllus or, at least as likely, by Thrasyllus himself. Tarrant, *Thrasyllan Platonism*, argues that Thrasyllus may have set out his full tetralogical schema in an 'Introduction to the reading of Plato's dialogues'. However, the present fragment would be unlikely to derive from a work of precisely that character, since it is clearly focusing ultimately on just one dialogue, the *Theaetetus*, rather than on the tetralogy or tetralogies as such. The author pays special attention to the *Theaetetus*, not only by going into greater detail about its content and function, but also by referring to it as 'this dialogue, the *Theaetetus*' (fr. 1.i 6, ὁ Θεαίτ]ητὸς οὑτοcί). The deictic pronoun, if correctly read here, opens the possibility (kindly suggested by Professor A. Pierris) that the text was in fact a commentary on that dialogue, even if no commentaries by Thrasyllus are attested in our sources. If so, the fragment would almost certainly come from the commentary's introductory section—corresponding to Anon. *In Platonis Theaetetum* (*CPF* III) 2.11–3.25, where in his own introductory section this Middle Platonist commentator compares two rival views as to how the *Theaetetus* is related to the *Sophist*, neither of them being exactly the Thrasyllan view proposed in the present fragment.

Fr. 1 Col. i

1–4 These lines defy exact reconstruction. But the theme seems to be the harmonized study (ἁρ]μοστὴν . . . [πραγμ]ατείαν) that the four dialogues combine to offer. This musical metaphor, which will continue with προ]ῄιδετο in 4, may have already started in lines 1–2, where με]θοδικ[ὸν ᾇιc]μα could be restored. Fittingly, harmonic theory was Thrasyllus' own major area of specialization (texts in Tarrant, *Thrasyllan Platonism* 222–7).

3]ατων. Since the tetralogy is meant to be about philosophical method, one might expect ζητημ]άτων or θεωρημ]άτων.

4–6 Cf. DL 3.57, quoting Thrasyllus with regard to the first tetralogy: διπλαῖς τε χρῆται [sc. Plato; see first paragraph of 11–14 n.] ταῖς ἐπιγραφαῖς καθ' ἕκαστον τῶν βιβλίων, τῇ μὲν ἀπὸ τοῦ ὀνόματος, τῇ δὲ ἀπὸ τοῦ πράγματος. In then setting out the tetralogies, Thrasyllus systematically gives each dialogue its full disjunctive title, for example (58) Κράτυλος ἢ Περὶ ὀρθότητος ὀνομάτων, as echoed in the present passage, albeit without its explicit use as title plus subtitle. Thrasyllus (see 11–14 n.) believed the subtitles to go back to Plato, and they certainly predated Thrasyllus himself by centuries (cf. Mansfeld, *Prolegomena* 71–4), because that of the *Phaedo*, Περὶ ψυχῆς (for which cf. also Anon. *In Plat. Tht.* 48.9–10, possibly close in date to Thrasyllus), was already used by Callimachus (*Epigr.* 23.2–4).

4 προ]ῄιδετο: the imperfect suggests that the author purports to be describing the regular practice of the early Academy.

5 δ[ιδασκ]αλίαν is due to Professor Tarrant, who also suggests περι|[άπτων ('joining on'?) in 5–6. For the latter, περι|[λαβών, 'incorporating', is another option, and a third is περι|[έχων, 'including' (suggested by Professor Carlini, who cites the parallels of DL 1.112 and Diodorus 2.1.1). This last fits the lacuna, provided we assume that it was followed by a space like that in line 11. The first two treat the *Cratylus* as appending an extra topic to the ensuing trilogy, the third as simply including it in its contents. Since the topic of 'correctness of names' was recognized as the theme of the *Cratylus*, one might hope to avoid a reading which makes this topic merely 'included' in it, and hence prefer one of the first two suggestions. The author considers the methodology of attaining knowledge to be the dominant theme of the whole tetralogy, and this would make it natural for him to treat the official topic of the *Cratylus*, correctness of names, as somehow subsidiary or ancillary ('joined on' or 'incorporated') to the tetralogy's purpose. On the other hand, he could, if περι|[έχων were read, have it in mind that the question 'How are we to obtain knowledge?' is already becoming a focal question by the end of the *Cratylus* (337d–340e), a point of view from which it would indeed be true that correctness of names is merely 'included' among the dialogue's themes.

6 The restoration of this line is primarily due to Professor Pierris.

6–11 Following the *Cratylus*, the ensuing trilogy of *Theaetetus, Sophist, Statesman* is seen as turning to the methodology by which knowledge is to be attained. The latter two, being supreme exhibitions of definition by the method of division, are direct lessons in philosophical method. The *Theaetetus*, which is prefaced to them (for the use of ἐπί in 7, see n. below), is only indirectly or covertly about method, since in it Plato's main aim is to eliminate Theaetetus' wrong definitions of knowledge and thus prepare the ground for what will emerge from the entire trilogy as the correct account of knowledge. Knowledge, in the author's view, turns out to depend on the full articulation of our innate concepts by the process of recollection, a process that is presumably here identified with the dialectical mapping of interrelated Forms through the method of division. The *Theaetetus*, with its portrayal of Socrates as midwife, sketches the correct means of arriving at knowledge as one of intellectual parturition from our own innate resources; and the *Sophist* and *Statesman* go on to show in detail what the complete attainment of that parturition is like.

7 The unusual ἐπί + dative, used here to describe dialogues as 'following' others in a tetralogy, concurs with Albinus' report of Thrasyllus' first tetralogy (*Prolog.* 4.10), ἐπὶ τούτοις [sc. *Euthyphro* and *Apology*] τὸν Κρίτωνα κτλ.). As Professor Most has plausibly suggested to me, it could be a usage derived from the title Ἐπινομίς. This title had already been applied in the early Academy to the dialogue believed to have been compiled by Plato's secretary Philip of Opus, which was accepted by Thrasyllus in his ninth tetralogy as the authentic sequel to the *Laws*, Νόμοι (DL 3.60). It may be meant (as Professor Manetti suggests to me) to express a closer continuity than the simple ἑξῆς δὲ τούτωι in line 6. The latter describes the relation of the *Cratylus* to a trilogy that it prefaces without either significantly anticipating its content or being part of a single dramatic sequence.

11–14 It is unclear from the run of the text whether the subject of βούλεται . . . [δε]ῖξαι is (a) 'the *Theaetetus*' or (b) 'Plato', the reverential omission of whose name is a common feature of Platonist literature. But a striking parallel from Diogenes Laertius may help. DL 3.57 is reporting Thrasyllus' tetralogies: πρώτην μὲν οὖν τετραλογίαν τίθησι τὴν κοινὴν ὑπόθεσιν ἔχουσαν. **παραδεῖξαι γὰρ βούλεται** ὁποῖος ἂν εἴη ὁ τοῦ φιλοσόφου βίος. It has generally been held (and argued by Tarrant, *Thrasyllan Platonism* 91) that the subject of this latter passage is Thrasyllus, but the parallel in the papyrus now favours taking it either, in correspondence with option (a), as 'the tetralogy', or, with option (b), as 'Plato'. Of these, the second is marginally favoured by the fact that in the next sentence of Diogenes Laertius (quoted above, 4–6 n.) the unnamed subject said to use double titles for dialogues is not very likely to be 'the tetralogy' but could very well continue to be 'Plato'. On either reading, it is Plato whose intentions are in both texts said to be didactic: his first tetralogy started off the entire didactic project by displaying Socrates' conduct in his last days as a paradigm of the philosophical life; the second continued by teaching how we too can attain philosophical knowledge.

For the author's definition of knowledge, including the suggested completion ἀνά|[πτυξιν], cf. Anon. *In Plat. Tht.* 47.37–48.7: ἐν δὲ τῷ διδάσκειν αὐτοὺς [παρ]εσκεύαζεν (sc. Socrates) [τοὺς] μανθάνοντας [λέγει]ν περὶ τῶν π[ραγ]μάτων, ἀναπτύ[c]cων αὐτῶν τὰς φυcικὰς ἐννοίας καὶ διαρθρῶν. καὶ τοῦτο ἀκόλο[υ]θον τῷ δόγματι τῷ τὰς λεγομένας μαθήcεις ἀναμνήcεις ε[ἶ]ναι[ι] κ[αὶ] πᾶcαν ἀνθρώπου ψυχὴν τεθεᾶcθαι τὰ ὄντα καὶ δεῖν αὐτῇ οὐκ ἐνθέcεως μαθημάτων ἀλλὰ ἀναμνήcεως. Like this author, our author turns out to hold this same Middle Platonist position that knowledge is acquired by 'unfolding' or 'articulating' one's innate (ἔμφυτοι or φυcικαί) ἔννοιαι into full-scale definitions, an interpretation that combines the Platonic theory that all learning is recollection, the portrayal of Socrates in the *Theaetetus* as an intellectual midwife bringing to birth others' embryonic ideas, and the elaborate methodology for articulating definitions deployed in the *Sophist* and *Statesman*.

With the author's view of the *Theaetetus'* strategy, cf. Anon. *In Plat. Tht.* 2.52–3.25, according to whom Plato uses the dialogue to refute a series of wrong views about what knowledge is, converging on but deliberately stopping short of the correct one.

14 ἐκ τῆc] μνημονεύcεως. This rare noun is otherwise attested only in Epicurus, *Nat.* 25 (34.19.2 Arrighetti[2]) and Origen, *In Ev. Io.* 206.3, 208.6. In neither author does it refer to Platonic recollection, simply meaning 'memory' or 'remembering', a sense that however is perfectly suitable to the present passage. It is possible that a compound should be restored instead: either ἐκ cυμ]μνημονεύcεως or ἐξ ἀπο]μνημονεύcεως. However, neither term has any link to Platonic recollection that would commend it as obviously preferable. The former is a Pyrrhonist technical term for *joint*-memory of two or more items, and the latter very rare word would be more likely to connote 'recounting' than simple remembering. A final possibility would be ἐξ ἀνα]μνημονεύcεως, but not only is the noun unattested but the cognate verb ἀναμνημονεύω has only three attestations, none of them linking it to Platonic recollection; and the prefix would sit awkwardly with the immediately following ἀνα- compound.

D. N. SEDLEY

4942. Zenobius, *Epitome of Didymus and Lucillus of Tarrhae*, Book i

29 4B.48/B(2–4)b   12.4 × 9.5 cm   Third century
                                                                     Plate VI

The tops of two consecutive columns from a papyrus roll, written across the fibres on the back of a document. The line beginnings of the first column are not preserved, but the second column is almost complete in width, with only a small lacuna in the first four lines and a few letters missing from the end of lines. The intercolumnium ranges between 1.5 and 2 cm. The papyrus, irregularly broken on all sides, has an upper margin 2 cm high. Over the centre of col. ii, at the top of the margin, there appears an incomplete and uncertain trace of ink (an ascending oblique), which probably represents a column number (on the practice of numbering columns in papyrus rolls, see **4935** introd.). The exact number of lines missing from the bottom of the columns is uncertain. The document on the front appears to be a land survey (names, cardinal points, *aroura* symbol, numbers) written in a second-century hand.

The text is written in a medium-sized, slightly sloping specimen of the 'severe' or 'formal mixed' style, but the contrast between broad and narrow (ε, θ, c) letters is not as pronounced as in e.g. *GLH* 19b (dated to the first half of the third century because of a land survey 'most probably of the reign of Gallienus' on its back). The hand is only roughly bilinear. ρ, γ, φ, ψ, and occasionally τ have long descenders relative to other letters, which sometimes curve leftwards at the bottom (cf. *GMAW*² 27). λ is consistently angular. ε has a protruding midstroke. ξ (i 11) is made in three strokes. φ has angular flanks, its left-hand side being markedly larger than the right-hand one. The center of ω is almost flat, with only a slight rise. The hand may be assigned to the early third century.

The only lectional signs in evidence are three diaereses over ι (ii 9, 12) and υ (ii 8), which are employed organically to separate vowels between words. The scribe writes iota adscript at the one place we expect it (i 10). Elision is effected, but not marked (i 7, 14). There are some minor mechanical errors in the text (see i 13–14 n. on Μεc]ϲηνί⟨αι⟩, ii 11 n. on ἁδὺ ὕδωρ), but whether they are due to the scribe or his exemplar cannot be determined with any certainty.

The text belongs to a paroemiographical treatise, that is, a discursive collection of proverbs (*paroimiai*) appearing in literature, accompanied by explanations of their origins and usage. The following *paroimiai* are expounded in the preserved portions of the papyrus (for ease of reference I will be referring to these proverbs by the numbers assigned to them here):

1) The end of a discussion of the proverb πάντ' ὀκτώ (i 1–7).
2) A group of quotations from Menander that invoke Ἀράβιοι as paradigms of garrulity (i 8–16), whose explanation is not extant:
   (a) [Ἀράβιος α]ὐλ[ητ]ής (for the restoration see i 8–14 n.), a known proverb that is newly attributed to the *Kanephoros*, followed by two thematically related verses:
   (b) Ἀράβιον ἐξεύ[ρηκα cύ]μβουλον πάνυ from an unknown play (fr. 634 K.–A.; πάνυ is new and completes the verse);
   (c) Ἀράβιον [ἆρ' ἐγὼ κεκίν]ηκ' ἄγγελ[ον (fr. 31 K.–A.) from the *Messenia*.
3) A digressive story illustrating the saying πρὸc δύο οὐδ' ὁ Ἡρακλῆc (ii 1–11). The proverb itself is not preserved and must have been cited in the lost lower portion of col. i, but it is clearly deducible from the explanation in col. ii (see ii 1–12 n.).

All these proverbs recur in the directly transmitted paroemiographical collections (on which see generally K. Rupprecht, R.-E. XVIII.4 1735–78, s.v. *Paroimiographoi*). Their order of presentation in the papyrus, however, is almost identical to that evinced by the so-called 'Athoan recension' of Zenobius, the early-second-century author of a paroemiographical work in three books (cf. *Suda* ζ 73, s.v. Ζηνόβιοc, and see W. Bühler, *Zenobii Athoi Proverbia* i (1987) 33–7). This group of manuscripts, which takes its name from a fourteenth-century codex discovered by Emmanuel Miller in 1864 on Mt. Athos (now Par. suppl. 1164 = M), is believed to represent a more faithful version of the work of Zenobius than the so-called 'vulgate recension' known since the Renaissance (all of whose representatives ultimately descend from Par. 3070 = P; henceforth 'Zen. vul.' = Leutsch et Schneidewin, *Corpus paroemiographorum graecorum* i 1–175). Unlike the latter, the Athoan recension preserves a non-alphabetic ordering of the proverbs, contains many superior readings, and separates the proverbs of Zenobius (collections 1–3), in what is probably their original book division, from those of other collections (collections 4–5, containing Ps.-Plutarch's proverbs and an anonymous collection, all of which are mixed up in the alphabetized vulgate tradition). Unfortunately, all the representatives of the Athoan recension are incomplete and omit a number of proverbs that very probably occurred in Zenobius; moreover, the explanations of proverbs offered therein are often severely abridged versions. The 'Athoan recension', therefore, despite being more reliable than the vulgate tradition, does not necessarily correspond to Zenobius' original work in its full breadth and *ipsissima verba*.

The coincidences in the order of the proverbs between **4942** and the Athoan recension of Zenobius are as follows:

1) πάντ' ὀκτώ ~ Zen. Ath. I 3 (= Zen. vul. v 78)
2) [Ἀράβιος α]ὐλ[ητ]ής ~ Zen. Ath. I 4 (= Zen. vul. II 39)
3) (πρὸς δύο οὐδ' ὁ Ἡρακλῆς) ~ Zen. Ath. I 5 (= Zen. vul. v 49)

(Book I of the Athoan recension of Zenobius has not yet been edited by Bühler, who produced only an edition of Book II to date in his *Zenobii Athoi Proverbia*, but the readings of M can be consulted for now in M. E. Miller, *Mélanges de littérature grècque* (1868) 349; see also Bühler, in *Serta Turyniana* (1974) 430, for some minor variants among manuscripts of the Athoan recension in relation to these three proverbs.) Menander's frr. 634 and 31 K.–A. are admittedly not present in the Athoan Zenobius; but this can be easily attributed to the latter's abridged state. In effect, the two Menandrian verses are quoted as derived from the saying Ἀράβιος αὐλητής in the heterogeneous medieval paroemiographical collection known as the *Proverbia Coisliniana* (see i 8–14 n.). Furthermore, the lemma Ἀράβιος ἄγγελος, based on one of the Menandrian verses (fr. 31 K.–A.), appears with an explanation deriving it from the proverb Ἀράβιος αὐλητής in the vulgate recension of Zenobius (Zen. vul. II 58) as well as in the *Suda* and Hesychius (s.v. Ἀράβιος ἄγγελος). The conclusion is hard to avoid that Menander's verses had occurred originally in Zenobius, but fell out from the abridged version of the Athoan recension; only the fragment of one of the verses (Ἀράβιος ἄγγελος) survived in lemmatized form in the vulgate tradition.

Not much can be said about the discussion of the first two groups of proverbs, given the damage and incompleteness of the first column. The remains of the discussion of πάντ' ὀκτώ do not seem to correspond in any obvious way to the account found in the medieval recensions of Zenobius (see i 5–7 n.), but this can easily be ascribed again to an abbreviation of the entry in the medieval manuscripts. Since only the end of the discussion is preserved in the papyrus, nothing excludes that the explanation found in the medieval manuscripts was presented beforehand; this is especially supported by the mention of τῆς προκει[μένης] αἰτίας (sc. of the proverb) at i 3–4.

What is striking is that the digressive explanation of the third proverb, the most extensive and the best preserved in our papyrus, corresponds up to a point almost exactly to the explanation of the same proverb found in a scholion on Plato's *Phaedo* (see ii 1–12 n.). The beginning of the explanation at the bottom of col. i is not preserved, but it may be presumed to have been identical too. **4942** begins to diverge from the scholion just before the break of col. ii (11) with a mention of Euphorion instead of the scholion's further citation of some historians. The medieval recensions of Zenobius give a condensed summary of the scholion's and the papyrus' explanation up to precisely this point. Now, L. Cohn, *Untersuchungen über die Quellen der Plato-Scholien* (Jahrb. Suppl. 13; 1884) 836–52 (esp. 840), had argued that the great majority of the paroemiographical scholia on Plato, i.e. all those that are not clearly Neoplatonic, derive from none other than Lucillus of Tarrhae, one of the sources of Zenobius' epitome, who composed three books Περὶ παροιμιῶν around the middle of the first century AD (Steph. Byz. s.v. Τάρρα p. 604.9 M; see Bühler, *Zenobii* i 36 n. 16, with further bibliography). As Bühler, *Zenobii* i 300, notes, however, Cohn's arguments about the source of the paroemiographical scholia on Plato are not definitive, and there are compelling reasons to think that the scholia are based directly on Zenobius rather than Lucillus. The correspondence between **4942** and, on the one hand, the order of proverbs in the Athoan recension of Zenobius and, on the other, the scholion on *Phaedo*, would reinforce this hypothesis. The divergence of **4942** from the scholion after ii 11 could then be ascribed to the scholiast's use of additional sources or to his abbreviation of Zenobius.

Assuming Zenobian authorship, **4942** would provide direct evidence of the heavily abridged and contaminated nature of the medieval recensions of this author. It would also confirm modern scholars' suspicion that a post-Zenobian tradition is responsible for the alphabetization of proverbs in the vulgate recension; see especially O. Crusius, *Analecta ad paroemiographos Graecos* (1883) 70 ff., 95–6, and cf. Rupprecht, loc. cit. 1753–4, Bühler, *Zenobii* i 35. **4942** i 8 suggests that proverbs were cited in lemmatized form (see i 8–10 n.), although subsequent related proverbs (in this case the two Menandrian verses) were incorporated within the text. It has been argued that Zenobius ordered his epitome by literary genre, but there is no evidence that the first and third proverbs of the papyrus belong to comedy or Menander. The group of quotations from Menander shows at least that proverbs of similar content and authorship were cited together, as has been already surmised on the basis of the order of proverbs in the Athoan recension (cf. Crusius, *Analecta* 87–90, on *paroimiai* from Attic comedy in the Athoan recension that are linked by common authorship).

Since the proverbs of **4942** recur near the beginning of the first collection of the Athoan recension of Zenobius, and the first three collections of the latter probably reflect the original tripartite book division of Zenobius (see above, §4), the papyrus must come from Book 1 of the *Epitome*.

I am grateful to Professor Colin Austin and Mr Nigel Wilson for some helpful suggestions.

Col. i

```
        ]ωνεπιφ.νουν               [   c.7   τ]ῶν ἐπιφωνούν-
      ].π.οειρημενην               [των τὴ]ν προειρημένην
      ]πο.της.ροκε.[               [   c.6  ]που τῆς προκει-
      ]αι.ιαϲεϲτινευ               [μένηϲ] αἰτίαϲ ἐϲτὶν εὐ
5     ].νεπιτωνομοι            5   [   c.6  ].ν ἐπὶ τῶν ὁμοί-
      ].αϲινενκυρουν               [οιϲ πράγ]μαϲιν ἐνκυρούν-
      ].ε[....].παντοκτω           [των...].ε[....]. "πάντ' ὀκτώ".
      ]..[..].ϲταυτην              [Ἀράβιοϲ α]ὐλ[ητ]ήϲ· ταύτην
      ].μενανδροϲεν               [   c.6  ]ν Μένανδροϲ ἐν
10    ]κανηφορωιεντε          10  [δράματι] Κανηφόρωι, ἔν τε
      ].τωϲαραβιονεξευ             [   c.5  ο]ὕτωϲ "Ἀράβιον ἐξεύ-
      ].βουλονπαννεν              [ρηκα ϲύ]μβουλον πάνυ", ἐν
        ].ηνιαρα....[             [τε τῆι Μεϲ]ϲηνί⟨αι⟩ "Ἀράβιον [ἆρ'
        ].κ.γγε.[                 [ἐγὼ κεκίν]ηκ' ἄγγελ[ον"
15      ].ϲαρχε[             15   [         ]ηϲ ἀρχε[
        ].ων[                     [         ]ρων[
```

.   .   .   .

Col. i

1 φ.ν, horizontal base flanked by inward leaning obliques: ⲁ or ω   2]., top of upright
π.ο, foot of descender, then part of right arc at two-thirds height: ρ or φ   3 ο.τ, γ with damaged left arm   ϲ.ρ, two parallel uprights: π   .[, lower half of upright   4 ι.ι, horizontal bar of τ   5]., part of right arc at one-third height   6]., ascending oblique joining an upright at two-thirds height: right-hand half of ⲙ   7]., foot of descending oblique: ⲁ, λ, or ⲁ   ]., dot level with letter tops (top of upright?)   8].., first, ascending oblique at two-thirds height: right arm of γ (too steep for κ or χ); second, thick ascending oblique with bottom flattened to the left, then short descending oblique (slightly displaced): ⲁ or λ   ]., top of upright   9]., right-hand half of ⲛ   11]., ascending oblique at top: right arm of γ   12]., top of upright (with join at top?)   13]., horizontal speck level with letter tops   ....[, first, lower loop of ⲃ; second, foot and top of upright; third, speck at two-thirds height; fourth, thick dot level with letter tops (top of upright?)   14]., crossbar and second upright of ⲏ   κ.γ, ⲁ or (less

likely) λ   .[, ᴀ, ᴧ, or λ   15]., crossbar and second upright of ʜ   16]., faded small loop at top: ᴩ?

Col. ii

<table>
<tr><td></td><td>ητ[. . . . .]αικατατην[</td><td></td><td>ἠτ[τηθῆν]αι κατὰ τὴν [ἐπ᾿ Αὐ-</td></tr>
<tr><td></td><td>.εα[. . . . . . .] . ανδιωχθεντ . [</td><td></td><td>γέα[ν στρατε]ίαν, διωχθέντα [δὲ ἄ-</td></tr>
<tr><td></td><td>χριτ . [. . .] . πρασιδοσκαι . [</td><td></td><td>χρι τῆ[ς Βο]υπράσιδος καὶ π[ερι-</td></tr>
<tr><td></td><td>βλεψα . . νονωσουδεισε . [</td><td></td><td>βλεψάμενον ὡς οὐδεὶς ἐξ[ίκε-</td></tr>
<tr><td>5</td><td>τοτωνπο . εμιωναναψ . [</td><td>5</td><td>το τῶν πολεμίων ἀναψῦ[ξαί</td></tr>
<tr><td></td><td>τεκαιεκτουπαραρρεον[</td><td></td><td>τε καὶ ἐκ τοῦ παραρρέον[τος πο-</td></tr>
<tr><td></td><td>ταμουπιονταπροσαγορ[</td><td></td><td>ταμοῦ πιόντα προσαγορ[εῦσαι</td></tr>
<tr><td></td><td>τουτοναδυϋδωρουνυν[</td><td></td><td>τοῦτον "ἁδὺ ὕδωρ". ὃ νῦν [δεί-</td></tr>
<tr><td></td><td>κνυταιϊοντωνεκδυ . [</td><td></td><td>κνυται ἰόντων ἐκ Δύμ[ης</td></tr>
<tr><td>10</td><td>εισηλινκαλουμενο . [</td><td>10</td><td>εἰς Ἦλιν, καλούμενον [ὑπὸ τῶν</td></tr>
<tr><td></td><td>εγχωριωναδυϋδωρκ . [</td><td></td><td>ἐγχωρίων "ἁδὺ ὕδωρ". κα[ὶ Εὐ-</td></tr>
<tr><td></td><td>φοριων . . . . . οσηϊνα . [</td><td></td><td>φορίων . . . . . ος ἢ Ἴναχ[</td></tr>
<tr><td></td><td>. . . [*c*.5   ] . [.] . [.]ρπε . [</td><td></td><td>. ε . [*c*.5   ] . [.] . [.]ρπε . [</td></tr>
<tr><td></td><td>[   ] . . . [</td><td></td><td>[   ] . ε . [</td></tr>
</table>

Col. ii

2 .ε, ᴦ or ᴛ   ]., bottom of upright   .[, thick foot of ascending oblique   3 .[, upright with foot flattened to the left   ]., foot of descender: ᴩ, ʏ, φ, or ✝   .[, ᴦ or ᴨ   4 *a* . .*ν*, first, upright, then dot at line level; second, foot of upright with a right hook: ε or ϲ   ϲ in ουδεις corr.?   .[, left end of horizontal level with letter tops   5 ο .ε, lower half of λ or χ   .[, short thick descending oblique at top, then upright: left part of ʏ   9 .[, thick upright leaning to the right (with join from the right at top?)   10 .[, first upright and mid-stroke of ɴ   11 .[, dot at line level: foot of ascending oblique or upright leaning to the right?   12 *ν* . . . . .*o*, first, short ascending oblique at mid-height, then upright extending slightly above letter tops: most likely the top left angular quadrant and central upright of φ, but ᴧ is perhaps also possible; second, small upper arc level with letter tops; third, dot level with letter tops (the second and third traces could be part of the same letter); fourth, end of short ascending oblique at mid-height and horizontal (or gently descending oblique) near line level (bottom of ᴈ? arms of κ, χ? Left arm and base of ω?); fifth, thick upright or very narrow oval letter: ι? θ?   .[, upper tip of steeply descending oblique, below it foot of ascending oblique: extremities of left arm and foot of χ (not λ)   13 . . .[, first, apex of two obliques: ᴀ, ᴧ, or λ; second, upper half of ε; third, top of upright slightly above letter tops   ] . [, top of upright   ].[, descending oblique   .[, speck at line level   14] . . ., first, top of thick upright; second, top of oval letter open to the right and short horizontal at two-thirds height: ε; third, triangular junction of ascending oblique and horizontal base, then slightly displaced descending oblique: ᴧ or ω

Col. i

'. . . some of those who say the aforementioned . . . of the cause stated above it is well . . . It is concerning those who encounter the same affairs that (the proverb) "All eight" is said.

'"The Arabian *aulos*-player": Menander mentioned this proverb in the play *Kanephoros*, and in . . . (he said) as follows: "I have found a thoroughly Arabian councilor", and in the *Messenia*: "It seems I've aroused an Arabian messenger" . . .'

Col. ii

' . . . (Heracles) was defeated in the expedition against Augeas, and having been pursued as far as Bouprasis he looked around, and as none of the enemy had caught up with him he recovered; and when he drank from the river that was flowing by, he addressed it "Sweet water!". This river is now shown when (people) go from Dyme to Elis and is called "Sweet water" by the locals. Euphorion also . . . Inachus . . .'

Col. i

1–4 These lines imply that a different explanation of the proverb πάντ' ὀκτώ was discussed in the previous column; on the proverb and its explanations, see below, i 5–7 n. Before τ]ῶν ἐπιφωνούν[των] restore e.g. ἔνιοι or τινές, and in 3 perhaps [ῥῆcιν ὁ]ποῦ (C. Austin).

5–7 ἐπὶ τῶν ὁμοί[οιc πράγ]μαcιν ἐνκυροὺν[των . . .] . ε[. . . .] . "πάντ' ὀκτώ": in 7 perhaps restore καὶ] λέ[γετα]ι or γὰρ] λέ[γετα]ι (with postponed γάρ; cf. Denniston, *GP* 97–8); for the collocation ἐπὶ/κατὰ τῶν . . . λέγεται sc. ἡ παροιμία (also in reverse order), cf. e.g. Zen. Ath. II 42, 43, 58, 84, 105, 107.

The proverb πάντ' ὀκτώ was subject to various explanations among ancient authorities, none of which seems to correspond to the present one. Pollux, *Onom.* 9.100, Photius, *Lex.* (π 378), and the *Suda* (π 225) relate it to the tomb of Stesichorus, whose steps, columns and corners each numbered eight (this explanation is also imputed by Erbse to the Atticist Pausanias, *Lex.* π 7; these texts can be conveniently consulted in *PMGF* Stes. TA36–7). Although the proverb's usage is not discussed, Photius and the *Suda* seem to imply that it applied to extravagant displays of wealth (cf. πολυτελῶc), in the context of burial at least, while Pollux connects it with a dice throw of eight called Cτηcίχοροc (cf. also Suetonius, Περὶ παιδιῶν p. 67 Taillardat = *PMGF* Stes. TA38). Zen. Ath. I 3 = Zen. vul. v 78, quoting Evander, traces the proverb to τοὺc πάντων . . . κρατοῦντac θεοὺc (whom he names) or, according to others, to the eight Olympic contests. Finally, some philosophical and scientific writers claim that the proverb refers to the eight spheres encircling the earth (see Lloyd-Jones and Parsons on *SH* 397A for references). None of these explanations specify under what circumstances the proverb was used. **4942** implies that the proverb applied to people who kept on encountering the same situations. The preceding explanation (see above, i 1–4 n.) perhaps corresponds to one of the extant explanations found in the medieval recensions of Zenobius.

6 ἐνκυρούν-: read ἐγκυρούν-; cf. ἐγχωρίων in ii 11.

7 πάντ' ὀκτώ: the elided form is given only by Pollux, *Onom.* 9.100; all the other instances cited in i 5–7 n. have πάντα ὀκτώ. Could the elision hint that the proverb was part of a verse (as suggested by Prof. Bärbel Kramer)?

8–14 This section quotes proverbial sayings from comedy that invoke Ἀράβιοι as exempla of loquaciousness. The proverbs apply ἐπὶ τῶν ἀπαυcτὶ διαλεγομένων according to later explanations (see the references in i 13–14 n.). All are attributed to Menander and are in fact cited together by the so-called *Proverbia Coisliniana* p. 124 §40 (ed. Gaisford, *Paroemiographici Graeci* i 120–54; cf. Bühler, *Zenobii* i 277–9): "Ἀράβιος αὐλητής". [. . .] ἀπὸ τούτου ἐλήφθη ἡ παροιμία, ἣν μεταλλάξας Μένανδρος "Ἀράβιον" φηcὶν "ἐξεύρηκα cύμβουλον" καὶ "Ἀράβιον ἐγὼ κεκίνηκ' ἄγγελον". The first verse of

Menander (fr. 634 K.–A.) has fallen out in the other explanations of the proverb Ἀράβιος αὐλητής or Ἀράβιος ἄγγελος; see above, introd., and below, i 13–14 n.

By claiming that Menander derived frr. 634 and 31 K.–A. from the saying Ἀράβιος αὐλητής, the paroemiographical tradition implies that the saying was not itself by Menander. This now appears to be erroneous, for **4942** states that it occurred in Menander's *Kanephoros* (i 8–10). The later paroemiographical tradition's confusion can be plausibly explained. The phrase Ἀράβιος αὐλητής is itself based on the fuller joke (ὁ Ἀράβιος αὐλητής) δραχμῆς μὲν αὐλεῖ, τεττάρων δὲ παύεται, which is suspected to be a comic fragment (fr. adesp. 920 K.–A.). Whether an older comic verse or not, Menander alluded to this proverb by having one of his characters mock another as an Ἀράβιος αὐλητής in the *Kanephoros*. When explaining the further extensions of the proverb by Menander in frr. 31 and 634 K.–A., the paroemiographical tradition at some point confusedly substituted the longer proverb δραχμῆς μὲν αὐλεῖ, τεττάρων δὲ παύεται with Menander's own Ἀράβιος αὐλητής as the origin of these verses.

The ultimate socio-historical basis of this group of proverbs is unclear. Various explanations are offered by the paroemiographical literature, none of which is plausible (see the references in i 13–14 n. and cf. Steph. Byz. s.v. Ἀραβία). For a similar joke, cf. Cantharus fr. 1 K.–A. κιθαρῳδὸν ἐξηγείρατ' Ἀράβιον † τὸν χορὸν τοῦτον, which shows that the proverb must go back at least to the fifth century BC. The brief discussion of these passages in T. Long, *Barbarians in Greek Comedy* (1986) 66, is not particularly illuminating.

8–10 [Ἀράβιος α]ὐλ[ητ]ής· ταύτην [*c*.6]ν Μένανδρος ἐν [δράματι] Κανηφόρωι: [Ἀράβιος α] ὐλ[ητ]ής is restored here because the following two Menandrian verses are derived from it in the paroemiographical tradition (see above, i 8–14 n.). This restoration makes sense with the continuation ἔν τε at 10 and suits the traces. It is slightly too long assuming a regular left-hand margin, so I suspect that it must have been set in *ekthesis* by two or three letters, a procedure sometimes used to mark new entries (see *GMAW*² p. 8). With ταύτην understand τὴν παροιμίαν, which is too long to restore at the beginning of 9; for a similar ellipsis cf. Zen. Ath. II 81, Zen vul. I 50, VI 43, and see the comment of Bühler, *Zenobii* iv 407. A verb of saying is required at the beginning of 9, *exempli gratia* [εἴρηκε]ν. The restoration of δράματι is due to C. Austin.

11–12 Ἀράβιον ἐξεύ[ρηκα σύ]μβουλον πάνυ: Men. fr. 634 K.–A. = 757 Koerte (the papyrus does not support van Herweden's emendation of ἐξεύρηκα to ἐξηύρηκα). This iambic verse (minus πάνυ; see following note) is preserved only by the *Proverbia Coisliniana* p. 124 §40, along with the following verse (Men. fr. 31 K.–A.); see above, i 8–14 n. The play to which the verse belongs must have been cited in the lost beginning of 11 (5 or 6 letters). Kassel and Austin cautiously suggest attributing the verse to the *Messenia*; but see below, i 13–14 n., on the impossibility of restoring this title here.

12 πάνυ: this adverb is lacking in the quotation of the verse by the *Proverbia Coisliniana* and completes the metrically defective fragment.

13–14 Ἀράβιον [ἆρ' ἐγὼ κεκίν]ηκ' ἄγγελ[ον: Men. fr. 31 K.–A. = fr. 30 Koerte. *Proverbia Coisliniana* §40 omits ἆρ'. The complete iambic verse is quoted by the *Suda* s.v. Ἀράβιος ἄγγελος; the lemma Ἀράβιος ἄγγελος also appears in Zen. vul. II 58, Hesychius s.v. (α 6927) and later medieval paroemiographers (Apostolius III 70–71; Macarius II 37, 67), none of whom cites the whole verse nor mentions Menander. The *Suda* ascribes the verse to Menander's Ἀνατιθεμένη ἢ Μεσσηνία. Meineke (quoted in *PCG* VI.2, p. 60), followed by Koerte (II 24) and Kassel–Austin, thought that these are unlikely to be alternative titles of the same play, for they are elsewhere always cited individually, sometimes even by the same author. The fact that *Proverbia Coisliniana* §40 cites two Menandrian verses that derive from the proverb Ἀράβιος αὐλητής would suggest that each verse comes from one of these plays, and that the *Suda* (or its source) omitted one of the verses but retained the title of both plays. Under this hypothesis, it was not clear to which of the two plays each fragment ought to be attributed, and Koerte and Kassel–Austin arbitrarily ascribed the present verse to the *Anatithemene*. If the restoration of τῆι Μεϲ]ϲηνί⟨αι⟩ at the beginning of 13 is correct, however, fr. 31 K.–A. should be attributed to the *Messenia*. The restoration, which presupposes a 'saut du même au même' if the scribe's exemplar had iota adscript or a one-letter haplography with the following Ἀράβιον if not, is plausible, for none of the attested play titles by Menander are third-declension words in -ης, -ηνος (for a convenient list, see Sandbach's OCT edition, pp. 339–40). This ascription, however, does not automatically imply, as Meineke's reasoning would, that fr. 634 K.–A. belongs to the *Anatithemene*, for this long title would not fit the space at the beginning of 11 (5 or 6 letters). The possibility remains open, therefore, that *Messenia* and *Anatithemene* are alternative titles of the same play. For another play by Menander referred to by alternative titles, the second of which is an ethnic, cf. Ἀνδρόγυνος ἢ Κρής.

Col. ii

1–12 Up to ὕδωρ in 11, these lines correspond almost exactly to a section of a scholion on Plato, *Phaedo* 89c (p. 13 Greene), explaining the proverb πρὸς δύο οὐδ' ὁ Ἡρακλῆς (οἷός τε εἶναι) (on some variants, see the notes below). The present explanation invoking the fight of Heracles against the Molionidai is attributed by the scholion to Echephyllidas (*FGrHist* 409 F 1). A report of the explanation of Douris (*FGrHist* 76 F 93) that precedes the account of Echephyllidas in the scholion may have stood in the lower part of **4942** col. i. Following ὕδωρ at **4942** ii 11, the scholion continues differently, naming other authorities (Pherecydes fr. 79a Fowler = 78 Dolcetti; Comarchus *FGrHist* 410 F 2; Istrus *FGrHist* 334 F 42), but it is unclear whether these writers are cited because they generally related the story of Heracles' defeat by the Molionidai or because they specifically explained the proverb in this way. There follows a further digression on the consequences of Heracles' defeat, which is not germane to the explanation of the proverb, as well as yet another explanation by Herodorus (*FGrHist* 31 F 23 = fr. 23 Fowler) and Hellanicus (*FGrHist* 4 F 103 = fr. 103 Fowler). **4942**, on the other hand, appears to mention Euphorion at 11–12, perhaps as one of the loci wherein a version of the proverb or the narrative just related occurs (see below, ii 11–12 n.). Whether it then mentioned some of the authorities cited by the scholion and the third explanation of Herodorus and Hellanicus cannot be determined. Now, both the Athoan and vulgate recensions of Zenobius offer a heavily compressed and corrupt summary of the first two explanations found in the scholion, namely those of Douris and Echephyllidas (the authorities are not named in this abridged version); to give the example of the Athoan manuscript M (1 4): οἱ μὲν ἐν Ὀλυμπίᾳ φασὶ τὸν Ἡρακλέα ὑπὸ Λαΐου καὶ Φεράνδρου ἡττηθῆναι ἀγωνιζόμενον, οἱ δὲ ὑπὸ Κτε{ν}άτου καὶ Εὐρύτου, καὶ διὰ τοῦτο τὴν παροιμίαν ταύτην κρατῆσαι (cf. Zen. vul. v 49; note the corruption of Ἐλάτου > Ἐλαίου > Λαΐου and the erroneous implication that the Molionidai Cteatus and Eurytus also beat Heracles in an athletic context). If this evidently abridged explanation roughly mirrors Zenobius' original passage, it would correspond to the scholion on Plato and **4942** up to line 11, which is precisely the point at which the papyrus begins to diverge from the scholion.

For further citations of the proverb in question, see Leutsch and Schneidewin on Zen. vul. v 49. For similar proverbs based on Heracles' limitations, cf. e.g. Zen. Ath. II 78, 84. The direction of the narrative seems geared towards an aetiology of the name of the river from which Heracles drank after his setback. This was probably its original intention (e.g. in one of the historians cited by the scholion on Plato) before it was incorporated into the paroemiographical tradition to expand the explanation of the proverb πρὸς δύο οὐδ' ὁ Ἡρακλῆς, since the aetiology of the river's name is not necessary for the understanding of the proverb.

1–2 [ἐπ' Αὐ]γέα[ν: so Hermann (see Erbse's apparatus ad Paus. Att. π 32 p. 205). MSS of the sch. on Plato have ἐπ' Αὐγείᾳ, which is retained by Greene as well as Fowler and Dolcetti in their editions of Pherecydes (fr. 79a Fowler = 78 Dolcetti).

8 τοῦτον "ἁδὺ ὕδωρ": MSS of the sch. on Plato have τοῦτο ἡδὺ ὕδωρ. The papyrus' reading is a welcome improvement of the scholion's text, for the Doric form ἁδύ is closer than the Attic-Ionic

ἡδύ to the river name that is aetiologically derived from this exclamation (Caδὺ ὕδωρ or Baδὺ ὕδωρ according to different authorities; the papyrus wrongly keeps ἀδὺ ὕδωρ as the river's name; see below, ii 11 n.). Greene takes τοῦτο as belonging to the quotation ('This (is) pleasant water'), while Erbse, Fowler, and Dolcetti understand it as introducing the quotation ('he addressed the following: "pleasant water"'). The papyrus' masculine accusative implies τοῦτον sc. τὸν ποταμόν as the object of προσαγορεῦσαι ('he addressed this river "pleasant water"').

11 "ἀδὺ ὕδωρ": MS T of the sch. on Plato has "Caδὺ ὕδωρ" (preferred by Greene and adopted by Dolcetti and Fowler). But some recentiores read "Baδὺ ὕδωρ", which agrees with Pausanias v 3.2 (Pausanias gives a completely different aetiology of the name, but it is also implicitly connected to ἀδύς/ἡδύς; cf. ὑπερηcθέντεc). The papyrus' ἀδὺ ὕδωρ is a simple repetition of Heracles' exclamation at ii 8. The true reading is probably Baδύ, for F was often represented by β in the post-classical period; see C. D. Buck, *Greek Dialects* (1955) § 51, and A. Thévenot-Warelle, *Le Dialecte grec d'Élide* (1988) 73–5. The precise location and identification of the river are uncertain; see G. Maddoli and V. Saladino's BUR commentary on Paus. v 3.2.18–20 (p. 194).

11–12 κα[ὶ Εὐ]φορίων . . . . . οc ἦ Ἴναχ[: the restoration of the third word is uncertain (a personal name?). If it is a second-declension nominative, Ἴναχ[οc could be restored at the end of the line; the nominatives in turn would imply that this is a direct quotation of Euphorion. The scholar-poet is cited in the papyrus either because he offered a different explanation of the name of the river—apparently involving Inachus the first king of Argos or the homonymous Argive river—or because he used a variant of the proverb πρὸc δύο οὐδ' ὁ Ἡρακλῆc. It is notable that Euph. fr. 121 Powell = 125 van Groningen mentions the city of Dyme (poem and precise context unknown), which also figures in the foregoing explanation of the proverb.

The mention of Inachus points to Euphorion's poem of that name (Euph. fr. 32 Powell = fr. 33 van Groningen). The title is known from a scholion on Clement of Alexandria, which relates the colonizing mission of Caranus from Argos to Aegae in Macedonia. The only point of contact with Inachus is the common origin of both in Argos. The reference to Caranus in the *Inachus* must therefore have been a learned digression rather than a central part of the poem. The scholion also attributes the same story to Euphorion's (?) *Histie*, about which nothing is known (cf. E. Magnelli, *Studi su Euforione* (2002) 94 n. 4).

A. BENAISSA

4943–4944. DICTYS CRETENSIS, *BELLUM TROIANUM*

Together with P. Tebt. II 268 (Pack² 338) and XXXI **2539**, these two texts form a group of papyrus manuscripts of the Greek prose version of the account of the Trojan War that passed in antiquity under the authorship of Dictys of Crete. We possess the corresponding Latin version in a translation or adaptation by a certain Septimius, transmitted in the medieval tradition, that is most likely to be dated to the fourth century AD; a dating in the third or even second century (unlikely) has not been completely excluded by S. Merkle, *Die Ephemeris belli Troiani des Dictys von Kreta* (1989) 86, 263–83; id., 'Telling the True Story of the Trojan War: The Eyewitness Account of Dictys of Crete' in J. Tatum (ed.), *The Search for the Ancient Novel* (1994) 183–96; id., 'News from the Past: Dictys and Dares on the Trojan War' in H. Hofmann (ed.), *Latin Fiction* (1999) 155–66. **4943** now establishes the existence of the Greek version as early as the second century. (For the putative date of discovery of Dictys' work, see **4943** introd.) Its text attests a passage corresponding to book II of the Latin version, while **4944** attests the conclusion and authorial *sphragis* known from book V of the Latin, thus adding another copy of that book in the Greek version in addition to the two of book IV previously afforded by P. Tebt. II 268 and XXXI **2539**. As has already been observed by the editors of P. Tebt. II 268, and Merkle (op. cit. 113 ff.) for the two previously published papyri of Dictys, the Latin text for the most part follows the Greek faithfully, however with several alterations, omissions, and additions. It remains uncertain whether these Greek texts bore the title Ἐφημερίς, as the transliteration *Ephemeris* in the Latin version suggests; but there is nothing to intimate that they did not. Other stylistic features present in **4943–4** (narration in present tense, simple syntax) are consistent with those expected from a 'diary' or 'daybook' (compare Caesar's *Commentaria*). Narration in the present tense, close parallels with Homeric commentaries, D-scholia, and testimonia for the lost poems of the Epic Cycle, together with rationalizing explanations and the absence of direct involvement of the gods—all make their appearance in **4943–4**, thus confirming what have come to be recognized as the hallmarks of Dictys and his Latin reception, on which see (in addition to the studies by Merkle cited above) the commentary of H. J. Marblestone, *Dictys Cretensis: A Study of the Ephemeris belli Troiani as a Cretan Pseudepigraphon* (diss. Brandeis 1970); P. Venini, *Ditti cretese e Omero* (1981). The Greek version of Dictys, as known from Ioannes Malalas and later to Ioannes Tzetzes, was studied before the light shed by papyrus discoveries by F. Noack, *Der griechische Diktys*, Philologus Suppl.-bd. vi.2 (1892); cf. N. E. Griffin, 'The Greek Dictys', *AJPh* 29 (1908) 329–35. The Greek fragments (including P. Tebt. II 268 and XXXI **2539**) were re-edited, as far as they were known, under the pseudonyms of their various authors by F. Jacoby in FGrHist, and more recently by K. Dowden for the *New Brill Jacoby* (Brill online).

In **4943–4** by Dictys is meant the Greek version; Septimius (hereafter Sept.) refers to the Latin text, quoted according to the edition of W. Eisenhut, *Dictys Cretensis: Ephemeris belli Troiani* (Leipzig 1973²). In the notes we cite corresponding portions of the Latin that suggest a line of reconstruction for the Greek text. We further refer to relevant parts of Ioannes Malalas (hereafter Mal.), *Chronographia*, ed. I. Thurn (Berlin and New York 2000); his anonymous excerptor in the Ἐκλογὴ Ἱστοριῶν (as *Ecl. Hist.*), ed. J. A. Cramer, *Anecdota Graeca* ii (Oxford 1839) 165–230; Georgius Cedrenus (as Cedr.), *Historiarum compendium*, ed. by I. Bekker (Bonn 1838); the *Suda*, ed. by A. Adler (Teubner 1928–38); and the Hypothesis to Homer's *Odyssey* (*Hyp. Od.*), ed. by G. Dindorf, *Scholia Graeca in Homeri Odysseam* (Oxford 1855) 3–6; all of which borrow from Dictys. The material from the last two works is considered to represent fragments from the work of Ioannes Antiochenus (see Griffin, *Dares and Dictys* (1907) 36–37), for which see the editions of U. Roberto (2005) and S. Mariev (2008).

The related narratives in Ioannes of Antioch, Malalas, Cedrenus, and the

Ἐκλογὴ Ἱστοριῶν, which are known to have drawn on Dictys, are too compressed to afford any parallels for **4943**, as they do for P. Tebt. II 268, XXXI **2533**, and **4944**. Cedrenus is the only one who briefly includes in his history the plague in the Achaean army (*PG* 121.256D). Several texts from the Homeric commentary tradition are relevant, however, especially for *Il.* 1: two hypotheseis, namely P. Achm. 2 (Pack² 1159, re-edited by M. van Rossum-Steenbeek, *Greek Reader's Digests?* (1998) no. 29) and P. Bon. 6 (Pack² 1157, re-edited by F. Montanari, *Anagennesis* 2 (1982) 273–84), both of III–IV AD, and the medieval Hyp. II. The other three extant ancient Homeric hypothesis to *Iliad* 1 are not quoted, because LVI **3829** (later II AD) and LXXI **4814** (IV AD) offer the same text as P. Achm. 2, and P. Berol. 17598 (ed. by W. Luppe and G. Poethke, *Archiv* (1998) 214–15) of I BC does not afford any parallels to **4943**. We cite scholia minora preserved in P. Oslo. II 12 (Pack² 1160), P. Berol. 5014v (Pack² 1158), P. Achm. 2, XXIV **2405** (Pack² 1162), and the scholia D from the proekdosis of Van Thiel (www.uni-koeln.de/phil-fak/ifa/vanthiel/scholiaD. pdf); paraphrases to the opening lines of the *Iliad* composed by Plato *Rep.* III 393d and Aristides (ed. Spengel, *Rhet. Gr.* ii 510), the 'elaborate retelling' of *Il.* 1–21 preserved in the tablets T. Bodl. Gk. Inscript. 3019 1b+4a (ed. P. J. Parsons, *ZPE* 6 (1970) 135–41), the text of Tab. Iliaca Paris E after IGUR 4, 1620, and A. Sadurska, *Les Tables iliaques* (Warszawa 1964), along with four prose paraphrases of the *Iliad* compiled by Byzantine scholars, the first quoted after I. Bekker, *Scholia in Homeri Iliadem* (1827) Appendix 1, and the rest after the partial edition by A. Ludwich, *Aristarchs' Homerische Textkritik nach den Fragmenten des Didymos* ii (1885) 490 ff.: PB by Michael Psellos (known as Bekker Paraphrase), PM by Manuel Moschopoulos, PG by Theodorus of Gaza, who reworked the Moschopoulos paraphrase, and finally PA, the interlinear paraphrase contained in Codex Venetus Graec. 454.

4943. Dictys Cretensis, *Bellum Troianum* II 29–30

27 3B 39/B(1–3)c	7.3 × 13.6 cm	Second century
		Plate I

A fragment from a papyrus roll with top of column and upper margin preserved (at least 2.8 cm, possibly complete) together with intercolumnium to the right measuring *c.*1.5 cm. Across the fibres are fourteen lines from Dictys of Crete's account of the Trojan War. As reconstructed, 4–5 letters are missing from the beginning of the lines. The original column-width may be estimated at *c.*7.5 cm. About 25 columns may have preceded this one, on a rough calculation, assuming that the roll began at the same point as the second book of the transmitted Latin *Ephemeris belli Troiani*, and if each column contained *c.*35 lines. A central horizontal and two vertical creases are visible. On the other side and along the fibres are eleven lines of proceedings (?) in a documentary cursive, not far off in date, containing frequent abbreviations. For literary texts written on the back of documents, and the difficulty in speculating on their origins, see W. Clarysse, *Egypt and the Hellenistic World* (1983) 45–6; M. Lama, *Aegyptus* 71 (1991) 55–120.

The text is written in a sure, rapid, medium-sized, and well-spaced script (height about 3 mm), with a slight slant towards the right. Its style is characterized by curves (apparent even at times in ı) and long tails, normally curved upward at bottom, often descending to the top of the line below. The scribe slips easily into ligature (e.g. ΑΙ, ΕΙ, ΑΡ), and certain combinations of letters touch each other. Cursive influence is obvious in some forms, for instance, some Α at line-end, curved Υ, ο sometimes is left open, almost round ϲ, Μ with curved legs and deep middle. The right hasta of Η descends curved from its cross-bar without surpassing it. Α frequently keeps its angular shape; Ε is large and executed in two parts. Χ, ω, and Δ are broad, the latter resting on the baseline. Β is written without lifting the pen with squashed upper part. Bilinearity is infringed only by Ρ, φ, some ı, and once by the unique forked Υ (7). The handwriting shows some affinities with that of Roberts, *GLH* 15a, dated to AD 117, although some individual letters vary. The general impression is also similar to that of the hand of the *Gnomon of the Idios Logos* in BGU 1210 (plate in Norsa, *Scrittura letteraria* 12b), dated to AD 150–61; within the same tradition could be placed the hand in Norsa, op. cit., 12a, dated to AD 85. **4943** could be assigned to the second century, perhaps in the first half of it. Its writing is thus closer to AD 66 (the 13th year of Nero's reign, when, according to the *Prologus* of the *Ephemeris belli Troiani*, Dictys' tomb at Cnossos was supposedly opened and the tablets of his diaries were discovered and translated or transliterated by order of the emperor) than the two other extant papyri of Dictys, namely P. Tebt. II 268 (Pack² 338), written on the back of revenue returns of AD 206 (P. Tebt. II 340), and thus dated to the early third century AD, and XXXI **2539**, assigned to the late second or early third century.

The scribe marked an angular rough breathing on the first vowel of the diphthong in 9 (form 2 in *GMAW*² p. 11), the base of which is deliberately extended over the initial letter of the following word, although there is no marking of the breathing in 3 ἡμερῶν. Punctuation in the form of a high short stroke is employed three times as strong punctuation (1, 9, 12), and once (second instance in 1) superfluously as a comma. The scribe failed to write iota adscript in 1, the only opportunity to observe it. Elision occurs tacitly in 5 (probably) but *scriptio plena* in 8 and 13. No errors or corrections are in evidence. A χ of the same size as those in the text but in fainter ink and perhaps by different hand is placed at about the mid-height of the top margin, and centred over the column's width (as reconstructed). A column-number (= 600) may be excluded. χ appears commonly as a siglum in the right margin, for the various functions of which see K. McNamee, *Sigla and Select Marginalia* (1982) 19 ff. and Table F: it is employed either as a reference mark directing the reader to a commentary, or as an indication for something notable. For occurences of χ placed in the top margin, see IX **1182** (*GMAW*² no. 67, I/II AD) and LXVII **4577** (later III AD), where its meaning is still undetermined; 'it may have been marked by a second hand just to check or to mark something, e.g. the number of columns already corrected by a διορθωτής or covered by a reader' (LXVII **4577** introd.). Perhaps here it is to be correlated with a section break discernible in Sept. after 11 29, and at **4943** 1 after]αυτῷ, where punctuation is also marked in the text.

As preserved, the text relates, as does the Latin version, events familiar from *Il.* 1.33–53, Chryses' withdrawal from the Greek camp and the plague that follows. There are no references to Chryses' prayer to his patron god Apollo asking for revenge or to the latter's violent reaction against the Achaeans that actually caused the disease where we would expect them, apparently because the narrator is 'Dictys' who, as an Achaean soldier and supposed scribe of Idomeneus at Troy, could not yet have been aware of Chryses' invocation to Apollo nor of the latter's reaction by shooting arrows to the Greek camp.

As far as style is concerned, the present text is consistent with the two previously published papyri of Dictys, namely P. Tebt. II 268 and XXXI **2539**. It consists of single sentences linked by simple connective particles, namely καί (3, 9, 11), δέ (13) with adversative force (λαῶν . . . βαcιλέων) perhaps preceded by μέν in l.10, οὔτε . . . οὔτε / οὐδέ (13–14) preceded by οὐδείc for strong negation, and the transitional μὲν οὖν (1); see Denniston, *Greek Particles* (1950²) 472–3. Hiatus is tolerated in 3, 7, and 9. Finite verbs are in present (whether historic or actual), although not without exception: as restored, ἐνό[μιcαν (8–9), and the uncertainly read ἐνόcη[cεν and διε[φθάρη (13–14). No subordinate clauses are in evidence. The articular infinitive may have been employed (5), and participles of various usage often occur, sometimes instead of subordinate clauses: genitive absolute with temporal force (3–4 ἡμερῶν διαγε[νομ]ένων), a circumstantial participle (1–2 ἀ[τιμ]αcθείc) to express both time and cause, and attributive participle (7 ἐμπεcούcηc with νόcου). An instance of hyperbaton is evident at the end of colon: ἡμερῶν . . . ὀλίγων. (J. Palm, *Über Sprache und Stil des Diodoros von Sizilien* (1955) 131 ff., notes that hyperbaton is more common in Hellenistic prose than before.) Litotes is employed in 5 (see n.), perhaps to avoid repetition of the adjective ὀλίγων. There is assonance in 7 with the repetition of the syllable cου, possibly to place stress upon the plague. Although the syntax is not complicated, the word order is fairly symmetrical. The vocabulary is formal and carefully chosen; μῆνιν, νόcου, and λαοί are retained from the Homeric text; the phrase ἡμερῶν διαγενομένων with a numeral or a quantitative adjective, as well as the verb ἐμφοροῦμαι, come into vogue in later Greek, from the first century AD and the first century BC respectively (see 3–4 n., 5 n.).

A comparison between **4943** and the corresponding Latin text suggests nothing to refute the claim of Sept., in his introductory letter to Rufinus (*Epistula*, p. 1 ll. 16–17), that he wished to make a free translation into Latin during his spare time, feeling that he had no special talent (*Latine disserere, non magis confisi ingenio, quam ut otiosi animi desidiam discuteremus*). A difficult Greek expression in 5 is replaced in Sept.

by a simple, general phrase. The effect of the plague upon the people is described with more words in Sept. than in Dictys. Sept., not satisfied by the plain and short wording of Dictys, apparently added some commonplace details to intensify the narrative. Frequently in Sept. the plain, tight syntax of Dictys is mirrored: subordinate clauses are employed instead of participles or of single sentences, the latter being once replaced by an ablative absolute in Sept. (9–11, cf. II 30.4–5). A more detailed account of the differences between **4943** and Sept. is offered in the commentary below.

χ

]αυτω‘χρυϲηϲμενουν‘α
].ϲθειϲαπερχεταιπροϲ
]ονκαιημερωνδιαγε
]ενωνολιγωνειτεδια
5].λλωνεμφορηθηναι
]νειτεδιαμηνιντινα
]ννοϲουεμπεϲουϲηϲ
]πολλωναααιτιονενο
]όιλαοιειναί‘καιαρχε
10].τοκακοναποτων
].ποδωνκαιδιαφθει
]τωνλαωνπολλοί‘βα
]δεουδειϲουτεε . . . .
].δ..[*c.*7   ]..[*c.*5

*c.*3]αυτῷ. Χρύϲηϲ μὲν οὖν ἀ-   II 30
τιμ]αϲθεὶϲ ἀπέρχεται πρὸϲ
οἶκ]ον καὶ ἡμερῶν διαγε-
νομ]ένων ὀλίγων εἴτε διὰ
5 τὸ Ἀπ]όλλων’ ἐμφορηθῆναι
μηδὲ]ν εἴτε διὰ μῆνίν τινα
θᾶϲϲο]ν νόϲου ἐμπεϲούϲηϲ
τὸν Ἀ]πόλλωνα αἴτιον ἐνό-
μιϲαν] οἱ λαοὶ εἶναι· καὶ ἄρχε-
10 ται μὲ]ν τὸ κακὸν ἀπὸ τῶν
τετρ]απόδων καὶ διαφθεί-
ρονται] τῶν λαῶν πολλοί, βα-
ϲιλέων] δὲ οὐδεὶϲ οὔτε ἐνόϲη-
ϲεν οὔτ]ε διε[φθάρη *c.*3]..[*c.*5

2]., short line, almost horizontal at mid-letter-height, compatible more with the extension of the right oblique of ⋏ than of the middle stroke of ϵ   5]., speck of ink, assignable to many letters   10].τ, the extension of τ leftwards may distort the shape of the first visible letter of the line, which should be either ϲ or ɴ, of which part of the oblique and the right-hand side vertical can be seen   11].π, high speck of ink just below the left-hand side extension of the horizontal of π, suggestive of the extension of ⋏   13 ϵ...., tiny traces from the top of one or two letters, followed by the top of a semicircle and of a vertical   14]., part of a middle horizontal and of a high slightly curved line, which, if projected, would form an acute angle, suits well ϵ   δ.., speck from the top of a narrow letter, perhaps ι, followed by left-hand upper part of a letter, probably of ϵ rather than ϲ   ]..[, right-hand side oblique slightly curved compatible with ᴍ, ⋏, λ, followed by left-hand semicircle, suggestive of ο, φ, ρ, and less likely ω or ϲ

'. . . to [or for] him. Chryses therefore insulted departed homewards, and after few days, either because Apollo was not at all satisfied or due to wrath, a disease soon fell upon them and the soldiers considered Apollo to be responsible. The pestilence originated with the animals, and many soldiers perished, nevertheless none of the kings became sick or died . . .'

For comparison: the Latin version by 'Septimius'

(II 29) *Ceterum Achilles in ore omnium ipsumque et Menelaum contumeliis lacerabat.* (30) *Igitur Chryses ubi iniuriam perpessus ab Agamemnone domum discessit neque multi fluxerant dies, incertum alione casu an, uti omnibus videbatur, ira Apollinis morbus gravissimus exercitum invadit principio grassandi facto a pecoribus, dein malo paulatim magis magisque ingravescente per homines dispergitur. tum vero vis magna mortalium corporibus fatigatis pestifera aegritudine infando ad postremum exitio interibat. sed regum omnino nullus neque mortuus ex hoc malo neque ademptatus est.*

2 fluxerunt *Eπβ ex* fluxerant G² *cf. Br.* 7; *Frie.* 57   incertum est P   an *om.* B   3 morbus . . . principio *om.* σ   facta G¹ *corr.* G²   4 magisque] ac magis V   tum] Fuit V   5 interibat E¹V *corr.* E² *v.adn.cr.*   omnimodo σ   malo] morbo P   neque] atque EV

1]αυτῷ: sc. Ἀγαμέμνονι, according to Sept. (*ceterum Achilles in ore omnium ipsumque et Menelaum contumeliis lacerabat*). The context is presumably Agamemnon's decision not to return Chryseis to her father, and his abusive behaviour towards the latter that prompted the challenge by the Achaean leaders including Achilles.

1–2 ἀ[τιμ]αϲθείϲ. Cf. Sept. *iniuriam perpessus ab Agamemnone*, and *Il.* 1.11–12 οὕνεκα τὸν Χρύϲην ἠτίμαϲεν ἀρητῆρα Ἀτρεΐδηϲ. Less probable would be ἀ[χθ]εϲθείϲ, as regards space and the thickness and position of the middle stroke of the assumed ε. The same syntax with circumstantial participle is also offered in P. Bon. 6 απο]πεμπτειϲ (l. αποπεμφθειϲ) υπο τ[ου Α]γαμεμνονοϲ, and Hyp. II ἀλλὰ καὶ μεθ' ὕβρεωϲ ὑπὸ Ἀγαμέμνονοϲ ἀποδιωχθείϲ. (For Hyp. II we give the readings of the majority of MSS.) At this point the additional variations are reported in A. Ludwich, *Textkritische Untersuchungen über die mythologischen Scholien zu Homer's Iliad* i (1900) 8–9 διωχθείϲ, ἀποδιενεχθείϲ, ἀποπεμφθείϲ, ἀνιαθείϲ. Cf. also D, P. Oslo II 12.2.10, P. Berol. 5014v.17, P. Achm. 2, and the four Byzantine paraphrases of *Il.* 1.11, which offer ἀτίμωϲ or ἄτιμοϲ followed by a verb to denote Agamemnon's behaviour towards Chryses.

ἀπέρχεται. The present tense has not been preserved in Sept., who offers the perfect *discessit*. The same Greek verb in the imperfect is employed for Chryses' departure from the Greek camp in the paraphrases of Plato *Rep.* III 393d and Aristides (ed. Spengel, *Rhet. Gr.* ii, p. 510), and in the aorist in PM and PG.

3 οἶκ]ον. Both οἶκ]ον and δόμ]ον would correspond to the Latin *domum* and suit the space. δόμοϲ is a poetic word, but it could have been retained from memory of the Homeric text. However, οἴκοιϲ glosses δόμοιϲ at P. Strasb inv. Gr. 1015 (published by O. Plasberg, *Archiv* 2 (1903) 185–228) 5.15 (on *Il.* 5.198). Owing to the perspective of this narrative, namely that of an Achean soldier, which is completely different from that of the narrator of the *Iliad*, Chryses' withdrawal to the shore (as well as his prayers and the ensuing actions of Apollo) in the Homeric text would not have been known to the Achaean camp, cf. *Il.* 1.34 βῆ δ' ἀκέων παρὰ θῖνα πολυφλοίϲβοιο θαλάϲϲηϲ.

3–4 διαγε[νομ]ένων. Cf. P. Tebt. II 268.18. The participle as genitive absolute expressing lapse of time is attested in a number of later authors, e.g. Plutarch, Longus, Aristeides, Xenophon, Origen, and Porphyry, as well as in the New Testament. διαγε[γενημ]ένων is not attested in this phrase, and would be too long. In Sept. the absolute construction is replaced by a time clause: *(ubi) neque multi fluxerant dies.* The time reference in 3–4 would not be simply transitional, or even pedantic. Some time may have reasonably elapsed between the string of the related events, and presumably the effect of the disease upon the Achaeans could not have been made visible immediately after Chryses' departure so as to allow any connections.

5–6 τὸ Ἀπ]όλλων' ἐμφορηθῆναι [μηδὲ]ν. The same name is written with *scriptio plena* in 8; presumably the scribe was inconsistent in his practice. Restoring τὸ μὴ π]ολλῶν at the start of 5 would be too long for the available space, unless one assumes a scribal error, e.g. the omission of τό or μή. Likewise too long are θυϲιῶ]ν, εὐχῶ]ν, or ἀγαθῶ]ν, though cf. *Il.* 1.65 and 93 εἴ τ' ἄρ ὅ γ' εὐχωλῆϲ ἐπιμέμφεται ἠδ' ἑκατόμβηϲ, and XXIV **2405**, containing scholia minora on this line, as well as D and the four Byzantine paraphrases ad loc., which gloss εὐχωλῆς and ἑκατόμβης as εὐχῆς (D + δεήσεως) and (μεγάλης PB / τελείας D PA) θυcίαc respectively. Sept., who has *alione casu* here, is not as close as elsewhere, perhaps because ἐμφορηθῆναι proved difficult for the translator.

5 ἐμφορηθῆναι. The unusual verb ἐμφοροῦμαι, attested once in a document, P. Lips. 119 ii 6 (III AD), unlike here, is normally used of negative attributes, as Professor D. Mastronarde observes.

7 θᾶcco]ν could be considered here as standing for the positive, as it frequently does in Homer and poetry in general. As an alternative, one could consider restoring a modifier of μῆνιν, e.g. κακὴ]ν or ὀλοὴ]ν (cf. *Od.* 3.135), but the unecessary emphasis conveyed by this word order makes such a supplement less likely. Sept. has simply *ira Apollinis*, while the adjective *gravissimus* refers to *morbus* and is absent from Dictys.

νόcου ἐμπεcούcηc. Cf. *Il.* 1.10 νοῦcον ἀνὰ cτρατὸν ὦρce κακήν and Cedr. (Bekker 1 222.7–8) λοιμώδουc νόcου ἐνcκηψάcηc τῷ cτρατῷ. Similar structure but as genitive absolute recurs in Hyp. II: λοιμοῦ γενομένου (a variant reading is λοιμοῦ ἐνcκήψαντοc; see Ludwich, *Textkritische Untersuchungen* (1900) 9), and slightly different with transitive verb in Tab. Iliaca Paris. E του απολλωνοc . . . λοιμον εμβαλοντοc). Sept. rejects the participial construction in favour of a whole clause, supplemented with fairly obvious details (*morbus gravissimus exercitum invadit*). The issue of the plague occurs more accurately as λοιμόc and not νόcοc in the structure of the main clause also in P. Achm. 2 (διοπερ λοιμοc κατεcχεν τουc ελληναc) and P. Bon. 6 (ο δε θεοc επακουcαc λ[οιμ]ον επεcκηψεν τοιc αχαιοιc). Scholia minora and paraphrases on *Il.* 1.10 normally offer νόcον (with the exception of Par. A, which offers ἀρρωcτίαν).

8 τὸν ᾽Α]πόλλωνα: alternatively perhaps θεὸν ᾽Α]πόλλωνα? Cf. sch^bT on *Il.* 1.64: τῶν αἰφνιδίων θανάτων αἴτιόν φαcιν εἶναι Ἀπόλλωνα.

8–9 ἐνό[μιcαν] οἱ λαοί. Sept. is again here not very literal. The impersonal construction in a parenthetical clause of the Latin text *uti omnibus videbatur* corresponds to the personal Greek ἐνό[μιcαν] οἱ λαοί, while the rest, that is τὸν Ἀπόλλωνα αἴτιον εἶναι, is implied in the preceding lines. Dictys' explanation fills a logical gap in the Homeric narrative. People themselves (the generalization perhaps prompted by Achilles' assertion at *Il.* 1.65) arrived at the conclusion (ἐνόμιcαν) that the plague was Apollo's means of punishment, for the commonest reason of ritual errors or an old wrath, since nothing in the *Iliad* explains the source of people's certainty on this matter, especially when it is not connected with Chryses' mistreatment. Although not mentioned in the text, people may have thought of Apollo in the first place, because he was normally considered responsible for sudden death for men, as his sister, Artemis, was for women, often in childbirth (e.g. *Il.* 24.604 ff.; *Od.* 11.171–3). In the use of the verb ἐνόμιcαν may be detected a rationalizing attitude on the part of Dictys towards the divine, similarly evident in Dares Phrygius' *De excidio Troiae historia*, and the Homeric hypothesis 'with no gods' published by J. J. O'Hara, *ZPE* 56 (1984) 1–9. However, the rationalizing here appears less thoroughgoing than Sept. at 1 19, where the reasons of the plague at Aulis are given as *neque multo post irane caelesti an ob mutationem aeris corporibus pertemptatis lues invadit*.

10 μὲ]ν. Alternatively, οὖ]ν (cf. 1 μὲν οὖν), but μέν correlates better with the clause beginning in 12–13 βα[cιλέων] δέ.

τὸ κακὸν. Cf. *Il.* 1.10 (see 7 n.) and *malo* Sept. (II 30.5).

11 τετρ]απόδων: *a pecoribus* Sept.; cf. *Il.* 1.50: οὐρῆαc μὲν ἐπῴχετο καὶ κύναc ἀργούc. τετράποδα of animals occurs frequently in the Homeric scholia; cf. also Thuc. II 50.1, where τὰ τετράποδα are also mentioned in a context of plague. At this point the simple construction of a single sentence in Dictys has been rendered in a more complicated way in Sept. by means of ablative absolute and gerund as noun (*principio grassandi facto a pecoribus*).

11–12 διαφθεί[ρονται. Cf. *Il.* 1.10 ὀλέκοντο δὲ λαοί; 1.52 αἰεὶ δὲ πυραὶ νεκύων καίοντο θαμειαί. The same verb but as genitive absolute in Hyp. II καὶ πολλῶν, ὡc εἰκὸc διαφθειρομένων (variant reading: καὶ τῶν Ἀχαιῶν φθειρομένων; see Ludwich, *Textkritische Untersuchungen* (1900) 9), while the circumstantial participle κακουμενοι appears in P. Bon. 6. In the paraphrases the verb διαφθείρομαι is employed in T. Bodl. 3019.29–30 υφ' ης οι ελληνες καταπολεμουμενοι διαφθειροντο (l. διεφθ-) and Aristides, op. cit.: πολλοὶ μὲν . . . πρὸ ὥρας διεφθάρηςαν. The plain ἐφθείροντο is employed in the PM and PG of *Il.* 1.10. At this point, Sept. becomes verbose by comparison: II 30.11–15 *dein malo paulatim magis magisque intravescente per homines dispergitur. tum vero* **vis magna mortalium** *corporibus fatigatis pestifera aegritudine infando* **ad postremum exitio interibat**, of which only the boldface text corresponds to Dictys. In Sept., the translation of Dictys' λαῶν into *mortalium* (which refers both to the soldiers and the animals) is not accurate.

13–14 βα[cιλέων] δὲ οὐδεὶc οὔτε ἐνόcη[cεν οὔτ]ε διε[φθάρη. The reconstruction here is guided by Sept. *sed regum omnino nullus neque mortuus ex hoc malo neque adtemptatus est*, but, if correct, there is a change in Sept. of the order of the two parts of the negation.

14 διε[φθάρη c.3] . . [. The two traces visible in the remainder of 14 are too meagre to allow reconstruction, although they would allow λο[ιμοῦ or λο[ιμῷ; cf. Sept. *morbi* (II 30.17) and the variant attested at II 30.16 in P (a manuscript of the 15th century) *(ex hoc) morbo*. Professor Parsons, however, suggests τὸ ὅ]λο[ν here, which would correspond nicely to *omnino* in Sept. As a soldier, Dictys, unlike Homer, marks the contrast between the many common Achaean soldiers who died from the plague and their kings of whom none even fell ill.

R. HATZILAMBROU

4944. Dictys Cretensis, *Bellum Troianum* v 15–17

100/6 (a)	Fr. 1 26.8 × 31.5 cm	Early third century
	Fr. 2 5.2 × 7.5 cm	Plate VII

Three fragments from a papyrus roll, the main ensemble (probably the end of the roll) showing the first fourteen line-ends of a column, followed by two columns at full height but for the most part lacking line-ends. Two smaller fragments, plus two scraps with exiguous if any remains, are of uncertain placement. The backs are blank. The Greek text corresponds to the final chapters of book v of the Latin version by 'Septimius' of the account of the Trojan War attributed to Dictys of Crete and, notably, includes the fifth book's conclusion with its authorial *sphragis*. Traces about 1.5 cm above the initial letter of the third column could be remains of a column number, although the equivalent at the same position in the second column is not discernible. Top, bottom margin and intercolumnar space measure 3.0, 5.8, and *c.*1.5 cm. respectively. In fr. 1, col. ii consists of 54 lines, while col. iii has 55. Lines average 20–21 letters at an average length of *c.*8 cm. (In the text below of fr. 1, continuous line-numeration is given for cols. ii–iii, to which line-numbers without designation of fragment or column in the discussion and notes below refer; citations of Sept. without book number are to book v.)

The text is written in a mature, medium-sized, almost upright specimen of the 'Severe Style', comparable to the third century hands of *GLH* 20a = *GMAW*² 84 (on its date, see BL VIII 133 and IX 183 under VII **1044**; L. C. Youtie, *ZPE* 21 (1976) 7 ff., with the qualifications of J. Rowlandson, *ZPE* 67 (1987) 290) and Seider II 33. Visible shading and ornamentation by means of hooks and serifs favour a date in the early third century. ⋏ rests on a long baseline, and its right oblique is extended upwards. The middle stroke of ε sometimes touches the following letter. z has a wavy baseline, and θ is narrow with middle stroke protruding both ways. μ is large with shallow belly, and ν has short right vertical. ξ is elegant with long baseline and middle part of the form of a comma. The horizontal of τ starts off with pointed acute angle, when at the beginning of a line. The middle part of φ is elliptical.

Iota adscript is not normally written, but is perhaps inserted by the same hand in the fragmentary line 92. Diairesis is always marked inorganically on initial ι and υ (2, 13, 36, 66, 86). Elision is tacitly effected in lines 18, 43 (probably), 47 and 75, while *scriptio plena* is preferred in lines 27, 28, 70, 93 and 107. Strong punctuation is sometimes indicated by space of one letter, noticeable in lines 17, 21 and 71. Accents are placed infrequently, acute: 16, fr. 2.10 (on the first vowel of a diphthong, as usual); grave: 107. The end of the book is elaborately marked by a decorated or 'forked' *paragraphus* (i.e. same shape as the *diple obelismene*: see *GMAW*² p. 12 with n. 60) extending underneath the initial letter of the last line of the book (92), dividing off the epilogue with its authorial *sphragis* that follows. No other lectional or critical signs or corrections are in evidence.

4944 preserves the second longest text of Dictys after P. Tebt. II 268, i.e. longer than XXXI **2539** and **4943**. Its standard format and bookhand further attests to the popularity of this unusual work in Graeco-Roman Egypt. The fact that its end coincides with the end of the fifth book in the Latin version gives a strong indication that the division of the Greek original into books up to this point in the work was as described by Sept. (*Epistula*, pp. 1.17–2.2) *itaque priorum quinque voluminum, quae bello contracta gestaque sunt, eundem numerum servavimus*. Internally, some differences in structure from Sept. may be observed: 13–15, for example, do not seem to contain the strong pause expected for the transition to a new section as in Sept., where the section-beginning may have been imposed by the Latin adaptor. **4944** also confirms that the close of the book, together with the authorial *sphragis* (93–109, cf. Sept. v 17 p. 119.8–18) that concludes the narrative of the war corresponding to the Homeric *Iliad* (and in Sept. precedes the narratives of the *nostoi* in book vi, cf. **4944**.25–6), was present in the Greek version. (On the *sphragis* and its function, especially in Greek and Latin Poetry, see W. Kranz, 'Sphragis: Ichform und Namensiegel als Eingans- und Schlussmotiv antiker Dichtung', *RhM* 104 (1961) 3–46, 97–124.)

In this epilogue Dictys openly introduces himself in the first person by name, and comments on the language, script and historiographical method employed in his work; cf. the briefer account of this earlier in Sept. (i 13 p. 11.14–20). Here Dictys sheds some light on the complex problem of the putative original language of Dictys' work, which is difficult to understand in Sept. (on the problem see further W. Eisenhut, *Mittellateinisches Jahrbuch* 18 (1983) 19–20; S. Merkle, *Die Ephemeris belli*

Troiani des Diktys von Kreta (1989) 109–113). It may be that Dictys intentionally left the specification of the language vague (or subject to the reader's suspension of disbelief), given the difficulty of determining which specific language or dialect was expected to be used by Dictys, a supposed Cretan-speaker of the time of the Trojan War. In **4944** Dictys' explanation draws on the discussion of Cretan dialects at Hom. *Od.* 19.172–83 (see 96–7 n.), where there are said to be various ethnic groups on Crete who speak both Greek and non-Greek languages or dialects. Dictys describes himself as Dictys of Cnossos, follower of Idomeneus, the leader of the Mycenaeans (Achaeans), who dominated central Crete according to the tradition presented at *Il.* 2.645–52. Accordingly, it was possible in theory for the Achean Dictys to employ a Greek dialect (cf. 96 ἐφικτό[ν), but the author of the Greek work did not risk naming it.

Sept. certainly understood from Dictys' epilogue (and perhaps the original Greek prologue) that the language used by Dictys was Greek, and he more explicitly stated this in his *Epistula* p. 1.12 *nam oratio Graeca fuerat*. In the Latin Prologue, which was either translated from the Greek or composed at some point by someone other than Sept., the language is never specified, while the use of the Phoenician alphabet (pp. 2.13, 3.4–5) is stressed. However, vagueness regarding this matter is retained and emphasized by two controversial references to the Phoenician language: (i) *Dictys . . . peritus vocis ac litteris Phoenicum* (p. 2.7–8); and (ii) *(Nero) iussit in Graecum sermonem ista transferri* (p. 3.8–9). Malalas, who may be expected to have read the original Greek beginning of the work, wrote ambiguously (*Chronographia* x p. 189.65) καὶ (Νέρων) ἐκέλευcεν μετὰ τὸ ἀνοῖξαι καὶ γνῶναι, τί ἐcτιν μεταγραφῆναι (which could mean both 'transliterate' and 'translate') αὐτὰ καὶ ἐν τῇ δημοcίᾳ βιβλιοθήκῃ ἀποτεθῆναι αὐτά. It is tempting to conclude that the author of the Greek original on purpose avoided specifying the language or dialect in which Dictys had supposedly written his diary.

Since vagueness on this point may be detected in both the Latin Prologue and Malalas, we are of the view that Sept. on his own account took pains in the process of adaptation to interpret and specify the language used by Dictys. One may, of course, still agree with Sept., and understand *Graecum sermonem* as meaning the *koine*: cf. *Epistula* p. 1.12 *commutatos litteris Atticis*, and Sept. 17 p. 119.11–13 *neque sit mirum cuiquam, si quamvis Graeci omnes diverso tamen inter se sermone agunt*, where *sermo* should be understood in the sense of 'dialect'. For discrepancies between the *Epistula* and the *Prologus*, see N. E. Griffin, *Dares and Dictys* (1907) 117–120; Eisenhut, art. cit. 18–22; Merkle, *Die Ephemeris* 98–109.

The style of **4944** is in conformity with that of the three previously published papyri of Dictys, so that we are now in the position to shape a clear idea of Dictys' plain and compressed style, suitable for the genre of the work, the main features of which are: few subordinate clauses but many participial ones, frequent use of genitive absolute and historic present, tendency to place the finite verb towards the end of the sentence, parataxis and dull connection of the clauses mainly through δέ, and plain diction that does not avoid repetition of vocabulary (see 20 and 21, 43 and 47).

4944 confirms for Sept. by comparison the general impression formed by the other three papyri of Dictys, namely that the Latin text is a rendering in which only limited parts of the Greek text are rendered into Latin with accuracy (cf. 21–24, 72–77). Sept. indulged in elaboration and amplification of the Greek text, where he felt that his original was too compressed (see e.g. 7–9, 14–15, 20–21, 41–45, 49–53, 59–60). However, there are a few points where the Latin text appears condensed in comparison to Dictys (47, 54–5, 68–9), and there are two instances (32–3 and 82–92), where elements of the Greek text of **4944** have been totally omitted in the Latin. In other places, especially in col. iii at the end of the narrative before the epilogue, limited space in the papyrus suggests that the Greek text is far more compressed in relation to the Latin, making certain restoration impossible (61 ff., 81–92 n.). Here we have adopted a conservatively restored text, relegating promising supplements to the notes (see commentary). Closer in scale and diction to Dictys' text is the epilogue with its authorial *sphragis* in Sept., allowing for a more fully restored text of the close of the book.

It is interesting that Sept. (or his Greek exemplar) critically opted for a different tradition regarding the location of Hecuba's grave (18–19), and he also appears to have corrected Dictys (11–12) on the way Diomedes gained the Palladion. Notable is the effort in Sept. to improve the connection of clauses by often using in his text *ita(que)*, *ceterum*, *per idem tempus*, *quippe*, *inter quae*, *praeterea*, *tunc*, *dein*, *exin*. The addition of a final transitional sentence of book v in the Latin text (see above) may be seen as a stylistic and structural embellishment in Sept., and was probably never present in **4944**.

It is interesting for the interrelation of the Byzantine authors who make use of Dictys (see introd. to **4943–4944**) that the narratives of Cedrenus, *Hyp. Od.* and *Suda* (s.v. Κυνὸς Cῆμα) in their account of Odysseus' departure and Hecuba's death, are very close to each other and in agreement with Dictys as attested in **4944**, while a reference to the end met by Hecuba (present in **4944**) is missing from Malalas (and the *Ecloge*).

Fr. 1

Col. i		Col. ii		Col. ii		
. . .		τριεν . [		τριενδ[	c.15	(v 15)
]η		εισϋδ . [		εἰς ὑδρ[ίαν	c.12	
]		να[c.4] . ι . [		να[c.4] . ιδ[	c.12	
]ε		ερο . [c.3] . . αυ[		ερο . [c.3] . . αυ[	c.10	
]	5	καιδ[c.3] . [	5	καὶ δ[c.3] . [	c.13	
]		. . . [c.4]ομ[		. . . [c.4]ομ[	c.12	
]ν		πρι̣[c.5]ονα̣λ . . . [		πρὶ[ν τὸ Ἴλι]ον ἁλῶνα̣[ι, οὔκ-		
]ιν		ουν̣ ν̣ετιεπολεμης[. .]α .		ουν ἂν ἔτι ἐπολέμης[αν] αὖ		
]		τουςβαρβαρουςφρυγ[. .]η		τοὺς βαρβάρους Φρύγ[ας.] ἤ-		
]	10	δηοδυσσευςφοβουμ[. .]ος	10	δη Ὀδυσσεὺς φοβούμ[εν]ος		
]		τουςελληνασδιομη[		τοὺς Ἕλληνας Διομή[δους		
] .		αφελομενουαυτου[		ἀφελομένου αὐτοῦ [τὸ Παλ-		
]		λαδιονεισιμαρον . [		λάδιον εἰς Ἴσμαρον . [c.5		
]ς		τουγενομενησεκαβ . [. .] .		του γενομένης Ἑκάβη[c. κ]α̣-	v 16	
. . .	15	κηγορουσαγαραπαντ[. .] . η	15	κηγοροῦσα γὰρ ἄπαντ[ας . .] . η		
		παρ . μενηάπονος . [. . . . .] .		παραμένη ἄπονος . [. . . . .] ἀ-		
		τειμωσανη . εθη εγ . [		τείμως ἀνηρέθη. ἐγέ[νετο		
		δαυτησταφοσενμα . [		δ' αὐτῆς τάφος ἐν Μαρ[ωνείᾳ		
		τηςχερρονησουοκυν[		τῆς Χερρονήςου, ὃ Κυν[ὸς Cῆ-		
	20	μαλεγεταιεπειαυτη[	20	μα λέγεται, ἐπεὶ αὐτὴ[ν κυ-		
		νογλωσσονελεγον ε . [		νόγλωccον ἔλεγον. ἔν[θεος		
		δεγενομενηκασσαν[		δὲ γενομένη Καccάν[δρα c.3?		
		μυριαεισαγαμεμνο[		μυρία εἰς Ἀγαμέμνο[να προλέ-		
		γειφονονπρομηνυο . [		γει, φόνον προμηνύου̣[ca c.3?		
	25	επιβουληνκαικακο . [	25	ἐπιβουλὴν καὶ κακὸν [νόc-		
		]ιcαλλοιςβαcιλ[		τον το]ῖ̣c ἄλλοιc βαcιλ[εῦcι.		
		]νωρδεαματοις[		Ἀντή]νωρ δὲ ἅμα τοῖς [αὐτοῦ		
		]οαυτωνμηδιε[		ἐδεῖτ]ο αὐτῶν μὴ διε[ρίζειν		
		] . cθαιτοcουτον . [		ἀνάγ]εcθαι τοcοῦτον . [c.4		
	30	]νηcανταcκαλω[	30	c.2 δειπ]νήcαντας καλω[c.2		
		] . cαυτουσκαιδωρ[		c.6] . c αὐτοὺς καὶ δωρ[c.1		
		] . ωνειδεπαρ . [		c.3 cυμ]φω̣νεῖ δὲ παρα̣[c.4		
		]εcτωραναπει . [		c.7 Ν]έcτωρ ἀναπείθ[c.2		
		]cυμπλεινα[. .]οιc		c.2 Αἰνείαν] cυμπλεῖν α[ὐτ]οῖc		
	35	] . ιcχνουμεν[	35	c.8 ὑ]πιcχνουμεν[c.3		
		]ϊcομοιριαπ[		c.9]ϊcομοιρίᾳ π[c.3		

].ξημεν...λε	*c.*9].ξημεν...λε
].ολεμο..ου.[	*c.*5 Νεοπ]τόλεμος τοὺς[*c.*2?
]παραχ.ρει.[..].	*c.*10]παραχωρεῖ.[..]ν
40].νελληνωνχρυ	40 *c.*9]ων Ἑλλήνων χρυ-
].ονερχονται	σὸν καὶ ἄργυ]ρον. ἔρχονται
]γορανομοθυμα	*c.*5 εἰς ἀ]γορὰν ὁμοθυμα-
]εσεπ..ντι	δὸν *c.*6]ες ἐπ' Αἴαντι
]ησα.[..].λομε	*c.*4 ἐπένθ]ησαν [τι]λλόμε-
45]δεη...αμε	45 νοι *c.*6]δεη. Ἀγαμέ-
]χειρου.παν	μν- *c.*7] χείρους παν-
]σεπαιαντικαι	των *c.*6]ς ἐπ' Αἴαντι καὶ
]ωσον.[.]ζον	*c.*9]ως ὀνίδ[ι]ζον
].θενιδασδεη	*c.*5 Πλει]σθενίδας δεη-
50]νλαωνχρωνται	50 θέντες τῶ]ν λαῶν χρῶνται
]ιλεωναυ[	*c.*6 βασ]ιλέων αυ[*c.*5
]γεινον.[*c.*4].	*c.*10]γείνοντ[αι *c.*2].
]αιαντο[*c.*4].	*c.*10]Αἴαντο[ς *c.*3].
]αυκηστ.[*c.*4].	*c.*6 ἐκ Γλ]αύκης τ.[*c.*4].

Col. iii	Col. iii
55 εκουςη..[	55 ἑκούςης.[*c.*13
εκτεκμη[	ἐκ Τεκμή[ςςης *c.*10
αςοιελλην[	ας οἱ Ἕλλην[ες *c.*6 χει- V 17
.ωναμελλ[	μῶνα μέλλ[ο- *c.*11 ἀ-
..γονται.[	νάγονται.[*c.*7 κομί-
60 ςαν...[	60 ςαντες[*c.*12 ἀπο-
πλε[.]ςαντω[	πλε[υ]ςάντω[ν δὲ τῶν Ἑλλή-
νωναινειαςα[	νων Αἰνείας ἀ[πολειφθεὶς
εντωδαρδαν[	ἐν τῷ Δαρδάν[ῳ *c.*10
θεςθαιαντην[	θέςθαι Ἀντήν[ορα *c.*7
65 καιτωνενχερ.[	65 καὶ τῶν ἐν Χερρ[ονήςῳ *c.*4
μηϋπακου..[	μὴ ὑπακου..[*c.*11
νωνμαθωνϋ.[	νων μαθὼν ὑπ[ὸ ἀγγέλου τὰ γε-
νομεναδιορ[	νόμενα διορ[*c.*11
αυτωζωης...[	αὐτῷ ζωης...[*c.*10
70 ταδεαυτονε.[	70 τάδε αὐτὸν εἰ[ς τὸ Ἴλιον οὐ δέ-
χονται χωριζ[	χονται. χωρίζ[εται δὲ *c.*4
αινειαςτον..[	Αἰνείας τὸν πα[τρῷον βίον

<table>
<tr><td></td><td>ϲυναυτωκομ[</td><td></td><td>ϲὺν αὐτῷ κομ[ίζων, πολλοῦ δὲ</td></tr>
<tr><td></td><td>]αρβαρουεωϲ[</td><td></td><td>β]αρβάρου ἕως [Ἀδρίαν συνέτυ-</td></tr>
<tr><td>75</td><td>]. τιζειδα . [</td><td>75</td><td>χεν.] κτίζει δ᾽αὐ[τόθι, σὺν δὲ</td></tr>
<tr><td></td><td>]ωλαοιπολ[</td><td></td><td>αὐτ]ῷ λαοὶ πολ[λοί, πόλιν Κόρ-</td></tr>
<tr><td></td><td>]ανμελα[</td><td></td><td>κυρ]αν Μελα[ίναν λεγομένην.</td></tr>
<tr><td></td><td>]δετωντρ[</td><td></td><td>ὅϲοι] δὲ τῶν Τρ[ώων   c.8</td></tr>
<tr><td></td><td>]παρμεν[</td><td></td><td>c.3]παρμεν[c.12</td></tr>
<tr><td>80</td><td>]ϲινερχ[</td><td>80</td><td>c.3]ϲιν ἔρχ[ονται πρὸς τὸν Ἀν-</td></tr>
<tr><td></td><td>]. ρακαια[</td><td></td><td>τήν]ορα καὶ α[c.11</td></tr>
<tr><td></td><td>].. [</td><td></td><td>c.5].. [c.14</td></tr>
<tr><td></td><td>]. [</td><td></td><td>]. [</td></tr>
<tr><td></td><td>ϲυνε[</td><td></td><td>ϲυνε[c.17</td></tr>
<tr><td>85</td><td>τεϲε . [</td><td>85</td><td>τεϲε . [c.16</td></tr>
<tr><td></td><td>ϊλιον . [</td><td></td><td>Ἴλιον . [c.15</td></tr>
<tr><td></td><td>μενο[</td><td></td><td>μενο[c.17</td></tr>
<tr><td></td><td>αναδ[</td><td></td><td>αναδ[c.17</td></tr>
<tr><td></td><td>πριαμ[</td><td></td><td>Πριαμ[c.16</td></tr>
<tr><td>90</td><td>ηδη[</td><td>90</td><td>ηδη[c.18</td></tr>
<tr><td></td><td>τοδε . [</td><td></td><td>τοδε . [c.16</td></tr>
<tr><td></td><td>νειαι . [</td><td></td><td>νειαι . [c.15</td></tr>
<tr><td></td><td>ταυτα . εε . [</td><td></td><td>ταῦτα δὲ ἐγ[ὼ ϲυνεγραψάμην,</td></tr>
<tr><td></td><td>δικτυ[.]κνωϲϲι[</td><td></td><td>Δίκτυ[ϲ] Κνώϲϲι[οϲ, Ἰδομενεῖ</td></tr>
<tr><td>95</td><td>ϲυνεπ[..]μενοϲ[</td><td>95</td><td>ϲυνεπ[ό]μενοϲ [c.10</td></tr>
<tr><td></td><td>ωϲεμ[..]εφικτο[</td><td></td><td>ὡϲ ἐμ[οὶ] ἐφικτὸ[ν ἦν, Κάδμου</td></tr>
<tr><td></td><td>καιδα[.]αουγρ . [</td><td></td><td>καὶ Δα[ν]αοῦ γρά[μμαϲιν. οὐ</td></tr>
<tr><td></td><td>γαρμι . χρωντ[</td><td></td><td>γὰρ μιᾷ χρῶντ[αι γλώϲϲῃ οὔτε</td></tr>
<tr><td></td><td>παντ . . οιελλ . [</td><td></td><td>πάντεϲ οἱ Ἕλλη[νεϲ οὔτε πάν-</td></tr>
<tr><td>100</td><td>τεϲοιβαρβαροι . [</td><td>100</td><td>τεϲ οἱ βάρβαροι, ἀ[λλὰ μεμι-</td></tr>
<tr><td></td><td>γμενητουτοδ[</td><td></td><td>γμένη. τοῦτο δ[ὲ θαυμαϲτὸν</td></tr>
<tr><td></td><td>μηδειϲηγειϲθ[</td><td></td><td>μηδεὶϲ ἡγείϲθ[ω εἶναι, ἐπεὶ</td></tr>
<tr><td></td><td>καιημειϲοιεν[</td><td></td><td>καὶ ἡμεῖϲ οἱ ἐν [Κρήτῃ οὐ πάν-</td></tr>
<tr><td></td><td>τεϲχρωμεθατη[</td><td></td><td>τεϲ χρώμεθα τῇ [αὐτῇ γλώϲϲῃ.</td></tr>
<tr><td>105</td><td>ταμενουνϲυμβ[</td><td>105</td><td>τὰ μὲν οὖν ϲυμβ[άντα τοῖϲ Ἕλ-</td></tr>
<tr><td></td><td>ληϲικαιτοιϲβαρ[</td><td></td><td>ληϲι καὶ τοῖϲ βαρ[βάροιϲ πάν-</td></tr>
<tr><td></td><td>ταειδ . [..]. [</td><td></td><td>τα εἰδὼ[ϲ α]ὐ[τὸϲ ϲυνεγραψά-</td></tr>
<tr><td></td><td>μηνπερι[</td><td></td><td>μην, περὶ [δὲ Ἀντήνοροϲ παρὰ</td></tr>
<tr><td></td><td>ελληνων[</td><td></td><td>Ἑλλήνων [ἄλλων ἀκηκοώϲ.</td></tr>
</table>

Fr. 2

<pre>
          ·   ·   ·   ·
        ].[   ].[
        ].ωο[   ].ωο[
        ].α...[   ].α...[
        ]αιμη.[   ]αιμη.[
   5   ].....[5   ].....[
        ]..ρο.[   ]..ρο.[
        ]ναξτουμονοcτυ.[ἄ]ναξ τοῦ μόνοc τυ.[
        ]ωιμοιξ. · [..].....[ ]ωιμοιξ. · [..]....[
        ].τοικα.[   ].τοικα.[
  10   ]αcόυc.[10   ]αcόυc.[
        ]οcουcτ[   ]οcουcτ[
          ]εκα.[   ]εκα.[
          ]βηι.[   ]βηι.[
          ].αιμ..[   ].αιμ..[
  15   ].....[15   ].....[
          ·   ·   ·   ·   ·   ·
</pre>

Fr. 3

<pre>
          ·   ·   ·
        ].εμ.[
          ·   ·   ·
</pre>

Fr. 1   Col. i
    12]., extension of horizontal as of mid-stroke of ε

Col. ii

    1 .[, acute angle at lower left suiting ⋏   2 .[, part of upright as of ʜ, м, ɴ, π, ρ   3 .ι., horizontal at mid- to upper-level intersecting with descender at right, as of г, ε, τ   after ι acute angle at lower left as of ⋏   4 .[, upright joining curved line near top as of м or ʜ   ].., horizontal joining upright at right, π or гι   5].[, curving left side of oval shape with horizontal connecting at mid-level, θ or ε   6 ...[, feet of two uprights and part of oblique ascending to right, parts of two or three letters, the last as ⋏   7 λ..., low curve at the line compatible with ω, followed by three low traces of two letters   8 ν., low oblique descending to left   α., a speck of ink at mid-level as of upright above prolonged tail of ⋏   13 .[, speck of ink at line-level 14 .[, low speck of ink   ]., short horizontal   15]., descender ligatured into following ʜ 16 ρ.[, part of oblique descending to left and part of arc as of ⋏   .[, pointed tip of horizontal at upper left   ]., end of horizontal   17 η., speck of ink in upper part of writing space   .[, thick vertical stroke intersecting with fine horizontal protrusions to right at top and bottom, as ε (perhaps corrected from ι?)   18 .[, upright   21 .[, two traces in vertical alignment as part of upright   24 .[, part of horizontal   25 .[, part of upright   29]., part of high

horizontal and scattered traces as of ε   .[, low trace   31 ., speck of ink as end of an oblique descending to right   32]., small arc   .[, end of oblique ascending to left   33 .[, low trace and part of horizontal at mid-level compatible with ϑ   35]., traces in vertical alignment 37]., short oblique at mid-level ascending to right   ν..., first ε¹ *prima facie* (but could also be н corrected from ε by the addition of an upright), then low trace, then extension of a letter ligatured with λ   38]., tip of short horizontal at mid-level   ..ο, part of upright, then speck of ink   υ., speck of ink in lower part of writing space   39 χ., scattered traces of ink   ι., circlet resting on horizontal at mid-level   40]., short vertical in upper part of writing space   41]., disruption of fibres obscuring roundish letter   43 π..., scattered traces   44 .[..]., scattered traces   45 η..., short horizontal at top, then specks of ink   46 υ., specks of ink 48 υ.., foot of upright and scattered traces   49]., trace of ink   52 .[, part of horizontal at upper-level   ]., horizontal   53]., upper part of upright   54 ., ε or н   ]., traces suggesting extension of a stroke

Col. iii

          55 η. .[, low trace with another in vertical alignment, second a vertical below line-level 58 .ω, scattered traces at line-level   59 ..γ, feet of three uprights and short oblique of the second letter   ι., speck in upper part of writing space   60 ...[, high horizontal as of two letters followed by high speck   65 .[, stem of vertical   66 ..[, foot of descender curving to right suiting ε and c, then a low trace   67 .[, scattered specks as of single letter   69 ...[, two verticals, then edge of oblique descending to left and speck at same level   70 .[, vertical   72 ..[, upright curving to left and top part of oblique suggesting π and λ   75]., horizontal stroke at mid-level   κ.[, short oblique at upper-level descending to right suiting left arm of γ   81]., blob of ink in upper part   82]..[, apex suggesting λ or ᴅ, or combining with following trace as of м   83].[, low speck   85 .[, lower half of vertical   86 .[, trace in upper part   91 .[, foot of vertical   92 ι., upright slightly curving to right   93 α., short oblique descending to bottom right   .[, lower half of vertical   97 .[, bottom of oblique ascending to left   98 .χ, foot of oblique ascending to left   99 ..ο, curve as of back of ε followed by tiny low trace   λ., upright   100 .[, high speck   107 δ`, top of upright in left part under grave accent   ].[, lower part of upright descending below the line and curving back to left at bottom

Fr. 2

          1].[, low curve at line as of ω   2]., upper and lower extremity of descender, upper extremity of ascender, as of κ or χ   3]., tiny trace at line-level   α...[, remains of two or three letters: lower extremity of upright, trace in lower part possibly upright, lower part of upright, lower part of ascender   4 η.[, trace at upper-level   5]...., first lower part of an ascender; second part of high horizontal; third, high horizontal with its middle in vertical alignment with small right-hand arc in lower part, suggesting ᴣ; fourth two very tiny traces close to each other at upper-level   6]., short horizontal at lower-level   .ρ, fibres disturbed: unclear traces in upper part ο., thick trace at line-level   7 μον, over a descending diagonal as of grave accent, too low for part of descender from line above   τυ., remains of ascender   8 ξ., tiny mark in upper part of writing space as though high stop   ]...[, scattered traces on damaged fibres   9]., short tiny vertical in upper part   α.[, ascender   10 ουc.[, high horizontal with horizontal connecting to right as of ᴣ or τ   12 α.[, short arc   13 ι.[, remains of arc as of c   14]., arc as of c   μ., remains of upright with horizontal connecting at mid-level as of ε   .[, faded traces at line-level   15]....[, first tiny trace in upper part; second top of round letter, third remains of arc, fourth remains of triangular letter

Fr. 3

1] ., two uprights of single letter e.g. π, or of two different letters e.g. ι and τ   μ.[, two traces in lower part as of upright

Fr. 1

16–17 l. ἀτίμως   48 l. ὠνείδιζον   52 l. γίνοντ[

'. . . in an urn . . . before Ilion had been taken, they could certainly no longer have been able to fight anew the barbarian Phrygians. Odysseus, fearing that the Greeks [had] already [fled] to Ismarus, and since Diomedes had deprived him of the Palladion and Hecuba had become . . . [*verb missing*]. For since she spoke ill of everyone, [so that] she did not remain a slave . . . , she was dishonourably stoned and so relieved of the necessity of labour. Her tomb was raised at Maroneia in the Chersonesos, and is known as Cynossema (The Tomb of the Bitch), for they used to call her dog-tongued. Cassandra inspired by the god foretold countlessless [evils?] for Agamemnon forewarning murder and (*or* because of) a plot and a bad homeward journey for the rest of the kings. Antenor along with his men urged them (i.e. the kings) not to strive with each other to such an extent . . . to sail (*or* in sailing). . . . those having invited them to dinner he also bestowed gifts on them. . . . And . . . Nestor agreed . . . [they] tried to persuade [Aeneas] to sail along with them . . . promising . . . with equal share [in everything] . . . Neoptolemus granted the [sons of Hector to Helenus] gold and silver [by common consent?] of the Greeks. They came with one accord . . . to an assembly in honour of Ajax . . . they mourned by plucking out their hair . . . Agamemnon . . . more difficult than all . . . for Ajax and . . . were reproaching [them] as sons of Pleisthenes, fearing the army they used (?) . . . among the kings . . . they became . . . . [The sons] of Ajax [Aiantides] born of Glauce by her consent (?) . . . [and Eurysaces] born of Tecmessa . . . . The Greeks were about to [delay?] [because of] the winter, they set sail carrying off [with them] . . . . After [all?] the Greeks had sailed off, Aeneas who had been left behind at Dardanum [tried? wished?] to [drive?] Antenor [away] and [urged?] the inhabitants of Chersonesos . . . not to obey [him]. Having learned what (had) happened through [a messenger Antenor] . . . . And [then] they did not accept him [into Ilion]. So Aeneas departed carrying with him the paternal [property], and he passed by [many] barbarians as far as [the Adriatic Sea]. And he founded [there] together with many people a [city called] Corcyra Melaina (Black Corcyra). [All] the Trojans [who] . . . remained . . . approached [Antenor] and . . . together . . . Ilion . . . Priam . . . .

'I, Dictys of Cnossos, accompanying [Idomeneus recorded] this account in [this language?], as it was possible for me, in the letters (i.e. alphabet) of [Cadmus] and Danaus. For neither all the Greeks [nor] all the barbarians use a single [language], but rather, a mixed one. And no one should [marvel] at this, [for] we also, the [Cretans, do not] all use the same language. I have recorded everything that happened to the Greeks and the barbarians based on my personal knowledge, [but] about [Antenor after having heard it from other] Greeks.'

1–6 Cf. Sept. v 15 pp. 116.28–117.2 *interim Neoptolemus advecta ligni materia Aiacem cremat reliquiasque urnae aureae conditas in Rhoeteo sepeliendas procurat brevique tumulum extructum consecrat in honorem tantis ducis*; Mal. 93.77–80 (and *Ecl. Hist.* 216.12–15) λοιπὸν ὁ Πύρρος ἑωρακὼς πάντας ἀποπλεύσαντας, τεφρώσας τὸν Τελαμώνιον Αἴαντα καὶ βαλὼν ἐν ὑδρίᾳ ἔθαψεν μετά τιμῆς μεγάλης πλησίον τοῦ τύμβου Ἀχιλλέως, τοῦ ἐξαδέλφου αὐτοῦ, πατρὸς δὲ τοῦ Πύρρου εἰς τόπον λεγόμενον Cίγριν; cf. also the burials described in XXXI **2539** 3–7, P. Tebt. II 268.69–76, 89–95 and Sept. IV 18 p. 95.21–5, and IV 13 pp. 91.8–92.6, IV 15 pp. 92.1–93.3 respectively. Other burial scenes in Sept. are: II 2 pp. 21.31–22.1–3, II 4 p. 23.14–16, II 15 p. 31.21–3, II 32 p. 45.6–8, II 41 p. 51.18–21, III 12 pp. 68.28–69.3, III 14 p. 70.7–11, IV 8 p. 87.12–18, IV 18 p. 95.21–5.

1 τριενδ[. Perhaps πα]τρὶ ενδ[. There could be a reference to the fact that Ajax was cousin of

Achilles, the father of Neoptolemus, or that Neoptolemus honoured Ajax as his father; on the latter, cf. Sept. IV 17 p. 94.21–3.

2 εἰς ὑδρ[ίαν c.12: possibly εἰς ὑδρ[ίαν χρυσῆν c.6. On the probable use of the preposition, see K.–G., *Grammatik*, ii 1§432 1.1 a (p. 469) with the meaning 'an einem Orte versammeln'.

7–9 Cf. Sept. 15 p. 117.2–5 *quae si ante captum Ilium accidere potuissent, profecto magna ex parte promotae res hostium ac dubitarum de summa rerum fuisset.* Here there is clearly what appears to be amplification of the Greek original.

9 βαρβάρους Φρύγ[ας. It is revealing of Dictys' prejudice towards the Trojans, that he often characterized them as barbarians. This epithet is frequently omitted in the corresponding element in Sept. for obvious reasons, especially when it refers to the Trojans alone; cf. also below 100, P. Tebt. II.268 4–5, 30 and 61.

10–11 Cf. Sept. 15 p. 117.5–6 *igitur Ulixes veritus vim offensi exercitus clam Ismarum ausfugit.* Ismarus (on this Thracian city, see *RE* IX 2 3 §§2134–5) is reported to have been the first stop in Odysseus' νόστος at *Od.* 9.39–40, 197–198 and Sept. VI 5 pp. 123.29–124.1. On Odysseus' hasty departure from Troy, see also Mal. V 85.15–19, *Ecl. Hist.* 208.5–8, Cedr. 232.10–13 and *Hyp. Od.* pp. 3.23–4.3.

11–13 Διομή[δους] ἀφελομένου αὐτοῦ (sc. Ὀδυσσέως) [τὸ Παλ]λάδιον. Cf. Sept. 15 p. 117.6–7 *atque ita Palladium apud Diomedem manet.* It appears that in Dictys' account Diomedes had previously deprived Odysseus of the Palladion. Sept. (14–15 pp. 115.7–117.7) relates the outcome of the Palladion-strife (equivalent to the Iliadic Ὅπλων Κρίσις) as follows. The contest was initially between Ajax, Diomedes, and Odysseus. Diomedes later yielded to Ajax, but Agamemnon and Menelaus favoured Odysseus, to whom the Palladion was finally offered. On the following day, Ajax was found stabbed, and Odysseus, under heavy suspicion for his murder, decided to depart, leaving the Palladion behind to Diomedes. The Byzantine authors' accounts (Mal. 84.9–18, *Ecl. Hist.* 207.27–30, 208.2–5, Cedr. 232.3–10, and *Suda* s.v. Παλλάδιον) differ slightly from Sept.: the Greeks decided that Diomedes should safeguard the Palladion until the following day, when a decree was expected over whether it should be given to Ajax or Odysseus. However, during that night Ajax was stabbed to death, and Odysseus had to leave in haste.

13–21 Cf. Sept. 16 p. 117.8–13 *ceterum post abscessum Ulixi Hecuba, quo servitium morte solvere, multa ingerere maledicta imprecarique infesta omina in exercitum. qua re motus miles lapidibus obrutam eam necat sepulchrumque apud Abydum statuitur appelatam Cynossema ob linguae protervam impudentemque petulantiam*; Cedr. 232 13–16 τὴν δὲ Ἑκάβην καταρωμένην τῷ στρατῷ οἱ μετὰ Ὀδυσσέως λίθοις βάλλουσι καὶ τῇ θαλάσσῃ ῥίπτουσιν εἰς χώραν λεγομένην Μαρώνειαν, ἣν καὶ κυνὸς σῆμα ὠνόμασαν; *Hyp. Od.* p. 4.4–9 = *Suda* 2722 s.v. Κυνὸς Σῆμα· ὡς οὖν Ὀδυσσεὺς εἰς τὴν ἰδίαν ἠπείγετο πατρίδα περιπλεύσας εἰς χώραν λεγομένην Μαρώνειαν καὶ συγχωρούμενος τῶν νεῶν ἀποβῆσαι διακρίνεται τούτοις πολέμῳ, καὶ λαμβάνει τὸν πλοῦτον αὐτῶν ἅπαντα. ἐκεῖ δὲ τὴν Ἑκάβην καταρωμένην τῷ στρατῷ καὶ θορύβους κινοῦσαν λάθων βολαῖς ἀνεῖλε καὶ παρὰ τὴν θάλασσαν καλύπτει ὀνομάσας τὸν τόπον Κυνὸς σῆμα. Μαρωνειάδα is the name of the place reached by Odysseus at Mal. V 85.19–23, and *Ecl. Hist.* 208.11, but with no reference to Hecuba's grave.

13–14 .[c.5]του. There is no space to fit both a finite verb corresponding to *ausfugit* (Sept.) and a predicate for Hecuba in agreement with γενομένης. Perhaps the finite verb was accidentally omitted, in which case ἀ[φορή]του could be supplied with γενομένης. Hecuba is reported to have been allotted to Odysseus at Sept. 13 p. 115.3–4.

14–15 κ]ακηγοροῦσα γὰρ ἅπαντ[ας. The verbosity of Septimius at this point is remarkable: *multa ingerere maledicta imprecarique infesta omina in exercitum.*

15–17 . .]. η παραμένη ἄπονος. ὡς] μὴ is attractive before παραμένη ἄπονος. But if a final clause is to be restored, its exact sense is uncertain. Sept. appears to have understood that the enslaved Hecuba through her behaviour was intentionally provoking her murder (*quo servitium morte solvere*). A less probable alternative could be that Odysseus' soldiers punished her for her curses, so that she did not remain an ἄπονος slave. The position of ἄπονος is crucial: if it is part of the main clause, it should agree with Sept. and mean 'relieved' or 'freed from the necessity of labour', cf. Plat. *Tim.* 81e ὁ δὲ μετὰ γῆρας ἰὼν ἐπὶ τέλος κατὰ φύςιν ἀπονώτατος τῶν θανάτων καὶ μᾶλλον μεθ' ἡδονῆς γιγνόμενος ἢ λύπης. If it is taken as part of the subordinate (final?) clause, its sense should be 'unpunished'.

16 . [. . . . .]. λ[ίθοις] is a possible supplement.

18 ἐν Μαρ[ωνείᾳ is restored after Cedrenus and *Hyp. Od.* = *Suda*, loc. cit. (n. 13–21). Cf. Strabo VII 55 ἔςτι δ' ἐν τῷ περίπλῳ τούτῳ τῷ μετὰ Ἐλαιοῦντα ἡ εἰςβολὴ πρῶτον ἡ εἰς τὴν Προποντίδα διὰ τῶν ςτενῶν, ἣν φαςιν ἀρχὴν εἶναι τοῦ Ἑλληςπόντου. ἐνταῦθα δ'ἐςτὶ τὸ Κυνὸς ςῆμα ἄκρα, οἱ δ' Ἑκάβης φαςί. καὶ γὰρ δείκνυνται κάμψαντι τὴν ἄκραν τάφος αὐτῆς, and Procl. *Chrestom.* 297–298 (ed. A. Severyns, vol. iv), where Odysseus is reported at Maroneia in Thrace. On this city, see *RE* XIV 2,1 1912–13, which later commentators and lexicographers wrongly identified with the neighbouring city of Ismarus (see n. 10–11). Sept., however, or his Greek exemplar, preferred another tradition, which placed Hecuba's grave on the Asiatic side of the Hellespont, near to the well-known city of Ἄβυδος (*RE* I, 1.1.129–130): cf. Strabo XIII 1 28 ἔςτι τοίνυν μετ' Ἄβυδον ἥ τε Δαρδανὶς ἄκρα, ἧς μικρὸν πρότερον ἐμνήςθημεν, καὶ ἡ πόλις ἡ Δάρδανος, διέχουςα τῆς Ἀβύδου ἑβδομήκοντα ςταδίους. μεταξύ τε ὁ Ῥοδίος ἐκπίπτει ποταμός, καθ' ὃν ἐν τῇ Χερρονήςῳ τὸ Κυνὸς ςῆμά ἐςτιν, ὅ φαςιν Ἑκάβης εἶναι τάφον.

19 ὅ. The gender of the relative (neuter instead of masculine in agreement with τάφος) is attracted by that of the predicate, cf. K.–G., *Grammatik* ii 1.369.4c.

19–20 Κυν[ὸς Ϲῆ]μα. A well-attested tradition, inaugurated by Euripides, who first identifies the Κυνὸς Ϲῆμα in the Thracian Chersonesos with the tomb of Hecuba (Eur. *Hec.* 1273).

20–21 ἐπεὶ αὐτὴ[ν κυ]νόγλωςςον ἔλεγον. Dictys here offers a rationalizing explanation for the name of Hecuba's grave, positing an etymological *aition* different from the traditional one of her canine metamorphosis: see *PMG* 965, Eur. *Hec.* 2171–3, Ovid *Met.* XIII 565–71 et al. Cf. also the rationalizing schol. Lycophr. 315 ςκύλακα τὴν Ἑκάβην λέγει, ὣς φηςι μυθικῶς Εὐριπίδης . . . καὶ Ἀςκληπιάδης περὶ τοῦ τόπου, οὗ ἀνῃρέθη, ὃ καὶ Κυνὸς καλοῦςι δυςμόρου ςῆμα. καὶ ταῦτα μὲν τὰ μυθικά, τὸ δ'ἀληθὲς οὕτως ἔχει. μετὰ τὴν τελευτὴν Πολυξένης ὕβριζε καὶ κατηρᾶτο τοὺς Ἕλληνας, οἱ δὲ ὀργιςθέντες ὡς κύνα αὐτὴν ἀνεῖλον. The adjective κυνόγλωςςος, meaning 'one who howls like a dog', 'who talks bitterly' is a *hapax*; cf. the two late attestations of the verb κυνογλωςςέω in Lampe, *Patristic Greek Lexicon*, and Sophocles, *Greek Lexicon of the Roman and Byzantine Periods*, s.v. An interpretation by Sept. of Dictys' aetiological explanation has been amply incorporated in his paraphrase *ob linguae protervam impudentemque petulantiam*.

21–6 Cf. Sept. 16 p. 117.13–18 *per idem tempus Cassandra deo repleta multa in Agamemnonem adversa praenuntiat: insidias quippe ei ex occulto caedemque domi per suos compositam; praeterea universo exercitui profectionem ad suos incommodam exitialemque.*

21 ἔν[θεος. Cf. Eur. *Troiad.* 255 and 366.

22 Καςςάν[δρα *c.*3? Perhaps κακά could be restored at the end of the line corresponding to the Latin *adversa*.

24 προμηνύου[ςα *c.*3? Here καὶ corresponding to the Latin text, or perhaps διὰ could be supplied at the end of the line.

27–30 Cf. Sept. 16 p. 117.18–20 *inter quae Antenor cum suis Graecos orare, omitterent iras atque urgente navigii tempore in commune consulant.*

28 αὐτῶν: sc. τῶν βαςιλέων.

29–30 . [*c.*6 δειπ]νήςαντας. We expect a genitive participle, in agreement with 28 αὐτῶν. μ[ελλόντων, 'as they were delaying so long in setting sail' could be considered; however, this has no corresponding element in Sept.

30–32 Cf. Sept. 16 p. 117.20–21 *praeterea omnes duces ad se epulatum deducit ibique singulos quam maximis donis replet.* A similar scene is described at Sept. II 44 p. 54.7–9.

30 δειπ]νήςαντας. We might have expected the future participle.

31 *c*.6] ̣ ̣ς. ἄπαντ]ας is a possible supplement.

31–2 δωρ[. δῶρ[α δίδωςι or ἔδωκε is likely.

32–3 References to agreement and to Nestor are not now present at this point in Sept. Nestor could here be the subject of ϲυμ]φωνεῖ. We might have expected a comment to the effect that Nestor agreed either with Antenor (27–30) or with the Greeks to invite Aeneas to set sail with them to Greece (33 ff.). It appears from Sept. that Dictys often cited Nestor's opinion, for he considered him along with his master, Idomeneus, the most judicious man in the Greek camp; cf. Sept. I 20 p. 18.13–16, II 19 p. 34.1–3, IV 22 p. 99.11–16, and VI 2 p. 121.6–9.

33–8 Cf. Sept. 16 p. 117.22–4 *tunc Graeci Aeneae suadent, secum uti in Graeciam naviget, ibi namque ei simile cum ceteris ducibus ius regnique eandem potestatem fore.*

33–4 Ν]έϲτωρ ἀναπείθ[*c*.4. After Ν]έϲτωρ one could either place a strong pause and restore ἀναπείθ[ουϲι corresponding more or less exactly to the Latin *suadent*, or restore ἀναπείθ[ειν as complementary to 32 ϲυμ]φωνεῖ.

35 ὑ]πιϲχνουμεν[. Probably ὑ]πιϲχνουμέν[οιϲ.

36–7]ἰϲομοιρία π[.]ἰϲομοιρία π[ᾶϲι or π[άν|των?

37] ̣ξημεν ̣ ̣. If the letter after ν could be read as ⲏ corrected from ⲉ, η]ὐξημένη would be attractive.

38–41 Sept. 16 pp. 117.24–118.1 *Neoptolemus filios Hectoris Heleno concedit, praeterea reliqui duces auri atque argenti quantum singulis visum est.*

38 *c*.5 Νεοπ]τόλεμος. Possibly *c*.2 ὁ δὲ Νεοπ]τόλεμος.

38–39 τοὺϲ ̣[*c*.12. τοὺϲ Ἕ[κτορος Ἑλένῳ could perhaps be restored.

39–40 ̣[̣ ̣]ν[*c*.9]ων. ἐ[κό]ν[των τε πάντ]ων may be restored, since the remains of 40 point to a genitive absolute construction. The limited space suggests that the Greek text is again far more compressed in relation to the Latin.

41–5 Cf. Sept. 16 p. 118.1–4 *dein consilio habito decernitur, uti per triduum funus Aiacis publice susciperetur. itaque exactis his diebus cuncti reges comam tumulo eius deponunt.* Similar mourning scenes in Sept. IV 1 pp. 81–2 (for Hector), IV 21 p. 98.5–9 (for Achilles), VI 15 p. 130.24–7 (for Odysseus). There is insufficient space to accomodate all the information given in Sept.

43 *c*.6]εϲ. ἄπαντ]εϲ is a plausible supplement.

45–9 Cf. Sept. 16 p. 118.4–6 *atque exin contumeliis Agamemnonem fratremque agere eosque non Atrei sed Plisthenidas et ob id ignobiles appelare.*

45–6 Ἀγαμε[μν-. Most probably Ἀγαμέ[μνονα.

45–8 Menelaus (i.e. Μενέλαον or ἀδελφόν) is expected in these lines.

47 ἐπ' Αἴαντι. This could be the justification of the army's hostility towards Agamemnon and Menelaus: they were considered responsible for the death of Ajax, since they had openly supported Odysseus in the competition over the Palladion (Sept. 14 pp. 115.19–116.1). In the Latin text there is no mention of this; perhaps it is implied in *exin*.

48–9 Suggested restorations: οὐκ Ἀτρέ]ωϲ ὀνίδ[ι]ζον [ἀλλὰ Πλει]ϲθενίδαϲ or ἀτίμ]ωϲ ὀνίδ[ι]-ζον [αὐτοὺς Πλει]ϲθενίδαϲ.

49 Πλει]ϲθενίδαϲ. Agamemnon and Menelaus are the sons of Pleisthenes in Hesiod, *Κατάλογοι Γυναικῶν sive Ἠοῖαι* fr. 194 M.–W., cf. also Aesch. *Agam.* 1569 and 1602, *TGF* 625–33 (*argumentum* of the Πλειϲθένης), scholia D on A7, B249. Sept., probably following Dictys, consistently maintains this tradition: see I 1 p. 4.1–9, I 9 p. 8.22, III 3 p. 61.26, with the exception of the *Prologus* p. 2.7. According to Mal. 68.53–6, Menelaus was the only son of Pleisthenes, who had been brought up in the palace of Atreus together with the latter's son, Agamemnon. Thus they were both called Atreidai; cf. also Mal., 70.6, 80.73, 80.76, 84.97–8, Cedr. 217.10–13, 218.11 and *Ecl. Hist.* 198.18–20. See further *RE* XXI.1.199–205 for the problem of the place of Pleisthenes in the family line of Tantalus.

49–53 Cf. Sept. 16 p. 118.7–10 *quare coacti, simul simul uti odium sui apud exercitum per absentiam leniretur, orant, uti sibe abire e conspectu eorum sine noxa concedant. itaque consensu omnium primi navigant deturbati expulsique ab ducibus.* The Latin text appears much inflated.

50–51 χρῶνται [*c.*6. χρῶνται [ναυcί may be restored.

51–2 αὐ[*c.*5. αὐ[τοὶ πρῶτοι corresponding to the Latin *primi*. However, Odysseus was actually the first to set sail (cf. above 10–13).

53–7 Cf. Sept. 16 p. 118.10–12 *ceterum Aiacis filii, Aeantides Glauca genitus atque Eurysaces ex Tecmessa, Teucro traditi*, and Mal. (quoting chiefly Sisyphus of Cos) 100.89–93 καὶ ἀναστὰς περιεπλάκη τῷ Πύρρῳ ὁ Τεῦκρος καὶ ᾔτησεν αὐτὸν τοὺς τοῦ Αἴαντος, τοῦ αὐτοῦ ἀδελφοῦ, λαβεῖν υἱούς, τὸν Αἰαντίδην τὸν ἀπὸ Γλαύκης, τῆς προτέρας γυναικὸς Αἴαντος, καὶ τὸν Εὐρυσάκην τὸν ἀπὸ τῆς Τεκμήσσης, καὶ αὐτὴν Τέκμησσαν. καὶ παρέσχεν αὐτῷ ὁ Πύρρος. καὶ λαβὼν ὁ Τεῦκρος εὐθὺς ἀπέπλευσεν ἐπὶ τὴν Cαλαμῖνα.

53–6 could be tentatively partially restored as follows: υἱοὶ | παῖδες] Αἴαντο[ς Αἰα]ντ[ίδης ἐκ Γλ]αύκης τε[χθεῖ]ς ἑκούσης α[ὐτῆς Εὐρυσάκης τε] ἐκ Τεκμή[ccης Τεύκρῳ. At this point the Latin text is perhaps slightly more compressed.

Col. iii

57–60 Cf. Sept. 17 p. 118.13–17 *dein Graeci veriti, ne per moram interventu hiemis, quae ingruebant, ab navigando excluderentur, deductas in mare naves remigibus reliquiisque nauticis instrumentis complent. atque ita cum his, quae singuli praeda multorum annorum quasiverant, discedunt.*

57–8 διὰ τὸν χει]μῶνα μέλλ[οντες or μέλλ[ουσι could be restored, but there is probably not sufficient space to restore διατρίψειν after it.

58–60 Suggested restoration: ἀ]νάγονται ς[ὺν αὐτοῖς κομί]σαντες [πᾶσαν τὴν λείαν; cf. 73 below.

60–67 Cf. Sept. 17 p. 118.18–20 *Aeneas apud Troiam manet. qui post Graecorum profectionem cunctos ex Dardano atque ex proxima paene insula adit, orat, uti secum Antenorem regno exigerent.*

60–62 Probably ἀπο]πλε[υ]σάντω[ν δὲ τῶν Ἑλλή]νων, or ἀπο]πλε[υ]σάντω[ν πάντων τῶν Ἑλλή]νων.

63–7 These could be supplemented *exempli gratia* ἐν τῷ Δαρδάν[ῳ ἐκποδὼν θέσθαι Ἀντήν[ορα πειρᾶται or βούλεται or κελεύει] καὶ τῶν ἐν Χερρ[ονήσῳ πάντας] μὴ ὑπακούει[ν αὐτῷ (sc. Ἀντήνορι) παραι]νῶν. However, 63 here appears shorter than expected.

63 ἐν τῷ Δαρδάν[ῳ. Aeneas was the leader of the Dardanians, based in the foothills of Mt. Ida; cf. Hom. *Il.* 2.819–820 and 20.215 ff.; also Mal. V 1.3–6 ἐν δὲ τοῖς χρόνοις τοῦ Δαβὶδ ἐβασίλευσεν τοῦ Ἰλίου, ἤτοι τῆς Φρυγῶν χώρας, Πρίαμος, υἱὸς Λαομέδοντος. ἐν δὲ τῇ αὐτοῦ βασιλείᾳ τότε καὶ τὸ Ἴλιον καὶ τὸ Δάρδανον καὶ ἡ Τροία καὶ πᾶσα ἡ χώρα τῆς Φρυγίας πορθεῖται ὑπὸ τῶν Ἀχαιῶν, *Ecl. Hist.* 197.8–10, and Cedr. 216.11–12.

67–71 Cf. Sept. 17 p. 118.21–3 *quae postquam praeverso de se nuntio Antenori cognita sunt, regrediens ad Troiam imperfecto negotio aditu prohibetur.*

68–9 Suggested reconstruction: διορ[γιcθεὶς Ἀντήνωρ] αὐτῷ.

69 After ζωης, although space and traces could accommodate three letters, πα[and πλ[are also possible readings. This and the following lines have no analogue in Sept.

69–70 ἔπει]τα δὲ could be supplied.

70 [τὸ Ἴλιον. [τὴν Τροίαν would be preferable (cf. the Latin text), but it is longer than space would allow.

71–5 Cf. Sept. 17 p. 118.23–5 *ita coactus cum omni patrimonio ab Troia navigat devenitque ad mare Hadriaticum multas interim gentes barbaras praevectus.*

72 πα[τρῷον. πα[τρικὸν could be considered as an alternative.

73–4 [πολλοῦ δὲ β]αρβάρου: synecdoche.

75–7 Cf. Sept. 17 pp. 118.25–119.1 *ibi cum his, qui secum navigaverant, civitatem condit appelatam Corcyram Melaenam.*

75 [cὺν δέ: *exempli gratia*, since καὶ cὺν is also a possible supplement here.

76–7 Κορκύρ]αν Μελα[ίναν. See *RE* XI.2.3.1416–17.

77 [λεγομένην: *exempli gratia*; cf. 20. Alternatively, καλουμένην could be restored here.

78–81 Cf. Sept. 17 p. 119.1–4 *ceterum apud Troiam postquam fama est Antenorem regno potitum, cuncti qui bello residui nocturnam civitatis cladem evaserant, ad eum confluunt.*

79]παρμεν[.]παρμέν[ουcι or]παρμέν[οντεc are likely supplements.

81–92 Cf. Sept. 17 p. 119.4–7 *brevique ingens coalita multitudo. tantus amor erga Antenorem atque opinio sapientiae incesserat. fitque princeps amicitiae eius rex Cebrenorum Oenideus.* Part of the Greek appears to have been omitted or abridged in Sept. Perhaps Dictys made reference to the character and the kind behaviour of Antenor towards the Greeks; cf. Sept. 1 6 p. 7.16–18, 1 11 p. 10.17–20, 1 12 p. 11.6–7, III 26 p. 80.10–14, IV 22 pp. 99.10–101 8, V 1 p. 101.13–18.

81–2 The gist of these lines may be that the Trojans who had survived the slaughter recognized Antenor as their king. Very tentatively, 81 could be restored καὶ α[ὐτὸν βαcιλέα.

93–7 Cf. Sept. 17 p. 119.8–11 *haec ego Gnosius Dictys comes Idomenei conscripsi oratione ea, quam maxime inter tam diversa loquendi genera consequi ac comprehendere potui, litteris Punicis ab Cadmo Danaoque traditis.*

93 [cυνεγραψάμην: *conscripsi* Sept.; cf. 107–8, where Sept., conscious of a need for rhetorical variation, has *retuli*. cυνεγράφω would have historiographical connotations.

95 cυνεπ[ό]μενος [*c*.10. The line could be restored with a reference to the language employed, e.g. γλώccῃ τῇδε or ταύτῃ corresponding to the Latin *oratione ea*. There appears to be no room for Φοινικείοιc representing *Punicis*, which, if restored here, would leave no space for the expected reference to the language used (cf. the explanatory γάρ in 98). Finally, we have resisted restoring Φοινικικῇ (sc. γλώccῃ), which, if it had been written in the Greek original, would have been translated clearly by Sept.; cf. also his *Epistula*, p. 1.11–12 *qui (Praxis) commutatos litteris Atticis, nam oratio Graeca fuerat.*

96–7 [Κάδμου] καὶ Δα[ν]αοῦ. Cf. *FGrHist* 1 F20 τῶν cτοιχείων εὑρετὴν ἄλλοι τε καὶ Ἔφοροc ἐν δευτέρῳ (II) Κάδμον φαcίν. οἱ δὲ οὐχ εὑρετήν, τῆc δὲ Φοινίκων εὑρέcεωc πρὸc ἡμᾶc διάκτορον γεγενῆcθαι, ὡc καὶ Ἡρόδοτοc ἐν ταῖc Ἱcτορίαιc (V 58) καὶ Ἀριcτοτέληc (F 501 Rose) ἱcτορεῖ. φαcὶ γὰρ ὅτι Φοίνικεc μὲν εὗρον τὰ cτοιχεῖα, Κάδμοc δὲ ἤγαγεν αὐτὰ εἰc τὴν Ἑλλάδα. Πυθόδωροc (IV) δὲ [ὡc] ἐν τῷ Περὶ cτοιχείων καὶ Φίλλιc ὁ Δήλιοc (II) ἐν τῷ Περὶ Χρόνων πρὸ Κάδμου Δαναὸν μετακομίcαι αὐτά φαcιν. ἐπιμαρτυροῦcι τούτοιc καὶ οἱ Μιληcιακοὶ cυγγραφεῖc Ἀναξίμανδροc (9 F 3) καὶ Διονύcιοc (III) καὶ Ἑκαταῖοc, οὓc καὶ Ἀπολλόδωροc ἐν Νεῶν καταλόγῳ (II) παρατίθεται. Dictys compromised the two traditions about the introduction of the Phoenician alphabet to Greece by Kadmus or Danaus; cf. *Prologus*, p. 2.9–10 *quae a Cadmo in Achaiam fuerant delatae*, and *Epistula*, p. 1.3–4 *quae tum Cadmo et Agenore auctoribus per Graeciam frequentabantur*, perhaps influenced by, or at any rate related to Sept. 1 9 p. 8.23–24 (*Danaum enim atque Agenorem et sui et Priami generis auctores esse*). *Prologus* and *Epistula* are in agreement regarding the alphabet employed by Dictys: see *Prologus* pp. 2.13, 3.4–5, and *Epistula* p. 1.2–4 and 11–12. Cf. also Sept. 1 16 p. 13.26–7 *Punicis litteris Agamemnonis nomen designant.*

96 ὡc ἐμ[οὶ] ἐφικτὸ[ν ἦν: a Hellenistic prose expression, 'possible', 'accessible', cf. Theophr. *Lap.* 25, *Ign.* 70 καθ᾽ ὅcον ἐφικτόν; Polyb. 9.24.5 δι᾽ ἧc ἐcτιν εἰc Ἰταλίαν ἐλθεῖν ἐφικτόν; D. H. *A. R.* 2.34.4 ὡc οὐκ ἦν ἐφικτὰ αὐτοῖc.

97–104 Cf. Sept. 17 p. 119.11–15 *neque sit mirum cuiquam, si quamvis Graeci omnes diverso tamen inter se sermone agunt, cum ne nos quidem unius eiusdemque insulae simili lingua sed varia permixtaque utamur.* Dictys here alludes to Hom. *Od.* 19.172–7:

> Κρήτη τιc γαῖ᾽ ἔcτι μέcῳ ἐνὶ οἴνοπι πόντῳ,
> καλὴ καὶ πίειρα, περίρρυτοc· ἐν δ᾽ ἄνθρωποι
> πολλοὶ ἀπειρέcιοι, καὶ ἐννήκοντα πόληεc. —
> ἄλλη δ᾽ ἄλλων γλῶccα μεμιγμένη· ἐν μὲν Ἀχαιοί,
> ἐν δ᾽ Ἐτεόκρητεc μεγαλήτορεc, ἐν δὲ Κύδωνεc
> Δωριέεc τε τριχάϊκεc δῖοί τε Πελαcγοί.

See J. Russo, M. Fernandez-Galiano, A. Heubeck, *A Commentary on Homer's Odyssey* iii (1992) 83–4. The intertextual link between the two texts is emphasized by the use of the collocation γλῶcca μεμιγμένη, which in all probability to be supplied in 98 and 100–101. Dictys attests knowledge of verses 175–7, whose authenticity has been suspected, being omitted in quotation in a spurious Platonic dialogue (Ps.-Plat. *Minos* 319b); they were deleted by Hoffmann and others.

102 [ἐπεί: *exempli gratia*; alternatives include perhaps [οὕτωc or ὁμοίωc or ὡc.

103–9 Cf. Sept. 17 p. 119.15–18 *igitur ea, quae in bello evenere Graecis ac barbaris, cuncta sciens perpessusque magna ex parte memoriae tradidi. de Antenore eiusque regno quae audieram retuli.* On Dictys' procedure in the collection of his material, see Sept. 1 13 p. 11.16–20, vi 10 p. 128; Mal. 79–80.66–70, 91.91–2; *Ecl. Hist.* 213,11–12, 216.4–5; and Cedr. 223.4–13.

108–9 παρὰ] Ἑλλήνων [ἄλλων ἀκηκοώc: presumably because Dictys could not be expected to have been present for the events described in 62–92. Space in 108 would allow *scriptio plena* at line-end; cf. introd. The concern for eye-witness accuracy and evidential plausibility in reporting is a hallmark of Dictys' historiographical narrative.

At this point the column ends, and if [ἄλλων ἀκηκοώc or something like it completed the line, as seems very likely judging from the Latin, then the roll and book presumably ended at this point. A colophon may have followed (perhaps after an ἄγραφον) bearing title of work and, possibly, the author's name, although the latter is in particular uncertain, given the pseudepigraphical character of the work; the supposed author's name, and some indication of the genre, have, after all, just been stated in the epilogue (93–4). A final short sentence corresponding to the concluding, transitional sentence in Sept. (17 p. 119.18 *nunc reditum nostrorum narrare iuvat*) is unlikely to have occupied the first line of a following column alone; rather the scribe seems to have endeavoured to fit in the exact extent of text that one would have expected on the basis of the Latin (minus the transitional sentence) before the end of the column.

Fr. 2

Placement uncertain, although, if it is correct that 109 is the end of the book and roll, this fragment will have preceded fr. 1.

4]αιμη.[: κ]αὶ μὴν is one possibility among many.

7 τυ.[: τυχ- possible, e.g. τύχη, or from τυγχάνω, τυχών.

R. HATZILAMBROU

D. OBBINK

4945. LOLLIANOS, *PHOINIKIKA*

57/42(a)   8.4 × 20.4 cm   Third century
                                                                  Plate VIII

Remains of a single column of a papyrus roll. Horizontal fibres are stripped in 1–2, above which it is impossible to tell whether lines are lost to abrasion or a top margin is preserved to a height of 1.3 cm. The back is blank. Along the fibres are 41 lines of closely written prose. Line-beginnings, ends, and bottom margin are lost, so the original column width and number of lines is unknown. Further, there is no visible indication of how close or far the extant text is from the right or left margins of the column. Syntax in lines 9–22, however, may be completed most economically, but making continuous sense, by supplying no more than a word or two at end or beginning of lines. On this (admittedly hypothetical) reconstruction, the column would have contained 30–35 letters per line at a width of 7.5–9 cm, and at least 2–4 letters must be missing from both the right and left of the column at at its widest preserved point (see 13–14 n., 20–21 n.).

The handwriting is a spiky, angular, rapidly written version of the Formal Mixed variety or 'Severe Style', with a distinct slant to the right, and marked by the variety and inconsistency of angles at which what would otherwise be horizontal or oblique strokes are placed. The right-hand parts of ᴀ and ᴧ lift up off the baseline, and ᴧ conforms by having a base cocked at an angle to the line, as do the horizontal parts of ᴈ and (often, and more unusually) the middle element of ʜ. The middle element of ɴ, by contrast, sometimes approaches horizontal: e.g. 19 *cυν*. Similarly, the lower leg of ᴋ kicks up high off the line, so that it is virtually horizontal. ᴛ regularly has an angular tick on the start of its horizontal; γ regularly has a similar angular hook or serif on the top of its left-hand arm, as do ᴋ, ɪ, and ʜ on its first upright. The middle of ᴍ leans more toward the left than the right of its uprights. ᴏ and ω are diminutive and narrow, and the latter has but a slight rise in the centre. є is short and narrow (again, conforming to ᴏ), not tall, unlike ᴄ, which is inconsistently taller and narrow (i.e. oval), with a straight vertical back but curved top and bottom. There is sufficient connection between letters, especially ᴀ, ᴧ, ᴛ, ᴦ, π with the following letter, compounded by the unevenly executed contrast between tall, narrow letters and short, wide ones (see e.g. tall and wide x in comparison to the short, narrow є and ᴏ that flank it in 18), so that the handwriting has a hasty and hurried, though not entirely unprofessional look, not ameliorated by the narrowly cramped spacing of the lines (interlinear space less than half the average height of letters). Decenders of ᴘ and γ and the vertical of ϕ frequently clash with the tops of the letters in the line below. The hand may be compared with the similarly right-slanting II **223** (Roberts, *GLH* 21a), *Iliad* v, dated to the early third century (II **237**, a petition of 186 on the front), although **4945** is more closely written. A date in the first quarter of the third century or a little later may be assigned.

The scribe twice places diaereses over initial *υ* (14, 36) and uses a raised stop, followed by a slight blank space, to mark punctuation (11, 13, 25, 26); once a letter is corrected by overwriting (26), but there are otherwise no lectional signs. Iota adscript is not written, and the scribe does not elide final vowels, preferring *scriptio plena*, before word-initial vowels. However, he regularly assimilates consonants where we would expect, and his orthography is otherwise standard, with a preference for Attic forms (6 n., 29 n.).

There are no similarities, overlaps, or joins between **4945** and the two previously identified papyri of Lollianos' *Phoinikika*, apart from the shared element that all three papyri come from the late second or third century AD. Like XI **1368**, **4945** is a papyrus roll, couched in a similar hand. P. Colon. inv. 3328 is a single-column codex with very long lines, while the column of **1368** is narrower than that of **4945** and its text is written on the back (front: register).

The unusual name Glauketes (21; cf. 25 n.) establishes the identity of the text as part of Lollianos' *Phoinikika*. Glauketes' role as receiver of a message and instructions in **4945** is consistent with the previously known fragments (A. Henrichs, *Die Phoinikika des Lollianos* (Bonn 1972); S. A. Stephens and J. J. Winkler, *Ancient Greek Novels: The Fragments* (Princeton 1995) 314–57). (For the possible presence of the previously known Androtimos, see 10 n., but this is highly conjectural.) **4945** adds significantly to the growing cast of characters of this well-populated narrative: a new named female character, Arginna (11; cf. 16 n.), and at least one other, Myelos or Myrrhine, the latter a name from Old Comedy, together with an old woman and a friend or servant who acts as a messenger. A group of men referred to as exiting from the scene may be identifiable as one of the groups of brigands present in the previously known fragments (see 7 n.). The text changes from narration to direct speech (possibly monologue) and back again at least once, in a combination of tenses suitable in a narrative, fictional text. Subjects under discussion include longing and physical symptoms of love, love-sickness, death or its simulation (by sacrifice or magic?), lying awake during the night, confessions of love, arrangement of a love-meeting by a servant—all elements familiar from the Greek novel, especially of the exciting, violent sub-type of the genre exhibiting involvement with brigands and other unsavory characters and activities that is instantiated by Apuleius' *Metamorphoses*, its Greek originals, and Lollianos' *Phoinikika*.

The composition betrays a style that may be characterized as rapid narrative (perhaps even a complete change of topic from 4 to the end?). Even if the text contained events told by several different persons (see 11 n.), we would have a rapidly developing action: narration, love-sickness of Arginna, thoughts of a male, report and instructions to Glauketes, agreement, further plans. If **4945** indeed contained a monologue or something like one, this would be something new for Lollianus, inviting comparison with the rhetorical monologues in Achilles Tatius, Heliodorus, Apuleius, and his precursor LXX **4807**.

The language consists of simple syntax and mainly, short paratactic sentences, connected with ὁ μέν / ὁ δέ, ἀλλά, δέ, οὖν: 7, 11, 15, 25, 26 (see Henrichs, op. cit., 9). This is combined with abrupt change of tenses (see Henrichs 9 and 12 n. below). Hiatus, generally avoided in the Greek novelists, is admitted throughout (see further M. D. Reeve, 'Hiatus in the Greek Novelists', *CQ* 21 (1971) 514–39), as in the other fragments (Henrichs 9 n. 8).

It is sufficiently clear that the action of the fragment concerns romantic affairs, together with other calamities experienced by protagonists of the *Phoinikika*. Love at first sight, followed by the usual symptoms (12–16), apparently takes possession of a male character, who seems to confide his condition to another (16 ff.), then sends a messenger to Glauketes, who is in turn charged with making arrangements for a meeting (with Arginna?) in the evening with no witnesses present (22). Glauke-tes agrees to do as he is told, when the text begins to fade away.

Yet the passage contains a wealth of details that remain uncertain. The set-ting, changes of speaker/narrator, as well as a number of the participants elude identification. As far as can be seen, and assuming a minimal loss of text from beginnings and ends of lines as suggested above, the following skeleton of events emerges from the third-person narration: (i) someone has just returned (to the dwelling place of the brigands?). (ii) an old woman speaks in direct speech, adress-ing someone, with references to marrow/brain (or a person named Myelos) and myrtle ?wine (or a woman named Myrrhine) and water. (iii) A group of men leaves (the dwelling?), while someone else does something else with his head (covering it? in grief?) (iii) At the same time (and perhaps occasioning this reaction), a young woman turns pale and is on the point of death. Meanwhile, a woman, Arginna, burns with love for a male character (or inflames him with desire). (iv) Lying awake in the night, he confides his desire to one of his friends (or expresses it in a mono-logue) and forms a plan to meet her. (v) Then he directs his friend or a servant to go to Glauketes and tell him to (arrange this meeting) in the evening in a secret place. (vi) The messenger goes as instructed and reports the instructions to Glauke-tes. (vii) Glauketes agrees to do as asked. (viii) A reference to an intended sacrifice (perhaps in an attempt to secure the success of the love-meeting) is the only certain reference in the remaining lines 28–41 (see the commentary below for a few more clues and a suggested line of reconstruction). A setting for this scene in the large, mysterious building in which the brigands dwell, known from the other two pa-pyri of the *Phoinikika*, is one possibility (see 3 n., 7 n.), although this should not be regarded as certain. (Glauketes, for example, is apparently not present, or at least sufficiently distant in the large dwelling from the speaker of 21–6 or inaccessible to him to require the go-between of a messenger with instructions.) If correct, how-ever, **4945** is to be located in the *Phoinikika* somewhere after XI **1368** and before the leaves of P. Colon. inv. 3328.

For the texts and treatment of previously known fragments of Lollianos' *Phoinikika*, see Henrichs, op. cit.; Stephens and Winkler, op. cit., 495 f. with further bibibliography; M. Paz López Martínez, *Fragmentos papiráceos de novela griega* (Alicante 1998) 161–208. The commentary below contains suggestions on previews of the text by Professors G. M. Browne (GMB), A. Henrichs (AH), and others. We are grateful to Professor Stephen Bay for making available Professor Browne's notes from his unpublished papers.

```
].[..]....[
].ωρ.....[..].[
].ρα..αι·...γραυςη.[
].ιπενωϲδηεπιϲταμε[
```

```
].[..]....[
].ωρ.....[..].[
]ραπται· ἡ δὲ γραῦϲ ητ[
]. ιπεν ὡϲ δὴ ἐπιϲταμε[
```

5].μυελουαναστραφε.[	5 το]ῦ μυελοῦ ἀναστραφέν[τος
]..ιδεμυρρινησϋδατ[	]..ιδε μυρρίνης ὕδατ[
].ν·καιοιμενεξηεσα[	].ν· καὶ οἱ μὲν ἐξήεσα[ν
].ηνκεφαληνκα.[	]την κεφαλὴν κα.[
]ωκειηπαιδισκηαπο.[	ἐ]ῴκει ἡ παιδίσκη ἀπο.[
10]..μυελοσαποστραφεισα[.].[	10]..μυελὸς ἀποστραφεισα[.].[
]ν·τωδεαργιννααξεκαετο.[	]ν· τῷ δὲ Ἄργιννα ἐξεκαετο.[
]γαρωχρ.καιαποθνησκεινδο[	]γὰρ ὠχρὰ καὶ ἀποθνῄσκειν δο[
].ομωσαυτωεφαινετο·επεικ.[	]η ὅμως αὐτῷ ἐφαίνετο· ἐπεὶ κα[
]ν.ρωτοσϋπεκκαυμαπροσελαβ.[	]ν ἔρωτος ὑπέκκαυμα προσέλαβε[
15].ενουναγρυπνωντησνυκ.[	15] μὲν οὖν ἀγρυπνῶν τῆς νυκτ[ὸς
].εγ[....]..νατωνεαυτουετ.[	]λεγ[....]..νατων ἑαυτοῦ ετ.[
].υ[.].τεεμοιαυτηηγυνηοι[	].υ[.].τε ἐμοὶ αὕτη ἡ γυνὴ οι[
].μηκαιουτωσεχουση π.[	].μη καὶ οὕτως ἐχούσῃ π.[
].ρσυννεν.μαιραιον.οκ.[	γ]ὰρ συγγένωμαι, ῥᾷον δοκ.[
20].ι·αλλαπι.ικαιαπαγγε.[	20].ι· ἀλλὰ ἄπιθι καὶ ἀπάγγελ[ε
].λαυκετηνοπωσ.ο[	] Γλαυκέτην, ὅπως.ο[
].ηνεσπερανερημια[	]την ἑσπέραν ἐρημία[
]νκαιαυτονειτουτ.υ.[	]ν καὶ αὐτὸν, εἰ τούτου.[
]ουχηττονηειζω..[	] οὐχ ἧττον ἢ εἰ ζω..[
25].·ομενδηταυταπροστ[	25].· ὁ μὲν δὴ ταῦτα προστ[
].⟦ει⟧ηγγελλεν·οδεπροσ[	].ἤγγελλεν· ὁ δὲ προσ[
]..λογησενουτωπο.[	ὡ]μολόγησεν οὕτω πο.[
]εινειντηνε..[	]είνειν τὴν ε..[
]κατασφατ.[	] κατασφαττ[
30]ετηναπ.[	30]ετην ἀπο[
]νκαιτελ[	]ν καὶ τελ[
].πειτη.[	].πει τη.[
].σθατ.[	].σθατ.[
]..ηνικ[	]..ηνικ[
35].υτησα.[	35].υτης αγ[
].ϋποτο[	].ϋποτο[
]εκαικ[	]ε καὶ κ[
].υτοιν[	].υτοιν[
]εασ·ευ.[	]εασ· ευ.[
40]σετ..[	40]σετ..[
]...[	]...[

1] . . [, first, large blob, partly dirt?; second, descender below the line, as of γ   ] . . . . [, first, feint speck; second and third, tops of uprights; fourth, top of upright with upper arm attached, as of κ   2] ., oblique, as upper arm of κ or left side   δ . . . . [, high horizontal (z, ȝ), low horizontal with upright attached at base (ε, c), lower half of bowl as of o, speck at mid-level, high oblique (α, ᴧ, λ) .[, oblique, λ suggested   3] ., upright with horizontal extending right (ᴦ, τ) . ., three uprights . . ., upright followed by trace at mid-level, low oblique (left part of α ᴧ λ), lower half of tight bowl (ε o c) .[, foot of upright (not λ, ᴩ), centred as of τ   4] ., right end of a hair-line horizontal at mid-level, suiting ε or λ with its right leg rising high off the line, as elsewhere; however, there is possibly the faint trace of the right end of another horizontal just above, which (if it is in fact ink) would commend ε   5] ., upright descending low, suits γ .[, foot of upright (ʜ ɴ π)   6] . ., first low horizontal with diagonal connected on top, ᴧ, z, ȝ possible; then a speck at mid-level   7] ., tiny lower end of an oblique connecting to foot of first upright of ʜ, as of α, λ (not ɪ)   8] ., lower half of centred upright as of τ .[, left side of α, λ   9 .[, low speck in lower left quarter compatible with ε, ⊖, c   10] . ., right side of smallish bowl suiting o, dot at mid-level .[, foot of oblique inclining right as of λ   11 .[, specks forming curve as of lower half of tight bowl, as of ε, o, c   12 . ., two low specks, as of feet of uprights or obliques 13] ., upright with short horizontal connecting from right at mid-level suiting ʜ or ᴍ .[, foot of oblique inclining right and thicking, as of nose of α rather than λ   14]ν ., remains of a vertical projecting slightly downwards, then an oblique descending from the top left with an immediately attached vertical, then lower half of bowl as of ε, o, c .[, ink off-centre to left at mid-level, suiting ε, ⊖, o, c, ω   15] ., foot of upright .[, upright descending beneath the line as of τ or γ 16] ., oblique curving to horizontal into ε at mid-level, as α or λ   ] . ., trace of the lower part of an upright, then a full upright with a small left-facing hook at the top, in the middle of which a stroke coming from the left: ɴ, ᴦɪ, ʜ, ᴍ, τɪ? .[, lower angular part of ε or c   17] .ν, two obliques meeting at apex, the right one extending over the left, as of α λ   ] .τ, hairline horizontal entering from left and stopping under the left half of cross-stroke of τ, as of mid-stroke of ε or tail of α or right leg of λ   18] ., high speck .[, two obliques converging in apex at top, the right overlapping the left with the distinct hook, while the left descends below the line, λ suggested (no obvious ink inside the two arms as with α)   19] ., thin stroke entering from left near top line, suggesting α or λ with raised second element ν .μ, lower part of bowl ν .o, two obliques meeting at an apex with hook over left .[, left extremity of round letter as ε, ⊖, o, c, ω   20] ., oblique curving in from left at mid-level as of α, λ ɪ .ɪ, lower and left parts of round letter with horizontal ink at mid-level, ⊖ rather than ε, since the oval seems closed .[, two obliques converging at apex as of α, ᴧ, λ 21] ., high horizontal entering from left and touching λ at the convergence of its obliques c .o, two uprights connected by a sagging middle, as badly formed ʜ or ᴍ   22] ., high horizontal entering from left: ᴦ, τ, ȝ   23 τ .ν, bowl missing its right side, c suggested, but compatible with ⊖, o .[, high oblique stopping at mid-level, as though hook off apex of α, ᴧ, λ (not x)   24 .[, upright with curved stroke at bottom, c suggested, then another upright as of ʜ, ɴ, π   25] ., high trace with specks along edge, as though from an upright: ʜ, ɴ?   26] ., bottom part of round letter with a high horizontal stroke connecting into ʜ, c suggested η corrected from εɪ by writing over it, probably by first hand   27] . ., tops of two uprights, as of ɪɪ or if a single letter, ʜ or ᴍ .[, high trace and speck along edge suggesting upright   28 . .[, horizontal at mid-level as of ε, ⊖, ȝ; high speck   29 .[, high horizontal connecting to cross-stroke of τ, τ recommended   30 .[, left extremity of round letter off-centre left, as of ε, ⊖, o, c, ω   32] ., high trace suiting top of upright .[, upright with horizontal protruding at mid-level, ʜ suggested, ᴍ not excluded, probably not ɴ   33] ., top of upright (ɪ, ʜ?) .[, upright with horizontal connecting at mid-level and rising to right, prima facie ʜ, but compatible with ɪτ   34] . ., foot of oblique connecting with upright as of ɴ, ᴧɪ, αɪ   35] ., end of horizontal at mid-level as of ε, also suiting rising tail of

ᴀ, ʌ   .[, upright with horizontal extending to right at top, but without extending left, thus г better than π   36] ., end of high horizontal as of τ or cap of ᴄ, not π, ꙁ   38] ., end of horizontal entering somewhat under mid-level, as of tail of ᴀ, ʌ   39 .[, left side of round letter with tip of horizontal protruding left at mid-level as of ө   40 . .[, two uprights, the first most probably ı, the second with a horizontal extending right at top with hairline (connecting?) stroke to left, suggesting г, τ not excluded   41] . . .[, upright with finial as of ı, top half of round letter with horizontal at bottom connecting to following letter (є strongly recommended), top of upright as of ı

'³ has returned . . . now the old woman ⁴. . . said (*or* left), that knowing (*or* knowingly) . . . |⁵ . . . the marrow/brain having been brought back/turned around (*or* Myelos having returned again) . . . |⁶ . . . of Myrrine (*or* myrtle wine) the water . . . |⁷ . . .; and some went out . . . |⁸ . . . (covering?) the head . . . |⁹ . . . the young girl seemed (to be near death?) . . . |¹⁰ . . . the marrow/brain that had been brought back/turned around (*or* Mylelos who had returned again), . . . |¹¹ . . .; for him Arginna was burning up (or inflamed him) . . . |¹² . . . for she turns pale and seems to be near death . . . |¹³ . . . nevertheless, she seemed to him to be (beautiful?); since . . . |¹⁴ . . . he had gotten the fuel of love . . . |¹⁵ . . . He, then, lying awake during the night . . . |¹⁶ . . . said . . . of his own . . . |¹⁷ . . . for me this woman . . . |¹⁸ . . . although she may not be in the same condition (as me?) . . . |¹⁹ . . . for (if?) I meet with her, I expect very easily to . . . |²⁰ . . .; but go away and report (this?) |²¹ (to?) Glauketes and see to it that he (arranges the meeting?) . . . |²² in the evening in a secluded place . . . |²³ . . . and this/him too, if of this/him . . . |²⁴ . . . no less than if some (other animal?) . . . |²⁵⁻⁶ . . .; he, then, reported this . . . to (Glauketes?); |²⁷ . . . He assented that he would so do (it) |²⁸ . . . |²⁹ . . . sacrifices/slaughters . . .'

2] . ωρ: ῠ]δωρ (AH)? (cf. 6).

3]τραπται: e.g. ἀνέϲ]τραπται, 'she/he has returned'. -γραπται (AH) is not to be ruled out, but seems less likely in the context, since writing/inscription is not elsewhere mentioned.

ἡ δὲ γραῦϲ (AH): assuming γραῦϲ is to be read, as seems likely, this should be an old woman, perhaps performing the role of a guard or bodyguard of sorts in the dwelling of the brigands, based on resemblances with other Greek novels: cf. [Luc.] *Asin.* 20–24. She might also be responsible for performing a ritual or magical rite: cf. Theocr. 2.91 ἢ ποίαϲ ἔλιπον γραίαϲ δόμον ἅτιϲ ἐπᾷδεν;

4] . ιπεν: either εἶπεν (AH) or one of its compounds could introduce direct speech, e.g. by the γραῦϲ. In this case, someone would finish speaking in 3 with]τραπται, to be continued by ἡ δὲ κτλ. introducing the speech of the γραῦϲ: e.g. ὡϲ δὴ ἐπιϲταμέ[νωϲ εἴρηκαϲ (GMB), 'How knowingly have you spoken' (cf. Charit. 6.5.6). However, traces also allow -ἐ]λιπεν, followed by a causal clause: for ὡϲ δή 'because apparently' or (ironically) 'as if', see KG II 130; cf. Xen. Eph. 3.10.4 ἔξειϲιν ὡϲ δή τινοϲ χρῄζων, καὶ καταλιπὼν πάνταϲ ἐπὶ τὴν θάλατταν ἔρχεται. In this case: someone (perhaps the old woman) leaves because she/he knows (where or how to find/prepare the marrow/brain for the rite, i.e. as part of the elaborate illusion of a Scheintod?).

5 το]ῦ μυελοῦ ἀναϲτραφέν[τοϲ: either 'the marrow/brain having been turned upside down' or 'the brain having been brought back' or metaph. 'the inmost part (of a person) having been stirred up' (cf. Eur. *Hipp.* 255). Another possibility is that Μυελόϲ is here (and in 11) the name of a character, or a pet-name or term of endearment (= Lat. *Medulla*) for one: the meaning would be 'Myelos returned again' (cf. Plato, *Leges* 626e πάλιν . . . ἀναϲτρέψωμεν), although a different meaning would then seem to be required of the identical expression in 11 ('Myelos turned away'?). Is it possible that the expression 'turning again' described motions (real or metaphorical) in connection with a sympathetic magical rite or ritual involving sacrifice, killing/death, or dismemberment? Cf. 29 καταϲφαττ[, the ἴυγξ-spell in Theocr. 2, and, for the verb, the enigmatic magical spell published by E. G. Turner, 'The Marrow of Hermes' in *Images of Man in Ancient and Medieval Thought: Studia Gerardo Verbeke ab amicis et collegis dicata* (Louvain 1976) 169–73, ll. 1–4 ὥϲπερ ϲτρέφεται ὁ Ἑρμῆϲ τοῦ μυελοῦ . . . οὕτωϲ ϲτρέψον

τὸν ἐγκέφαλον καὶ τὴν καρδίαν, which he translated: 'As Hermes turns in his marrow . . . so too turn the brain and heart.' But there has been little agreement on the nature and meaning of this text. Following Turner in seeing the spell as a love-charm are e.g. J. G. Griffiths, *ZPE* 26 (1977) 287–88 and H. D. Betz, *The Greek Magical Papyri in Translation* (Chicago 1985) 312 ('PGM CIX'), while C. Faraone, *ZPE* 72 (1988) 279–86, and Suppl. Mag. II 56, emending μυελοῦ to μυλαίου, see it as a curse; H. S. Versnel, *ZPE* 72 (1988) 287–92 thinks of an effigy moulded from fat/brain. Note the article, as here. It is in either case perplexing why this expression should be repeated in 10 in virtually the same phrasing (different case-endings), unless perhaps this is because it is told by a speaker in direct speech (here?), but (in 10?) referred back to by a third-person narrator.

6]. . ιδε: the first letter could be ξ, which is not promising: [ἀλλὰ πά]ξ· (GMB), 'enough said' (cf. Menander *Ep.* 987); but the letter could also be δ, and we could have e.g. cὺ] δὲ ἴδε (ἴδε could be parenthetic, 'look', or 'here is x').

μυρρίνης: Μυρρίνη is instanced as a woman's name from the fifth century BC onwards, used for prostitutes, ἑταῖραι, and by Aristophanes for one of the Athenian women in *Lysistrata*. If a name, Lollianos uses the Attic form, which is rare in comparison with the Ionic Μυρc-. Possibly, in his choice of names he was indeed influenced by Aristophanic comedy: see on 21. For the influence of Old Comedy on the Greek novelists, see, e.g., Photios *Bibl.* cod. 166, p. 111 a 34 f. (regarding Antonius Diogenes): λέγει δὲ ἑαυτὸν ὅτι ποιητής ἐcτι κωμῳδίαc παλαιᾶc (for the influence of Aristophanes and Old Comedy on ancient romance elsewhere in the papyri, see e.g. LXX **4762** ii 9–12 n.). As a female character here, she could be the procuress or supplier of materials necessary for a rite, or the person performing it, if not identical with the γραῦc of 3 herself. Alternatively, we must reckon with the possibility that μυρρίνη here could be the plant 'myrtle', myrtle oil (as a magical substance?), or myrtle wine (Pollux 6.17, Athen. 1.328), e.g. a potion brewed by the γραῦc, or simply as refreshment (for whoever has arrived in 3?). μυρρίνη, 'myrtle' is, of course, also commonly used to fashion garlands and wreaths worn or presented at civilized drinking-parties, although of possible functions this seems the least likely here.

ὕδατ[: possibly ὕδατ[ι plus form of μίγνυμι, but its purpose remains uncertain: myrtle wine/oil mixed (or someone mixing it) with water? Or was the water used (by Myrrhine, genitive absolute?) in a rite involving the marrow/brain? In P. Colon. inv. 3328 fr. B1 verso 9–11, a man (wearing a crimson loincloth) cuts out the heart of a παῖc who has been sacrificed (either in reality or as an illusion), slices it, and then sprinkles the slices with oil (and perhaps barley groats) before giving these to initiates to eat as part of an oath-taking ceremony.

7 οἱ μὲν ἐξῄεcα[ν presupposes two groups of people, one of which leaves here (i.e. exits a building?), perhaps in order to do something with the head (8 κεφαλήν). A corresponding ὁ-/ἐκεῖνοc δέ, plus a verb like [ὠδύρετο] (GMB) as at Charit. 86.29 (cf. ἐλυπεῖτο Charit. 55.1; 86.14), may have stood in the missing portions of text after ἐξῄεcα[ν and before 9 ἐ]ῴκει. (11 τῷ δὲ could be the correlative with οἱ μὲν here, but seems too distant.) As in P. Colon. inv. 3328, οἱ μὲν implies that more than one group (of brigands?) is involved: similarly in P. Colon. inv. 3328 fr. B1 verso 29, after having split up into two groups, a gang leaves a building (ἐξῄεcαν ἔξω). Are οἱ μὲν here to be identified with one of those two groups?

8]την κεφαλήν. If τήν, whose head? A possible source of the μυελόc, 'brain' seems almost too macabre to contemplate. For a possible identification of the owner, see on 11.

κα. [: very likely a form of καλύπτω (e.g. καλ[υψάμενοc, which, followed by punctuation and e.g. [καὶ γάρ], would take up about the expected space before 9 ἐ]ῴκει) with τὴν κεφαλήν as object, whether of someone (contrasted with the exiting group of brigands) who has covered his own head (in grief?), or the head of a sacrificed victim? Cf. Charit. 1.13.11 cυγκαλυψαμένη τὴν κεφαλήν.

9 παιδίcκη: the word (if not the formation) is rare. The meaning is 'female slave' in the Greek novelists ([Luc.] *Asin.* 2; 51; Heliod. *Aeth.* 7.9.3), but elsewhere also 'young girl' or even 'prostitute'. The

article shows that the girl has already been introduced. Cf. XI **1368** 37–8 ὁ δὲ νεανίςκος ἠφανίςθη. If it refers back to a character, e.g. Μυρρίνη, any of the above meanings above might apply, since we would know almost nothing about her, except that she is not the main female character (if she is a character). It seems, however, equally possible that the παιδίςκη referred to here is another female, perhaps Ἄργιννα.

ἀπο̣.[: very likely ἀποθ[νήςκειν. The girl seems to die (or to be on the point of death), perhaps to the character contrasted with the exiting group in 7, who is agrieved at this sight (and so covering his head?); nevertheless (cf. 13 ὅμως), a male character is inflamed with love for her in 11 ff. If so, her near-fatal condition would seem to be due not to the action of a sacrifice, but to some other calamity. For the suspected illusion of a character's apparent death that turns out to be simulated or feigned, or the expectation of death subverted elsewhere in Lollianos and the extant novels, see the discussion of Stephens–Winkler (op. cit. 320–25), and further development by J. J. Winkler, *JHS* 100 (1980) 155–81.

10]..: After ἀποθ[νήςκειν in 9 a continuation like [μετὰ δὲ τοῦτ]ο̣ (Ach. Tat. 1.5.4, 8.10.4) is possible, which would suit the first trace here well; but if]ο is correct, we might instead have the article] ὁ here, as μυελός indeed does in the same expression (with different case-endings) in 5. But there is also a second trace afterwards, which looks like a a stop at mid-level: misplaced punctuation? For μυελὸς ἀποςτραφειςα̣[cannot not be the beginning of a sentence, unless a connective particle is missing.

ἀποςτραφειςα[.].[. Although reading ἀποςτραφεῖςα is possible in principle, ἀποςτραφεὶς coheres better with μυελός. At end, we could possibly have Ἀ[ν]δ̣[ροτίμου, which would introduce a character from previously known fragments of the *Phoinikika* (P. Colon. inv. 3328 frr. B 1 recto 18, B 1 verso 9); however, while the alpha looks all but certain, there are also other possibilities that would suit the final trace, e.g. ἀ̣[λ]λ[ὸ] (GMB) or related forms in ἀ̣[λ]λ̣[.

11 Ἄργιννα: A name hitherto unknown, but formed with the fairly productive suffix -ιννα, the origin of which is still disputed (see Chantraine, *La Formation des noms* (1933), 205 and Masson, *BSL* 81 (1986) 228 f.). For other names derived from ἀργε-/ι- (*ἄργος 'shine'), see Bechtel, *Die historischen Personennamen des Griechischen* (1917) 64.

ἐξεκαετο̣[: i.e. either ἐξεκάετο (e.g. ἔ[ρωτι], but the preceding τῷ is hard to construe) or ἐξέκαε το̣.[, e.g. τὸ ς̣[τῆθος] (GMB) or τος[οὕτως. Cf. Charit. 2.4.3, 3.1.8. The verbs καίω and καίομαι and their compounds, i.e. the metaphor of fire, are often used for love by the Greek novelists: e.g. Long. 1.14.1, Charit. 5.9.9, 2.4.4, Xen. Eph. 4.5.4, but never with the dative. See, e.g. Charit. 4.6.2 καὶ γὰρ αὐτὸς ἐκάετο τῆς Καλλιρόης (where LSJ, however, would supply ἔρωτι). We might, then, take τῷ as *dativus causae*, cf. Plat. *Leg.* 783a3 f. (ἔρως) ὁ περὶ τὴν τοῦ γένους ςπορὰν ὕβρει καόμενος—provided that the lost part of the sentence did not supply a cause. If this is correct, the reference of τῷ can hardly be to the 'marrow' or 'brain', but ought to be to a male character, perhaps one mentioned in the preceding lines (Myelos?). Another possibility would be a change of narrator somewhere within 10–11: Arginna would then fall in love with a male character who would have narrated the events recounted in the preceding lines. This would also account for the sudden change of topic from 10 to 11.

12 ὠχρά. Presumably Arginna is still the subject, in a description of her symptoms of love (cf. Heliod. *Aeth.* 4.7.7). Before it, we could have e.g. [πάνυ] (GMB), if not [ἡ] or [ὁ]. For the abrupt change of tenses as a characteristic feature of the author's narrative technique, see Henrichs, op. cit., 116 (on P. Colon. inv. 3328 fr. B1 recto, 10–12).

δο[: very likely δο[κεῖ or δο[κοῦςα, sc. Arginna.

13]η. If η (and not ῃ) is right, this would presumably be an adjective describing the girl, i.e. how she appeared to the desiring male character. The run of the sentence would then be: 'Although she seemed pale and on the brink of death, she nevertheless appeared x to him. Thus e.g. either [ἐραςτ]ή, 'lovely' (GMB) or [καλ]ή, 'beautiful'.

αὐτῷ: sc. the desiring male character.

ἐπεὶ κα̣[. ἐπεὶ κα̣[ὶ, introducing a main sentence (as it does at Luc. *Tox.* 38; Ach. Tat. 2.14.8, 8.5.3; see KG II 461 n. 1)?

13–14 If we restore ἐπεὶ κα̣[ὶ, the syntax could be most economically completed by restoring [αὐτὸ]ν, which would give a hypothetical line-length of about 30 letters, and if divided [αὐ|τὸ]ν, then the preserved beginning of 14 would be just two letters in from the left edge of the column. At the end of 13, one could allow for slightly more letters at the end of lines by restoring e.g. ἐπεὶ κα̣[ὶ διὰ αὐ|τὸ]ν or ἐπεὶ κα̣[ὶ ταυ|τὸ]ν. But much, including the exact point at which the lines divided, remains uncertain.

14 ἔρωτος ὑπέκκαυμα: 'fuel for love', cf. Xen. *Symp.* 4.25: ἔρωτος οὐδέν ἐστι δεινότερον ὑπέκκαυμα, imitated by Ach. Tat. 1.5.6 ὑπέκκαυμα . . . ἐπιθυμίας, 'fuel of desire'. For ἔρωτος, cf. P. Colon. inv. 3328 fr. A 2 recto, 34 ὄμμα ἔρωτος with Henrichs, op. cit., 111 ad loc.

προσέλαβε̣[: no doubt προσελάβε̣[το or προσέλαβε̣[ν. Cf. P. Colon. inv. 3328 fr. A 2 recto 14 ἄ]μφω ἔλαβε[ν] with the apparatus of Stephens–Winkler (op. cit.) ad loc.

15] μὲν: just before should come the subject, e.g. [ἔκεῖνος] or perhaps a name ([Μυελός]?).

15–16 Perhaps τῆς νυκτ[ὸς ἐκεί|νης] (GMB).

16]λεγ[: probably ἔ]λεγ[ε (sc. the desiring male?). With in ἀγρυπνῶν certain in 15, Ach. Tat. 4.10.5 ἀγρυπνῶν . . . ἔλεγον is very close to this. An attractive continuation would then be πρός] τινα τῶν ἑαυτοῦ ἑτα[ίρων (although it should be pointed out that the space would be filled, and the traces compatible with, reading Ἀργί]ννα/α̣ τῶν here). At the end, the traces, a high point of ink suiting the apex of ⋏ better than ε, rules out ἑτέ[ρων.

16–17 An address or monologue-like speech seems to begin.

17] υ[.] . : The first trace could be ⋏, ⋏, or ⋏, the second ⋏ (with its tail lifting off the line) or ε (with extended mid-stroke): thus e.g. [φίλε (GMB) ἡ]δύ[τ]α̣τε (AH) (for the form cf. Plut. *Mor.* 98ε with the Teubner app. crit. ad loc. vol. i p. 201.2), beginning an address, or [ἔ]λυ[π]ε τε (presuming a lost verb of similar meaning preceding this). In either case we would have the desiring male in direct speech describing to a comrade a desire he presumes that the girl shares. With the latter, the following words would provide subject and (indirect) object; with the former, we would need to restore a verb for these at the end, e.g. οἴ[στρεῖ] (GMB) (used of a woman: Ach. Tat. 2.37.8).

18] μὴ καὶ οὕτως ἐχούςῃ π̣ [: Assuming μή, as seems likely, the thought might be: 'although she doesn't feel it as I do'. Thus e.g. αὐτ]ὴ μὴ καὶ οὕτως ἐχούςῃ or αὐτ]ῇ μὴ καὶ οὕτως ἐχούςῃ. Either of these might have been introduced by e.g. [εἴη δὲ] (GMB) or some similar wish. Feel what? At end, the direct object ought to be expressed. Thus it is tempting to restore πά[θος ἐρωτικὸν] (Charit. 2.5) or [ἔρω|τος] or [ταυτὸν] (Xen. Eph. 1.9.1). However, the trace at the end slightly suits ⋏ better than ⋏, in which case perhaps πλ[εῖον e.g. πάθος] ('although she doesn't feel mo[re passion for me than for another]')?

19 γ]ὰρ cυνγένωμαι, ῥαιον δοκ̣ [: Perhaps [ἐὰν γ]ὰρ: 'If I meet with her, it seems that very easily . . .' (see below on 20 for a possible continuation). Thus the desiring male character proposes a meeting, then sends a messenger to tell Glauketes to arrange it.

ῥαιον: could be either the adverb ('easily') or the neuter participle of ῥαίω ('crushing'), although the former is far more likely here.

δοκ̣ [: δοκῶ or δοκῶ[ν or δοκε̣[ῖ would account for the final trace.

20] ι. The thought could be completed along the lines of: [(μοι) τοῦτο πυθέσθ]αι (GMB). Presumably the desiring male speaks the commands that follow. But who is the addressee of the imperatives? Either the speaker himself (if a monologue) or the friend or servant sent as messenger. If the speaker himself, 25 f. ὁ μὲν . . . ἤγγελλεν could also refer to him, narrating in the third person the action ensuing from the monologue.

20–21 With ἀπάγγελ[ε (cf. Ach. Tat. 4.8.1(4) ἀπαγγέλει μοι) we expect an object (e.g. [ταῦτα]) expressing what the speaker exhorts someone (or himself) to convey to someone else; or, if this is understood, perhaps [δή] (frequent with the imperative in the novelists) or [εἶτα] or [ἔτι]) to fill out the line. Then, presumably, the continuation in 21 is: [πρὸς τὸν] Γλαυκέτην. Cf. 25 ὁ μὲν δὴ ταῦτα πρὸς τ[ὸν ---].

21 Γλαυκέτην. The name is mainly known from Attic authors (in particular Ar. *Pax* 1008, Thesm. 1033, Dem. 24) and Attic inscriptions, but also attested elsewhere.

ὅπως ̣ο[. The uncertain letter is ineptly executed, and could be м (e.g. ὅπως μό[νη ᾖ or μό[νοι ὦμεν) or, perhaps more likely, н, e.g. ὅπως ἡ ὁ[μιλία γένη|ται] (GMB). For ὁ[μιλία cf. Charit. 2.5.3.

22]την ἑσπέραν: very likely [περὶ] τὴν ἑσπέραν, 'toward evening' (cf. Plat. *Resp.* 328a, Xenoph. *HG* 4.3.22).

ἐρημία[: e.g. ἐρημία[c οὔcηc/παρούcηc/τυχούcαc μοι] (or perhaps [ἐκεῖ] or [αὐτοῦ]? Still other ways of saying this might be contemplated (e.g. ἐρημία[ν ἐχόντων] or ἐρημία[c πίcτει, 'through the assurance of solitude' i.e. privacy, ἐρημία[c ἐν ἀcφαλείᾳ], etc.). The point must be that the planned meeting must be in a secret or deserted place.

23–6 Further instructions to be conveyed to Glauketes follow, of uncertain nature. One possibility is that he was instructed to make a sacrifice (for a propitious outcome to the love-meeting?). Thus 24 could begin [δεῖ δὲ θύει]ν, a command that would be fulfilled in 29 κατασφαττ[, and perhaps in 28 ἀποκτ]είνειν, or [προτ]είνειν, which could also refer to an offering of some sort (Henrichs, op. cit. 49 n. 11).

24 ζω ̣ ̣[: either ζωιο[ν (a reference to the animal to be sacrificed: a dove, περιcτερά, sacred to Aphrodite whose aid would thereby be sought, at Charit. 36.25, 39.33, 82.6, 86.12), or ζῶcι(ν) or ζῶcι- or ζώcῃ. However, we do not expect the scribe to write iota adscript, given his practice elsewhere, and the trace after ζω ̣ does not especially suit ο.

25–6 προcτ[: probably πρὸς τ[ὸν Γλαυ|κέτην προ]cήγγελλεν (see 20–21).

26–7 ὁ δὲ προc[. This must be a different person than the giver of the instructions: either the messenger who conveys the instructions, or more likely, Glauketes himself. Thus e.g. ὁ δὲ πρὸς [αὐτὸν ἀπο|πέμψας ὡ]μολόγηcεν.

27 ὡ]μολόγηcεν. Glauketes agrees to do what he is told.

27–8 οὕτω πο ̣[. The thought could then continue οὕτω ποι[ήcειν (or πο}ή[cειν?) καὶ | μέλλειν ἀποκτ]είνειν (or προτ]είνειν).

29 κατασφαττ[: The earliest occurrence of -ττ- instead of -ζ- in this word is Luc. *Sacr.* 12, but the simplex has it since classical times. Once again, the author prefers the Attic form (see above on 6).

30]ετην: very likely another mention of Glauketes. Given the accusative, and in conjunction with ἀπο[, one might conjecture [ὁ δὲ πρὸς τὸν Γλαυκ]έτην ἀπο[cτείλας].

35] ̣υτης ἀγ[: articulation uncertain, whether α]ὐτῆc/-α]ὐτης, or rather e.g. το]ῦ/-το]υ τῆc. In either case, for what follows, ἀγ[γελίας, or less likely, a form of ἀγ[γέλλω, looks promising; cf. 26.

D. OBBINK

IV. KNOWN LITERARY TEXTS

4946. DIONYSIUS HALICARNASSENSIS, *ANTIQUITATES ROMANAE* IV 77–8

100/112(a)   11.2 × 16.8 cm   Third century

Remains of a column of near full width, preceded by line-ends of the preceding column, written along the fibres of a papyrus roll in an informal, upright bookhand. Generous bottom-margin preserved to 5.5 cm. (probably original). On the back, written across the fibres and the other way up, are accounts of meat in a cursive hand of the later second century, scheduled for publication in a later volume.

The papyrus is the first to give the text of Dionysius' *Antiquitates* as witnessed by the medieval manuscripts. P. Ant. I 19 = Mertens–Pack[3] 2211, a fifth-century parchment codex, gives what may be an epitomized version of VIII 38–9 and 44–5, possibly from the shorter version that Photius (*Bibl.* 84) says Dionysius himself made of his lengthy *Antiquitates*, which was still extant in Photius' day, or from an another abridgement later than Dionysius. Unlike P. Ant. I 19, **4946** follows the transmitted text closely, although not without exception, in (relatively short) columns of 21 lines (as reconstructed). Presumably it gave the whole of the fourth book (which would have occupied about 120 columns in this format), since the book-divisions go back to Dionysius himself, who in Hellenistic fashion refers to the end of one book and the beginning of the next at the conclusion of each book. If the papyrus had contained a selection of speeches (cf. LXXI **4810** introd.), for example, or had given Brutus' speech only, the latter would not have begun with the top of a column in this format (as reconstructed). The fortunes of Tarquinius, Lucretia, and Brutus in book IV of the *Antiquitates* would have provided an exciting, dramatic narrative to some Greek readers at Roman Oxyrhynchus.

The hand is an oval version of the Formal Mixed style, with a slight slope to the left: м in four strokes and deep, but basically the same form as N but with an additional diagonal stroke added giving it an unnaturally extended appearance; н has the first upright higher than the second and the cross-stroke, i.e. the shape of a Roman h. The back of є is upright, tall, and only slightly curved. There are several different shapes of ᴧ (one virtually indistinguishable from ᴧ) and of ʏ. Hardly a single stroke in any letter is straight: almost all strokes, including most uprights, show some curvature. The scribe assimilated consonants where expected (ii 5, 10) and tacitly elides a final vowel before a word-initial one, but inconsistently writes *scriptio plena* in 13. Iota adscript is not written in the two places where we can tell. An unusual form of the filler-sign (=) is used to take up space at line-end in col. i, and is once used (i 9) to cancel a letter erroneously written (mis-syllabification?).

Punctuation is by blank space. For a suggestive parallel for the formation of letters, compare *GMAW*[2] no. 62, later second century (assigned), with Latin accounts on the back. **4946** may be assigned to a slightly later stage of development, probably in the third century, by comparison with the hand of P. Vat. Gr. 11 verso = tav. 13 in M. Norsa, *La scrittura letteraria greca dal sec. IV a.C. all'VIII d.C.* (Florence 1939), on the date of which see now A. Tepedino Guerra (ed.), *Il De exilio di Favorino di Arelate* (Rome 2007) 25–6.

   For reports of readings of the mediaeval manuscripts, and for supplementation of lost text *exempli gratia* to illustrate space where appropriate, we have used C. Jacoby's Teubner edition (vol. ii, Leipzig 1888). The papyrus exhibits at least two interesting new variants: a change of word order at ii 11–12, where a word proposed for deletion by Cobet is not present, and another at ii 13, where it omits a superfluous connecting particle (perhaps correctly).

Col. i

```
                                ] . ν              (77)
                                ]
                                ]
                                ]
 5                              ]
                                ] . . .
      c.3 εθιϲμουϲ και νομουϲ την]  δυ=
      ναϲτειαν καταϲχοντα ουτ]  επει
      δη κατεϲχεν οπωϲ δη ποτε]  λα⟦β⟧=
10    βων καλωϲ αυτη και βαϲι]λι
      κωϲ χρωμενον αλλ υπερβε]βλ⟦ . ⟧η
      κοτα παντας υβρει τε και]  πα
      ρανομια τους οπου δη ποτε γ]ενο
      μενους τυραννους αφελε]ϲθαι
15    την εξουϲιαν βεβουλευμε]θα=
```

Col. ii

```
      μεν ημιν χ[ε]ν̣ε̣ϲ[θ]α̣[ι π]ρ̣[ατ]τ̣[οντ      78
      ελευθεριαν τη πατριδι ηϲ ουτε π[ρο
      τερον ημιν εξεγενετο μεταλαβει[ν
      εξ ου Ταρκυνιοϲ την αρχην κατε[ϲ
 5    χεν   ουθ υϲτερον εαν νυν μαλα
      κιϲ[θ]ωμεν εξεϲται   ει μεν ουν̣
```

χρονον ειχον οσον εβουλομην

η προς αγνοουντας εμελλον λε

γειν απασας διεξ[ηλθον] ἀν τ[ας

10   του τυραννου παρα[νο]μιας εφ [αις

ουχ απαξ αλλα πολλακις ην α

πολωλεναι δικαιος   επειδη

δε ο καιρος ον τα πραγματα μο[ι

[δι]δωσι βραχυς εν ω λεγειν μεν

15   ολιγα δει πραττειν δε πολλα και

Col. i

6].‚.‚. : traces of four uprights, the last the shortest, the second to the last the longest, dipping slightly below the line; apparently not any part of ἡμων or (πατ)ριους as transmitted, but of an unattested variant that may have carried over into 7.

9 β has been overwritten by the filler-sign (=).

Col. ii

1 π]ρ[ατ]τ[οντ: the papyrus does not reveal its reading at line-end: πράττοντες AB: πράττοντας Stephanus.

2 ελευθεριαν: with AB: τήν added by Kiessling before ἐλευθερίαν, but not present in the papyrus as judged from space at the end of 1.

10 παρα[νο]μιας: ν is visible on a small detached scrap.

εφ [αις restored *exempli gratia* with AB. However, εφ [αις would have produced a line visibly longer than the surrounding line-ends by several letters, and it is not impossible that the papyrus read ἐφ' ᾗ, sc. generalizing to the singlular παρανομίᾳ, which reading would have conformed at any rate to the expected line-length judged from the surrounding line-ends. The scribe's attempt to keep an even right-hand margin is witnessed by the placement of filler-signs at the end of lines in col. i (lacking in col. ii at the preserved ends of 11, 12, 14 and 15).

11–12 πολλακις ην α|πολωλεναι δικαιος: πολλάκις ἄπασιν εἴη δίκαιος ἀπολωλέναι A: πολλάκις ἄπασι. δίκαιος ἀπολωλέναι B. The papyrus anticipates C. G. Cobet, *Observationes criticae palaeographicae ad Dionysii Halicarnassensis antiquitates romanas* (Leiden 1877) 91, who deleted ἄπασι and εἴη (producing a more direct and succinct formulation than the transmitted version with its deferred ἄπασιν in apposition with αἷς)—although he left δίκαιος standing before ἀπολωλέναι as in the mediaeval witnesses, whereas the papyrus has it afterwards, producing a word order different from that of any of the mediaeval manuscripts.

13 δε ο καιρος: δ' ὅ τε καιρός AB. The papyrus shows *scriptio plena*, and omits τε, possibly correctly: Dionysius in his rhetorical works proscribes excessive use of τε . . . καί.

D. OBBINK

4947. STRABO, *GEOGRAPHICA* V 4.12–13

87/313(b)   fr. 2 3.6 × 7.1 cm   Second/third century

Three fragments (fr. 1 is made up of three smaller scraps) from three columns of a roll; of the first column in fr. 1, there are only exiguous traces. Fr. 2 comes from the top of a column, and preserves 1.3 cm of the upper margin. The intercolumnium measures *c*.2 cm (fr. 1). About 13 lines are lost between frr. 2 and 3. Maas's law may be observed in fr. 1. The writing is along the fibres, on the back of a (tax?) register relative to sheep; of this document there are only exiguous remains, and no date is preserved, but the hand is a good second-century cursive.

The hand, informal in character and with occasional cursive features (e.g. κατα in fr. 2.1), is a distant relative of the 'Severe Style'. Letters often touch and are sometimes ligatured with each other. I should be inclined to place it in the second half of the second century or only slightly later; compare P. Fuad Univ. 19 = *GLH* 15b of 145/6, or the more pointed VI **852** = *GMAW*² 31, assigned with good reason to the late second or early third century.

There are several high points (frr. 1.11, 12, 2.2, 3.2). Elision is effected tacitly in the only case that can be verified (fr. 1.15). Iota adscript was inserted at a later stage, high in the line, in the two cases that require it (fr. 3.3, 10). There is one itacism of common kind (fr. 3.4).

Only three other papyri of Strabo have been published, all of them from Oxyrhynchus: XLIX **3447** (LDAB 3976), LXV **4459** (+ PL/III 294A, ed. *Eirene* 32 (1996) 96–7; LDAB 3979), and P. Köln I 8 (LDAB 3978). The Vatican palimpsest (LDAB 3980) is another witness from Late Antiquity. The text of **4947** is not transmitted by any of them.

The text of the papyrus has been collated with the edition of S. Radt, *Strabons Geographika* ii (2003). There are some textual points of interest: a new reading, possibly corrupt (fr. 1.9); an omission, most probably inadvertent (fr. 3.4 ff.); and agreements with the MSS against modern conjectures (fr. 3.1–2, 3–4). Purely orthographical variants and certain modern conjectures are not reported in the notes.

The line-divisions in frr. 2–3 are by no means certain.

Fr. 1

```
. .     .     .
]      τ[ε]ς [Cαβινοι πολυν χρονον          (4.12)
]      προς [τους Ομβρικους ηυξαν
]λ     το καθ[απερ των Ελληνων
]      τινε[ς τα γενομενα τω ετει
]   5  τουτω [καθιερωσαι νικη
```

```
]        ϲα[ντ]εϲ δε [των γενομε
]        νω[ν τ]α με[ν κατεθυϲαν
]        τα [δε κ]αθιε[ρωϲαν αφορι
].       αϲ δ[ε γε]νομ[ενηϲ ειπε
.  . 10  τ]ιϲ ωϲ εχρη[ν κ]α[θιερωϲαι
         κα]ι τα τεκνα· οι δ [εποιηϲαν
         το]υτο· και τουϲ [γενομε
         ν]ουϲ τοτε παιδ[αϲ Αρεωϲ
         επ]εφημι[ϲα]ν [ανδρωθεν
    15   τα]ϲ δ εϲ[τειλαν ειϲ
              .        .
```

Fr. 2

```
         ριθμο]ν κατα την [των δειπ      (4.13)
         νων α]ξιαν· Ανν[ιβα δ εξ εν
         δοϲεωϲ] λαβοντοϲ α[υτουϲ
         δεξαμ]ενοι χειμαδ[ιοιϲ την
    5    ϲτρατι]αν ουτωϲ ε[ξεθηλυ
         ναν ται]ϲ ηδοναιϲ ω[ϲθ ο Αν
         νιβαϲ ε]φη νικων [κινδυ
         νευειν] επι τοιϲ ε[χθροιϲ γε
         νεϲθαι γ]υναικα[ϲ αντι των
    10   ανδρων το]υϲ ϲτρ[ατιωταϲ
              .        .
```

Fr. 3

```
              .        .        .
         ϲ]αυνι[τιν μεχρι Φρεντα
         νω]ν· επ[ι μεν τη Τυρρη
         νικ]η'θαλα[ττη το των Πι
         κε]ντε[ινων εθνοϲ υπο Ρωμαι
    5    ω]ν μετ[ωκιϲμενον ειϲ τον
         Π]οϲειδω[νιατην κολπον οϲ
         νυν Πα[ιϲτανοϲ καλειται
         κ]αι η πο[λιϲ η Ποϲειδωνια
         Π]αιϲτοϲ [εν μεϲω τω κολ
    10   π]ω'κει[μενη ϲυβαριται
         με]ν ουν [επι θαλαττη
              .        .
```

Fr. 1

2 Ὀμβρικουϲ, restored with the MSS, would suit the space. Radt prints Ὄμβρουϲ, conjectured by Dittenberger, perhaps with good reason.

9 γε]νομ[ενηϲ: γενηθείϲηϲ MSS. The reading of the papyrus may be an influence from the earlier τὰ γενόμενα and τῶν γενομένων. In any case, the sense is the same.

Fr. 2

1–2 δειπνων is restored with the MSS. Of the conjectures recorded by Radt, only ϲυνδείπνων (Bekker) could perhaps be accommodated in the space available.

5 ουτωϲ: γ corrected from τ.

6 ω[ϲθ. The minimal trace does not immediately point to an ω, but there is no other evidence for a textual discrepancy here.

9 αντι των restored with AX by reason of space: ἀντί BC: ἀντ' Plan., Cobet (printed by Radt).

Fr. 3

1–2 [μεχρι Φρεντανω]ν is restored with the MSS (it would suit the space), but has systematically been emended or excised by editors, lastly by Radt.

3–4 Πικε]ντε[ινων is the reading of the MSS (Πικεντίνων). Modern editions print Πικέντων, an emendation (Kramer).

4 Between Πικεντίνων and ὑπὸ Ῥωμαίων, the received text has ἔθνοϲ οἰκεῖ μικρὸν ἀπόϲπαϲμα τῶν ἐν τῷ Ἀδρίᾳ Πικεντίνων, which is not present here. The omission is very probably due to a scribe's *saut du même au même*. I have considered but would exclude that the omission indicates that μικρὸν . . . Πικεντίνων is a later interpolation; there is no space for the words ἔθνοϲ οἰκεῖ in the break, and if one of them was omitted we would have to reckon with a different text.

5 I have restored *exempli gratia* μετ[ωκιϲμενον, an emendation, instead of the MSS' erroneous μετωκιϲμένων, in assimilation to Ῥωμαίων.

9–10 [εν μεϲω τω κολπ]ωι κει[μενη with ABC: ἐν μέϲῳ κειμένη τῷ κόλπῳ X.

N. GONIS

4948. ACHILLES TATIUS, *LEUCIPPE AND CLITOPHON* II 37.8–10, 38.4

24 3B.74/G(b)   5.8 × 13.5 cm   Third century

Parts of two columns written across the fibers of a papyrus roll. The bottom margin beneath col. i measures 2 cm, and the intercolumnium ranges from 0.9 to 1.8 cm on account of the irregular right-hand margin of col. i. On the back (scheduled for publication in vol. LXXVI), and across the fibres, are verse beginnings, identifiable from diction and the presence of a *coronis* as lyric poetry, written in a different but contemporaneous hand.

With an average of 24 letters per line, the number of lines per column may be calculated at 39–40. This would mean that the right-hand column was the last of the book, with the missing text following the preserved end of col. ii filling out the column to the bottom (in 10–12 lines). By extension, 18–20 lines must be missing from the tops of the columns. If this columniation were maintained for the whole work, a little over 217 columns would be required for the whole of the work, in eight books as transmitted in the medieval tradition. If book 2 circulated independently in this format, it would comprise a short roll of approximately 32 columns. (See the further discussion of W. A. Johnson, *Bookrolls and Scribes in Oxyrhynchus* (Toronto 2004) 145).

The hand is a relatively regular, upright version of the Formal Mixed variety or 'Severe Style', assignable to the third century. Letters are carefully formed, with occasional connection between letters and some shading. ω lacks a central element, as frequently in the developed phase of this type. The descenders of φ and γ are often given a stylized swerve to the left, while in other letters (ι, η, ν, τ) vertical strokes are made with orthogonal precision. The hand is precise and deliberate, but uneven in places.

Lectional signs are scarce: one apostrophe separating double consonants (i 2 γ]λωτ'ται)—a practice that only becomes common in the third century (*GMAW²* 11 with n. 50)—and a superscript dash representing final ν at line-end (i 6). A faint trace above the η of φιλημ[ατι in i 18 may be an acute accent. The scribe does not write iota adscript (i 11, ii 6). There is one iotacistic spelling (ii 6 Αφρο]δειτη).

Seven papyrus fragments of Achilles Tatius have been previously published, three of which come from Oxyrhynchus (for slight redatings of some of the hands, see G. Cavallo, in O. Pecere, A. Stramaglia (eds.), *La letteratura di consumo nel mondo greco-latino* (Cassino 1996) 16, 36–8): VII **1014** (early III) = Π⁷ (preserving IV 14.2–5), identified by M. Gronewald, *ZPE* 22 (1976) 14–17; X **1250** + LVI **3837** (II/III) = Π¹ (II 7–8, 2–3, 9), identified by E. G. Turner and P. J. Parsons as fragments of a multiple-roll set; LVI **3836** (early II) = Π⁵ (III 21–3); P. Schubart 30 (III) = Π² (II 2, 3–5), republished by G. Poethke, *APF* 48.1 (2002) 1–5; and P. Mil.Vogl. III 124 (II) = Π³ (VI 14–15); the Cologne/Duke papyrus (P. Colon. inv. 901 + P. Duk. inv. 722) (III) = Π⁴ (III 17–21, 23–4), republished by W. H. Willis, *GRBS* 31 (1990) 73–102. None of these papyri overlaps with **4948** or matches its hand. **4948** is the third papyrus to witness Book II.

For reports of readings from the medieval manuscripts, and for supplementation of the text *exempli gratia* to illustrate spacing and alignment in the papyrus, we have drawn on the Budé edition of J.-P. Garnaud (Paris 1991); for a more detailed exposition of the manuscript tradition, see the introduction of E. Vilborg (ed.), *Achilles Tatius: Leucippe and Clitophon* (Göteborg 1955). **4948** offers an improved reading in ii 6 (cυμπλοκάc for περιπλοκάc of the medieval manuscripts). The transmitted text cannot be faithfully accommodated in the lacunae of i 8–9, which suggests that the papyrus had readings different from the medieval manuscripts at this point. It is also unclear whether the omission of καί in i 16 is accidental or conceals a different text. Otherwise, the papyrus generally agrees with the majority of manuscripts, except in i 12 where it shares the contracted form χειλῶν solely with M. Note that codex D contains only excerpts from book 2, which do not include chapters 37–8 (see Vilborg, op. cit., pp. xxiv–xxv).

Col. i

.   .   .   .   .

     ] φ[ιλο]υ[cα   (2.37)

και μαινεται αι δε γ]λωτ᾿ται του

τον τον χρονον φοιτωcι]ν αλλη

λαιc ειc ομιλιαν και ω]c δυναν

5 ται βιαζονται κακειν]αι φιλειν

cυ δε μειζονα ποιειc τ]ην ηδονη(ν)

ανοιγων τα φιληματα π]ρ[ο]c δε το

     η] γυνη γενο

μενη (. . . . .) αcθμ]αινειν

10 υπο καυματωδουc ηδο]νηc το δε

αcθμα cυν πνευματι ερ]ωτικω

μεχρι των του cτοματοc χειλω[ν

αναθορον cυντυγχαν]ει πλαν[ω

μενω τω φιληματι και] ζητο[υντι

15 καταβηναι κατω αναc]τρεφο[ν

τε cυν τω αcθματι το φιλ]ημα μ̣[ι

χθεν επεται και βαλλει] τ̣ην καρ[δι

αν η δε ταραχθειcα τω] φιλημ[ατι

παλλεται ει δε μη τοιc] cπλαγ[χ

20 νοιc ην δεδεμενη ηκολ]ο̣υθη[cεν

αν και ανειλκυcεν αυτην αν]ω το[ιc

Col. ii

.   .   .   .   .

κ̣αι προ τ[ηc εν Αφροδειτη cυμπλο   (2.38)

κηc και ε̣[ν παλαιcτρα cυμπεcειν

και φαν[ερωc περιχυθηναι και

ουκ εχου[cιν αιcχυνην αι περιπλοκαι

5 και ου μα[λθαccει ταc ἐν Αφρο

δειτη cυμ̣[πλοκαc υγροτητι cαρ

κων αλλ [αντιτυπει προc αλλη

λα τ]α [cωματα και περι τηc

.   .   .   .   .

Col. i

 5 βιαζονται κακειν]αι: so WM V G F: κἀκεῖναι βιάζονται E.

 6 ηδονη(ν). The scribe wrote the final stroke of the first N over the first bar of H, perhaps to save space at the end of the line and so conform to the notional margin.

8 π]ρ[ο]ϲ . . . αϲθμ]αινειν. Restoration of the transmitted text in 8 (τέρμα αὐτῆϲ τῆϲ Ἀφροδίτηϲ) would result in a significantly longer line. Cobet had already expressed unease with αὐτῆϲ, which is unnecessary at this point, and proposed αὐτό instead. It is possible that αὐτῆϲ was omitted by the papyrus, which would fit the space nicely.

8–9 γενο||[μενη with WM VE: γινομένη G F. Indeed, the aorist is preferable, given the sense and syntax of the passage as preserved in the manuscript tradition, particularly in light of πέφυκεν. We cannot tell whether or not πέφυκεν was present in **4948**, but it is unlikely on grounds of space that **4948** agreed precisely with the manuscript tradition at this point (see next note); in any case a word similar in meaning and syntax to πέφυκεν is clearly required.

9 Conversely from 8 (see note), this line is slightly too short for the text as transmitted, so that the papyrus had either a (longer) variant word or an additional short word in this line.

12 χειλω[ν with M: χειλέων W VGE F. The final trace is clearly the left hand part of ω and is incompatible with ε.

16–17 το φιλ]ημα μ[ιχθεν. The papyrus omits the universally transmitted καί before μιχθέν (μ is virtually certain and is missing only the second upright). Coordination is necessary between ἀναϲτρέφον and μιχθέν. If the omission of καί is not simply accidental, the papyrus may have instead had τε (i.e. θ᾽) following μιχθέν as an alternative means of coordination.

21 αν]ω: omitted by WM.

Col. ii

1–2 και . . . [ϲυμπολ]οκηϲ: omitted by G.

5–6 [εν Αφρο]δειτη: omitted by G.

6 ϲυμ[: so the papyrus, the μ being more likely than ν; spacing supports the supposition that the papyrus read ϲυμπλοκάϲ: περιπλοκάϲ WM D VGE F. The new reading of the papyrus avoids the close repetition of περιπλοκαί at the end of the previous sentence (4) and echoes the expression τῆϲ ἐν Ἀφροδίτῃ ϲυμπλοκῆϲ five lines above. The corruption of the manuscripts must have been influenced by the preceding occurrence of περιπλοκαί seven words previously.

7–8 αλλ κτλ.: omitted by G.

D. OBBINK

Y. TRNKA-AMRHEIN

4949. AELIUS ARISTIDES, *PANATHENAICUS* 390, 392

5 1B.56/C(1)a	6.6 × 5.1 cm	Sixth century

A scrap from a papyrus codex, broken on all sides. Approximately 76 lines are lost between the last line of the ↓ side and the first of the →; the most economical hypothesis for the layout is that there were two columns per page of *c*.25 lines each, with a written height of *c*.18 cm and a width of *c*.7 cm. If we posited an intercolumnium of 2 cm, and reckoned with side margins totaling 5 cm (an arbitrary figure), we should have a page of *c*.21 × *c*.23 cm, which would bring it into Turner's Group 4 of papyrus codices (*Typology* 16); but note that most examples of this group are earlier in date than **4949**.

The hand is an example of the 'Alexandrian Majuscule', to be assigned to the later sixth century; it is fairly similar to the earliest dated specimen of this style,

P. Grenf. II 112 = *GBEBP* 37 of 577. The contrast between broad and narrow letters, which increases as the style matures, is not pronounced. The extremities of most vertical strokes are slightly thickened, but otherwise ornamentation is sparse. There are not very many papyri of non-Christian authors written in this script: see P. Bingen 23 introd. (p. 126 with n. 4).

There are some lectional signs: diaeresis, in the form of a short dash, over initial iota (→4), and a high point (→3).

This is the first papyrus of Aelius Aristides identified in the Oxyrhynchus collection (LXXII **4854** comes from one of the *spuria*), and only the fifth papyrus of this author to be published; see the overview in P. Bingen 24 introd. Three of these five papyri preserve portions of the *Panathenaicus* (the others are P. Ant. III 144 and P. Mich. inv. 6651; neither overlaps with **4949**).

Collated with the edition of Lenz in F. W. Lenz, C. A. Behr, *P. Aelii Aristidis Opera quae exstant omnia* i.1 (1976). There are no new readings.

↓

```
                  .     .     .     .
      οιμαι νομ]ιζου[ϲα                                    (§390)
      των] μεν οι[κετων
      ου τουϲ ευπ[ορω
      τατουϲ αλλα τ[ουϲ
  5   πιϲτοτατουϲ [βελ
      τιϲτου]ϲ νομιζ[ειν
      των δε ελευ]θε[ρων
                  .     .     .     .
```

→

```
                  .     .     .     .
      ].[
      εξε]ϲτιν [ωϲ αν τιϲ                                  (§392)
      βου]ληται· τι[μαϲθαι
      δε] και ϊϲχνειν ο[υ
  5   τοι]ϲ βουλομενο[ιϲ
      εϲ]τιν αλλα τοιϲ [εξ
      ητα]ϲ[με]ν[οιϲ και γαρ
                  .     .     .     .
```

↓

3–4 ευπ[ορω]τατουϲ with OPh: εὐπορωτέρουϲ U.
5–6 [βελτιϲτου]ϲ restored with OPh by reason of space: βελτίουϲ U.

N. GONIS

V. SUBLITERARY TEXTS

4950. *Post Eventum* Predictions for AD 69–70

103/154(b)   9.1 × 9.5 cm   Second century

The fragment preserves the upper parts of two columns, though of the second only a few letters from the beginnings of lines remain. The upper margin was at least 2 cm in height. The hand is regular, fluent, medium-sized, and rather informal, with a slight slant to the right. The right margin is generally tidily aligned. Letters are often ligatured, and towards the end of the line the writing tends to be rather cramped. ⲁ is written in a single sequence, and has quite a large loop. There are no accents or breathings, nor any punctuation; initial trema is regularly added (3, 6, 7, 10); iota adscript is not written. The itacizing spelling λειμανχου[μενοι (9) should be noted. Though the number of letters missing at the start of the line can be securely established only in 3, highly probable supplements in 8 and 10 indicate that the scribe began the line progressively further to the left ('Maas's Law'). The script appears comparable to the hands of VI **853** = Roberts, *GLH* 17a (his plate shows col. xvii, not col. xvi, and the transcript there must be ignored), a commentary on Thucydides Book 2, for which a *terminus post quem* is provided by one of the three documents on the verso of which it is written (VI **986** [131/2]), and XLIX **3452**, a Greek–Latin glossary; both these sub-literary texts are dated by their editors to the second century. The back is blank.

The text forecasts the arrival of Vespasian in Egypt, a further event dated on the 17th day after the rising of Sirius, i.e. early August 70, most probably his departure for Rome, and the sack of Jerusalem by Titus. No personal names are given, but the striking description 'a ruler with a mongoose's eyes' recalls Suetonius' reference to Vespasian's characteristically strained expression (*Ves.* 20), *vultu veluti nitentis*; on Vespasian's looks see further B. Levick, *Vespasian* (London and New York 1999) 208. Eubulus' riddle (F107 K–A) suggests that the mongoose's prominent eyes were a commonplace. The image is rather favourable to Vespasian in view of the animal's skill in dispatching snakes and other noxious vermin (cf. Ps.-Oppian, *C.* 3.407–48). In an Egyptian context the mongoose's association with Horus should not be overlooked; see further *Lexikon der Ägyptologie* 3.122 f. s.v. *Ichneumon*.

Vespasian took as his *dies imperii* 1 July, the day of his acclamation by the Egyptian legions, but we do not know when he actually arrived in Egypt, nor when he left, though he was still there on 21 June 70, at the time of the Capitol's refoundation (Tac. *Hist.* 4.53.2). No chronological conclusions can be based on Dio's report (66.8.1) that when Vespasian entered Alexandria the Nile rose in a day a palm higher than usual. No Roman emperor had visited Egypt since Augustus, and Vespasian's prolonged stay in Alexandria must have raised high hopes. It is not easy to suggest what the writer might have thought worth dating precisely to the seventeenth day after the rising of the Dog Star (l. 4), the beginning of the Egyptian year, if not some action of Vespasian's. The traditional date for the rising of Sirius was 25 Epeiph, equivalent to 19 July; early August would be as good a time as any to start on a voyage from Alexandria to Rome. The precision of this item in the prediction is interesting and suggests that there was some significance to the date, but it does not, of course, guarantee its truth. If the fall of Jerusalem is to be dated 8 September (see Griffin, *CAH* [2] xi 4, Levick, op. cit. 40–42), our writer takes rather a generous view of the period covered by the rising of Sirius; the destruction of the temple almost a month earlier would better fit this chronological detail, and it would not be surprising if a prophet's vision merged the two disasters. We should not see evidence of anti-Jewish feeling in this reference to the city's fall; the successful conclusion of this campaign was vitally important to justify Vespasian's bid for power. It is interesting that βαϲιλεύϲ is used of both Vespasian and Titus. For the assumption that they were equal rulers, we may compare Pliny, *NH* 3.66, 7.162, and Josephus, *Vita* 359, 361; for a more precise view of Titus' position, see Griffin, op. cit., 17–18, Levick, op. cit. 184–8.

Our sources report a proliferation of prophecies relating to Vespasian's accession. Thus Suetonius (*Ves.* 4): *Percrebuerat Oriente toto vetus et constans opinio, esse in fatis ut eo tempore Judaea profecti rerum potirentur. id de imperatore Romano, quantum postea eventu paruit, praedictum Judaei ad se trahentis rebellarunt*; cf. Tac. *Hist.* 5.13.2, Josephus, *BJ* 6.312–3. While it might be expected that predictions of Flavian rule, whether genuine or *post eventum*, would have ceased to be of interest at any rate by the end of the first century, the well-documented tendency for omen literature to survive far beyond the situations to which the predictions originally related (see Alexander Jones on LXV **4471**) makes it unsurprising that this text was judged worth copying in the second century.

Some sort of introduction to our piece seems needed, and presumably preceded; we cannot tell whether the prediction extended beyond col. ii. Lucian's Alexander (*Alex.* 27) kept ὑπομνήματα of his oracles, and he substituted more appropriate verses for prognostications to which events failed to correspond. This could more easily have been done if his prophecies were recorded on separate sheets of papyrus than if they were collected in one or more rolls.

I am indebted to Dr Miriam Griffin and Dr M. L.West for their help.

Col. i

] . ναιρεσει . [.] . ερωνβασιλεων
] . ϲελευϲε . αιειϲαιγυπτονβασι
]ϲϊχνευμονοϲοφθαλμουϲεχων
]ομικοϲτηδειζκυνοϲαϲτρου
5] . ϲ . ϲαιγυπτουκαιεϲταιβασιλευϲ
]αϲοϲκαθελειτομεγαϊεροντο
] . ουμενονϊεροϲολυματηαυτη
] . επιτοληκαιπαρεμβολαϲεπι
] . ειαπολουνταιγαρλειμανχου
10]δεαυτουτα . . . . [.] . (.)¨ . . (.) . .
]. [

Col. ii

ν[
ο[
μ[
ε[
τ[
φο[
κα . [
ϲτ . [
τη[
αϲ . [
ολο[
[.] . α . [

Col. i

. . . .] ἀναιρέϲειϲ [ἑ]τέρων βαϲιλέων
. . .] ϲελεύϲεται εἰϲ Αἴγυπτον βαϲι-
λεὺ]ϲ ἰχνεύμονοϲ ὀφθαλμοὺϲ ἔχων
. . . .]ομικοϲ, τῇ δὲ ιζ κυνὸϲ ἄϲτρου
5 . . . .]οϲιϲ Αἰγύπτου καὶ ἔϲται βαϲιλεὺϲ
. . .]αϲ ὃϲ καθελεῖ τὸ μέγα ἱερὸν τὸ
. . . .]λούμενον Ἱεροϲόλυμα τῇ αὐτῇ
κυνὸ]ϲ ἐπιτολῇ καὶ παρεμβολὰϲ ἐπι-
. . .]ϲει. ἀπολοῦνται γὰρ λειμανχού-
10 μενοι .]δε αὐτοῦ ταβο . . [.] . (.)ϊ . (.) . ν
c.6   ] . [

Col. i

1] . , right extension of ᴀ or ʌ   ι . , left arc, like back of ϲ   ] . , ᴦ or ᴛ   2] . , dot at line level   ε . , horizontal bar of ᴛ   5] . , right half of o; ᴘ also possible   ϲ . , faded traces of upright   7] . , lower part of right leg of ʌ; ᴀ also possible   8] . , contours of rounded letter   9] . , short horizontal base compatible with ϲ or ε   10 a . . . . , first, small loop like that of ʙ or ᴘ; second, upper semicircle thickening at the left; third, top of upright; fourth, top of upright touched by a long horizontal from the right   ] . (.)¨ . . (.) . ., two dots level with letter tops; top of upright below trema; high horizontal (ᴛ?); two thick traces level with letter tops (ʜ?); upper arc; ɴ or ᴍ   11] . , speck

Col. ii

7 . [, foot of upright   8 . [, upright, possibly with a join from the right near mid-height   10 . [, left half of ᴛ   12] . , ᴨ or o   . [, small trace about mid-height

'After the destruction of other rulers there will come to Egypt a ruler with a mongoose's eyes . . . On the seventeenth day after the Dog Star's rising . . . of Egypt. And there will be a . . . ruler who will destroy the great holy place, the famous (?) Jerusalem, at the same rising of the Dog Star, and he will (set up) military camps. For they will perish from hunger . . .'

1 μετά suggests itself at the start of the line.

2] . ϲ ἐλεύϲεται or] . ϲελεύϲεται?

3 κερτ]ομικόϲ (M. L. West; cf. Suet. *Ves.* 23)? οἰκον]ομικόϲ with an itacizing spelling (ἰκονο-), 'thrifty, frugal', would suit Vespasian's reputed parsimony, much resented in Egypt (cf. Suet. *Ves.* 16, Dio 66.8.2–6).

5 .]οϲιϲ: perhaps κάθα]ρϲιϲ or a compound of -δ]οϲιϲ (i.e. a noun governing Αἰγύπτου rather than a verb)? Just before Αἰγύπτου, what might be taken as a suprascript letter inserted before A, seems to be rather the displaced top of ᴀ.

6]αϲ: νεανί]αϲ would probably be too long.

7 θρυ]λούμενον M. L. West (cf. Tac. *H.* 5.2.1 *famosae urbis supremum diem tradituri sumus*).

8 παρεμβολάϲ: an increased Roman military presence was required to maintain order after the sack of Jerusalem.

8–9 ἐπι|[στή]ςει would satisfy space and sense.

9–10 λειμανχού|[μενοι: read λιμαγχούμενοι. Famine is a recurrent theme in Josephus' account of the siege; but Titus did not simply wait for starvation to deliver the city into his hands. It is awkward to take this as the first word of a clause of which δέ is the second; more likely Titus is the subject of what follows, and we should supply ὁ] δέ. Of the letters marked as doubtful in 10 only the tops remain, and it is not clear how to combine the traces.

S. R. WEST

4951. COMMENTARY ON A POETIC TEXT

22 3B.14/F(14–16)a   7.0 × 12.3 cm   First century
                                                                      Plate VIII

Twenty-three lines from the upper part of a column plus slight traces of the first letters of the first three lines of the following column. 1.2 cm of the top margin is preserved, with an intercolumnium of *c*.1 cm. In 1–8, where supplements of line beginnings are certain, quoted lemmata project about one letter-space into the left margin (although 10–12 and 14 seem to be aligned with 1, 4–5, and 8, and there are great uncertainties about 9 and 13). The back is blank.

The script is a medium-sized, upright, rounded book-hand, roughly bilinear (except for the long ascenders and descenders of φ, large ʒ, ρ protruding below, ι sometimes extending above or below the line, and occasionally high and tiny ο), with broad ᴧ, м (mostly deep and well rounded), and ω, but rather narrow ε and sometimes narrow oval ο (in two strokes). There is a marked mixture of cursive elements, and several letters are written in two shapes: triangular ᴀ besides a round and more cursive one; broad and rounded ε with long often detached central stroke (sometimes ligatured with the next letter) besides the common cursive type; κ with slightly detached diagonal strokes besides the rounded and cursive type executed in two movements; four-stroke м besides the type with central elements shaped by a curve (but between these two types there is not a clear-cut contrast); γ in two movements, with rightwards loop from which the upright departs, besides the type with rounded cup. ᴧ projects its right-hand diagonal over the apex; the central stroke of н is high, and the diagonal of ν sometimes almost horizontal. τ is split or even loopy, and the left extremity of its crossbar sometimes presents a hook. Hooks are also to be seen on the foot of н, ι, π, τ, γ, and φ. There are sequences up to five letters all in ligature. Some features appear to be quite early and are found in Roberts, *GLH* 9a (petition of 4–7 BC), although much less ligatured; cf. also XIX **2214**, Call. *Aitia*, assigned to the first century BC / first century AD. **4951**, slightly later by comparison, may be assigned to the first century AD.

Lemmata and commentary are usually separated by dicolon and blank space (4, 5, 8, 9, and 16; cf. 3, where dicolon occurs at line-end and therefore blank space is not needed). In one case (16) perhaps change of speaker is marked (although dicolon here apparently written by another hand, with different spacing). Long *ι* is spelled *ει* (11).

The commentary (on an unknown, apparently poetic text) is of an elementary nature, giving basic explanation of rare forms or words: *τετύκοντο* (2 f.), *βουcτάτιδοc* (5 ff.), *μυθιήταιc* (8 ff.). At least one, and probably two of these explanations are incorrect (see 1–4 and 4–8 nn.). For illustration the commentary cites Homer (1 ff.) and a new fragment of Sophron (14 ff.). If the reconstruction tentatively proposed below for 8–22 is correct, this fragment is further commented on in a note referring to Likymnios the mythical king of Argos (less likely the poet).

From the lemmata neither the contents nor the genre of the commented text can be determined with certainty, although it seems to be metrical. Two lemmata are preserved almost completely, but hardly form a continuous text. They would suit either a dactylo-iambic lyric metre or a comic trimeter (*ἐγὼ μὲν ἄρτι βουcτάτιδοc* ⟨× – ‿ –⟩ / *φίλοιc παρὰ μυθιήταιc* ⟨– ‿ –⟩, or *ἐ. μ. ἄ. β.* ⟨× –⟩ *φ.* / *π. μ.* or *ἐ. μ. ἄ. β.* ⟨× – ‿ – / × – ‿ – × – ‿ – × – ‿ – × –⟩ *φ.* / *π. μ.*, avoiding the verse with caesura; see M. L. West, *Greek Metre* (Oxford 1982) 88). If *βουcτάτιδοc* (5 with n.) conceals a Doric form, as the commentator would have it (probably wrongly), this would speak in favour of the first alternative. Otherwise, the style of the lemmata favours comedy. In 8 the restoration *μυ|θι⟨ή⟩θαιc* seems inevitable (see below 8–12 nn.). If this is a reference to the Samian revolutionary party, one might guess that the text, if comic, comes from Crates' *Samioi*, a play possibly referring to the Samian revolt in 423/2 BC. Possibly the speaker (in a military context?, see below 8–12 nn.) applies the name *μυθιῆται* to the Samians in general.

For the female speakers in Sophron and further on the transmission of his fragments see J. Hordern, *Sophron's Mimes* (Oxford 2004), reprinting (with some updating) an abbreviated version of Kassel–Austin's text and critical apparatus in *Poetae Comici Graeci* i; cf. Kaibel, *Comicorum Graecorum fragmenta* i.1 (1899); A. Olivieri, *Frammenti della commedia greca e del mimo nella Sicilia e nella Magna Grecia: Parte seconda* (1930, 1947²); J. Rusten–I. C. Cunningham, *Theophrastus: Characters; Herodas; Mimes; Sophron and Other Mime Fragments* (2002). Sophron has surfaced elsewhere in the papyri, most notably PSI IX 1214 (fragment of a mime) and P. Herc. 1014 (quotations of S. by Demetrius Lacon).

Col. i	Col. ii	Col. i
]. οιητηcαυταρεπειπ . [	.　　.	ὁ] ποιητήc· "αὐτὰρ ἐπεὶ πα[ύ-
]cαντοπονου . ετυκοντο	[	cαντο πόνου τετύκοντο
]τεδαιτατουτεcτινητοι:	[	τε δαῖτα". τουτέcτιν ἤτοι
]. αcαντο: εγωμεναρτι	[.].[	ἐ]δάcαντο. **ἐγὼ μὲν ἄρτι**
5　]. υcτατιδοc: βουcτατι	[	5　**β]ουcτάτιδοc·** βουcτάτι-

	] . οϲλεγειτην . ταϲιντην	[		δοϲ λέγει τὴν ϲτάϲιν τὴν
	]ωνβοωνουοιβουϲι	[		τ]ῶν βοῶν οὗ οἱ βοῦϲ ἵ-
	] . αντ . ι: φιλοιϲπαραμυ	κ[		ϲ] τανται. **φίλοιϲ παρὰ μυ-**
	] . αιϲ: τοιϲεκτηϲαυτηϲ	μ[		**θι⟨ή⟩]ταιϲ**· τοῖϲ ἐκ τῆϲ αὐτῆϲ
10	] . ξεωϲμοιουϲινοιϲει	[	10	τ]άξεώϲ μοι οὖϲιν οἷϲ εἰ-
	]θαμενομειλειντογαρ	. .		ώ]θαμεν ὁμ{ε}ιλεῖν. τὸ γὰρ
	] . θιζεινεπιτ . [			μ]υθίζειν ἐπὶ τ . [
	] . θαιτιθεαϲιν[			]ϲθαι τιθέαϲιν[
	] . φρον . μιμο . [			Ϲ]ώφρονι μιμου[
15	] . ϲτινγυναικεϲπο . . . [		15	]εϲτιν γυναῖκεϲ· "ποιου[
	] . . . ϲ . υθ . ζοντι: τοι[			] . ταϲ μυθίζοντι;" "τοι[
	] . . [. . .] . ταϲεβα . . ε[			] . . [. . .] . ταϲ ἔβαϲκε[. . . ".
	] . ιουτο . δε[			τ]οιοῦτοϲ δε[
	]οφητηϲηλθε . [			]οφήτηϲ ἦλθεν
20	] . υποτουλικυ		20	]ω ὑπὸ τοῦ Λικυ-
	] . φθενταϲπα[			μνίου c.3]. φθένταϲ πα[.]
	]νοτιτροπ . ν			]νοτι τρόπον
	] .			].

Col. i

1] ., faded remains of crossbar   . [, remains of small left-hand arc?   2 υ . ε, lower half of upright   4] ., lower extremity of descender?   5] ., extremely tiny dot in lower part of writing space   6] ., extremely tiny dot in lower part of writing space   ν . τ, vertical tiny trace in lower part of writing space   8] ., part of right-hand of crossbar in ligature with following α   τ . ι, remains of small bottom arc?   9] ., either Γ or Τ after loss of left-hand half of crossbar   10] ., descender in ligature with following ξ   12] ., small loop on tip of upper half of upright; 1 mm farther, tiny dot at line-level   τ . [, slightly curvilinear upright that may belong to left-hand arc   13] ., two tiny horizontal traces in upper part of writing space and at line-level respectively, possibly upper and lower extremities of a left-hand arc   14] ., upper half of descender (?) slightly curvilinear, possibly upper half of right-hand arc   ν . [, lower half of upright   μο . [, diagonal stroke slightly descending from left to right, whose lower extremity is in vertical alignment with tiny dot lying at mid-height   15] ., tiny diagonal trace, descending from left to right, in upper part of writing space, possibly belonging to top of left-hand arc; slightly below, 0.5 mm farther, right-hand extremity of horizontal at mid-height in ligature with following ϲ   πο . . . [, first, foot of upright with rightwards hook; second, horizontal trace just above line-level; third, extremely tiny dot at line-level   16] . . ., first, remains of left-hand arc; second, upright slightly curvilinear with rightwards convexity/arc; third, upper half lower extremity of descender   ϲ ., tip of upright   θ ., trace at line-level   17] . ., first, tiny trace in upper part of writing space; second, horizontal stroke in upper part of writing space   ] ., upper and lower extremity of left-hand arc   βα . ., first, lower half of left-hand arc? second, two short roughly horizontal strokes parallel to each other lying respectively in upper part of writing space and at line-level   18] ., bottom arc; in vertical alignment with its middle very tiny dot lying in upper part of writing space   το . ., extremely tiny and

blurred traces at line-level   19 θϵ‚‚ lower half of upright with tiny leftwards hook   20]‚, upright with leftwards lower extremity   21]‚, extremely tiny trace in upper part of writing space   22 τροπ‚, scanty remains of left-hand arc at mid-height   23]‚[, tiny trace in upper part of writing space, possibly tip of upright

Col. ii

4]‚, tiny diagonal trace, ascending from left to right, in upper part of writing space

'. . . as Homer (says): "After they finished the work and got the feast ready" (*Il.* 1.467 etc.). This is indeed instead of (saying) "they divided".

I, on the one hand, just now of an ox-stopping (one): By 'ox-stopping' he means the stopping of the oxen where the ox stands.

In rhetors who are our friends: These seem to me to be from the same rank as those with whom we are accustomed to converse. For, to utter . . . they place . . . by Sophron . . . represent(ed in a mime) . . . women . . . . A: "What kind (of people) do they call [x]?" B: "Did anyone speak ill (of such people as) [x]?" . . . such a [pro]phet came . . . by Likymnios . . . those (m.) speaking . . . manner . . .'

1 ὁ] ποιητής: sc. Homer.

1–3 "αὐτὰρ ἐπεὶ πα[ύ]||cαντο πόνου τετύκοντο | τε δαῖτα". *Il.* 1.467 (also 2.430 etc.) is quoted, but for what purpose is unclear. It is unlikely that the epic reduplicated aorist which is glossed should have stood in the commented text. The standard gloss on τετύκοντο in the Homeric scholia is παρεcκεύαζον (e.g. *Schol. in Il.* 1.467, 18.419 etc.; cf. also *EM* 755.15). Besides we find the middle-passive παρεcκεύαζοντο (e.g. Phot. 582.3; *Suda* τ 419), κατεcκεύαζον (e.g. Phot. 582,.4) or κατεcκεύαζοντο (Hesych. τ 674, *Suda* τ 420) and ἠτοιμάζοντο (Hesych. τ 673). But ἐδάcαντο seems suggested by the etymology of δαίc (cf. *EM* 525.5 f.) and by such a phrase as δαιτὸc εἴcηc. In particular the Homeric δαccάμενοι δαίνυντ(ο) (*Od.* 3.66) may have suggested that τετύκοντό τε δαῖτα refers to the distribution of the meal into equal portions. Perhaps commented text likewise referred to the distribution of a meal.

3 τουτέcτιν ἤτοι introducing the gloss is puzzling (cf. τουτέcτιν γυναῖκαc?, below 14 f.). τουτέcτιν, δηλονότι, ἤτοι, ἤγουν, ἀντὶ τοῦ are frequently interchanged, and τουτέcτιν ἤτοι may be the result of a conflation of two versions (perhaps via ἤτοι written above τουτέcτιν as a *varia lectio* or vice versa). Another possibility (suggested by N. G. Wilson) is that another gloss has fallen out before ἤτοι. Perhaps ἐδάcαντο is an alternative or further explanation of a standard gloss on παρ- or κατεcκεύαζον.

4–8 βουcτάτιδοc. The commentator takes this as derived from βούcταcιc. If correct, (1) we would have to assume a shift of the ι-stem to dental inflection (Schwyzer *GG* i 464.1). This is unlikely in a Doric form and hardly acceptable in a *deverbativum* in -τι/cι-. βουcτάτιδοc may be an easy corruption for the correct βουcτάτιοc (after βουcτάc, βουcτάδοc?). It seems however better to dismiss the explanation of the commentary and postulate a *nomen agentis* βουcτάτιc, fem. of βουcτάτηc (e.g. χοροcτάτιc Alcman, ὀβολοcτάτιc Plato, παραcτάτιc Plato Comic.). In this case the second element of βουcτάτιc could be taken transitive or intransitive (cf. E. Fraenkel, *Geschichte der griechischen Nomina agentis auf* -τηρ, -τωρ, -τηc (τ) i (Strassburg 1910) 49 f.) and mean either (2*a*) 'places' or 'stops' or (2*b*) 'weighs' (cf. ὀβολοcτάτιc, ζυγοcτάτηc Cerc.) or (2*c*) 'stands' in a certain position. βουcτάτιc then would mean (2*a*) 'someone who places an ox in a certain position' or 'someone who stops an ox' or (2*b*) 'someone who weighs an ox'. If -cτάτιc is taken as intransitive (2*c*) βουcτάτιc could mean theoretically either 'someone who stands like/as an ox' (cf. ὀρθοcτάτηc Eur.) or 'someone who stands on an ox' (λαυτοcτάτηc, Cratinus). However incorrect the derivation βουcτάτιδοc from βουcτάτιc may be, it is reasonable to assume that βουcτάτιδοc indeed refers to a place or at least that it stood in a context where it could refer to a place. Otherwise the explanation βουcτάτιc could hardly have been given.

Assuming βουϲτάτιϲ (2a) above, it is tempting see a place name in βουϲτάτιϲ along lines of the wide-spread legend where a cow leads settlers to the site of a new town (see F. Vian, *Les origines des Thebes*, Études et commentaires 48 (Paris 1963) 79; Th. Mommsen, *Die unteritalischen Dialekte* (Leipzig 1850) 173). Normally the indication essential for the foundation is the animal lying down (Vian, *Origines* 79 f., 88 f.), but the 'stopping' of the animal may have a special point in a story like that of Helenos' foundation of βούθρωτον (FGrH III A 274 F1), where the cow had been running away. Thus βουϲτάτιϲ may indicate the place 'that stopped the cow' perhaps by attracting its attention to a spring where it stopped to drink (for a spring in a story about a cow, cf. Call. fr. 42 Pf.) or by a rich pasture (cf. βούνειμα schol. Tz. ad Lyc. 800, Steph. Byz. s.v.; βουθερήϲ for a meadow S. *Tr.* 188; see H. Lloyd-Jones, *CQ* 4 (1954) 93). For a feminine *nomen agentis* referring to a place, Professor Parsons points to ἰχθυόπωλιϲ (sc. ἀγορά, cf. W. Judeich, *Topographie von Athen* (München 1931²) 359 f.), but I do not know of any example for a *nomen agentis* with τ-suffix (*nomina agentis* in -τηϲ may be used for material objects, namely instruments; see Fraenkel, *Geschichte der griechischen Nomina agentis* ii (Strassburg 1912) 7, 200; A. Debrunner, *Griechische Wortbildungslehre* (Heidelberg 1917) 174 f.).

Alternatively, βουϲτάτιδοϲ might be taken as a genitive depending on e.g. ἕδρα or πέδον and as referring to its resident, presumably the goddess dwelling in a place (perhaps the goddess even standing alone for the place belonging to her). Assuming that the line is a comic trimeter, one could think of something like ἐγὼ μὲν ἄρτι βουϲτάτιδοϲ ⟨λιπὼν ἕδραϲ / παρῇ⟩ φίλοιϲ παρὰ μυθιήταιϲ or ἐγὼ μὲν ἄρτι βουϲτάτιδοϲ ⟨ἀφιγμένοϲ / πέδον⟩ φίλοιϲ κτλ. (cf. ἐπὶ τὴν οἰκίαν / ἀφίγμεθ' ὄντωϲ τοῦ νέου θεοῦ; Ar. *Pl.* 959 f.), perhaps even something like ἐγὼ μὲν ἄρτι βουϲτάτιδοϲ ⟨ἐλθὼν⟩ φίλοιϲ κτλ. ('coming from the goddess βουϲτάτιϲ'). In this case βουϲτάτιϲ may still be connected with some story of a cow leading to a place where the temple or altar of a certain goddess had to be built, and this goddess was then worshipped there as the one 'who stopped the cow' or perhaps 'the one who placed the cow in position or on the spot to be sacrificed' (cf. the story of Βούνειμα mentioned above). If the text refers to Samos, one thinks of course of Hera.

8–10 **φίλοιϲ παρὰ μυ[θι⟨ή⟩]ταιϲ·**: The two Greek words that in principle can be restored in 8 f. are μύϲταιϲ and μυθιήταιϲ. The explanation by τάξιϲ (alternative restorations such as β]άξιϲ, λ]άξιϲ, ϲ]άξιϲ, perhaps πρ]άξιϲ, ϲτ]άξιϲ, φρ]άξιϲ hardly deserve to be mentioned) and by μυθίζειν decides for the latter (for the connection with μυθμύω see *EM* 493.43 ff.). Space excludes the restoration μυ|[θιή]ταιϲ, but μυθήτηϲ and μυθίτηϲ are usual spelling errors for μυθιήταιϲ (see E. Lobel, *CQ* 21 (1927) 50), the correct spelling being rather the exception (cf. Page's apparatus ad Anacr. 353). So there is nothing against restoring μυ|[θή]ταιϲ or μυ|[θί]ταιϲ here. The former is not excluded absolutely by the space, but μυ|[θί]ταιϲ fits much better. It may also be favoured by the μυθίζειν of the commentary (see below). Lobel, loc. cit., has shown that there is no evidence for a word μυθήτηϲ 'story teller', and μυθιῆται is hardly a general term for ϲταϲιάϲται/ϲταϲιῶται, as scholia and *etymologica* explain. μυθιῆται in this sense is confined to a political party at Samos alluded to by Anacreon fr. 353 (cf. also Antig. Car. 120 (132), p. 84 Giannini). Lobel does not mention, however, Phoenix fr. 7.1 (*Coll. Alex.* p. 231), where μυθιήτηϲ (Schweigh: μυθηήτηϲ sive μυήθηϲ codd. Athen. XII 530e) appears to mean simply 'rhetor'. The explanation τοῖϲ ἐκ τῆϲ αὐτῆϲ τάξεώϲ μοι οὖϲιν κτλ., however, seems to exclude this meaning of the word for our text. 'Rhetor' is the obvious meaning of the word: if this had made any sense in our passage even the most perverse commentator would hardly have explained the word in this obscure way. The commentator indicates that with μυθιήταιϲ the text must have referred to the Samian party of Anacr. 353, or perhaps to the Samians in general. οἷϲ εἰώθαμεν ὁμιλεῖν seems to be a fitting paraphrase for something like φίλοιϲ, i.e. the members of a ἑταιρία, but the use of a word like τάξιϲ is remarkable. Of course τάξιϲ can simply mean 'group, class' of men (LSJ s.v. IV), but one wonders why the commentator should use such a technical word if not in a technical sense. The choice of τάξιϲ is explicable if μυθιήταιϲ occurred in a military context. τάξιϲ is a gloss on ἴλη in *Schol. in S. Ai.* 1407b (cf. Hesych. ι 458). There the context is military, but it is interesting that another scholion on this verse (1407a) explains ἴλη as κυρίως δὲ φατρία, a word that is normally glossed as σύνταγμα, σύστημα in *etymologica* (e.g. Hesych. φ 234). μυθίζειν might have some relevance to the technical τάξις and thus throw some further light on the matter, but beside the loss of text in 13 it is hard to see how any conceivable explanation of μυθίζειν could refer to any known meaning of τάξις. μυθίζειν (NB not μυθέομαι) confirms that μυθιήταις not μύσταις or *μυθήταις has to be restored. Were it not for the ι in μυθιήταις it would hardly be necessary to take μυθίζειν instead of the common μυθέομαι or μυθεύεσθαι and to quote Sophron for illustration, especially if it is correct μυθίζειν can only have been quoted here in the sense 'to speak'. As μυθιῆται is commonly explained as στασιάσται/στασιῶται, one's first thought is of course to restore [τὸ γὰρ | μ]υθίζειν ἐπὶ τὸ [στασιά|ζε]σθαι τιθέασιν κτλ. But the space is too short for the supplement -ζε]σθαι, and it is difficult to connect this explanation of μυθίζειν with anything in the preceding explanation of μυθιήταις; in view of the connecting γὰρ it is impossible to separate the two explanations and take them as alternatives. The obvious link to μυθίζειν in the preceding phrase is ὁμιλεῖν if taken in its later meaning 'to speak', and the quotation from Sophron too suggests that μυθίζειν has to be understood in this sense (see below). Two very narrow letters before]σθαι can perhaps not be ruled out with certainty, but one letter is much more likely, and this of course very much limits the choice of suitable words. Probably [μυθέ|ε]σθαι is the best supplement. An alternative would be [μυθεύ|ε]σθαι, but then the middle would be hard to explain; for the uncontracted μυθέεσθαι cf. e.g. *EM* 30.34 ff. (αἰδέω, αἰδέομαι; uncontracted present forms of these verbs occur in Homer). The point of this 'gloss' seems only to be that μυθεῖσθαι has a 'Nebenform' of μυθίζειν, hence μυθιήταις. If correct, our commentary in a perverse way mixes explanation of the most elementary kind with obscurity and pedantry. Are comments such as 'μυθιῆται are people οἷς εἰώθαμεν ὁμιλεῖν', or that μυθίζειν is another form of μυθέεσθαι too implausible for a commentator who explains βουστάτιδος as τὴν στάσιν τὴν τῶν βοῶν οὗ οἱ βόες ἵστανται?

13 C]ώφρονι prevents us from restoring a case of μῖμος in 15.

15]εστιν in association with γυναῖκες suggests [του|τ]έστιν. A possibility is [αἱ παρὰ | C]ώφρονι μιμού[μεναι του|τ]έστιν γυναῖκες. The reason for attributing a special usage of a word to the author's characters rather than to the author himself could be in this case that this usage or something in the quotation is thought to be characteristic for μῖμοι γυναικεῖοι. The emphasis on this point would perhaps explain the otherwise rather pointless supplement τουτέστιν γυναῖκες.

ποίου[ς (the ς perhaps extending somewhat into the marginal space) seems to be the only compatible reading that makes sense with -τας in 16 as an accusative plural. The following τοι[, still belonging to the quotation (see below), points in the same direction. The traces before -τας in 16 suit ς or the curved vertical of н or, less likely, π. In 17 we have presumably the same accusative plural in -τας as in 16, and before it something like τοιούτους or τοιοῦσδε. The traces of two letters at the beginning of 17 suit the left-hand tip of γ and possibly a somewhat straightened cap of ς. τοι[ού|το]υς[would suit (assuming ΟΥ written narrowly at line-end).

17 ἔβασκε (or ἐβάσκε[τε): a Doric word according to *EM* 190.47 ff., presumably still part of the quotation. The dicolon in 16 probably indicates change of speaker. Presumably the dialogue ran: ποίους x μυθίζοντι; 'what kind of people do they call x' or 'of what kind of x do they speak?'— τοιούτους x ἐβάσκετε, or perhaps better ἐβάσκέ τις; '(What?) Did anyone call such people x' or 'speak ill of such people as x'. x must have some negative significance (cf. Hesych. β 296 βάσκειν· κακολογεῖν). If the following text refers to the quotation from Sophron, there should be some connection between the people called x and a προφήτης, but much concerning the sense of 18 ff. is uncertain.

18–22 It cannot be excluded that a new lemma begins with τ]οιοῦτος or πρ]οφήτης (or ὑπ]οφή-της), but 20 at any rate seems to belong to the commentary. The traces before ὑπό are most likely to come from ω. ο is not impossible, but one should expect the curve to be more rounded. If]θ were to be read, we should see part of the horizontal;]ρ, though not absolutely to be excluded, is extremely unlikely.

18 τ]οιοῦτος presumably refers back to ποίου[. . . τοι[ούτους (15 f.). Probably all the rest of the text from 18 onward belongs to the commentary and refers to the quotation from Sophron. τ]οιοῦτος apparently agrees with πρ]οφήτης and most probably a new sentence begins here δὲ (τοιοῦτος δὲ . . . προφήτης ἦλθεν).

19 πρ]οφήτης (or perhaps ὑπ]οφήτης) seems likely.

20 ὑπὸ τοῦ Λικυ[. A Likymnios, probably identical with the rhetor and poet (PMG 768–73 with additions in Campbell, *Greek Lyric* v; A. Henrichs, *ZPE* 57 (1984) 53–7) is mentioned in the Homeric scholia (schol. in *Il.* 2.106b). Janus Lascaris in his *Epigrams* (41.5; 42.15) and Musurus in Plat. 155 use the word ὑποφήτης in the sense of 'scholiast'. τρόπον in 22 might be used as a rhetorical term. If we restore e.g. ὑπ]οφήτης . . . ὑπὸ τοῦ Λικυ[μνίου . . .] φθέντας . . . [εἶπε]ν ὅτι τρόπον . . . , the commentator could be citing an explanation that rejects a view held by Likymnios. ὑποφήτης however is hardly a word to be expected in a commentary. Lascaris obviously derives it from such phrases as μουσαών . . . ὑποφήτας (Theocr. 16.29; for further examples see Gow ad loc.; cf. ὑποφήτωρ in the anonymous 'Encomium of Theon' VII **1015**.1, re-ed. Page, *Select Papyri* iii no. 130, p. 526). If our text is not part of a quotation from poetry, πρ]οφήτης is a much more likely supplement. Moreover ἦλθεν (19) suggests that here a story is told, so that ὑπ]οφήτης would suggest that the commentary refers to a story told by Likymnios in a poem. The structure of the sentence does not exclude this but rather points in a different direction (perhaps even toward Likymnios the poet/rhetor). It is perhaps easier to assume that Likymnios is part of the story. He is in this case probably the mythological king of Argos. A connection between him and a προφήτης is provided by the story in which he is sent to Delphi to inquire about Heracles after the incident with the poisoned robe (Diod. 4.38.3).

20 If]ω is correctly read, this can hardly be anything but a dative. We need at least two words: (1) the article or a noun with the participle in -φθέντας and (2) the dative in -ω. Not much space is available. There is hardly any other option than αὐτ]ῷ (sc. τῷ προφήτῃ). If the particle connecting ἦλθεν and εἶπεν came in the same line, only a very short supplement is possible, as perhaps τοὺς δ'αὐτ]ῷ κτλ. Presumably πα[would then be the beginning of a noun agreeing with -φθέντας, the accusative depending on εἶπεν. Perhaps it is better to insert the particle in 22 (καὶ εἶπεν ὅτι κτλ.) and to take πα[as a participle agreeing with ἦλθεν and governing -φθέντας. Nevertheless, space for a plausible supplement in 20 is rather small.

22]ν ὅτι is most promisingly separated, restoring a verb on which the ὅτι clause can depend, e.g. εἶπε]ν ὅτι. Alternatively, a completely different construction would result with δηλο]νότι.

τρόπον: might refer to the way in which Heracles and his friends must act (see on 20).

H.-C. GÜNTHER

4952. COMMENTARY ON ARCHILOCHUS' *TRIMETERS*

123/71(a)   9.2 × 8.2 cm   Third century
                                                                Plate IX

Two fragments from the middle part of two columns, written across the fibres, at the end of a papyrus roll. The fragments are apparently continguous, to be positioned side by side: fr. 1, containing 12 lines and the end of a prose text, and fr. 2, containing the title of the work, after a narrow ἄγραφον. A physically separate, third piece, containing an upper portion of the colophon, slots into place in the upper left corner of the latter fragment, without any gap, and so may be considered part of fr. 2. This seeeems to be confirmed by continuity of lines of writing on the front—a register of names in a respectable cursive documentary hand of the second century—although it is cannot be ruled out that a line or more has intervened in between the detached upper left part (containing line 1) and the lower portion (beginning with line 2). Orientation of fibres on both sides and continuity of lines of writing on the front suggest that fr. 2 should be positioned so that the last two lines of writing of the colophon are slightly lower than the last line in fr. 1. If this is correct, and the colophon was centred vertically as it is horizontally, then the text in fr. 1 (line 12 written only half-way) ended in the middle of its columnar space.

The format of the final column of the prose text (width *c.*6.5 cm, in lines of *c.*30 letters) may be reconstructed from fr. 1, which preserves beginnings (fr. 1.3–5) and ends (fr. 1.11) of different lines (and allowing that fr. 1.6 and possibly 7 may have stood in *ekthesis* by one or more letters into the left margin). The handwriting of this column is a diminutive informal, somewhat irregular version of the 'Formal Mixed' or Severe Style, with a slant to the right, showing the usual contrast between heights and widths of letters and shading of strokes, and a fair amount of connection between letters and some fluidity (ϻ in particular is oddly fashioned as though ε ligatured to ι, e.g. in fr. 1.4; ʒ in fr. 1.9 is flamboyantly large). Fr. 2, containing the colophon of the work, shows what is arguably the same hand, although written larger and more carefully, with the letters well-spaced and without connection. The handwriting, especially in the aspect illustrated by the final column of the commentary (fr. 1), may be compared with XXII **2341** = Roberts, *GLH* 19c, Legal Proceedings dated to 208 (not 202, as in Roberts), except that in **4952** the writing of the commentary is smaller and that of the colophon is larger. For the handwriting of the colophon, compare further that of the *sillybos* of the *Dithyrambs* of Bacchylides (VIII **1091**, P15 Caroli).

The same scribe made two supralinear corrections (fr. 1.9 and 11, the latter not very elegantly, combined with a correction by cancellation of a letter in the line of writing). Apostrophe is used to mark elision of a final vowel in fr. 1.7, although in 5 blank space serves the same function. Otherwise there are no signs of punctuation or other lectional signs. There is a quotation of the poet in fr. 1.6 (διμοιρίης, identifiable as a quotation from its Ionic dialect form), perhaps continuing in 7 (identifiable by the marked elision?). This may in fact constitute a quoted lemma (or internal-lemma), which is then provided with explanation by the commentator. Whether or not the text followed formatting conventions familiar from other papyrus commentaries on the poets (such as lemmata in *ekthesis* followed by blank space) is unknown due to the loss of the left margin in the lower portion of fr. 1.

This is the first commentary on Archilochus to come to light on papyrus. Apart from preserving a new expression of Archilochus, just enough survives of the commentary proper to show that it consisted partly of paraphrase of the poet's text, partly of autobiographical comment on the poet's family relations, and partly of ethical and/or rhetorical evaluation of his poetic language.

We are grateful to Professors G. Bastianini, F. Montanari, and A. Porro for discussion of the text.

↓

Fr. 1

```
          ·       ·        ·                          ·        ·       ·        ·
   .].αν̣[                                      .].αν̣[
   .].υϲ κ..[                                   .].υϲ κ..[
   ϲομενον.[                                    ϲομενον.[
   ουκαποκ[....]..[                            οὐκ ἀποκ[....]..[
 5 τ̣ιαλλ επικ[.].[.]...[                    5 τ̣ι ἀλλ’ ἐπικ[.].[.]...[
      ]ξ.διμοιριηϲ.[                              ]ξ. διμοιρίηϲ.[
      ]ειαδ’ω[.]δεκα.[.......].ρ̣ν̣[               ]ειαδ’ ω[.]δεκα.[.......].ρ̣ν̣[
      ]εταμ..ουϲθεντ[.].μ̣ενον[                    ]εταμ..ουϲθεντ[.].μ̣ενον[
      ]η̣’έαυ[.]..μητριωϲξενηνα..[            τ]η̣ ἑαυ[τ]οῦ μητρὶ ὡϲ ξενηνα..[
10 ].[....].τοϲειϲογεγραπ[τ]αιοϊαμ.[      10 ].[....].τοϲ εἰϲ ὃ γέγραπ[τ]αι ὁ ἰαμβ[
   ]..υ̣αρχιλοχουχαρακτηρα                  ].ου Ἀρχιλόχου χαρακτῆρα
      ]ϲπολλοιϲ                                ]ϲ πολλοῖϲ.
```

Fr. 2

```
      ]οϲτομ[                                   ]οϲτομ[
      τ..[                                       τῶν [τοῦ
      αρχιλοχ.[                                  Ἀρχιλόχο[υ
      τριμετρ..[                                 Τριμέτρων
 5    υπ( )                                5     ὑπ(όμνημα)
```

Fr. 1

1]. oblique stroke descending to right, as leg of κ, λ, χ   2]., tiny dot at mid-level, as of mid-stroke of ε or raised tail of z   .[, slight indistiguishable traces on matted fibres   3 ς, apparently bottom and top falling forward   .[, centred trace at baseline   4]..[, slight trace at mid-level, followed by higher trace capped by an arc-like hat vaguely suggesting ε or θ   5 before beginning of line, on a slightly higher level, traces suggesting the beginning and end of horizontal of τ   τι, or π, but the overhang of the horizontal at left and equal length of the uprights recommends the former   ].[, upright descending just beneath the line   ]...[, horizontal at mid-level as of н, connecting to arc left to right suggesting c, followed by an indistinguishable trace at mid-level 6 ξ., first the tiny round centre of the wide z that appears in 9, with a bit of its lower horizontal, then traces of two uprights separated by a hole, the first slightly lower than the second, taken together compatible with sides of ω, although the second not impossibly the left tip of ʌ   ι unusually curved like the back of ε   .[, right-hand part of ʌ, ʌ, λ   7]ε, mid-stroke ligatured to ι   ω, left side at top of middle   δ, apex of triangular letter   .[, upright suiting ι, but κ, н, not ruled out (not π, τ)   ].ρ̣ν̣[, bottom of upright, descending tail with tight bowl detached on split fibre to upper right, upright with oblique descending from top   8 .., faint traces originally at the top-level of the line of writing on a dangling fibre now pushed higher above the line   ].μ̣εν, bottom of upright descending below the line, upright with arced middle connecting suggesting м, bottom of round letter as of ε, ο   9]η̣, two uprights connected by oblique rising from left to right   ].., faint short

oblique, tail of descender below the line as of ρ, γ   supralinear ε in same hand as main text   . .[, two descenders below the line, the first with a horizontal crossbar on top as of τ, the second perhaps ι, but ρ not excluded   10] . [. . . .], tops of two uprights connected by arc as of μ   ] . , *prima facie* ν, γ also possible   . [, foot of upright curving left at bottom, with specks of ink across baseline, compatible with β, not λ   11] . . ʹύʹ, descender below the line, short oblique connecting to short upright (as ν, but angular ο not excluded), upright with short oblique connecting at top followed by equally short upright, ν suggested, perhaps cancelled with a horizontal stroke (γ written over this letter by the same(?) hand, but different form of υ)   12 ϲ, oval letter, open at right, with curved top wider than angular bottom strongly recommending ϲ

Fr. 2

1 μ[, upright with oblique descending from top which curves up slightly at bottom, suggesting μ and ruling out ν   2 . . [, horizontal stroke at baseline curving up at right into side of wide round letter, then two uprights, the second higher than the first and with a oblique connecting at bottom as of ν with raised right-hand part   3 . [, upper arm of χ ligaturing with a tight round letter as of ο   4 . . , two horizontal strokes curving inward pumpkin-like, as of ω, then two uprights, the second higher than the first as ν with raised right-hand part   5 υπ, the first smaller and superimposed on the second so that the arms and part of the upright emerge out of the middle of the crossbar of π (although the descender of γ sinking into the middle of π is no longer visible)

'. . . not (naming? revealing?) . . . but (blaming?) . . . "a double-share" . . . for/to/against his mother, as to how foreign . . . for which the iambic (poem?) had been written . . . the character (or: style) of Archilochus . . . for many.' (end of commentary)

'by   ]ostom[(author's name)

Commentary
on Archilochus'
Iambic Trimeters'

Fr. 1: Final column of commentary (not written to the bottom).

3 ϲομενον. To be articulated -ϲομενον or -ϲομεν ὅν or ϲομεν ὅν.

4–5 οὐκ . . . ἀλλ' . . . suggests an opposition in which two expressions (or ways of speaking) of Archilochus (or of his and another poet's) were compared as analogous or parallel, perhaps suggesting a line of continuity, opposition, or influence: thus οὐκ ἀποκ- . . . ἀλλ' ἐπικ- . . . .

4 ἀποκ[. . . .] . . [. ἀποκ[αλοῦ]με[ν- 'naming' (e.g. a personal enemy) or ἀποκ[αλυπ]το[μεν- 'disclosing', 'revealing' (e.g. potentially damaging private affairs) could be considered, assuming a parallel construction with ἀλλ' ἐπικ- in 5.

5 ἐπικ[α]λ[ο]υμε[ν-, describing the poet as engaging in the language of complaint or blame, for which early iambus was noted, would be apt here.

6]ξ . : perhaps -ξα or -ξε i.e. the aorist, although α and ε are both a little too short for the space, which suggests a wide letter with horizontal sides like ω (less likely η), thus perhaps ἔ]ξω, which could take the genitive διμοιρίης ('apart from a double-share') and could even have been part of the lemma quoted from Archilochus (cf. ἔξωθεν in Archil. fr. 194.1 W.2; elsewhere in iambics e.g. Soph. *OT* 1090 ἔξω κακῶν οἰκεῖν).

διμοιρίης: a 'double-share'; cf. Xen. *Ag.* 5.1.4; *An.* VII 2.36.2; 6.1.6; *Hel.* VI 1.6.8; *Lac.* 15.4.3). In Aeschylus we find the adjective form δίμοιρος (*Suppl.* 1070; *Th.* 850); cf. Antiph. Com. fr. 81.5 K–A. Hesych. δ 543 Latte has the entry μοῖρα (δειϲιάδα· τὴν μοῖραν. οἱ δὲ διμοιρίαν), and *Suda* (δ 1126 Adler): ἔϲτι δέ τιϲ καὶ ϲτρατιωτικὴ ἀρχή, ὡϲ λοχαγόϲ, διὰ τὸ παρ' ἄλλουϲ ϲτρατιώταϲ δύο μοίραϲ λαμβάνειν. οἱ δὲ διμοιρίαν καὶ ἡμιλοχίαν τὸ αὐτό φαϲι, either or both of which entries could be due to the presence of glosses on Archilochus' use of this word at an earlier stage in the lexicographical/commentary tradition, now instantiated by **4952**. In the Menander play III **409** i 28, the context is military and regards compensation for soldiery (see Gomme–Sandbach, *Menander: A Commentary* (1973) 424). Such a reference would clearly have a place in Archilochus' poetry, perhaps in the context of complaints by the poet that another person or persons (lampooned in his iambic verses) got a larger share (e.g. of pay, booty, drink, women) than he himself did.

7]ειαδ': the mark of elision may imply that this is part of the preceding lemma or a new or internal one. A number of completions are possible poetic expressions (γεν]ειάδ'? πελ]ειάδ'?).

9–10 ὡϲ ξενηνα . . [. Among possible articulations, ὡϲ ξένη would cohere nicely with μητρί ('to his mother as to how foreign she was'), a point that might have been being elucidated in commentary on the basis of the poetic text. Other possibilities include ἑαυ[τ]οῦ μητρί, ὡϲ ξένην αὐτ[, which would remove ξένη from the preceding syntactic construction and reference to his mother. But the former is favoured by the tradition that Archilochus himself had said that his mother was a slave named Enipo (Aelian. *VH* x 13, 4 on the authority of Critias 88 B 44 D.–K. = Archil. T 32 Campbell, *Greek Iambic Poetry*), which suggests derivation from a poem with an autobiographical frame, and which would fit well with fr. 1.10 'for which the iambic poem(?) had been written'.

10] . , prima facie N, thus a word in -ντοϲ; but Υ is also possible: ο]ὗτοϲ?

10–11 Possible completions include εἰϲ ὃ γέγραπται ο ιαμβ[οϲ, e.g. δηλῶν or ἐμφαίνων] τοῦ Ἀρχιλόχου χαρακτῆρα: 'for which the iambic poem had been written, thus demonstrating the style/character of Archilochus' (-β[is already one letter past the end of the line relative to the following line; but the scribe need not have been strict about ending the lines at precisely the same point). But we could also have ὁ ἰαμβ[ι|κὸϲ e.g. ποιητήϲ or ϲτίχοϲ, or e.g. ὁ ἰάμβ[ων | ποιητήϲ (cf. Theocr. *Epigr.* 21.1–2 = AP 7.664 Ἀρχίλοχον . . . τὸν τῶν ἰάμβων).

11 Clearly ΟΥ corrected from ΟΝ, with ν cancelled, possibly by the same hand as the main text, although the supralinear υ is in the V-shape familiar from documentary and informal hands of the third century, but different from elsewhere in the main text.

χαρακτῆρα is difficult to pin down in sense, since with it the commentator could be referring to (i) the personality of the poet, (ii) the character of the speaker in the poem, or (iii) the style of the poetry (i.e. in a rhetorical sense). Attestations for each of these three abound, although in literary criticism in commentaries and scholia (as opposed to, say, philosophical writing) it is sense (iii) that is the most frequently encountered: e.g. Dion. Hal., *Lys.* 10, 13; 15, 22; 20, 1; *Dem.* 9, 3; *Pomp.* 6, 8, 11; schol. Aristoph. *Ach.* 455 μιμεῖται τὸν Εὐριπίδου χαρακτῆρα τῷ λόγῳ; schol. Aristid. *Tett.* 226,12 ἵνα Πλάτωνοϲ μιμήϲηται χαρακτῆρα . . . ; schol. Eur. *Or.* 640,8 ἔνιοι ἀθετοῦϲι τοῦτον καὶ τὸν ἐξῆϲ ϲτίχον· οὐκ ἔχουϲι γὰρ τὸν Εὐριπίδειον χαρακτῆρα; schol. *Il.* XII 428 a 1 ἐμφαίνει Ὁμηρικὸν χαρακτῆρα. Ancient authors were much preoccupied with analysis and judgement on A.'s literary expressiveness and style (T 33–50 Campbell, op. cit.). If this was the sense here, the commentary was not simply of an elementary nature, but engaged in rhetorical analysis, which may have further figured e.g. in discussions of authenticity, dating of poems, and development of poetic expression.

12]ϲ: τοῖ]ϲ? In which case: ὡϲ δοκεῖν τοῖ]ϲ πολλοῖϲ, or some similar expression.

Fr. 2: Colophon (after ἄγραφον?).

1]οϲτομ[. On a detached but cognate piece of papyrus, which can be ranged vertically upwards by as much as several lines, but apparently fixed in this range horizontally. If the writing was centred like the lines below, only 2–4 letters can have followed in the line after]οϲτο . [, before blank surface resumes on the main part of fr. 2. As a result, there would not be room for a personal name, patronymic, or ethnic later in the line, although this could have occupied an intervening line. Normally we expect the name of the author in the genitive, dependent on the title ὑπόμνημα (fr. 2.5). Thus, we most probably have here the name of the author/commentator, e.g. Χρυϲ]οϲτόμ[ου? (less likely

Χρυϲ]οϲτόλ[ικου, for compatibility of the final trace). Dio of Prussa, although chronologically possible for the dating of the papyrus, and consistent with the rhetorical interest apparent in fr. 1, is not attested as having composed this type of work. An intriguing possibility (equally unattested for a commentary), suggested by Professor A. Porro, is a Latin name: Π]οϲτόμ[ου or Π]οϲτομ[ίου (variants: Πόϲτουμοϲ and Πόϲτυμοϲ, cf. II **283**.18, P. Lond. I 109 B 36; P. Ryl. II 182.8–9). But the likelihood of a Roman scholar, even a freedman grammarian, writing commentary on A. in or translated into Greek is not overwhelming. Neither Aristarchus, who wrote a commentary on Archilochus (Clem. *Strom.* 1.21.117), nor any of the ancient authorities known to have written treatises on him, including Aristotle (Hesych. Miles. *Vit. Aristot.* P. 16 Rose; Philod. *De poem.* iv col. 112), Apollonius Rhodius (Athen. 10.451c), or Aristophanes of Byzantium (fr. 367 Slater) can be made to fit the traces here.

2 τῶν. The genitive (dependent directly on ὑπόμνημα, less commonly with ὑπέρ) is standard for the work commented on in titles of *hypomnemata*, but the article is less common. See next note, with examples. Here it functions to form a substantive with Τριμέτρων in 4. But the article is frequently omitted in titles generally.

[τοῦ (A. Porro): Symmetry of format elsewhere suggests it (or another word of about this length) stood here. If correct, τ here did not descend as far as in the preceding τῶν, or its tail would have been similarly visible above the name of Archilochus in the preserved space above in the line below. It is not normally found with name of authors in titles of *hypomnemata* (just as the article with ὑπόμνημα would not be expected in a title), and its exact significance seems doubtful here: cf. P. Amh. II 12.17–20 Ἀριστάρχου | Ἡροδότου | ᾱ | ὑπόμνημα; XXIV **2392**.1–4 Διον[υ]ϲίου επο.[| Ἀλκμᾶνος | μελ[ῶ]ν δ' | ὑπ(όμνημα); XXXI **2536**.39–41 Θέω[νος] τοῦ [Ἀρ]τεμιδώρου | Πινδάρου | Πυθιονικῶν ὑπόμνημα.

4 Τριμέτρων: further confirms the organization of the Roman-period edition of Archilochus as into different books by metre, after the publication of LXIX **4708** (see introd. there). Whether such an organization goes back to Hellenistic times or was known to Alexandrian scholars remains unknown. Herodian. ap. Eustath. *Comm. in Il.* v 31 (518.24) and Harpocrat. 232.810 Dindorf s.v. παλίν-ϲκιον imply knowledge of a book of trimeters of Archilochus (not necessarily by this title). So also Theocr. *Epigr.* 21.1–2 (AP 7.664) Ἀρχίλοχον . . . τὸν τῶν ἰάμβων. As form of citation, already Herodot. 1.12 (Archil. fr. 7) ἐν ἰάμβῳ τριμέτρῳ; cf. Athen. 11.483d Ἀρχίλοχος ἐν ἐλεγείοις (similarly Orion *Etym.* col. 55.22 Sturz, and *Et. Gen.* s.v. ἐπίρρηϲις); see W. Crönert, *Archilochi Elegiae* (Göttingen 1911) on the classification of Archilochus' poems by metre in ancient editions. This scheme of organization ought further to imply a separate edition (and commentary) for the tetrameters, as we now know there existed for the elegiacs; whether there was yet another book for the polymetric poems is less clear.

5 ὑπ(όμνημα). The title of the work (per se) ὑπόμνημα is given in what must by the third century have already become the conventional form of its monogram abbreviation, ϒ written smaller over and into π, both occupying a single large letter-space. For this form, see e.g. XXIV **2392**, XXV **2433**.2, *Aristophaneia sillybos* P15 Caroli (all second century); P. Amh. II 18, 189, 275 (I–II AD). Monograms such as this in book titles must have come into existence in the same time period (post-first century BC: they are absent from the Herculaneum papyri) and same graphic environment as the monogram abbreviations for the names of authorit6ative Alexandrian and early Imperial scholars and editors that appear in the marginal scholia of our papyrus editions: for those of a slightly later period, see V. Gardthausen, *Das alte Monogramm* (Leipzig 1924).

D. OBBINK

VI. DOCUMENTARY TEXTS

4953. Petition to Strategus regarding Extortion

73/70(a)   7.5 × 16.5 cm   After September/October 48

A petition to the strategus Tiberius Claudius Pasion from Dius son of Peteuris, a weaver, complaining about the extortion by Ammonius, a former tax collector, of 40 drachmas in each of two consecutive years, Year 6 = 45/6 and Year 7 = 46/7. **4953** must have been submitted after September/October 48, when Dor[ion?], Pasion's predecessor as strategus, was still in office: see J. Whitehorne, *Strategi and Royal Scribes of Roman Egypt*[2] (2006) 91. It is one of a small group of texts of this type (II **284**, **393** descr. = SB XIV 11902; sim. **285**, **394** = **4954** below), but it is difficult to tell which is the earliest since they are all undated.

That four of these texts are addressed to the same strategus is likely to be an accident of preservation. There is no reason to suppose that this type of extortion was confined to a few years in the Oxyrhynchite nome or that Pasion was successful in stamping it out. Indeed the fact that each of the weavers lived in a different part of the city and they complained about different tax collectors (Apollophanes in **284** and **285**; Damis in SB 11902) shows how pervasive this type of extortion must have been. **4953** differs from the parallels in that the amount involved is much larger, and only here does the petitioner offer the extortion as an excuse for being in arrears in the payment of his weaver's tax for Year 7 (10–11).

There is no *kollesis*. The back is blank.

Τιβερίωι Κλαυδίω[ι Πα]ϲίωνι ϲτρα(τηγῷ)
παρὰ Δίου τοῦ Πετεύριος τῶν ἀπ' Ὀ-
ξυρύγχων πόλεωϲ γερδίων λαύ-
ραϲ Ποιμενικῆϲ. διαϲείϲθηι
5   ὑπὸ Ἀμμωνίου γ[εν]ομένου
πράκτοροϲ τῶι ϛ (ἔτει) Τιβερίου Κλαυδ(ίου)
Καίϲαροϲ Ϲεβαϲτοῦ Γερμανικοῦ
Αὐτοκράτοροϲ ἀργ(υρίου) (δραχμὰϲ) μ καὶ τῶι
ζ (ἔτει) κατὰ μέροϲ ἄλλαϲ ἀρ[γ](υρίου)] (δραχμὰϲ) μ,
10   ἐξ οὗ ἐφέλκομαι διὰ τὸ διάϲιϲ-
μα τὸ τοῦ ζ (ἔτουϲ) χειρονάξιν. διὸ
ἀξιῶι διαλαβ[ε]ῖν ὃϲ ἐάν ϲοι δό-
       ξηι.   (vac.)   εὐτύχ(ει).

1 ϲτρ˪   4 l. διεϲείϲθην   6, 9, 11 ϛ   8, 9 αργ⌐ϛ   10–11 l. διάϲειϲμα
11 l. χειρωνάξιον   12 l. ἀξιῶ, ὡϲ   13 ευτυ^χ

'To Tiberius Claudius Pasion, strategus, from Dius son of Peteuris, of those from the city of the Oxyrhynchi, of the weavers of the quarter of Poimenike. Ammonius, the ex-*praktor*, extorted from me in Year 6 of Tiberius Claudius Caesar Augustus Germanicus Imperator 40 drachmas of silver, and in Year 7, another 40 drachmas of silver, bit by bit. As a consequence, because of the extortion, I am in arrears for the trade tax for Year 7. I therefore request that you deal with (this) as you may see fit. Farewell.'

1 Although it cannot be dated precisely, this is perhaps the earliest attestation of Tiberius Claudius Pasion as strategus, since the text is likely to have been written after the end of Year 7 = 46/7 (line 9); cf. SB XIV 11902. His predecessor as strategus, Dor[ion?], is attested in office in September/October 48 (II **255** = W. *Chr.* 201) while the earliest secure date for Pasion himself remains 29 March 49 (I **37** i): see Whitehorne, *Strategi and Royal Scribes*² 91. The other texts, being undated, are of little help: **284** complains of extortion in Year 8, and so is Year 9 = 48/9 at the earliest; **285** refers to Years 1 (sic) and 9, and so is Year 10 = 49/50 at the earliest; SB XIV 11902 refers to the past Year 9, and so is also Year 10 at the earliest.

4 διαϲείϲθηι, l. διεϲείϲθην. Cf. 10–11 διάϲιϲμα. διαϲείω/διάϲειϲμα are the standard terms for extortion by officials; cf. Subatianus Aquila's edict, VIII **1100** (206) *passim*.

8–9 (δραχμὰϲ) μ. 80 drachmas over two years is a considerable amount, given that the weaver's tax was typically *c.*36 drachmas a year; see II **288** introd. The amounts in the parallels are much less: 16 drachmas over a year in II **284**, a linen tunic worth 8 drachmas plus 16 drachmas over a six-month period in II **285**, and 16 drachmas in Year 8 followed by 24 drachmas in Year 9 in II **393** descr. = SB XIV 11902.

9 κατὰ μέροϲ. Translated erroneously at **284** 10 as 'among other people'. In the context of a private account, J. R. Rea at LXIV **4436** i 3 n. suggests 'by instalments', which implies regular payments of a fixed amount. This is what happened in **285**, where 12 drachmas were extorted at 2 drachmas 'month by month', κατὰ μῆνα, over the six-month period. But this may not have been the case here. On analogy with κατ' ἄνδρα, 'man by man, person by person', κατὰ μέροϲ is rather 'bit by bit, part by part, severally'.

J. WHITEHORNE

4954. Petition regarding Extortion

Camb. UL Add. Ms. 4069   8.2 × 21 cm   *c.*49

This papyrus was first published in the form of a short description as II **394**: 'Conclusion of a similar petition [to **393** = SB XIV 11902] complaining of the extortion of 24 drachmae and a ἱμάτιον worth 16 drachmae' (P. Oxy. II p. 314). A full edition is given here since the text belongs to the same dossier as **4953**. We find a similar combination of extorted money and clothing (a linen tunic) in II **285**.

The back is presumed to be blank. The text was transcribed from a photograph, and is published courtesy of the Syndics of Cambridge University Library.

.   .   .   .   .

Γ]ερμανικοῦ Αὐτοκράτορος

κατὰ μέρος ἀργ(υρίου) (δραχμὰς) εἴκοςι

τέςςαρες ἀφαρπάςας

μου ἱμάτιον ἄξιον ἀργ(υρίου) (δραχμῶν) ις

5   ὥςτ᾽ εἶναι ἀργ(υρίου) (δραχμὰς) μ. δι̣[ὸ ἀ-

ξιῶι διαλαβε̣ῖν κατ᾽ αὐ-

τοῦ ὡς ἐάν ςο̣ι δοκῆι.

3 l. τέςςαρας   3, 4, 5 αργ ʹ   5–6 l. ἀξιῶ

'. . . Germanicus Imperator twenty-four drachmas of silver, bit by bit (?), having seized from me a cloak worth 16 drachmas, so that it is (in total) 40 drachmas of silver. I therefore request that you proceed against him as you may see fit.'

2–3 (δραχμὰς) εἴκοςι τέςςαρες was no doubt governed by a verb such as διέςειςε in the lost part of the line; cf. II **285** 12–13.

3 ἀφαρπάςας. Cf. **285** 10 ἀφήρπαςεν.

N. GONIS

4955. MILITARY ROSTER

32 4B.90/E(1–3)a   10.9 × 24.6 cm   Late first / early second century
                                                                                                    Plate X

One large and one smaller fragment that can be joined together. The left half of the smaller fragment, as well as some other bits, are lost. The papyrus preserves a left margin of *c.*2.3 cm and a bottom margin of 3.5 cm; top and right margins lost. A sheet-joint is visible 1.8 cm away from the left edge of the papyrus; the back is blank. The text is written along the fibres, in a so-called rustic capital. Such scripts are attested in several other Latin papyri dating from the first and second centuries AD (see below). In the left margin, there are remains of a few letters written in a cursive script, presumably by a different hand, which are clearly the ends of Roman *cognomina*. This suggests that we have a *tomos synkollesimos* of military reports or similar documents. There are no lectional signs or punctuation. The symbol used for *centuria* is attested, in various shapes, in other Latin papyri; see e.g. ChLA X 411.42 (156), IV 275.12 = **735** 12 (205), IV 270.12 (iii), XLII 1213 fr. b.10, and fr. *c.*5 (225–250). On Latin texts found in Oxyrhynchus, see J. D. Thomas in *Oxyrhynchus: A City and its Texts* 231–43.

Column ii is a list, in Latin, of the names of seventeen soldiers preceded by the centuries to which they belong (the names of five of these are preserved). The names are preceded by assignments to duty, which correspond to topographical locations, all but one probably civic or urban facilities: *castello, portico, amphothia*⟦*tur*⟧ (presumably *amphitheatro* was intended; see ii 20 n.), *fistulis* (water-pipes), *alabastrona* (quarry). In the smaller, upper fragment, the irregular line spacing suggests that some more topographical entries stood in the missing left part of the sheet. The names add up to seventeen, corresponding to the total given at the bottom of the sheet. Thus no names are missing at the top, although presumably there was originally some sort of heading, now lost. All *nomina* and *cognomina* appearing in this papyrus are found either in H. Solin, O. Salomies, *Repertorium nominum gentilium et cognominum Latinorum* (1994), or in I. Kajanto, *The Latin Cognomina* (1965). The presence of several Gaii Iulii (ii 10, 12, 27, and perhaps 15), as well as a Marcus Antonius (ii 2), points to the earlier first century. The four Titi Flauii (ii 6, 22, 24, 25), however, can hardly predate 69, when Vespasian became emperor. The names do not show any influence from later dynasties; notably there are no Ulpii or Aelii, which would point to the period 98–138. In P. Gen. lat. 1 (= CPL 106 = ChLA I 7 = S. Daris, *Documenti per la storia dell'esercito romano in Egitto* no. 10 = RMR nos. 9, 10, 37, 58, 68), a military register of 81–90, one finds names also attested here, such as Titus Flauius Valens (?) and Gaius Iulius Longus. In VII **1022** (= RMR 87), a Latin enrolment list of recruits dating from 103, Gaii Iulii appear twice (but no Flauii). A date in the late first or early second century therefore seems probable. It would suit the dating of the script, which is a less formal example of ChLA XXV 785 (= PSI XI 1183; 45–54). Other possible parallels are P. Herc. 817 (= Seider, *Pal. lat. Pap.* II.1 4; 31 BC – AD 79), ChLA I 7 (= P. Gen. lat. 1; 81/90), X 456 + XI 468 (95), XLI 1191 (i/ii), P. Mich. VII 430a (= Seider, *Pal. lat. Pap.* II.1 10; before 115), ChLA X 422 (= BGU VII 1689 = Seider, *Pal. lat. Pap.* II.1 9; 122–145). The names do not give any clue as to whether this was an auxiliary cohort or a legion.

This looks like a guard roster, parallels of which can be found in R. O. Fink, *Roman Military Records on Papyrus* nos. 12–19; see esp. 15 introd. The soldiers have been placed at strategic locations, either in pairs or singly. It is impossible to be certain of the town or region in question. The mention of an amphitheatre and of alabaster quarries makes it unlikely that we are dealing with Oxyrhynchus; on the theatre of Oxyrhynchus, see W. M. F. Petrie, *Tombs of the Courtiers and Oxyrhynkhos* (1925) 14–16 (repr. in *Oxyrhynchus: A City and its Texts* 52–4); A. Łukaszewicz, *Les Édifices publics dans les villes de l'Égypte romaine* (1986) 60, 170–71; D. M. Bailey in *Oxyrhynchus: A City and its Texts* 70–90. Antinoopolis might provide a better fit with some of the topographical features mentioned; A. Bernand, *Les Portes du désert* (1984) 29–46, quotes the description of the site of Antinoopolis made by E. Jomard in *La Description de l'Égypte*; Bailey, loc. cit. 70–71, listing a colonnade (33), an amphitheatre (34), baths (41) that could justify the presence of water-pipes, and quarries (44). However, the onomastics and the palaeography militate against a date after 130 (see above) and the 'amphitheatre' at Antinoopolis is in fact a theatre (*Descr. de l'Égypte* iv pl. 53). The only place in Egypt at which an amphitheatre is reasonably securely attested is Alexandria, close to Nicopolis; see J. McKenzie, *The Architecture of Alexandria and Egypt* (2007) 400 n. 49; D. M. Bailey, 'Classical Architecture in Roman Egypt', in M. Henig (ed.), *Architecture and Architectural Sculpture in the Roman Empire* (1990) 121–37, at 123. In that case, these soldiers would probably be legionaries. This, however, does not fit very well with the mention of an alabaster quarry; the nearest to Alexandria appear to be in the Fayum and south-east of Cairo (see ii 26 n.). Whatever the case, the papyrus could have found its way to Oxyrhynchus among the papers carried there by a veteran after his discharge; or it could have simply been discarded by a soldier who happened to be passing through Oxyrhynchus.

Col. i

```
          .     .
      ] . . . ens
      ]t. . . .
      ]
      ]
  5   ] . . us
      ]
      ]ṃanus
          .     .
```

Col. ii

```
                  .      .      .        .      .      .       .
(m. 2)                                  ]ị Q Voçonius Satu[rninus
                                        ] M Antonius Cl. [
          (topographical entry)         ]
          (century)                     ] M Tullius [
  5       (topographical entry)         ]
          (century)                     ] T Flauius [
          (topographical entry)         ]
          (century)                     ] M Dellius Quint[
          (topographical entry)         ]
  10      (century)                     ] C Iulius Firmu[s
          (topographical entry)         ]
          (century)                     ] C Iulius Crisp[
          (century)                     ] Q Vettius Pude[
          castello
  15      c(enturia) Faiani Crispi      Ç [. . . . .]. us Sç[
          c(enturia) Clodi Capitoni     C Annaeius Ḅ. [
              portico
```

c(enturia) Faiani Crispi	*P Vettius D*[
c(enturia) Septim[*i*]	*M Acillius Ṭ*[
20 *amphothia*⟦*tur*⟧	
c(enturia) Iuli Saturnini	*L Antoniụ*[*s*
c(enturia) Septimi	*T Flauius Vạ*[
fistuliṣ	
c(enturia) Faiani	*T Flauius Maio*[*r*
25 *c(enturia) Clodi Capitoni*	*T Flauius Sceuọ*[*la*
alabastrona	
c(enturia) Ti Iuli	*C Iulius Loṇ*[*g–*
sum(ma) XVII ededit P Ac.[	

.   .   .   .

14   *castellˢ*

(. . .)	Quintus Voconius Saturninus
(. . .)	Marcus Antonius Cl(. . .)
(Topographical entry)	
(Century)	Marcus Tullius (. . .)
5 (Topographical entry)	
(Century)	Titus Flauius (. . .)
(Topographical entry)	
(Century)	Marcus Dellius Quint(. . .)
(Topographical entry)	
10 (Century)	Gaius Iulius Firmus
(Topographical entry)	
(Century)	Gaius Iulius Crisp(us?)
(Century)	Quintus Vettius Pude(ns?)
At the reservoir:	
15 Century of Faianus Crispus	C(. . .)us Sc(. . .)
Century of Clodius Capito	Gaius Annaeius B(. . .)
At the colonnade:	
Century of Faianus Crispus	Publius Vettius D(. . .)
Century of Septimius	Marcus Acillius T(. . .)
20 At the amphitheatre (?):	
Century of Iulius Saturninus	Lucius Antonius (. . .)
Century of Septimius	Titus Flauius Va(. . .)
At the water-pipes:	
Century of Faianus	Titus Flauius Maior
25 Century of Clodius Capito	Titus Flauius Scaeuola
At the quarry:	
Century of Tiberius Iulius	Gaius Iulius Long(. . .)
Total of 17 (men). Publius Ac(. . .) presented (the list)	

Col. i

  1   ]...*ens*. Perhaps *Valens*, *Pudens* (see ii 13) or *C]lemens* (ii 2).

  7   ]*manus*. Perhaps *Ger]manus* or *Fir]manus*.

Col. ii

  1   Presumably the genitive ending of the name of the century at the left.

  8   *M Dellius Quint[*. The rather unusual *gentilicium* Dellius is listed in W. Schulze, *Zur Geschichte lateinischer Eigennamen* (1904, repr. 1991) 423.

  12   *Crisp[*. Presumably *Crisp[us* or *Crisp[inus*.

  13   *Pude[*. Presumably *Pude[ns*.

  14   The occurrence of *fistulis* in 23 suggests that *castello* here refers to a reservoir (a common meaning; cf. Frontinus, *Aq.* 106), rather than a fort or military installation, which would in any case be less likely to need a detail of a pair of soldiers on guard.

  15   *C* [.....] *us Sc[. C [Iul]ius* seems too short to fill the gap. *Se[* is possible, though less likely.

  16 and 25   *Clodi Capitoni*. One would expect *Capitonis*. Final *-s* is more stable than final *-m*; see J. N. Adams, *CQ* 53 (2003) 538. This genitive was apparently attracted by the 2nd decl. genitive *Clodi*.

  17   *portico*. For the shift to the (locatival) ablative singular, see J. N. Adams, *JRS* 85 (1995) 110, with parallels from Vindolanda. The word *porticus* usually belongs to the 4th declension. For parallels to the shift to the 2nd declension, see PSI IX 1026 B 1 (= *CPL* 117 = ChLA XXV 784; Caesarea Pal., 150) *in po[r]tico. CIL* VI 15048.6 *portico suo*. On colonnades in cities of Roman Egypt, see Łukaszewicz, *Les Édifices publics* 180–81, and LXIV **4441** *passim*.

  20   *amphothia⟦tur⟧*. This looks like a clumsy rendering of *amphitheatro*, although the Greek word ἀμφιθέατρον is not attested in papyri. The vowel change *amphi-/ampho-* is hard to explain, and there are no parallels either in Gignac, *Grammar* or in Mayser, *Grammatik*; there may be an analogy with e.g. ἀμφότεροι. For *-thia-* instead of *-thea-*, see Audollent, *Defix. tab.* 250b.16 *desub ampitiatri corona*. The scribe may have realized that his ending in *-tur* was improper, and crossed it out; apparently, he did not write *tro* for *tur*.

  21   *c(enturia) Iuli Saturnini*. A recruit named Gaius Iulius Saturninus is attested in VII **1022** 19 (103), probably not the same person. The different elements of the name are all too common to allow an identification.

  22   *T Flauius Va[*. A Titus Flauius Vale[is attested in P. Gen. lat. 1 = *RMR* 10.17 and 9.34.

  23   *fistulis*. The water-pipes could control the supply either of the baths or of a public fountain.

  24   *c(enturia) Faiani*. For the unusual *gentilicium* Faianius, see Schulze, *Zur Geschichte lateinischer Eigennamen* 185.

  26   *alabastrona*. This must derive from the Greek accusative of ἀλαβαστρών, as in SB I 4639.3–4 (209) καταδικασθέντα εἰς ἀλαβαστρῶ|να. The word is not attested in any papyrus from Oxyrhynchus, nor is the Latin form found either in *ThlL* or in *OCD*. In Plin. *Nat.* 5.61, *Alabastron* transcribes Greek gen. pl., whereas in 37.109, *Alabastrum* is acc. n. sing. For a parallel to the use of the Greek accusative without preposition in a similar context, see J. N. Adams, *Bilingualism and the Latin Language* (2003) 723–4; id., *CQ* 53 (2003) 551–2. The precise location of this quarry is uncertain. PSI VII 822.4–5 (ii), a document of unknown provenance, mentions Antinoopolis as well as quarry-workers: εὗρον | το[ὑ]ϲ ἀλαβαϲτρωνείταϲ. Alabaster quarries in Het-nub, close to Antinoopolis, are mentioned by K. Fitzler, *Steinbrüche und Bergwerke im ptolemäischen und römischen Ägypten* (1910) 108, although there is no ancient record for them; he also registers some in the neighbouring Hermopolite nome (121), where Alabastron polis was located. See also R. Klemm and D. D. Klemm, *Steine und Steinbrüche im alten Ägypten* (1993). The known alabaster quarries closest to Alexandria appear to be those at Wadi Gerrawi near Cairo (Klemm–Klemm 53, fig. 1, 200) and in the Fayum (Fitzler 110, and the quarry mentioned in SB

I **4639**, above). For a soldier of III Cyrenaica assigned to duty in a limestone quarry, see P. Gen. lat. I = *RMR* 9.d–e 4.

27 *C Iulius Lon̠[g—*. Presumably *Lon̠[gus*, although *Lon̠[ginus* is also possible. There are two occurrences of the name Gaius Iulius Longus in P. Gen. lat. I = *RMR* 9.11–12.

28 *sum(ma) XVII ededit P Ac̠* [.The total number of men listed in the document is indeed seventeen. See also P. Brook. 24.25 (Thebais, *c.*215) *summa qui decesserunt, mil(ites) XXX*, T. Vindol. II 154.25 *summa eor̠[um] X̠XXI*. For a parallel to *ededit* (instead of the regular *edidit*), see *CIL* VI 31850.8. Rather than resolving *sum(mam)* and regarding it as the direct object of *ededit*, we should understand a break in the sense after the numeral; the name of the person submitting the report is paralleled e.g. in T. Vindol. III 574. The verb *edo* does not seem to occur in Latin military documents, but see *OLD* s.v. 10.

P. SCHUBERT

4956–4957. Two Census Declarations

These two declarations are sufficiently similar, both extremely narrow like SB XXII 15465 and 15466 (11 and 7 cm wide, respectively), to raise the question whether they might have been part of a *tomos synkollesimos* together. But they concern different villages, Peenno and Sesphtha, in different toparchies; it is perhaps just chance that they also have in common that neither declarant has a legal father; the more complete (**4957**) lacks an address to any official, and it is altogether not obvious why they would have been filed together. Moreover, the second seems to preserve part of the original edges. Together, however, they add substantially to the small group of three Oxyrhynchite declarations previously known from the census of 145/6, for which see R. S. Bagnall, B. W. Frier, *The Demography of Roman Egypt* (1994) 232–3; no additional Oxyrhynchite declarations for that census have been published in the interim (see the addenda in the digital reprint, 2006). They follow, as far as preserved, the normal Oxyrhynchite formulary of the period for the κατ' οἰκίαν ἀπογραφή, for which see M. Hombert, C. Préaux, *Recherches sur le recensement dans l'Égypte Romaine* (P. L.-Bat. 5: 1952) 79, 91, 111, and 119–21.

4956. Census Declaration

75/22(a)   4.8 × 17.8 cm   146/7
                                                            Plate XI

The three fragments do not connect, but no more than a line or two is missing between the second and third fragments, depending on the degree of abbreviation. The amount lost between the first and second depends on how many (if any) persons were declared.

The hand is largely bilinear and detached, with some serifs, resembling a bookhand (cf. Roberts, *Greek Literary Hands* nos. 11, 13–14).

Fr. 1

```
      παρὰ Τνεφερ[ῶτος
      χρηματίζουσα [μητ(ρὸς) Cεν-
      παπῶτος Ἀντ[   c.5
      μετὰ κυρίο[υ τοῦ αὐτῆς
  5   ἀνδρὸς Πανεχ[ώτου
      Ἁρμιύcιος ἀμφ[οτέρων
      ἀπὸ Πεε(ννω). ἀπο[γράφομαι
      κατὰ τὰ κελ[ευcθέν-
      τα ὑπὸ Οὐαλερί[ου
 10   Πρόκλου το[ῦ ἡγεμ(ονεύcαντος)
      πρὸς τὴν τοῦ δ[ιελθόντος
      θ (ἔτουc) Ἀντωνί[νου
      Καίcαρος τοῦ [κυρίου
      κατ᾽ οἰκ(ίαν) ἀπογρ[αφὴν
 15   τὸ ὑπάρχ(ον) (πρότερον) Ψ[ενα-
      μούνιος Τ[   c.5
      τοῦ Ψεναμο[ύνιοc
      μητρὸς Τν[   c.5
      ἐν τῇ α(ὐτῇ) Πεε(ννω) [. . . μέ-
 20   ρος οἰκ(ίας) καὶ κα[μάρας
      καὶ αὐλ(ῆc) καὶ ἑτ[έρων
      χρηcτηρίων [κοι-
      νωνικ(ῶν) πρὸς [   c.5
      λων[. .]. .[
            .       .      .      .
```

Frr. 2–3

```
            .      .      .      .
      [   c.8    καὶ ὀμνύω]
      [Αὐτοκράτορα Καί-]
      cαρ]α Τ[ίτον Αἴλιον
      Ἁδριανὸν Ἀ[ντωνῖνον
  5   Cεβαcτὸν Εὐ[cεβῆ
      ἐξ ὑγι(οῦc) καὶ ἐπ᾽ [ἀληθείαc
      [ἐπιδεδωκέναι]
      [τὴν προκειμέ-]
      νην ἀπ[ογραφὴν
```

10   καὶ μήτε ἐπί[ξενον
        μήτε Ῥωμα[ῖον
        μήτε Ἀλεξ[ανδρέα
        μηδ᾽ ἄλ(λον) [μηδένα
        ο]ἰκ[εῖν μηδὲ

                .   .   .

Fr. 1

    2 l. χρηματιζούϲηϲ   7 Πε^ε   12 θ∫   14 οι^κ   15 υπαρ^χᾱ   19 ᾱ Πε^ε
20 οι^κ   22 αυ^λ   23 νωνι^κ

Frr. 2+3
    6 υγ^ι   13 α^λ

'From Tnepheros officially described as daughter of mother [Sen]papos daughter of Ant—, with as guardian her husband Panechotes son of Harmiysis, both from Peeno. I register according to the orders of the former prefect Valerius Proculus, for the house-by-house registration of the past 9th year of Antoninus Caesar the lord, the —th part belonging to me, formerly of Psenamounis son of T—, grandson of Psenamounis, mother Tn—, in the same Peeno, of a house and storeroom and courtyard and other appurtenances, owned jointly with . . . [break] and I swear by Imperator Caesar Titus Aelius Hadrianus Antoninus Augustus Pius that I have submitted the aforesaid declaration properly and truthfully and that neither foreigner nor Roman nor Alexandrian nor anyone else is living (in it) nor . . .'

Fr. 1

    2–3 [Ϲεν]παπῶτοϲ. The name had previously occurred in SB XXII 15441, a Theban mummy label of the third/fourth century: Ϲενπαπω(ϲ). (It is of course possible that Ϲιν-, common in the Oxyrhynchite nome, appeared instead of Ϲεν-.) Παπῶϲ is better attested (see the few instances in Preisigke, *Namenbuch*, and Foraboschi, *Onomasticon*, where the reference to P. Erl. 109.32 is to be deleted), but not apparently from the Oxyrhynchite. No Demotic version seems to be listed in Lüddeckens, *Demotisches Namenbuch*.

    2 χρηματίζουϲα, l. -ούϲηϲ. The idiom χρηματίζων/χρηματίζουϲα μητρόϲ is a distinctively Oxyrhynchite way of saying what in other parts of Egypt is expressed with the word ἀπάτωρ, i.e., with no legal father; see M. Malouta, *Pap. Congr. XXIV* (2007) 615 ff.

    3 Perhaps Ἀντ[ωνίου or Ἀντ[ᾶτοϲ.

    4 Perhaps abbreviated αυ^τ.

    7 Peenno was in the Middle toparchy; its attestations belong to the first three centuries of our era (Pruneti, *I centri abitati dell'Ossirinchite* 141). The last word in the line was perhaps abbreviated απογρ∫.

    9–10 On L. Valerius Proculus, see G. Bastianini, *ZPE* 17 (1975) 289–90 and 38 (1980) 82; W. Habermann, *ZPE* 117 (1997) 180–82. He is clearly described as former prefect in SB XXII 15466 and in **4957**, dated to 20 and 22 February 147, respectively; these are the earliest secure evidence for his having left office. One may thus safely resolve the abbreviations as ἡγεμον(εύϲαντοϲ) in P. Corn. 17 = SB XX 14304.6 and P. Bad. IV 75b.9, of 10 and 11 March, as Habermann has shown. It is likely that the aorist participle is to be restored here also, though cf. I **171** desc. = SB XXII 15353.5, also of Year 10 (146/7), which refers to him as τοῦ ἡγεμόνοϲ. The later date in BGU II 378 does not refer to Proculus, as Habermann has demonstrated. Proculus' successor, M. Petronius Honoratus, is not attested until summer.

15 μοι seems to have been omitted.

18 Probably Τυ[εφερῶτος] (perhaps abbreviated), as in the name of the declarant; the former owner of the part of a house was thus probably a relative.

19 It is possible that no portion was specified, given the limited space available.

20 κα[μάρας. κα[ταγείου is another, though statistically less likely, possibility. καμάρα is properly a vaulted room; see Husson, *OIKIA* 123–8. Whether it is distinguished from the house here because it was a basement and thought of separately (Husson 124 cites P. Lips. I 3, οἰκία . . . ὑφ᾽ ἥν καμάρα) or because it was a separate storeroom, the meaning it commonly takes on, is hard to say.

23–4 Ἀπολ]|λων[?

Frr. 2–3

14 This extended version of the oath formula is also found in SB XXII 15465.14–15, completed with ἔξω τῶν προκειμένων, and in 15466.35–7, where it is completed more fully with μηδὲ ἀπογρά(φεσθαι) ἔξω τῶν προκειμ(ένων) ὀνομάτ(ων) εἰ᾽ (l. ἤ) ἔνοχ(ος) εἴην τῷ ὅρκῳ.

4957. CENSUS DECLARATION

75/22(c)   8.5 × 18.5 cm   22 February 147

The hand of the body of the declaration is an irregular cursive, followed by a signature by a slow writer in an ungainly hand.

παρὰ Λεον[τ]ᾶτος χρηματίcαντ(ος)
μ[η]τ(ρὸς) Τανούφιος ἀπὸ C[έc]cφθα
τῆς κάτω τοπαρχείας. ἀπογ(ράφομαι)
τὰ κατὰ κελευουcθέντα
5   ὑπὸ Οὐαλερίου Πρ[ό]κλου
τοῦ ἡγεμονεύcαντος πρ[ὸ]c
τὴν τοῦ διελθόντος θ (ἔτους)
Ἀντωνίνου Καίcαρος τοῦ
κυρίου κατ᾽ οἰκε[ίαν ἀ]πογ(ραφὴν)
10   cημαίνω⟦. . .⟧ ἐμαυτὸν ἀναγραφόμενον ἐπὶ τῆς αὐτῆς Cέc-
cφθα ἐν τοῖc ἐπὶ κώμης ἀνα-
λαμμανομένοιc αὐτὸν ἐμὲ
Λεοντᾶν τὸν πρ[ογε]γραμμένο[ν]
15   ἄτεχνον ἄcημον (vac.) (ἐτῶν) μ[?].
πρ(οcγίνεται) Πμυcθᾶc υἱὸc μητ(ρὸc) Ἀρτέμιτος
(vac.)   (ἐτῶν) ιβ.   (vac.)
πρ(οcγίνεται) Πανετβεῦc ἀδελφὸc γονέων

τῶν αὐτῶν   (vac.)   (ἐτῶν) α.

20 γ(υναῖκες)· Ἄρτεμις Πανετβεῦς μητ(ρὸς) Cινπμυcτ( )
γυνή μου ἄτεχνος ἄcημος (ἐτῶν) λβ,
Τανοῦφις θυγάτηρ ἀμφοτέρων (ἐτῶν) ια.
καὶ ὀμνύω Αὐτοκράτορα
Καίcαρα Τίτον Αἴλιον Ἁδριανὸν
25 Ἀντωνῖνον Cεβαcτὸν Εὐcεβῆν
ἀληθῆ εἶναι τὰ προγεγραμμέ-
να. (ἔτους) ι Αὐτοκρᾳ[τορος] Καίcαρος
Τίτου Αἰλίου Ἁδ[ρια]ν̣οῦ Ἀντωνίνου
Cεβαcτ̣[οῦ Εὐcεβοῦ]c Μεχεὶρ κη̄.
30 (m. 2) Λεοντ[ᾶc ὁ προγε]γραμέ-
νοc ἐπιδ[έδωκα καὶ ὀμώ-
μεχα τὸν̣ [ὅρκον.

. . . . . .

1 χρηματιcαν^τ	2 μ[η]^τ	2, 11–12 l. Cέcφθα	3 l. τοπαρχίας		3, 9 απογ⟨
4 l. κατὰ τὰ κελευcθέντα	7 θ^L	9 l. οἰκίαν	10 ε of ἐμαυτόν written over original μαι?		
13 l. -λαμβανομένοιc	15, 17, 19, 21, 22, 27 L	16, 18 ρ̂	16 μη^τ	l. Ἀρτέμιδος	
20 γ̄ l. Πανετβεῦτος μη^τcινπμυ^{cτ}		25 l. Εὐcεβῆ	30 l. προγεγραμμέ-	32 l. -μοκα	

'From Leontas officially described as son of mother Tanouphis, from Sesphtha of the Lower toparchy. I register according to the orders of the former prefect Valerius Proculus for the house-by-house registration of the past 9th year of Antoninus Caesar the lord, declaring myself, registered in the same Sesphtha in the property registered in the village, myself Leontas the aforementioned, without a trade, without scars, 40[+?] years old. Additionally, Pmysthas my son by mother Artemis, 12 years old. Additionally, Panetbeus his brother from the same parents, 1 year old.

'Women: Artemis daughter of Panetbeus and Sinpmyst( ), my wife, without a trade, without scars, 32 years old. Tanouphis, daughter of both (of us), 11 years old. And I swear by Imperator Caesar Titus Aelius Hadrianus Antoninus Augustus Pius that the aforewritten facts are true. Year 10 of Imperator Caesar Titus Aelius Hadrianus Antoninus Augustus Pius, Mecheir 28.

(2nd hand) 'I, Leontas, the aforementioned, have submitted and sworn the oath.'

1 For χρηματίcαντ(ος), see **4956** fr. 1.2–3 n. The aorist is surprising; when it appears in such phrases, it usually stresses a change of legal designation intervening since a point in the past or at least (as in II **271**, where it refers specifically to being Πέρcης τῆς ἐπιγονῆς) the fact that a particular status was held at the time of a past transaction. Although the sigma and alpha are damaged, reading ζο is not possible.

2 I have not found another instance of Cέcφθα with doubled sigma, although forms omitting sigma altogether are known and theta is sometimes dropped. For gemination of sigma generally see Gignac, *Grammar* i 159. The village is attested over virtually the entire Graeco-Roman period (Pruneti, *I centri abitati* 174).

4 The inversion of κατά and τά is striking; despite damage to the surface, it does not seem possible to read the remains otherwise. This formula was new in the Oxyrhynchite in this census

(Hombert–Préaux, *Recherches* 111), and the scribe was evidently not yet accustomed to it. For the form κελευουϲθέντα, cf. Gignac, *Grammar* i 215.

5 For Valerius Proculus, see **4956** Fr. 1.9–20 n.

12–13 I do not know of a parallel for this phrase in the census declarations, but Hombert–Préaux, *Recherches* 111, note that Oxyrhynchite declarations give more information about the origin of ownership of property than those from other nomes. For ἀναλαμβάνω in the sense of 'porter dans les rôles', see P. Thmouis I 69.20 n., citing Preisigke, *WB* I 94 s.v. (12).

16 At the start (also in 18), a rho surmounted with a curve concave downward, suggesting πρ( ). For the use of πρ(οϲγίνεται) to indicate an additional person in a declaration I can cite no direct parallel, but cf. the Oxyrhynchite *gerousia* declaration PSI XII 1240a.9 and b.7, where it stands after the name but before the characteristic ἄτεχνοϲ ἄϲημοϲ.

The name Πμυϲθᾶϲ, otherwise unattested, is simply the well-known name Μυϲθᾶϲ prefixed with the masculine definite article. It is characteristic of the Arsinoite rather than the Oxyrhynchite, but as Dr Gonis points out, Sesphtha was not very far from the Arsinoite. The grandmother's name in line 20 is evidently formed by prefixing 'the daughter of' in its characteristic Oxyrhynchite form to this name, although with tau instead of theta at the end.

18 The younger son has been named after his maternal grandfather.

19 The indication of the age of the younger son has been corrected, but how is not clear. There is a clear alpha written above the horizontal of the year sign. This is followed by a mass of downward strokes, some apparently sinusoidal but one vertical. The ages otherwise never have markings after them, and it is possible that the scribe at first mistook an original eta, or age 8, for an alpha followed by a sinusoidal curve. That would not, however, explain why he did not (upon realising his error) alter the first part of the letter to look more like an eta.

19–20 The paragraphos is written just on top of γ(υναῖκεϲ) and barely distinguishable from its horizontal abbreviation stroke.

20 γυναῖκεϲ as heading for the section of women is found in (e.g.) SB XXII 15465 (145-Ox-1); the sequence of male and female household members in separate sections is typical of the Oxyrhynchite nome. For Artemis' mother's name, not previously attested, see 16 n. The sigma seems to have been written over the upper right part of the upsilon as an afterthought.

30–32 The verbs of oath and submission are given in reverse order in SB XXII 15466.42–3. The deformation of the second verb is striking, but it is paralleled in a number of texts; see Gignac, *Grammar* ii 304, with examples of ὀμώμεχα and ὠμόμεχα. The papyrus is broken off at the bottom, but it is possible that nothing is lost.

R. S. BAGNALL

4958. APPLICATION TO ACTING STRATEGUS

74/27(a)   7.5 × 25.5 cm   21 February 148
                                                            Plate XII

An application to Ischyrion, royal scribe and acting strategus, from Onnophris son of Sambas, a tenant farmer seeking to continue cultivating a holding of royal land.

The lease of the land had originally been granted to Sambas, Onnophris's deceased father, and Onnophris had apparently expected to take over the lease on the same terms on his demise; in fact he had already sown the land (19–20). But an overbid for the right to cultivate the land had been put in by Sarapion, freedman of Petosorapis (9), by offering an additional payment (18, 22, 25: for the possible resolution of the abbreviation, see 18 n.).

Onnophris, as 'the former tenant who has already sown the land' (18–20), now claims the right to continue as lessee for the present Year 11 = 147/8. He undertakes, 'according to the customary usage of the nome' (21), to match Sarapion's additional payment, on condition that it is removed from him after that year (23–5), that the right of farming the land in future will remain with him on the original terms which he had paid for the preceding Year 10, and that an appropriate deduction will be made for any land left unflooded or artificially irrigated in the following Year 12.

The inclusion of these standard clauses in lines 26–32 shows that Onnophris intended to continue farming the land himself. This may not have been the case with Sarapion. Initial applications to lease public lands, e.g. P. Sarapion 45 = P. Strasb. I 78 (Herm., 127) and P. Flor. III 383 (Ant., 232), appear to show that the payment of the additional amount might entitle the successful overbidder to sublet to a third party rather than work the land himself. So this may have been what attracted Sarapion's opportunistic overbid in the present case.

For some discussion of related texts, see Th. Kruse, *Der Königliche Schreiber und die Gauverwaltung* (2002) 578–81, but the only parallel to **4958**, and then not a close one, appears to be SB I 5672 (Herm., 156/7; not discussed by Kruse). This too is a petition to the strategus concerning a lease of public land; there is reference to the offer of an additional payment, and the complainants also describe themselves as προγεωργοί, but the text is too broken to be of much help.

There is no *kollesis*. The back is blank.

Ἰσχυρίωνι β(ασιλικῷ) γρ(αμματεῖ) διαδεχ(ομένῳ)
   καὶ τὰ κατὰ τὴν στρα(τηγίαν)
παρὰ Ὀννώφριος Σαμβᾶτος
τοῦ Ὀννώφρ[ιος μητρὸς
5   Σοήριος ἀπὸ κ[ώ]μης Ταν[ά]ε-
   ως. προσπέπτωκέ μοι Σα-
   ραπίων ἀπελεύθερος Πετο-
   σοράπιος ἀπ' Ὀξυρύγχων πόλεως ὑπερβαλὼν τῷ ἐνεσ-
10   τῶτι ια (ἔτει) τὸ ἀναγραφόμενον εἰς τὸν μετηλλαχότα
   μου πατέρα Σαμβᾶν Ὀννώφριος τοῦ Ὀννώφριος
   περὶ Σεφω ἐκ τοῦ Ἐπιμέ-

15 νους κλήρου βασιλικῆς
γῆς (ἄρουρ) . d, προσενεγκὼ[ν
πρὸς μόνον τὸ ἐνεστὸς ι[α] (ἔτος)
ε . ( ) ἕν. ἐγὼ οὖν προγεωργὸς
ὢν καὶ προεξυλαμηκὼς
20 τὴν γῆν, ἀναδέχομαι κατὰ τὸ τοῦ νομοῦ ἔθος
τὸ προκείμενον ε . ( ) ἕν,
ἐπὶ τῷ μετὰ τὸ ἐνεστὸς ια (ἔτος)
περιαιρεθήσεται ἀπ' ἐμοῦ
25 τὸ προκείμενον ε . ( ) ἕ[ν
καὶ μενεῖ μοι ἡ γεωργία
ἐπὶ μόνοις τοῖς τὸ διελθ(ὸν)
ι (ἔτος) τελεσθεῖσι τελέςμαςι.
ἐὰν δέ τις ἀπ[ὸ το]ῦ εἰςι[ό]ντ[ος
30 ιβ (ἔτους) ἄβροχος ἢ ἐπηντλημέ-
νη γένηται, παραδεχθήςε-
ταί μοι. (ἔτους) ια Αὐτοκράτορος
Καίσαρος Τ[ίτο]υ Αἰλίου
Ἁδ[ρ]ιανοῦ Ἀντωνείνου
35 Cεβαστοῦ Εὐςεβοῦς,
Μεχεὶρ κϛ. Ὄννωφρις
Cαμβᾶτος ἐπιδέδωκα.

1 βϛγρϛδιαδεͯͦ   2 cτρᴸ   10, 28, 32 Ⅼ   16 ⲧ   17, 23, 30 ʃ   27 διελᶿ
34 l. Ἀντωνίνου

'To Ischyrion, royal scribe acting also in the post of the *strategia*, from Onnophris son of Sambas the son of Onnophris, whose mother is Soeris, from the village of Tanais. It has come to my notice that Sarapion, freedman of Petosorapis from the city of the Oxyrhynchi, has made an overbid for the present Year 11 for the landholding registered to my deceased father Sambas son of Onnophris the son of Onnophris in the vicinity of Sepho, from the *kleros* of Epimenes, n ¼ aroura(s) of royal land, having offered a single ... for the present Year 11 only. So as I am the former tenant farmer and have sown the land beforehand, according to the customary usage of the nome I undertake (sc. to pay) the aforementioned single ..., on the terms that the aforementioned single ... will be removed from me after the present Year 11, and the right of farming will remain with me on the terms of only the payments paid for the past Year 10, and if from the coming Year 12 any land should become either unflooded or artificially irrigated a deduction will be made for me.
'Year 11 of Imperator Caesar Titus Aelius Hadrianus Antoninus Augustus Pius, Mecheir 26. I, Onnophris son of Sambas, have submitted (this).'

1–2 This is the first attestation of Ischyrion as acting strategus of the Oxyrhynchite nome. He is otherwise known as royal scribe only from I **171** descr. = II p. 208 = SB XXII 15353: J. Whitehorne, *Strategi and Royal Scribes of Roman Egypt*[2] 162.

5–6 κ[ώ]μης Ταν[ά]εως. Tanais was located in the Middle Toparchy, Sepho in the adjacent Thmoisepho Toparchy: P. Pruneti, *I centri abitati dell'Ossirinchite* s. vv. and map.

14–15 Ἐπιμένους κλήρου. The *kleros* of Epimenes is otherwise known from PSI X 1118.7; see Pruneti, *Aegyptus* 55 (1975) 176.

16 (ἀρουρ) . ∂. The unread figure might be ε or ι. One might even consider reading Ⳑ (½), which would correspond to τὸ ἀναγραφόμενον in 10–11. However, it would make no commercial sense for Sarapion to offer such a large additional payment as 5 artabas (see below, 18 n.) for the right to lease only ¾ aroura.

18, 22, 25 ε ( ) ἕν. The initial epsilon is definite, with its tip continuing upwards into a vertical stroke cut through by a horizontal dash above, similar to that which marks the numeral in 16. Its resolution remains uncertain.

J. L. Rowlandson, who had not seen the papyrus, pointed out that the standard term for an additional sum offered as an overbid in offers to lease or purchase public lands or property is ἐπίθεμα; see P. Ryl. II 97.5 n. for discussion of the term, and cf. III **500** (130, lease of public land), IV **721** and **835** (13/14, sale of crown land), P. Flor. III 368 (Herm., 96). P. Amh. II 85 (Herm., 78), which is an application to the *exegetes* to lease land held in trust for orphans, stipulates a period of 10 days allowed for the offer of an ἐπίθεμα. The word would give the required sense for the context and fit with the preceding neuter singular τὸ προκείμενον in 22 and 25. But it is questionable whether one could refer to 'a single additional payment' without specifying an amount. Nor does it seem possible to take the abbreviation mark as ἐ(πίθεμα) or ἐπ(ίθεμα).

K. A. Worp has suggested that the abbreviation may be the name of a dry measure, the amount of which constituted the overbid. If this is the case, the only likely candidate worthy of consideration here seems to be (πεντ)(αρτάβιον); the word is not attested, but cf. XIV **1760** 8–9 (II), where we find the adjective πενταρταβιαῖον, used of a sack of this size. Compare also the common term ἡμιαρτάβιον. For its abbreviation cf. XII **1445** 3, 11 (ii) or P. Graux II 14.8 (pl. VII), where the term πενταρταβία, '5 art. percentage', is written as ε followed by the symbol for artaba. An argument in favour may be that 5 artabas are also offered as the ἐπίθεμα in III **500**. The public land applied for there was 20 ¼ arouras, suggesting that 5 artabas as a lump sum may have been a standard amount for such an overbid. ε ( ) ἕν might accordingly be understood as 'one (or 'a single') 5 art. measure full.' We should not therefore be looking here for a one-to-one correspondence with the land area of 5 (or 10) ¼ arouras in 16.

19 προεξυλαμηκώς. *προξυλαμᾶν is an *addendum lexicis*.

28 τελέσμασι. Cf. VII **1031** 22.

J. WHITEHORNE

4959. LETTER OF AMMONIUS TO HIS PARENTS

43 5B.66/F(1–2)a   13.5 × 20.5 cm   Second century

Ammonius, who is or has been a gymnasiarch, wrote this letter to Demetria and Dius, whom he calls his mother and father (very probably but not certainly his parents), concerning his brother Theon. Theon had written to them that he had caught a chill but had recovered. Demetria and Dius, however, were apparently still worried about Theon's health, and Ammonius tries to reassure them. He swears to the gods that Theon has fully recovered, and no residue of his illness has remained.

The letter shows a very good command of Greek. There are no errors, save for a common phonetic spelling (4, 14). Iota adscript is used whenever required. The sophisticated language borders on the literary and has some prominent atticistic elements. On atticism in Greek private letters and letters written by educated individuals, see S. Witkowski, *Aegyptus* 13 (1933) 529–41, and W. Döllstädt, *Griechische Papyrusprivatbriefe in gebildeter Sprache aus den ersten vier Jahrhunderten nach Christus* (1934).

The two opening lines are spaced out more generously than the rest of the text. The scribe sometimes leaves a space between sentences as if to signify a change in context. In his effort to make the layout as regular as possible, the scribe uses angular filler signs at the ends of some lines (4, 14, 17, 19). In this he is fairly consistent, though there are a couple of lines that are shorter than others and have no filler signs (especially 12). The filler sign is of standard format, found often in literary papyri, similar, for example, to those in *GMAW*^{2} 67, but with the lower stroke more elongated. The size of some letters is occasionally exaggerated (even in the middle of words).

The main text is written in a distinctive script that can be parallelled in early examples of the 'chancery' style; for the main discussion of this style, see G. Cavallo, *Aegyptus* 45 (1965) 216–49. Cf. in particular P. Brem. 5–6, two formal letters of recommendation addressed to Apollonius, strategus of the Heptanomia in 117–19 (P. Brem. 5, pl. in *ed. pr.*; P. Brem. 6 is pl. 1 in Cavallo's article); P. Giss. Univ. Bibl. III 20, an official letter of *c.*113–17 (see J. D. Thomas, *The Epistrategos in Ptolemaic and Roman Egypt: The Roman Epistrategos* (1982) 187; pl. 1 in *ed. pr.*). P. Rain. Cent. 70, assigned to the late second third or early third century (J. Chapa, *Letters of Condolence in Greek Papyri* (1998) 87, pl. 5), is also somewhat similar. These parallels are different translations of the same principle. They are all influenced by the chancery script, but are less pretentious versions of the flamboyant official documents (see, for example, plates III–IV in Cavallo's article). A date for our letter in the early second century seems acceptable.

The document seems to have been thoroughly revised and corrected by a second hand, which is cursive and of variable size. Extensive parts of the text have been crossed out, and an alternative version has been added over each of the crossed-out lines. At the end of the main text, four additional lines were penned by the second hand. On the back, below the address, which was written by the first hand, the second hand added a docket stating the name and capacity of the sender.

A big X, starting from all four corners of the sheet, cancels the whole of the text. This is not an unusual feature in documents that have to do with loans, but it is very rare among letters (cf. XLII **3057**, where such a letter is possibly mentioned, but the editor thinks that it is more likely that the word κεχιαϲμένην refers to some kind of sign rather than that the letter was crossed out). It is not easy to tell who made the corrections, or even why, but it is even more difficult to speculate on who drew the **X**, for, though it is possible, it does not necessarily follow that it was the same person who did both.

To return to the corrections, a possible scenario would be that Ammonius, being or having been a gymnasiarch, was a man of above-average literacy, but not necessarily skilled in calligraphy. He hired a scribe, and dictated to him the letter, which the scribe finished and added the address. After that, Ammonius must have looked through the letter and perhaps thought that it was not convincing enough. Thus he took it upon himself to make the corrections in his own hand. It would be plausible to assume that, after he had made the corrections, he gave it back to the scribe to rewrite it, and either of them could have crossed it out. However, the letter seems to have been folded as if about to be sent (there are regular vertical fold marks), and also contains a docket under the address, stating the name of the sender. Maybe Ammonius wrote the docket, giving back the letter to the scribe, for filing purposes. It is not impossible that the letter was sent, despite its state, as Ammonius seemed to think it was urgent. Besides, the main text in **3057** starts with ἐκομιcάμην τὴν κεχιαcμένην ἐπιcτολήν, which, if it means 'I received the crossed-out letter', and not 'the one bearing the sign of the cross' (see P. J. Parsons in R. Pintaudi (ed.), *Miscellanea Papyrologica* (1980) 289; G. R. Stanton, *ZPE* 53 (1983) 50 ff.), suggests that, even if not a usual practice, it was conceivable that such letters were sent.

Ἀμμώνιος Δημητρίαι τῆι μητ[ρ]ὶ
 καὶ Δίωι τῶι πατρὶ χαίρειν.
ἐξήρκει μὲν καὶ τὰ Θέωνος τοῦ ἀδελφοῦ γράμματα
 δι' ὧν ὑμεῖν ἐδήλου ὅτι ψυγμῶι ληφθεὶς ἐκ
5 βάθους καὶ ἐκλύcει τοῦ cώματος ⟦καὶ⟧ ἐν ἀγωνίαι ποι-
 ήcας πάντας ἡμᾶς οὐ τῆι τυχούcηι, διὰ τοὺς θεοὺς αὐτῆς ὥρας ἀνέλαβεν καὶ τέλεον ἀνεκτήcα-
 το, ὥστε καὶ λούcαcθαι αὐτῆς ἐκείνης τῆς ἡμέ-
 ρας καὶ μηδὲν ἔτι αὐτῶι τοῦ cυμβάντος ἐνκατά-
       (m. 2) ἵνα ⟦[. . ₁ .λ]⟧λο . . π . . . . . .αιτε αὐτοῦ τοῖc
10 λειμμα εἶναι. ὅτι μὲν οὖν ἀληθέcτατα ταῦτα
 γρ]άμμαcιν ὡc ἄρα χαριζόμενος ὑμεῖν [ἐ]πέcτειλε κἀγὼ γέγραφα
 ⟦ὑμεῖν ἐπιcτέλλομεν⟧ τοὺς θεοὺς πάντας ἐπό-
       ὅπως δ' ἂν
 μνυμαι. ⟦ἵνα⟧ δὲ [. .]παρ' ἄλλου ᾿τ[ι]νόc᾿ πυθόμενοι τῶν
       ]. . .[. . .]. .ω . . .ε
 εἰωθότων ᾿μή᾿ τὰ ἀληθῆ λέγειν ἀν[α]γκαῖον ἡγηcά-
  . η
 . α μεθα φθάcαντες αὐτὸ τοῦτο δῆλον ὑμεῖν ποι-

15 ἦϲαι. ⟦δι’ ὅπερ μηδὲν ἐκταρα[χθ]ῆτε, ὡϲ κάλλι-
ϲτα ἔχοντοϲ τοῦ ἀδελφοῦ Θέω[νοϲ] καὶ τὰ ϲυνήθη
πάντα ποιοῦντοϲ.⟧ προϲαγορεύει ὑμᾶϲ ἡ θυγάτηρ ὑμῶν καὶ ὁ ἀδελφόϲ μου ‘ὁ̣’ ϲ̣ώταϲ. Πτολε-
μαῖον καὶ Ἀντίοχον τοὺϲ ἀδελφοὺϲ ἀφ’ ἡμῶν
20 ἀϲπάζεϲθε. (*m.* 2) ἐρρῶϲ̣θ̣αι ὑμᾶϲ εὔχομαι,
[τ]ι̣μιώτατοι, παν[ο]ικηϲίᾳ εὐτυχοῦνταϲ
κ . . . . ἐπόμνυμαι ὅτι καλῶϲ πά̣νυ
ἔχει ⟨ὁ⟩ ἀδελφὸϲ Θέων καὶ τὰ ϲυνήθη πράϲ-
ϲει.

Back, downwards, along the lines:

25 . . . . α . . . . .α̣.
(*m.* 2) πα(ρὰ) Ἀμμωνί(ου)
γυμν(αϲιαρχ)

1 δημητριαΙ   4, 14 ϋμειν; l. ὑμῖν   4, 14, 17, 19 ⁊ at line end   9 l. ἐγκατά-
10a ϊνα: ι corr. from ε?   11a l. ὑμῖν   12 ϊνα   17 ϋμαϲ   18 ϋμων

'From Ammonius to Demetria, his mother, and Dius, his father, greetings. The letter of my brother Theon should have been enough, in which he informed you that, having got a chill deep within and a general weakness of the body, which made us all worry greatly, he immediately recovered, thanks to the gods, and was in perfect form again, so that he even bathed on that very same day, and no residue of his illness still remains. I swear to all the gods that these things ~~that I am sending you~~ are very true. *In order that . . . you would . . . that he sent his letter to you just to please you, I have also written.* However, in order that you ⟨do not⟩ hear about this from one of those people who have the habit of not telling the truth, I thought it necessary to let you know of this before they did. . . . ~~Therefore, do not be upset, since Theon, my brother, is in perfect condition and carries out all his usual activities.~~ Your daughter and my brother Sotas send you their greetings. Give my best to Ptolemaeus and Antiochus, my brothers. *I wish you good health, my most honoured (parents), and good fortune to the entire household . . . I swear that my bother Theon is very well and doing his usual activities.'*
    Back: (illegible remains of the address followed by) '*from Ammonius, (ex-?)gymnasiarch.'*

    1 Ἀμμώνιοϲ. Ammonius is called a (former?) gymnasiarch in the docket. There are numerous gymnasiarchs of this name, in Oxyrhynchus and elsewhere, but it is hard to propose an identification.
    3 ἐξήρκει. The use of this verb is one of the examples of accurate choice of wording and fine grammar in this letter. The ϲχῆμα Ἀττικόν is not always used already in the Ptolemaic papyri, and subsequently it is used less and less until it disappears completely (Mayser, *Grammatik* ii.3 28, §151). The plural is used mostly with neuters indicating persons, while the singular is found with non-personal subjects, as well as abstracts and pronouns (Blass–Debrunner–Rehkopf, *Grammatik des Neutestamentlichen Griechisch* 110, §133).
    The imperfect here is potential and expresses something unreal, which is common in Attic Greek; see Kühner–Gerth, *Grammatik* ii.1 204, §391.5, but they only refer to impersonal verbs or the like. A close parallel is Basil. *Epist.* 325.1 ἐξήρκει καὶ τὸ γράμμα τῆϲ ϲεμνότητόϲ ϲου πᾶϲαν ἡμῖν ἐξεργάϲαϲθαι εὐφροϲύνην.

4 ψυγμῶι. This word in the papyri usually refers to a special place in a pottery, where pots are left to cool off after they have been fired (see e.g. L **3595–7**). Here, however, it has the meaning of a 'cold' or 'ague'. There seems to be only one example of this meaning in the papyri, P. Oxy. Hels. 46 (i/ii), a private letter ending οὐ γὰρ ἠδυνήθην ἐπὶ τοῦ | παρόντος γράψαι οὐδενὶ διὰ τὸ ἀπὸ νόσου ἀναλαμβάνειν καὶ ψυγμοῦ | μεγάλου καὶ μόγις ἠδυνήθην καὶ ταῦτα γράψαι βασανιζ[ό]μενος (its inventory number, 43 5B.71/G(42–43)b, indicates that the papyrus was found during the same season of excavations as **4959**, and arranged in the same box, but that the two papyri were not found together).

In the medical writers, the term ψυγμός implies a medical condition, but it is not altogether clear what exactly that is; it can refer to a symptom of a disease, a cause of a disease, or the disease itself. Gal. 11.519 seems to use this term for a condition opposite to fever: τινὰ μὲν ἐπὶ τὸ θερμότερον ἐκτετράφθαι σώματα . . . , τινὰ δὲ ἐπὶ τὸ ψυχρότερον, ὡς ἐν τοῖς καλουμένοις ἤδη συνήθως ὑπὸ πάντων ἀνθρώπων ψυγμοῖς. On the other hand, Orib. *Syn.* 1.19.8, takes it as a cause of fever and refers to τοῖς ἀπὸ ψυγμοῦ πυρέττουσιν. The word also appears in *Sch. Nic. Ther.* 43a, where it seems to refer to a cold in the head, or the sniffles: ἔστι δὲ καὶ πόα δυναμένη ψυγμὸν ἀπελάσαι, εἴ τις τρίψας τρὶς προσενέγκῃ τῇ ῥινί. Aët. 2.3, as well as others, connects ψυγμοί with hip diseases (πρὸς ἰσχιάδα καὶ πάντας τοὺς περὶ τὰ νευρώδη μόρια ψυγμούς), and Dsc. 5.11.2, uses the word in the sense of 'shiver': τὰ τῶν θηρίων δήγματα, ὅσα τρόμους καὶ ψυγμοὺς ἐπιφέρει. Paul. Aegin. *Epit.* 1.100.3, associates ψυγμοί with diseases of the chest: ὅταν δέ τι περὶ τὸν θώρακα μέλλῃ γίγνεσθαι . . . ἀλγήματα γίγνεσθαι . . . ψυγμοὶ στήθους καὶ βραχιόνων.

4–5 ἐκ βάθους. In medical writings ἐκ βάθους often has the sense of 'within the body' or 'from deep within': Aët. 5.7, defines fever as θερμότης παρὰ φύσιν καρδίας καὶ ἀρτηριῶν . . . ἀναφερομένη τε ἐκ βάθους καὶ δριμεῖα. Sever. *Περὶ τῶν κωλικῶν φαρμάκων* p. 34 Dietz, in explaining the causes of dysentery, writes: ἡ δὲ αἰτία αὕτη οὐκ ἔξωθεν τὴν βλάβην κινεῖ, ἀλλ᾽ ὥσπερ ἐκ βάθους ἀνακύπτει.

5 ἐκλύσει. Durling, *Dictionary of Medical Terms in Galen* (1993), explains ἔκλυσις as 'feebleness, faintness'. In Galen, the word refers either to a general condition (4.437, καὶ γὰρ οὖν καὶ αὐτὸ τοῦτο τὸ ὕπτιον κατακεῖσθαι σημεῖόν ἐστιν ἐκλύσεως) or to specific parts of the body (7.602, ἐν ἐκλύσει καρδιακαῖς τε καὶ στομαχικαῖς). In the Corpus Hippocraticum the word often occurs with σῶμα, as it does in **4959**. The word is used in Hesychius and the *Suda* in the context of mental feebleness.

⟦καί⟧. Palaeography, sense, and style suggest that this may be the only correction made by the first hand, whereas all the others (10a, 11, 12, 15–17) are due to the second hand.

5–6 ἐν ἀγωνίαι ποιήσας πάντας ἡμᾶς οὐ τῆι τυχούσηι. This postponement of the negative expression / *litotes* is common enough, but here it has been displaced even more than would be expected. In J. D. Denniston, *Greek Prose Style* (1952) 50ff., in the discussion of *hyperbaton*, this case would fall in the category of 'deliberate separation of logically cohering words'. In this way, ἀγωνίαι features as the main point of the sentence, while τῆι τυχούσηι is emphasized by the postponement of its attributive position. For a similar construction, cf. P. Ryl. II 136.11–12 (34) ὕβριν μοι συν|εστήσατωι (l. -ατο) οὐ τὴν τυχοῦσαν.

6–7 διὰ τοὺς θεούς. Not found elsewhere. According to Mayser, *Grammatik* ii.2 426, διά with the accusative, apart from its instrumental and causal uses, can also have the sense 'in the name of'; as an example, he cites UPZ I 62.6 διά τε τ[ὸν] Σάραπιν.

7 ἀνέλαβεν. Although this verb is often attested in the papyri, there are not many passages in which it has a medical sense, 'to recover', as it does here: P. Zen. Pestm. 51.3 (257 BC), PSI IV 333.3 (256 BC), P. Bad. II 17.12 (i BC), P. Oxy. Hels. 46.17 (i/ii), XLVI **3313** 7 (ii). In classical Greek it can have a medical meaning, but always in the construction ἀναλαμβάνειν ἑαυτόν. What distinguishes later examples is the omission of the accusative. Examples illustrating this meaning are usually followed by an adverbial modifier: in Philo *De congressu* 39, *Legum allegoriarum* II 60, *De praemiis et poenis* 21, and Dsc. 5.6.16, ἀναλαμβάνειν is followed by the expression ἐκ νόσου, and in Plu. *Pyrrh.* 12.6, by ἐξ ἀρρωστίας.

τέλεον. τέλειος and τέλεος are both attested in the papyri, and the adverbial use of the neuter appears in either form. See Kühner–Gerth, *Grammatik* i.1 137–8.

7–8 ἀνεκτήσατο. This verb usually means 'to re-acquire, 'to take back', or 'to restore'. In this use it is mostly transitive. In the papyri it occurs rather rarely, and refers to land or the working of land, or sums of money changing hands. There are however two cases that are similar to the present one, denoting recovery from some sort of evil, though neither refers specifically to an illness: UPZ I 110.127 (164 BC) τοὺς ἀνθρώπους ἐκ . . . καταφθορᾶς . . . ἀνακτωμένους; and P. Fay. 106 = W. *Chr.* 395.18–19 (*c.*140) ἐμαυτὸν ἀνακτήσασθαι ἀπὸ τῶν καμάτων. In the latter passage, which comes from a letter written by a doctor, καμάτων refers to debts rather than physical exertion. The text also contains the word ἐξησθένησα, which works in the same motif.

In literature, the closer parallels to the present one come from theological writers, who tend to use the verb transitively. A good example is offered by Jo. Chrys. *In Epist. ad Rom.* 13.6 (PG 60.516), who uses the two verbs we have here in the same context: πῶς ὁ Δαυιδ πεσών, ἑαυτὸν ἀνεκτήσατο; πῶς ὁ Πέτρος ἀρνησάμενος, ἑαυτὸν ἀνέλαβε; The *Suda* (α 2243) explains the one from the other: ἀνεκτησάμην· ἀνωρθωσάμην, ἀνελαβόμην.

8 λούσασθαι. It is doubtful whether this was part of the curing process (some medical writers suggest bathing and then anointing oneself with oil or wine as a cure for ψυγμός; e.g. *Hippiatrica Parisina* 1082). It is more probable that it is mentioned to show that Theon's state of health was so good that he was capable of taking a bath (or simply that he would do so: when a doctor's advice can have the form 'in November, μὴ λούεσθαι τὸ σύνολον' (Aët. 12.69), it would be a brave thing to do just after recovering from an illness). This is supported by the fact that, after the assurance that Theon has fully recovered (16), he is reported to be carrying out all his usual activities. Presumably bathing was one of them.

9–10 ἐνκατάλειμμα. The primary meaning of this word is 'remnant', 'residue' or 'trace' (LSJ s.v. 1). It has previously occurred only once in papyri, P. Petr. II 4 (11).2 (255 or 254 BC [HGV]), where it seems to refer to a 'sediment' or 'silting up' (LSJ s.v. 4; W. Schubart, *Ein Jahrtausend am Nil* (1912) 18, renders ἐνκατάλειμμα γέγονεν as 'ist ein Rest unvollendet geblieben'). In a medical context the word usually refers to residual traces of a disease (e.g. Aët. 6.8 εἰ δ' ἐγκατάλειμμα εἴη τῆς διαθέσεως ἐπὶ τὸν λευκὸν ἐλλέβορον ἐλθέ; Paul. Aegin. *Epit.* 6.36 στηπτικοῖς φαρμάκοις ἐκδαπανᾶν τὸ ἐγκατάλειμμα). The example that best illustrates the particular use of the word in a medical context is in Paul. Aegin. *Epit.* 3.77.4 ἐγκαταλείμματος τῆς νόσου μείναντος.

10 ἀληθέστατα. The superlative has not occurred in any other papyrus.

10a ἵνα ⟦. . ι λ⟧λο . . π . . . . . . αιτε. The text written by the original scribe is 'Anyway, what we are writing to you is the absolute truth; I swear by all the gods'. Of this, only ὑμεῖν ἐπιστέλλομεν is deleted, but it would seem more likely that the inserted text is meant to replace the whole of the original text from ὅτι to ἐπόμνυμαι, since this makes better sense. However, since only two words were deleted it is conceivable that the corrector meant to leave in the phrase ὅτι μὲν οὖν ἀληθέστατα ταῦτα (sc. ἐστί) τοὺς θεοὺς πάντας ἐπόμνυμαι.

The readings of the suprascript material must follow the same pattern of absolute assertion of truthfulness: after ἵνα we expect a verb in the subjunctive, or indeed the optative, in accordance with the letter's atticistic attributes (Mandilaras, *The Verb* 272). That may be the word ending in -τε. If the following words αὐτοῦ τοῖς [γρ]άμμασιν belong to this clause, and they refer to the brother's letter, then the -τε verb should (i) refer to the parents, (ii) govern a dative, and (iii) describe their reaction to the letter. Since Ammonius thought it necessary to write again, that reaction must have been incredulity. Therefore the missing word should mean 'believe' or '(not) disbelieve'. If the former, then the obvious verb would be πιστεύσητε/-αιτε; if the latter, there must have been a μή after ἵνα, and the traces belong to a form of either ὑποπτεύω or ὑπονοέω. But none of these verbs can be read in the traces. In any case ἵνα must be followed by a conjunction.

10–11a τοῖϲ γρ]άμμαϲιν could be the object of the (unread) verb. Otherwise it may be taken as an instrumental dative, i.e., 'so that you may believe / not disbelieve him by his letters . . .'.

11a ὡϲ ἄρα χαριζόμενοϲ. The assumption is that this is the beginning of a clause dependent on a verb of suspecting or believing in the inserted line above. An alternative would be to take ὡϲ to mean 'since' (causal), but then χαριζόμενοϲ would have to be understood differently: 'so that you should believe/not disbelieve his letter, since he sent you a letter out of kindness, I too have written . . .'.

12 ἵνα. The word is cancelled by the second hand, who wrote ὅπωϲ over the line. In Classical Greek the two particles express different nuances, which in later Greek are more or less ignored. ἵνα introduces an abstract final expression, whereas ὅπωϲ expresses a psychological preoccupation. Classical authors often use a combination of the two, in the form οὐχ ἵνα . . . ἀλλ' ὅπωϲ (ἄν), to exclude a presumed intention and confirm the authenticity of another. In Attic Greek, ὅπωϲ replaces ἵνα only when the clause expresses subjectivity, uncertainty, particular circumstances, etc.; see S. Amigues, *Les Subordonnées finales par ὅπωϲ en attique classique* (1977) 103.

The correction appears even more impressive if one considers that in later Greek ἵνα is used increasingly at the expense of ὅπωϲ, since it is overall more straightforward and easy to use (Amigues, *Subordonnées finales* 105–6). Nevertheless, the writer of the letter knew about it and how to use it, unless he only made the correction in view of the fact that he had just inserted a ἵνα clause a few lines above and did not want to repeat the word.

Such corrections are found in two other texts: P. Petr. II 13 (18a).13 (257–249 BC [HGV]), where the correction was made, as in **4959**, as part of a general revision of the text; and in P. Got. 12.4 (iii/iv). The opposite occurs in P. Cair. Zen. II 59256 = SB III 6993 (252/251 BC) γέγρ]αφα οὖν ϲοι ⟦ὅπωϲ⟧ ἵνα̣ εἰδῇϲ, and P. Cair. Zen. III 59375 (c.258–256 BC), with ὅπωϲ ἄν replaced by ἵνα.

τ̣[ι]νόϲ, written over the line by the first hand, is an addition rather than a correction, since ἄλλου is not crossed out. Another similar addition is μή in 13.

πυθόμενοι. The expression πυνθάνομαι παρά τινοϲ does not have many occurrences in the papyri, but this is rather due to the fact that the agent is usually not mentioned than that it is expressed by a different construction (the alternative being the verb followed by genitive). It seems worth noting that the usual construction of the agent after forms of the verb based on the aorist stem (πυθ-) is almost always παρά τινοϲ, whereas the construction following verbs based on the present stem (πυνθ-) is almost always the genitive.

13 εἰωθότων. The ultimate meaning of this should be 'so that you do [not? worry?] by getting news from some other person of the kind who tend not to speak the truth, I have thought it . . .'. If indeed there was a 'not' (μή), it could well be what is missing after the ἵνα δέ of the original text. We also need a verb ἵνα δέ or ὅπωϲ δ' ἄν; this might have been added by the second hand, and we would expect it (possibly with μή, if it was not written in 12) somewhere in the unread traces over line 13.

15 ἐκταρα̣[χθ]ῆτε. This compound has occurred only in one other papyrus, P. Gen. I 1.12 (213), a letter of a senior Roman functionary.

17 προϲαγορεύει. The use of the singular instead of the plural in verbs followed by more than one subject is not uncommon in the papyri; see Mayser, *Grammatik* ii.3 30–33.

18 ὁ̣ ϛώταϲ. The putative omicron is written above ϲω. However, the article is not expected, unless Sotas was mentioned in the corrections over line 13, which have not been read. This would explain why the article was added later.

21 παν[ο]ικηϲίᾳ. This is the Attic equivalent to πανοικί, according to the Atticist Moeris (I. Bekker, *Harpocration et Moeris* (1833) 207). Döllstädt, *Griechische Papyrusprivatbriefe* 15, describes the latter as belonging to literary as well as everyday κοινή, and adds a further form, πανοικίᾳ (or -ίῃ), which he classifies as Ionic and poetic. Indeed πανοικίᾳ is only attested in Ptolemaic papyri, unless one includes P. Flor. II 273.25 (260) πανοικηνίᾳ, whereas πανοικ(ε)ί, though common enough, does not occur before the Roman period (in BGU II 450.27 (ii/iii), πανοικ(ίᾳ) should probably be resolved differently).

πανοικηϲίᾳ (or -εϲίᾳ) has fewer attestations than πανοικί, ranging in date from the second to the fourth century. All of them occur in documents that show good command of Greek, but as far as one can see, none of them has obvious atticistic affinities.

παν[ο]ικηϲίᾳ εὐτυχοῦντας. The two words often occur together at the close of private letters of the Roman period: see XLII **3084** 7, P. Berl. Zill. 11.23–4, P. Flor. II 273.24–5, P. Giss. Univ. III 32.30, P. Iand. II 8.14–15, P. Princ. II 68.15–16, 69.7–8, III 185.15, P. Ryl. II 434.12, PSI XIII 1335.30, SB V 7629.9, etc.

22 This must be a repetition of the oath in line 11, and the beginning of this line would read something along the lines of καὶ θεοὺς ἐπόμνυμαι, which suits the space and the sense.

M. MALOUTA

4960. Letter to a *Stolistes*

48 5B.32/E(1–3)b   14 × 16.5 cm   Second century

This letter concerns a victory in a law court, which resulted in the cudgelling of a man called Petseis, and which would have been a cause for celebrations. The sender, whose identity is uncertain, reports on those proceedings, and gives the date of the hearing and a summary of the outcome. The recipients are a ϲτολιϲτήϲ and a πλῆθοϲ of uncertain composition; the context points to some priestly guild. The legal procedures referred to in lines 6–8 are difficult to understand and interpret fully.

The text is evenly spaced, apart from the first two lines (2–3), which are closer together, and the closing greeting, which is spaced down after one line left blank. In the one remaining line of the prescript the words are divided by large spaces. There is some spacing between words and sentences in the main text, but not done consistently.

The hand recalls examples of the chancery script, on which see **4959** introd. The letters are formed separately. They are written with a wide-tipped pen and leftward slant. A date in the second century would suit.

It is unclear whether the address on the back is in the same hand as that responsible for the main text; the pen looks different, and the script is generally narrower and slants to the right.

The text is written along the fibres. The sheet exhibits regular vertical as well as horizontal fold-marks, including a deep horizontal fold. This would indicate that the letter must have first been rolled and squashed flat in the expected fashion, from right to left (see LIX **3989** introd.), but at some later point, it must have been opened and then folded again at right angles to the previous folding.

     .   .   .   .

τῷ̣ [(*vac.*) π]λ̣ήθει (*vac.*) χαίρειν.
πρὸ μ[ὲν] παντὸϲ εὐχόμεθα ὑμᾶϲ

ὑγιαί[νειν]. γεινώςκειν ὑμᾶς θέ-
λομε[ν ὅτ]ι τῇ ἕκτῃ διηκού-
5   ϲθη[μ]ε[ν] κ̣α̣ὶ ἐνεικήϲαμεν κ̣α̣ὶ
ἐξυλοκοπήθη Πετϲεῖς ἐπι-
κηρυϲϲομένου "μὴ ϲταϲια . . .
ἀλλ' ἔμμενε τοῖς κεκριμέν̣ο̣ις".
διὸ γράφομεν ὑμεῖν ὅπως
10   εὐωχῆϲθε καὶ εὐφραίνεϲθε
καὶ ϲ]τεφανηφορίαν ἄξετε
ϲὺν] παν̣τ̣ὶ τῷ πλήθει καὶ
c.6–7]ν καὶ παίδων.
          (vac.)
ἐρρ]ῶϲθαι ὑ(μᾶς) εὐχ(όμεθα). Θὼθ ϛ̄.

Back, downwards along the fibres:

15   (m. 2?)]ϲτ̣ο̣λ̣ιϲτῆι καὶ τῷ πλή[θει

2 υμας: υ corr. from ϲ?   3 l. γινώϲκειν   5 l. ἐνικήϲαμεν   8 l. ἔμμενε
9 l. ὑμῖν   12 παντι: ν corr. from α?   14 Υευˣ

'. . . the *gathering*, greetings. First of all we wish you health. We want you to know, that on the sixth our case was heard through, and we won. Petseis was flogged, while a herald cried "do not cause trouble, but abide by the judgement (of the court)". Therefore we write to you, so that you can rejoice and be merry and conduct a wreath-wearing (festival), together with the whole *gathering*, both of . . . and of children. We(?) pray for your health. Thoth 6.'

Back: '. . . the [. . . ?]*stolistes* and the *gathering* [. . . ?].'

1 τῷ [π]λήθει. Cf. 12, 15. In 12–13 the noun is defined by genitives, -ω]ν καὶ παίδων; in the address it is preceded by]ϲτ̣ο̣λ̣ιϲτῆι (or a compound), which shows that the letter was addressed to an individual as well as the group. We should allow for two lines lost at the top; there will have stood a proper name or names in the nominative, a name in the dative, and (—)ϲτολιϲτῆι καί.

There does not seem to be any other example of πλῆθος as addressee in papyrus letters. The 'collective address' is elsewhere expressed in the opening formula in more precise terms, as e.g. in P. Amh. II 40.1–3 (ii BC) Ἡπιόδωρος τῶι λεϲώνει καὶ τοῖς ἱερεῦϲι τοῦ Ϲοκνοπαίου χαίρειν, and in the closing formula in terms such as ἐρρῶϲθαί ϲε εὔχομαι πανοικεί. Otherwise, as in LV **3809** 12–13 ἀϲπάζου τοὺς ϲυμμαθητὰς πάντας, the internal coherence of the πλῆθος is accurately specified.

The word πλῆθος can have several connotations. In a few cases it can mean 'crowd', 'mob' in general (e.g. BGU VI 1214.24). More often it refers to a group of things or animals: πλῆθος προβάτων (P. Cair. Zen. III 59394.3–4), βιβλίων (P. Fam. Tebt. 15.89), οἰκιῶν (P. Hib. II 197 i 4), ἀργυρίου (P. Tebt. III 772.6), etc. The cases of human πλήθη usually refer to priests: πλῆθος ἱερέων (CPR XV 17.9; P. Bacch. 24.8; P. Lond. VII 2188 iii 56; P. Mert. II 73.3; P. Tebt. II 310.4), but also there are πλήθη ϲτρατιωτῶν (CPR VII 25.5), γερδίων (P. Mich. II 124 ii 19), ἀνδρῶν ἀτάκτων (L **3581** 18), κακούργων (LVIII **3926** 5–6), νεανίϲκων (P. Panop. 27.20).

All passages in which a πλῆθος ἱερέων occurs suggest that more than a mere crowd is meant.

The expression denotes an organized corporation, which has legal status in itself (cf. esp. P. Tebt. II 310, where Thaubastis surrenders some temple land to the corporation of priests, and P. Lond. VII 2188, where the priests of Pathyris sue for redress as a corporation). It is doubtful whether πλῆθος should be seen as a technical legal term; it would be more convincing to conclude that the word does not have such connotations in itself, but is used to describe a group which has internal coherence. This argument may be supported by P. Bacch. 24.8 διὰ τὸ τοὺς ἱερ⟨ε⟩ῖς ἀπὸ πλήθους εἰς ὀλίγους κατηντη[κέναι, which uses the same word but in its commoner meaning.

2 ὑμᾶς. υ is a correction from c. The error probably occurred because the scribe was more used to writing to a single recipient, that is, cε.

4–5 διηκούϲθη[μ]ε[ν]. C. B. Welles, *Royal Correspondence in the Hellenistic Period: A Study in Greek Inscriptions* (1934) 235, notes the use of the verb for listening to envoys and judicial hearings, and comments that 'in both connections, the verb belongs to the *koine*, but the uses are only a slight extension of the Attic meaning "to hear through"'. The same verb is used of a judicial hearing in NT Acts 23.35 (the arraignment of Paul at Caesarea), and commonly in papyri, e.g. P. Yale I 42.31 ὁ γὰρ βαϲιλεὺϲ αὐτὸϲ καθήμενοϲ διακούει.

6 ἐξυλοκοπήθη. The verb occurs in several Ptolemaic documents in the sense of 'to cut wood', and refers to a particular agricultural activity; see M. Schnebel, *Die Landwirtschaft im hellenistischen Ägypten* (1925) 22. Later on the meaning of the word seems to have changed radically, and κόπτω reverts to the definition 'to smite, strike' rather than 'to cut'. The meaning 'to cudgel' or 'to cudgel to death' appears in papyri of the Roman period, mostly in reference to illegal use of violence, for which retribution is sought (see the evidence collected by B. Kelly, *The Repression of Violence in the Roman Principate* (diss. Oxford 2002) 316–29, but note that it excludes military violence). However, in IV **706** = M. *Chr.* 81.12–13 (73?; see BL IX 181), a report of proceedings before a prefect, we find ἐάν ϲε μέμψηται . . . ξυλοκοπηθῆναί ϲε κελεύϲω.

The practice of beating people with sticks or rods seems to have been a Roman custom, especially in a military context. *Castigatio* was performed in the form of flogging, employed with no distinction of rank or position (cf. Frontinus *Strategemata* 4.1; C. E. Brand, *Roman Military Law* (1968) 103–5), and took several forms according to the seriousness of the transgression, as well as the official carrying out the punishment. The most brutal form of cudgelling, and one resulting in death, was *fustuarium*, a punishment for soldiers proven not to have been doing their duty. This is explained in modern literature as the beating of the condemned soldier with clubs, *fustes*, by his fellow soldiers (for an overview of military punishments see P. Southern, *The Roman Army* (2007) 146–8). Plb. 6.37, however, describes the procedure of ξυλοκοπία as the accused soldier being touched by an official's club, as a sign of condemnation, and then being stoned to death by his comrades. A similar punishment was whipping with rods, *virgae*, performed on criminals before their execution, and considered a great disgrace (Brand, *Roman Military Law* 80). Roman soldiers were also cudgelled by the centurion, who used a vine staff, *vitis*. It seems that this was a more 'everyday' kind of punishment, for less serious crimes and without implications of disgrace (Brand, ibid.).

The principal occurrences of the word in Greek literature, mainly in Polybius (6.37.1, 2, 38.1, 3), identify ξυλοκοπία with *fustuarium*. The word also appears in Epictetus (3.7.32, 4.4.38) applied to the beating of donkeys. Philo *In Flaccum* 10 gives first an example of official violence and then describes the practice behind it. E. A. Sophocles, *Greek Lexicon of the Roman and Byzantine Periods*, relates ξυλοκοπία to ξύλοιϲ παίω, citing D. H. *Ant. Rom.* 9.50.7 ξύλοιϲ παιόμενοι διεφθάρηϲαν.

There is little evidence for official use of force against private citizens (IV **706**; P. Flor. I 61; SB V 7523, on which see below). R. S. Bagnall, *BASP* 26 (1989) 213, argues that these are cases of threats, and they are recorded but never actually carried out. However, he adds that even though physical abuse of free citizens was forbidden by official edicts, official violence even against free persons did exist and was to be feared. In the present case it is unlikely that Petseis is a slave: there is evidence that the transgressions of slaves do not become legal cases, since their masters have the right to discipline them themselves (ibid. 207). It is likely that Petseis falls somewhere between the two extremes: if he is not a slave, he is obviously not a Roman citizen either. As an Egyptian, or 'Greek', he could be subjected to corporal punishment.

Little is known about penalties inflicted on people by the courts of Roman Egypt. It seems that for slaves and men of low status, the penalty for very serious crimes would be hard labour in an army camp, mine or quarry. Also prisons are mentioned as well as guard duty there (N. Lewis, *Life in Egypt under Roman Rule* (1985) 194). There are a few references to beatings ordered for the violation of court orders (ibid.), and based on the contents of the ἐπικήρυξις, one can assume that the document in question is such a case. R. Taubenschlag, *Opera minora* ii (1959) 737–41, gives several examples of court-ordered floggings, and differentiates between corporal sentences as *Erpressungsmittel* or *Strafe*. One interesting case is SB V 7523 (153), where a Roman citizen is being cudgelled on orders of a strategus (on this papyrus see H. Horstkotte, *ZPE* 111 (1996) 256–8).

Πετϲεῖϲ. A Greek transliteration of a Demotic name, likely to mean 'the one whom the goddess Shay has given' (suggested by Professor W. J. Tait). This form is unparalleled in the papyri, although one can find variations of it such as Πετϲέϲιϲ, Πετϲεῦϲ. The common Πετϲεῖριϲ, though similar in Greek, involves Osiris rather than Shay. For such names see E. Lüddeckens, *Demotisches Namenbuch* (1992) iv 280, 308, 344 (cf. v 298); J. Quaegebeur, *Le Dieu égyptien Shaï dans la religion et l'onomastique* (1975).

6–7 ἐπικηρυϲϲομένου. There are several possible ways of articulating the letters within this sentence. In this edition it has been interpreted as an impersonal passive compound in the genitive absolute, of which the subject is the following sentence. Though there is no reason for doubting this construction, two other ways of interpreting it should also be mentioned: ἐπὶ κηρυϲϲομένου (τινόϲ), i.e., in the presence (of someone) who announced, in which case the next sentence would be the object; ἐπικηρύϲϲομεν· "οὐ μὴ ϲταϲια . . .". The grammar of ἐπὶ κηρυϲϲομένου is not impossible, and ultimately it does not make much difference concerning the sense. Nevertheless, it is more probable that it was meant to be one word, given that in the surviving documents forms of κηρύϲϲειν almost always appear as compounds. The second alternative is even less likely. It does not make good sense, and would create unnecessary and clumsy *asyndeta*, to have a first person subject for any form of ἐπικηρύϲϲειν, and certainly not in the present tense.

7 ϲταϲια . . . . The second of the unread letters is a round one. If there is another letter after it (there is some scattered ink), this would disallow the most obvious guess, ϲταϲίαζε (ϲταϲιάζειν, ϲταϲιάϲηϲ, or ϲταϲιάϲαι are all palaeographically impossible). Based on palaeography, one might also suggest ϲταϲίαϲον, but μή with the 2nd-person singular aorist imperative would be unexpected. There is only one isolated and uncertain example in the papyri, P. Lond. VI 1915.36 (c.330–40) μὴ οὖν ἀμ[έ]-ληϲ[ο]ν (Mandilaras, *The Verb* 300, questions the reading, but according to the editor the final ν seems secure; see BL VII 93).

8 ἔνμενε τοῖϲ κεκριμένοιϲ. The easiest conclusion drawn from this phrase is that Petseis has transgressed against a previous court decision; he is being punished now, to learn that he must comply with the ruling of the court the first time round. Similar phrases occur in P. Mert. III 104.18, of the early Roman period, οὐκ ἐμμένει τοῖϲ κεκριμ(ένοιϲ); I **38** = M. *Chr.* 58.16 (49/50) μὴ βουλομένου ἐνμεῖναι τοῖϲ κεκριμένοιϲ; SB VI 9252.9 (118) ὅπωϲ πείθονται τοῖϲ κεκριμένοιϲ. It is plausible to assume that in all these cases the process is more or less the same, though none of them contains any indication of physical violence applied or threatened as a means of coercion.

10 εὐωχῆϲθε καὶ εὐφραίνεϲθε. εὐφραίνεϲθε occurs most often in the phrase ἐρρῶϲθαί ϲε εὔχομαι καὶ εὐφραίνεϲθαι, as for example in P. Mich. VIII 465.46. Here no form of ῥώννυμι could match the traces, but a form of εὐωχεῖϲθαι suits both the traces and the sense: this verb is associated with feasting and dining, which is very appropriate to the setting of a ϲτεφανηφορία (εὐφραίνομαι does not seem to have this particular sense).

10–11 εὐωχῆϲθε . . . εὐφραίνεϲθε . . . ἄξετε. A curious parataxis of three verbs, which seem to be in the present subjunctive, present indicative, and future indicative (or aorist imperative) respectively. The sentence is intended to be a secondary pure final clause introduced by ὅπωϲ. The normal construction of this kind of clause after a verb in the present tense is with a verb in the subjunctive. The problem is the second verb, since ὅπωϲ is not normally construed with the present indicative. F. Blass, A. Debrunner, F. Rehkopf, *Grammatik des neutestamentlichen Griechisch* (1979) 298–9, consider ἵνα with present indicative to be a scribal mistake, but do not mention the possibility of a similar construction with ὅπωϲ. Gignac, *Grammar* ii 385–9, argues that forms of the indicative frequently substitute those of the subjunctive, and partly attributes this phenomenon to the phonological identification of several endings (-ειϲ/-ηϲ, -ει/-ῃ, etc.). He gives many examples in clauses introduced by ἐάν, εἰ, and ἵνα, but he too does not mention ὅπωϲ. One example however can be found in Mayser, *Grammatik* ii.1 231, from PSI IV 382.17, which has ὅπωϲ followed by a verb in the present indicative, ὅπω⟨ϲ⟩ δὲ ἐργαζόμεθα; but ἐργαζόμεθα could be a phonetic version of ἐργαζώμεθα.

An alternative hypothesis is that εὐφραίνεϲθε is imperative. According to H. Ljungvik, *Beiträge zur Syntax der spätgriechischen Volkssprache* (1932) 49–50, there are examples in the papyri of the imperative taking the place of the subjunctive, in clauses introduced by ἵνα, ἐφ' ᾧτε, and ὅπωϲ.

As for the third verb, Mandilaras, *The Verb* 197, argues that the future indicative can sometimes replace the subjunctive in pure final clauses, but limits the statement by saying that this only occurs with ὡϲ and ἵνα, and that ὅπωϲ with future indicative occurs only in classical Greek. There is, however, one fragmentary example in P. Col. IV 93.9 (mid III BC [HGV]), ὅπωϲ μοι ὑπάρξει, which possibly is a final clause. In Blass–Debrunner–Rehkopf, *Grammatik* 298–9, ὅπωϲ with such a construction in pure final clauses is considered normal.

A final consideration is the possibility that the third verb is not part of the same sentence. If the restored καί that connects it with the previous line were not there, one could punctuate after εὐφραίνεϲθε and restore τήν; however, this would imply that it was a particular ϲτεφανηφορία being referred to. It is also risky to take a strong position on whether the *asyndeton* created by this hypothesis is possible or not; though there are no *asyndeta* elsewhere in the text, the sample is too small to allow judgement on the author's style. But even if καί were accepted, it would not be impossible that a new sentence started at this point, though admittedly it would be a very inelegant structure.

The overall impression that the document gives about the literacy of its author is a very good one. Therefore, the confusion of tenses and moods in this sentence cannot be simply dismissed as a grammatical mistake.

11 ϲ]τεφανηφορίαν. The word or cognates have occurred in VII **1021** 15 (54) διὸ πάντεϲ ὀφείλομεν ϲτεφανηφοροῦνταϲ καὶ βουθυτοῦνταϲ θεοῖϲ πᾶϲι εἰδέναι χάριτα; P. Giss. 27 = W. *Chr.* 17.9 (c.115 [HGV]) καὶ ϲτεφανηφορίαν ἄξω καὶ τοῖϲ θεοῖϲ τὰϲ ὀφειλομέναϲ ϲπονδὰϲ ἀποδῶ; LV **3781** 14 (117) εὐχόμ[ενοι] οὖν πᾶϲι θεοῖϲ αἰώνιον αὐτοῦ τὴν διαμονὴν ἡμεῖν φυλαχθῆναι ϲτεφανηφορήϲομ(εν) ἐφ' ἡμ(έραϲ) ι'; BGU II 646 = W. *Chr.* 490.23–4 (193) πανδημεὶ [θ]ύο[ν]ταϲ καὶ εὐχομένουϲ ὑπέρ τε τοῦ διηνεκοῦϲ Αὐτοκράτουϲ κ[αὶ το]ῦ ϲύνπαντοϲ οἴκου ϲτεφα[νηφ]ορῆϲαι ἡμέραϲ πεντεκαίδε[κα. Cf. also Dittenberger, OGI I 6.22 (311 BC) τὴν δὲ θυϲίαν κα[ὶ] τὸν ἀγῶνα καὶ τὴν ϲτεφανηφορίαν, 56.40 (239/8 BC) ἡμέραϲ πέντε μετὰ ϲτεφανηφορίαϲ καὶ θυϲιῶν καὶ ϲπονδῶν καὶ τῶν ἄλλων τῶν προϲηκόντων.

In most examples ϲτεφανηφορία is connected with some major political event, and all the documents cited above are official announcements: **1021** is a notification of the accession of Nero; P. Giss. 27 is a private letter in which Aphrodisius proposes to celebrate a victory of the strategus Apollonius (probably against the forces of the Jewish revolt); **3781** is an announcement of the accession of Hadrian; W. *Chr.* 490 refers to the celebration of the rule of Pertinax; OGI I 6 mentions ϲτεφανηφορία as part of the festivals in honour of Alexander; OGI I 56, the Canopus Decree, is a decree of the Egyptian priests in honour of Ptolemy III and Berenice. Moreover, or perhaps consequently, in all these texts ϲτεφανηφορία has clear religious connotations. This becomes even clearer by the fact that the word is accompanied by a mention of sacrificing to the gods or something similar. Also in some of these cases the number of days that the 'wreath-wearing' will last is specified. In religious festivals wreaths were worn by the people taking part, by the sacrificial animals, and were also used to adorn temples on important occasions (S. Price, *Rituals and Power* (1984) 108–12).

The fact that a στεφανηφορία usually is part of a major event, should not lead to the conclusion that the flogging of Πετσεῖς was of such great importance as to be celebrated in a way comparable to the accession or the birthday of an emperor. The most likely interpretation would be that the πλῆθος was preparing a great celebration involving a στεφανηφορία, and Πετσεῖς was for some reason an obstacle. Now that he has been punished for it, the priests can go on performing their duties. A remoter possibility would be that the expression στεφανηφορίαν ἄξετε is meant figuratively; cf. PSI XII 1247.8 ff. ἐὰν κομίζωμαι ὑμῶν γράμματα, ἑορτὴν ἄγω. This argument, however, is weakened by the fact that the particular στεφανηφορία is described further: σὺν] παντὶ τῷ πλήθει καὶ | [*c.*6–7]ν καὶ παίδων. This would be exaggerated in the case of a metaphorical expression.

13 *c.*6–7]ν καὶ παίδων. The context seems to be very much connected with priests and temples (cf. the address on the back), so that [ἱερέω]ν would seem appropriate. Besides, a πλῆθος ἱερέων is the most usual form of a πλῆθος in the papyri. In any case, the word to restore depends on what one takes those 'children' to be. A tracing, however, does not easily confirm the supplement, unless all the letters in this word were horizontally elongated and spaced out (which is not impossible, but does not seem justified, especially since all but ω are very narrow letters). [ἀνδρῶ]ν would seem more likely, albeit still too short for the break. On the other hand, if the idea of some kind of a priestly πλῆθος is still to be assumed, it is difficult to see what the actual word was, since στολιστῶν or any other specific priestly rank is too long.

The 'children' are part of the πλῆθος. It is not clear whether they are children or slaves. If the former, they could be sons and daughters of the priests (assuming that the πλῆθος did consist of priests), living in the temples; they could be pupils at the temple school; or they could themselves be priests. D. J. Thompson in M. Beard, J. North, *Pagan Priests* (1990) 101, notes that the sons who inherited the priesthood from their fathers were often very young.

Such 'children' may be mentioned in BGU I 176 = W. *Chr.* 83.9 ἀποσπᾶσθαι τοὺς παῖδας ἀπὸ τῶν ἱερέων. The meaning of the word παῖδας is disputed: sons of priests (Krebs, Wessely) or slaves (Otto, Wilcken)? Wilcken's argument is that if they were sons of priests, the expression would be τοὺς παῖδας ἀπὸ τῶν πατέρων or τοὺς υἱοὺς ἀπὸ τῶν ἱερέων. However, even if ultimately Otto and Wilcken could be right, the particular argument does not sound convincing (ἱερῶν, proposed in place of ἱερέων by K. F. W. Schmidt, BL III 9, should be ignored; Wilcken states that he has re-examined the original). It seems probable that the reference is made to an association of priests. Within those associations, the age of becoming a member is not specified. Some became members together with their sons, and it seems that this was common practice; there are several terms in Demotic which describe those young people or novices who were part of the association (F. de Cenival, *Les Associations religieuses en Égypte d'après les documents démotiques* (1972) 150). What is more interesting in this case, is that apparently there were formations within the association consisting of some sort of chief and the young members, and there even exists an expression for this, *p, ꞌts n mnh2·w*, 'the chief (some sort of chief; the exact meaning of *ts* is unclear) and the young ones/novices'; see de Cenival, *Les Associations* 173.

14 Thoth 6 = September 2/3.

15]στολιστῆι. In the papyri there are attestations of στολισταί, πρωτοστολισταί, δευτεροστολισταί, ἰβιοστολισταί, ἱεροστολισταί, or ἱερόστολοι. With the exception of the last, each of the other words could be the one in this document. For the rank of στολιστής see W. Otto, *Priester und Tempel im hellenistischen Ägypten* (1905) 83–4 and J. A. S. Evans, *YCS* 17 (1961) 188–9.

M. MALOUTA

4961. Authenticated Copy of a Petition to the Prefect

23 3B.12/A(1)+(2)   19.5 × 42 cm   14 November 223

Despite the large size of this papyrus, it is certain from the restorations in A 2–3 (cf. B 35–7) that even in the best preserved lines rather less than half the width is preserved, and considerably less than this in many of the other lines. What we have is a partially preserved authenticated copy or rather two copies of a petition to the prefect with his *subscriptio*. It is comparable in format to the text that I published as LXV **4481**, with a discussion in the introduction of this type of document and a list of parallels. Since then one further text of this type has appeared: P. Horak 13, published with an important introduction by Guido Bastianini. See also Tor Hauken, *Petition and Response* (1998) 98–105. The 'outer' text (B) occupies lines 35 ff.; above this, written in the same hand but in noticeably smaller writing, is the 'inner' text (A). There is a gap of 2.5 cm between A and B. The inner text would have been tightly rolled (shown clearly by the formation of the worm-holes), and sealed and signed on the back by the witnesses. Three of the signatures still survive, though none of the seals. These signatures start at the top of the outer document and run downwards at 180° to the direction of the text on the front. Both sides of the papyrus are written *transversa charta*. There is a *kollesis* 22.5 cm from the upper edge. On 'double documents' in general, see now, in addition to the remarks and bibliography in **4481** introd., the important discussion by Dominic Rathbone in *Essays and Texts in Honor of J. David Thomas* (2001) 102–5.

The general structure of the document is clear. It begins with the statement regarding certification (A 2–3, B 35–7); the petition itself occupies almost the whole of what follows (A 3–33, B 37–82); at the end is a copy of the prefect's *subscriptio* (A 33–4, B 83–5). This format is almost the same as that found in BGU II 525 + III 970 = M. *Chr.* 242 (177) and XVII **2131** (207); and very close to that in LXV **4481** (179) and BGU XI 2061 (207), which differ in that the certification clause comes once only, between the two copies. **4961**, however, has three unexpected features. In the first place, above the first line of the document proper, in what would have been close to the centre of the original papyrus, is the numeral $\iota\theta$; see further 1 n. Secondly, the documents just mentioned all have the prefect's *subscriptio* written in the same hand as the petition. In **4961** the hand changes for the *subscriptio*, as is most clear in B 84–5. In A the change of hand can be seen earlier than this, in the statement concerning Agathus Daemon (A 33), and presumably will have changed at this point in B. So little survives of this second hand in both copies, and it is so abraded in B, that one hesitates to insist that it is the same in both copies, though this is what we should expect. It is not too surprising that a *subscriptio* should have been copied later, after the petition and its *subscriptio* had been publicly displayed. This is almost certainly what happened in XLVII **3364** (see *Tyche* 18 (2003) 204–5) and no doubt in other cases. We could suppose that two copies of the petition were prepared in advance and that once the *subscriptio* had been posted, there was added to each of them (by Agathus Daemon?) a copy of this *subscriptio*.

The third peculiar feature in **4961** is that on the back there appear to be several lines of writing, along the fibres at right angles to the direction of the witnesses' signatures, one set of lines underneath the signatures, another set several centimetres below them. These are in fact offsets from the 'inner' text on the front, which was clearly rolled and sealed while the ink was still wet.

The difficulty of calculating the amount lost in the larger lacunas is complicated. In A 3, where the restoration ought to be certain (i.e., we expect ἀντίγραφον to be followed immediately by the imperial titles), we have 195 letters, but in no other line of A can we be confident of the restoration. B is more useful. The restorations should be certain in B 36, giving 123 letters to the line, B 37, giving 124 letters, B 42 (cf. A 6–7), giving 134 letters, and B 47 (cf. A 9–10), giving only 110 letters. However, if we count the letters in the part that survives before the break in the papyrus in those lines where the break comes earliest, which amounts to about one-third of the original line, we find that the first ten lines of B (ignoring B 35; see below) have about 44 letters; this number reduces over the same area to about 36 letters over the next ten lines and to about 34 letters over the remainder. This suggests that at first the scribe was writing about 120–25 letters in each line but by the later part of the text this was no more than about 105. The same thing seems to have happened in A: counting the letters up to the same point as in B gives an average of 67 letters in the first ten lines (ignoring A 2; see below), only 59 in the next ten, and no more than 55 in the last ten. This would point to a reduction in lines length from about 190 letters at first to no more 170 later. There is a further complication. In lines A 2 and B 35 what would seem to be the standard formula gives 227 and 133 letters respectively, with only 2–3 letters in *ekthesis*, and this is without the alias name for Diogenis. Restorations based on these lines, therefore, would suggest at least 20 letters more in A and 10 more in B. I do not see how to reconcile this with the length of line suggested by B 36 and 37 and by A 3 (though cf. A 2 n.). In B 37 nothing is expected between ἀντίγραφον and the imperial titles, though there may have been a *vacat* (a small *vacat* does indeed survive), but there is no obvious place for such a *vacat* in B 36 (there is a *vacat* in A 9 and in what seems to be the wrong place in B 46). From all this it will be clear that the number of letters suggested in the text for the longer lacunas should be treated as no more than a rough guide.

Since so much of the papyrus is missing, there is no hope of producing connected sense. What is clear is that the document contained two copies of a petition by a certain Aurelia Diogenis to the prefect M. Aedinius Iulianus. After the standard formula relating to the copying of the petition, which had been posted publicly in Alexandria (A 2–3, B 35–7), Diogenis prefixes to her petition imperial constitutions that were no doubt intended to support her case (A 3–9, B 37–45). Apparently these constitutions stated (1) that no *praeiudicium* exists if a petitioner has lied, and (2) that parents and children are in certain circumstances permitted to take action if they believe they have been wronged. On the use of imperial decisions as precedents, see R. Katzoff, *SZ* 89 (1972) 273–8. The format of **4961** in this respect, with imperial decisions quoted before the petition proper, is found in several other petitions, e.g. SB X 10537; the editor's comment in the *ed. pr.* (*BASP* 6 (1969) 17) that this is 'a rather unusual procedure' is incorrect—such a procedure was the norm (cf. Katzoff, loc. cit.). For a petition preceded by a combination of imperial rescripts and an edict (as in **4961**) see P. Flor. III 382. For judicial decisions issued by Severus on his visit to Alexandria in 199–200, see LXVII **4593** introd. Cf. also Jean-Pierre Coriat, *Le Prince législateur* (1997) 123–5.

The petition proper begins with a general introduction (A 9–12, B 47–51). Diogenis then proceeds to recount her case in great detail, much of which we can no longer comprehend. It is certain that she is or had been in dispute with her father over some property. It seems that this property originally came to her as a gift (A 12–14, B 51–4), but before something or other took place (ἐν τῷ μεταξὺ χρόνῳ B 55), her father had remarried and had children by his new wife (A 15, B 55–6). Urged on by Diogenis' stepmother, her father brought a petition against his daughter, no doubt alleging that she had not shown proper filial duty towards him (A 16–18, B 57–61). He obtained the *subscriptio* partially preserved in A 19, B 62. This seems to have led to a court hearing that resulted in her father losing his case; this at any rate seems to be the implication of ἡττήθη in A 21. Whereupon her father brought a further petition and obtained another *subscriptio*, the end of which is preserved (A 21–3: τὴν δέουσαν πρό[ν]οιαν ποιήσεται). After this the text becomes even more difficult to interpret, as the papyrus, especially in B, is less well preserved. It seems likely that Diogenis' father died (A 24) and that her stepmother had in some way deprived Diogenis of some property, probably because of the terms of the will that Diogenis' father had made, which she claims is illegal (A 28). We then come to the concluding part of the petition (A 30–32, B 78–81). In his *subscriptio* the prefect probably said little more than 'petition the epistrategus' (see B 84–5 n.).

In view of the large amount of the text that is lost, the legal situation is far from clear. On this I am grateful for advice which I have received from Prof. A. M. Honoré; I have also benefited greatly from discussing the problems with Dr Antti Arjava. There are many things we do not know: for example, whether Diogenis was married or what her age was, or whether she had full brothers or sisters (she certainly had at least one half-brother or sister (15)). If she had a husband, she does not mention him (unless his name occurs in 14 or 30; neither seems very likely). We cannot be certain that it was Roman law which was being applied. By the date of **4961** the parties were of course Roman citizens, and there is explicit mention of ὁ νόμος τῶν Ῥωμα[ίων (B 75). But we are only some ten years after the *Constitutio Antoniniana*, and Arjava has sought to demonstrate in several places that in Roman

Egypt people only gradually came to use Roman law, which did not become common until towards the middle of the third century. Thus in *Women and Law in Late Antiquity* (1996) 49, he remarks, 'In principle, the papyri should now [i.e., after 212] refer to Roman institutions. Sometimes "the law of the Romans" is explicitly mentioned. In practice the situation was, of course, much more complicated: the documents can present either local law, official Roman law, or any popular interpretations of it.' Cf. also *JRS* 88 (1998) 156; similarly *Pap. Congr. XXI* 30, and *ZPE* 126 (1999) 202–4. Most recently Arjava has treated the 'Romanization of the Family Law' in J. G. Manning, J. G. Keenan, U. Yiftach-Firanko (eds.), *Law and Society in Egypt from Alexander to the Arab Conquest* (forthcoming). However, two of the persons mentioned were citizens of Alexandria or one of the other Greek cities (ἀϲτή, A 13, B 56), who might be thought to have readily adopted Roman law. On the other hand, Diogenis insists that she is not the child of an 'unwritten marriage' (A 26), a concept that had no meaning in Roman law. Whether the use of the word προίξ is an indication that Roman law was being applied is uncertain; see 25 n.

If, as seems probable, the papyrus is to be considered as being based on Roman law, or at any rate on what the petitioner or her lawyers thought was Roman law, several consequences follow. Firstly, Diogenis would have been in *patria potestas* (a concept that non-Romans not surprisingly found particularly difficult to understand; cf. Arjava's article in *Law and Society* cited above), unless she had been emancipated, of which there is no mention in the extant parts of the text. If she were *in potestate*, in theory no legal case between her and her father could have arisen: Dig. 5.1.4, *lis nulla nobis esse potest cum eo quem in potestate habemus, nisi ex castrensi peculio.* Despite this, there are several passages in the Legal Codes that relate to fathers seeking the assistance of provincial governors to exercise control over recalcitrant children (e.g. Dig. 1.16.9.3, CJ 8.46.3, 5, 9.1.14, CTh 9.13.1); see also BGU VII 1578 and Arjava, *JRS* 88, 153 with n. 37. Secondly, if Diogenis was *in potestate*, she could not own any property; all her property in law belonged to her father. This applied even to maternal inheritance, on which see *Women and Law* 98–100, *JRS* 88, 151–2. We do not know whether maternal inheritance was involved in the present case, but there is a reasonable argument for thinking that it was; see A 12–14 n. This would make good sense, since conflict between father and children often arose in connection with maternal inheritance; see *Women and Law* 101, *JRS* 88, 152. Thirdly, if Roman law is involved, Diogenis' father would not have been legally entitled to disinherit her, unless there were exceptional circumstances: see *Women and Law* 46–7, *JRS* 88, 154 (**XXXVI 2757**, where apparently the right of a father to disinherit any of his children whom he wished is recognized, seems not to be based on Roman law). Possible exceptional circumstances were the failure of a child to show proper respect and affection to the parent, and this may well be precisely what Diogenis' father alleges against her (cf. especially A 18–19 and note). If a father disinherited offspring, thus depriving them of the one-quarter of their share on intestacy to which the children were legally entitled as a minimum, the child could raise a *querela inofficiosi testamenti* (see Dig. 5.2, CJ 3.28), by seeking to prove that he/she had acted properly towards his/her father, cf. CJ 3.28.28: *liberi de inofficioso querelam contra testamentum parentum mouentes probationes debent praestare, quod obsequium debitum iugiter, prout ipsius naturae religio flagitabat, parentibus adhibuerunt.* A court would then need to decide the matter (*JRS* 88, 154). One may add that the difficulties step-mothers could make were well known to Roman law (cf. *Women and Law* 172–4), e.g. CJ 9.22.4, 9.32.3, 9.33.5, and especially Dig. 5.2.4: *non est enim consentiendum parentibus, qui iniuriam aduersus liberos suos testamento inducunt: quod plerumque faciunt, maligne circa sanguinem suam inferentes iudicium, nouercalibus delenimentis instigationibusque corrupti.* This seems to apply closely to the circumstances we can deduce for **4961**.

As a parallel for a dispute between a daughter and her father one naturally thinks first and foremost of the celebrated petition of Dionysia (II **237**). However, in this case, as well as there being a property dispute, Dionysia's father is attempting to break up her marriage. More importantly, the petition dates from 186, and it is abundantly clear that it is Egyptian law that is being invoked, not Roman law. A better parallel is BGU VII 1578. There a veteran complains to the acting prefect about τὰ εἰϲ ἐμὲ κα[τ]ὰ ἀϲέβιαν ὑπὸ τῆϲ θυγατρόϲ μου . . . [τ]ολμηθέντα (8–9). In this instance, however, the father states explicitly of his daughter ὑποχειρίαϲ μοι οὔϲηϲ κατὰ τὸν νόμον (9), a fact that, he says (14–16), may have annoyed her and caused her behaviour towards him. Another partial parallel is P. Turner 34 (216), where a son alleges that his 'father's wife', presumably his stepmother, has obtained property resulting from an illegal will made by his deceased father.

4961 does not enlighten us very far on the much discussed concept of 'unwritten marriage', which has recently been studied in detail by Uri Yiftach-Firanko, *Marriage and Marital Arrangements* (2003) chap. 5. Here again the *locus classicus* on the subject is the petition of Dionysia, II **237**; see also CPR I 18 = M. *Chr.* 84 = SPP XX 4 = Meyer, *Juristische Papyri* 89. Both texts concern, in part at least, the power of fathers over their children, power that seems to be less when the child is the offspring of a written marriage. Similarly the implication of line 26 of the present text is that Diogenis has certain rights that she might not have had if she had been the child of an unwritten marriage. See Yiftach-Firanko, *Marriage* 84–91, who concludes (p. 91), 'much yet remains mysterious concerning the institution of *agraphos* and *engraphos gamos* and their effect on the capacity of the father over the person and property of his children'.

A possible scenario is the following. Diogenis had acquired property, which included slaves (A 27), probably given to her by her mother. This property in law belonged to her father, since she was still in his *potestas*, but he had agreed to register it in her name as a gift. However, Diogenis' mother died (or was divorced), and her father married again and had children by his second wife, Diogenis' stepmother. The stepmother induced Diogenis' father to bring an action against her on the grounds that she had not shown him due filial respect. This led to a court case in which the father's charges were dismissed as false. But he immediately made a new petition against her, again egged on by the stepmother, and this time obtained a *subscriptio* that was favourable to him and unfavourable to Diogenis. He then died, leaving a will in which Diogenis was either completely disinherited or at any rate deprived of the property already mentioned, a will that Diogenis claimed was illegal. She claims that she had not behaved badly towards her father and was being plotted against by her stepmother. She therefore petitioned the prefect asking him to ignore the *subscriptio* that was favourable to her father (and to her stepmother), on the grounds that it had been obtained by misrepresenting the facts (and therefore could not serve as a 'precedent' to be used against her), and to take action to enable her to recover her property that had been appropriated by her stepmother. It must be stressed that this is only a hypothetical reconstruction.

In the text that follows, readings that appear solely in B are given in boldface. The superscript figures in lines 2–34 are the line numbers in B. A vertical bar (|) marks the point at which the papyrus breaks off in A.

1   ιθ [

2   ³⁵ἔτους τρίτου Αὐτοκράτορος Καίσαρος Μάρκου Αὐρηλίου C[ε]ουήρου Ἀλεξά[νδρου Εὐσεβοῦς Εὐ]τυχοῦς Cεβαστοῦ μηνὸς |[Ἀθὺρ ιζ. ἐμαρτύρατο ἑαυτὴν Αὐρηλία Διογενὶς ἡ καὶ c.?] ³⁶**ἐξιληφέναι καὶ προσαντιβεβληκέναι ἐκ τεύχου**[c] **cυνκολλ**[ηcίμων βιβλειδίων ἐπιδοθέντων τῷ λαμπροτά-

3   τῳ ἡγεμόνι Αἰδεινίῳ Ἰουλιανῷ καὶ προτεθέντων ³⁷ἐν τῷ ταμικῷ **τῇ ἐνεcτώcῃ** ἡμέρᾳ οὗ ἐστιν ἀν[τίγ]ραφ|ον· [Αὐτοκράτωρ Καῖcαρ Λούκιος Cεπτίμιος Cεουῆρος Εὐcεβὴς Περτίναξ Cεβαcτὸς Ἀραβικὸς Ἀδιαβηνικὸς] ³⁸**Παρθικὸς Μέγιcτος καὶ Αὐτοκράτωρ Καῖcαρ**

4   Μᾶρκος Αὐρήλιος Ἀντωνεῖνος Εὐcεβὴς Cεβαcτὸ[c] Εὐδαίμονι .υ[… ἀπὸ Ἑρ]μ[ο]ῦ πόλεως τῆς μεγάλης· εἰ καθ|[ὼς φῂς *c*.10 ἐν τῷ] ³⁹**βιβλειδίῳ ἐψεύcατο ὁ ἀντίδικός cου οὐδὲν πρόκριμα ἔcται ἐκ τῆ**[c δο]**θείcης** ἀ.[*c*.20–30

5   φθη βιβλειδίῳ ἐπιδοθέντι Μαικίῳ Λαίτῳ τῷ ἡγ[εμον]εύ⁴⁰cαντι **ὑπὸ Cαρ**απιάδος τῆς καὶ Κυρίλλης κα[ὶ .. .[…..]. **ὑπογραφ|ῆc οὕτως ἐχούcης**..[*c*.65–75] ⁴¹**εὐτυχίαιc ἀλήθει**-

6   αν ἀποκρυψαμένους καὶ διὰ τοῦτο κατὰ ἀκολουθείαν ὧν ἠξίωcαν ἀντιγραφῶν τυχόντες κατ|[*c*.45–50]⁴²**εcτιν καὶ ἀcεβίας ἐνκλήματι τοὺς τοιούτο**[υc] **εἶναι ἐνόχους· καὶ ἐκ θεί**[ου διατ]**άγματο**[c τῶν

7   αὐτῶν θεῶν Cεουήρου καὶ Ἀντωνείνου προτεθέντος ἐν τῇ [λαμ]προτάτῃ

Ἀλεξαν⁴³δρείᾳ ἔτου|ϲ η Φαρμοῦθι ιη ἐπὶ μέρουϲ οὕτωϲ· πολλὴ μὲν
τοῖϲ ἡμετέροιϲ νό[μ]οι̣[ϲ   *c*.60–70

8   . νόμων ⁴⁴ϲυνκεχωρηκότων παιϲὶν καὶ γονεῦϲιν ἂν ἀδικει̣ϲθαι νομίζωϲιν
τῶν καθηκ[*c*.9]..ρυ|[*c*.45–55   ]⁴⁵καιοιϲ περὶ τέκνων καὶ γονέων
βουλ[ε]ύεϲθαι καὶ δεον.[*c*.35–45

9   μοι κελεύουϲι καὶ τὰ ἑξῆϲ (*vac.*) Μάρκῳ Αἰδιν̣[ίῳ] ⁴⁶Ἰουλιανῷ ἐπάρχῳ
Αἰγύπτου ⟨παρὰ⟩ Αὐρηλίαϲ Διογενίδοϲ τ|ῆϲ καὶ̣.[*c*.60–70   ]
⁴⁷ραϲ ἀπ' Ὀξυρύγχων πόλεωϲ. αἱ θεῖαι αὐτοκρατορικαὶ

10   διατάξειϲ διαγορεύουϲι τοὺϲ ψευϲαμένουϲ ἐν τα[ῖ]ϲ ἐντεύξεϲι̣..[*c*.10   ]
νουϲ τὰϲ ⁴⁸ἀληθείαϲ μη|δὲν πρόκριμα γενέϲθαι ἐκ τῆϲ δοθε̣ίϲηϲ
αὐτοῖϲ ὑ̣[πογραφῆϲ   *c*.55–65

11   ⁴⁹νουϲ δικαίωϲ γράφειν τὰϲ διαθήκαϲ καὶ ἐξῖναι πα⟨ι⟩ϲὶ καὶ γονεῦϲι
.[*c*.9   ]. νομίζῃ τῶν καθηκο.|[*c*.30–35   ]⁵⁰θαι τὰϲ διαθήκαϲ·
ἅπερ πᾶϲι προϲκυν..ντα προέταξα ἰϲχυριζομέν[η   *c*.15–20

12   ειμι ϲοι τῷ ἐμῷ δεϲπότῃ δεομένη ἀπὸ ϲοῦ [τῆϲ] ἐκ τούτ[ων βο]⁵¹ηθείαϲ
τυχεῖν. κατὰ γὰρ τοὺϲ ἔτι ἄνωθ|εν χρόνουϲ ηδ.[....]ϲ̣α̣ ἐπ[*c*.55–
60   ] ⁵²τοῦ Ἀϲκληπιάδου ἀπὸ τῆϲ αὐ-

13   τῆϲ πόλεωϲ μητρὸϲ Διογενίδοϲ Ἀπολλων[ίου] ἀϲτῆϲ κατ[ὰ δ]ημόϲιον
χρηματιϲμὸν [*c*.8]. υγχ.|[*c*.10–15   ]⁵³διὰ τοῦ καταλογείου
κατέγραψέ μοι κατὰ χάριν ἀναφαίρετον ἐν[*c*.40–45

14   Μεγίϲτου τοῦ Ϲποκέωϲ ⁵⁴μητρὸϲ Τϲενοϲείριοϲ ἀπὸ κώμηϲ Κερκεθύρεωϲ
ἑκαϲ|τ[.]ϲ [*c*.60–70   ] ⁵⁵τοῦ δὲ πατρόϲ μου ἐν τῷ μεταξὺ χρόνῳ
ἐπιγήμαντοϲ

15   τῇ μητρί μου καὶ ἐπιτάξαντόϲ μοι μητρυιὰν Αὐρηλία[ν Ϲαρ]απιάδα τὴν
καὶ Χαριτ..|[*c*.5–10   ] ⁵⁶Ϲαραπίωνο̣ϲ τοῦ Πλουτάρχου ἀϲτὴν ἐξ
ἧϲ ἐπαι[δοπο]ι̣ήϲα[το   *c*.60–65

16   ⁵⁷ἐνεργείηϲ τῆϲ μητρυιᾶϲ ὁ πατήρ μου εἰϲ τοϲοῦτον ἐλήλ[υ]θεν ὥϲτε μετὰ
το.ε.[.]...[..].τω|[*c*.30–35   ] ⁵⁸ἀμέμπτωϲ ὑπ[..]..υ.[...].υ
.ατ̣. [*c*.7]ατ[*c*.30–40

17   χρόνον μέχρι τοῦ διελθόντοϲ [[δευ]] β′ ⁵⁹⟨ἔτουϲ⟩ μηνὸϲ Παχὼν [*c*.6]
.....τ..ηϲ μου τῆϲ οἰκίαϲ ε.ε.τ|[*c*.50–60   ]⁶⁰μου δι' ὧν τὰ
ἅπαντα παρελ[ο]γίϲατο καὶ ἐψεύϲατο.[....]..[*c*.5–10

18   ἐπὶ τῇ τῆϲ μητρυιᾶϲ πιθῶ ἀγένητα ἐγκλήματα καὶ ἰκῇ [*c*.8] κατ'
ἐμοῦ ⁶¹ἐνέτ[α]ξ|εν δι' ὧν βιβλειδίων ἔτυχεν ὑπ[ο]γραφῆϲ τῆ[ϲ]δε
[*c*.60–70

19   ϲι εὐ⁶²ϲέβιαν μὴ ἀπονέμῃ ϲοι ἐντευχθεὶϲ πρὸ βήματοϲ τὸ δ[*c*.7]
Ῥωμαϊκά. κολ(λήματοϲ) μα |[*c*.35–45   ] ⁶³καὶ αἰϲθόμενοϲ ἧϲ διὰ
παντὸϲ π[ρο]ϲέφερον αὐτῷ ὡϲ πατρ̣[ὶ   *c*.5–10

20   βίας καὶ cυνελαυνόμενοc τῇ ἀληθείᾳ οὐ[. . . .]ξενα[*c.*5] . . . ο ⁶⁴κατ᾽ ἐμοῦ
     ἐκ τῆc τῆc μητρ|υι[ᾶc τό]λμηc κ . . [.].[..] . . . . [*c.*65–80

21   τ᾽ ἐμοῦ ψεύδη καὶ ἡττήθη· καὶ τῆc διαμε . [. . .] . ηc ἀφέμ[ε]νοc πάλιν δι᾽
     ἑτέρων β[ιβλειδίων . .]η . .|[*c.*25–35   ]⁶⁶.**ν προτερ** . . . . [. . . . .]
     θ . [.] . . [.]**ạ** . [*c.*40–50

22   παρατεθῆναι τοῖc τῶν ⁶⁷ἐνκτήcεων βιβλιοφύλαξι ακ . [. . .]c καὶ κατ᾽
     ἐρήμου κατ . |[*c.*110–120

23   cεωc cου τὴν δέουcαν πρό[ν]οιαν ποιήcεται· καὶ τούτοιc μ[ὴ ἀ]ρκεcθίcηc
     τῆc μητρυ|[ιᾶc   *c.*105–115

24   δι⁷⁰καcτήριον διαθήκην θέcθαι ἥτιc δια[. . . .].τελευcαντ[..] τοῦ πατρόc
     μου τῇ λ᾽ τοῦ δι[ελθόν]τοc μ|[ηνὸc   *c.*35–45   ]⁷¹.**εναι ἐπ᾽ ἐμοῦ**
     ἀνακ**αλ**ει**c** . [*c.*12   ] . **ελομεν**[.]**ν**α . **πεμ**[*c.*?

25   τά τε ὑπ᾽ αὐτοῦ μοι καταγραφέντα κα . [.] . [. . . . .] . ινα . [. .] . [*c.*9   ]
     . . προοικεὶ καὶ τα . νη|[*c.*?]⁷²**εντα μοι ὑπὸ τῆc** [. . . . .] . [. . . .]**ου**
     μητρὸc οὐ προ[c]**ηκόντ**[ωc   *c.*35–50

26   να τρόπον τῷ καὶ μὴ εἶναί με ἐξ ἀc⁷³υνγράφων γάμων καὶ . [. . .]
     τῇ μητρυιᾷ ⟨μου⟩ Cαραπιά[δ]ι |**τῇ κ**[αὶ Χαριτ   *c.*60–75   ]
     ⁷⁴**ἐνδομενίαν ἐν πλείcτῳ**

27   τιμήματι οὖcαν καὶ ἀποθέτοιc οὐ μόνον ἀλλὰ καὶ ακ . [*c.*7 δουλ]ικὰ
     cώματα πάντα α . |[*c.*20–30   ⁷⁵**ἐ**]**τύγχανεν ὄντα** . . . **ωc ὁ νόμοc**
     τῶν Ρωμα[ίων   *c.*10–15

28   πολειτευόμεθα δια{α}γορεύει ἅπανταc[. . . .] δουλου[c *c.*5] . . .
     cθαι· παρὰ⁷⁶νόμου οὖν οὔc|**ηc τῆc διαθήκηc αὐτοῦ καὶ ματαίαc**
     τῆ[c   *c.*50–60

29   . ων καταγραφέντων ⁷⁷ὑπαρχόντων τε **κ**αὶ δούλων **c**ωμάτων ἐκ τῶν
     νόμ|[ων   *c.*80–95   ]⁷⁸`.´ . . **μου**

30   ἀνόμωc **πρ**α**χθέ**ντα κα[.] . . . . υηθ . . [. . .]ιτευ . [.]ε . ατα . . . . |
     [*c.*65?   ]⁷⁹ . . . . [.] . . [..] . . . . **Cαραπίωνα τὸν καὶ Δημη**[*c.*5?

31   νον ἐν τοcούτῳ δὲ ε . . [*c.*8   ] . . . . . [. . . .] . . [..] feet of *c.*12 letters
     |[*c.*20–25?   ]⁸⁰ . **α** . **ου γὰρ περὶ ὀλίγου μοί ἐcτιν** [*c.*40?

32   cα τυχεῖν τῆc ἀπὸ cοῦ [β]οηθείαc ⁸¹ἵν᾽ ὦ εὐεργετημ[έν]η. διευτύχει. πρὸc
     δὲ τὴ|**ν τοῦ βιβλε**[ιδίου ἐπίδοcιν   *c.*?

33   ⁸²Αὐρήλιοc Θέων ἔγραψα ὑπὲρ αὐτῆc μὴ εἰ[δυίαc γράμματα.] (*m.* 2)
     Αὐρήλιοc Ἀγαθ[ὸc] Δαίμων ὁ διαδε|[*c.*?   ⁸³ . **αρ**[..] . . [*c.*?   ]
     ⁸⁴(**ἔτουc**) **γ**// **Ἀθὺρ ιζ μηδενὸc** [ἐπεχομένου *c.*?

34   . ω . ⁸⁵τῷ κρατίcτῳ ἐπιcτρατήγῳ ἔντυχε [κολ(λήματοc)] . ξ τό[μ(ου) *c.*5]
     (*vac.*)

B

35 ἔτους τρίτου Ἀὐτοκράτορος Καίϲαρος Μάρκου Αὐρηλίου Ϲ[εουήρου
ἐξιληφέναι καὶ προϲαντιβεβ[λ]ηκέναι ἐκ τεύχου[ϲ] ϲυνκολλ[ηϲίμων
ἐν τῷ ταμικῷ τῇ ἐνεϲτώϲῃ ἡμέρᾳ οὗ ἐϲτιν [ἀντίγ]ραφον· [
Παρθικὸϲ μέγιϲτοϲ καὶ Αὐτοκράτωρ Καῖϲαρ Μάρκοϲ Αὐρήλιοϲ
Ἀντ[ω]ν[εῖνος] Ε[ὐϲ]εβ[ὴς
βιβλειδίῳ ἐψεύϲατο ὁ ἀντίδικόϲ ϲου οὐδὲν πρόκριμα ἔϲται ἐκ τῆ[ϲ
δο]θείϲηϲ ἀ [
40 ϲαντι ὑπὸ Ϲαραπιάδος τῆϲ καὶ [Κυ]ρ[ί]λληϲ καὶ [.]. . . . ὑπογραφῆϲ
οὕτωϲ ἐχούϲηϲ . . [
εὐτυχίαιϲ ἀλήθειαν ἀποκρυψαμένουϲ καὶ διὰ τ[οῦ]το κατὰ ἀκολουθείαν
[ὧν ἠξί]ωϲαν ἀ[ντιγραφῶν
εϲτιν καὶ ἀϲεβίαϲ ἐνκλήματι τοὺϲ τοιούτο[υϲ] εἶναι ἐνόχουϲ· καὶ ἐκ
θεί[ου δ]ι[ατ]άγματο[ϲ
δρείᾳ ἔτουϲ η Φαρμοῦθι ιη ἐπὶ μέρουϲ οὕτωϲ· πολλὴ μὲν τοῖϲ
ἡμετέροιϲ νόμοι[ϲ
ϲυνκεχωρηκότων παιϲὶν καὶ γονεῦϲ[ι]ν ἂν ἀδικεῖϲθαι νομίζωϲ[ι]ν [
45 καιοιϲ περὶ τέκνων καὶ γονέων βουλ[ε]ύεϲθαι καὶ δεον[
Ἰουλιανῷ ἐπάρχῳ (vac.) Αἰγύπτου παρὰ Αὐρηλίαϲ Διογ[εν]ίδοϲ τῆϲ καὶ . [
ραϲ ἀπ᾽ Ὀξυρύγχων πόλεωϲ. αἱ θεῖαι αὐτοκρατορικαὶ διατάξ[εις
ἀληθείαϲ μηδὲν πρόκριμα γενέϲθαι ἐκ τῆϲ δοθείϲηϲ αὐτοῖϲ ὑ[πογραφῆϲ
νουϲ δικαίωϲ γράφειν τὰς [δι]αθήκαϲ κ[α]ὶ ἐξῖναι παι[ϲ]ὶ κα[ὶ γο]νεῦϲιν . [
50 θαι τὰϲ διαθήκαϲ· ἅπερ πᾶϲι προϲκυν . ντα προέταξα ἰϲχυριζομέν[η
ηθείαϲ τυχεῖν. κατὰ γὰρ τοὺϲ ἔτι ἄνωθεν χρόνουϲ ηδ . [. . . .]ϲα ἐπ[
τοῦ Ἀϲκηλπιάδου ἀπὸ τῆϲ αὐτῆϲ πόλ[ε]ωϲ μητρὸϲ Διογενίδοϲ
Ἀπολλ[ωνίου
διὰ τοῦ καταλογείου κατέγραψέ μοι κατὰ χάριν ἀναφαίρετον ἐν[
μητρὸϲ Τϲενοϲείριοϲ ἀπὸ κώμη[ϲ] Κερκεθύρεωϲ ἑκαϲτ[.]ϲ [
55 τοῦ δὲ πατρόϲ μου ἐν τῷ μεταξὺ χρόνῳ ἐπιγήμαντοϲ τῇ μη[τρὶ
Ϲαραπίωνοϲ τοῦ Πλουτάρχου ἀϲτὴν ἐξ ἧϲ ἐπαι[δοπο]ιήϲα[το
ἐνεργίαϲ τῆϲ μητρυιᾶϲ ὁ πατήρ [μου] εἰϲ τοϲο[ῦτον] ἐλή[λυθεν
ἀμέμπτωϲ ὑπ[. .] . . ν . [. . .] . υ . ατ [c.7] ατ[
ἔτουϲ μηνὸϲ Παχὼν [c.5]ο . [c.5]οϲταϲμ . [
60 μου δι᾽ ὧν τὰ ἅπαντα παρελ[ο]γίϲατο καὶ ἐψεύϲατο . [. . . .] . . [
ἐνέταξεν δι᾽ ὧν βιβλειδίων ἔτυχεν ὑπ[ο]γραφῆϲ τῇ[ϲ]δε [
ϲέβιαν μὴ ἀπονέμῃ ϲοι ἐντευχθεὶϲ πρὸ βήματοϲ τὸ δ[
καὶ αἰϲθόμενοϲ ἧϲ διὰ παντὸϲ π[ρο]ϲέφερον αὐτῷ ὡϲ πατρ[ὶ
[.] . . [. . .] κατ᾽ ἐμοῦ ἐκ τ[ῆϲ τῆϲ] μητρυι[ᾶϲ τό]λμηϲ κ . . . . [.] . . . . . [

65　　[　*c*.8　].εμ..[　　　*c*.16　　　].[.].κν..[

　　　[　*c*.8　].ν προτερ....[.....]θ.[.]..[.]α.[

　　　[ἐνκτήϲε]ων βιβλι[ο]φύλαξι [

　　　[　*c*.7　]τη.[

　　　[　*c*.7　]..νε[

70　[καϲτήριο]ν διαθήκ[η]ν θέϲ[θαι　　　*c*.11　　　]....[　　*c*.7　].. [

　　　[　*c*.6　].εναι ἐπ' ἐμοῦ ἀνακαλειϲ.[　　　*c*.12　　　].ελομεν[.]να.πεμ[

　　　[　*c*.6　].εντα μοι ὑπὸ τῆϲ [.....].[....]ου μητρὸϲ οὐ προ[ϲ]ηκόντ[ωϲ

　　　[με ἐξ ἀϲ]υνγράφων γάμων καὶ.[...] τῇ μητρυιᾷ μου Ϲαραπιάδι τῇ

　　　　　　　　　　　　　　　　　　　　　　　κ[αὶ Χαρίτῃ

　　　[　*c*.6　]ἐνδομενίαν ἐν πλείϲτω [τιμ]ήματι οὖϲαν καὶ ἀποθέτοιϲ 'ο[ὐ]'

　　　　　　　　　　　　　　　　　　　　　　　　μ[όνον

75　[　*c*.5　ἐ]τύγχανεν ὄντα....ὡϲ [[ονομωϲ]] ὁ νόμοϲ τῶν Ῥωμα[ίων

　　　[θαι· παρα]νόμου οὖν [ο]ὔϲηϲ τῆϲ διαθήκηϲ αὐτοῦ καὶ ματαίαϲ τῆ[ϲ

　　　[γραφέντων] ὑπαρχόντων τε καὶ δούλων ϲωμάτων [ ].τ...[

　　　[　　*c*.10　　]'.´...μου ἀνόμωϲ πραχθέντα καὶ δ[..].εντ.ϲ..[

　　　[　　*c*.11　　]..........[.]..[..]....Ϲαραπίωνα τὸν καὶ Δημή[τριον

80　[　　*c*.22　　].α.ου γὰρ περὶ ὀλίγου μοί ἐϲτιν [

　　　[ἵν' ὦ εὐεργετημένη. διευτ]ύχει. πρὸϲ δὲ τὴν τοῦ βιβλε[ιδίου

　　　[　　*c*.22　　Αὐρή]λιοϲ Θέων ἔγραψα ὑπὲρ αὐτ[ῆϲ

(*m.* 2?)　[　　　*c*.16　　　].αρ[..]..[*c*.4]　(*vac.*)

　　　(ἔτουϲ) γ// Ἁθὺρ ιζ μηδενὸϲ [

85　　　τῷ κρατίϲτῳ [ἐπ]ι[ϲ]τρατή[γῳ

Back, across the fibres:

B 86　(*m.* 3)　Αὐρήλιοϲ Ὠνήϲιμοϲ ἐϲφρ(άγιϲα)
　　　　　　　(*vac.*)

　　　(*m.* 4)　Αὐρήλιο[ϲ] Τριάδελφοϲ ἐϲφράγιϲα
　　　　　　　(*vac.*)

　　　(*m.* 5)　　　]...[....]ϲ ἐϲφρ(άγιϲα)

　　　　　.　　　.　　　.　　　.　　　.

2 l. ἐξειληφέναι, ϲυγκολληϲίμων βιβλιδίων　　　4 l. βιβλιδίῳ, so 5　　　5 l. ἐντυχίαιϲ? (see note)　　　6 l. ἀκολουθίαν, τυχόνταϲ, ἀϲεβείαϲ ἐγκλήματι　　　8 l. ϲυγκεχωρ-, ἐάν　　　11 l. ἐξεῖναι　　　14 1st ε of Κερκεθύρεωϲ a correction　　　16 l. ἐνεργείαϲ　　　17 β′ (see note)　　　18 l. πειθοῖ, ἐγκλήματα, εἰκῇ, βιβλιδίων　　　19 l. εὐϲέβειαν　　ἐντευχθείϲ: τευ corrected from τυ; θειϲ corrected, perhaps from ειϲ or θιϲ　　Ῥωμαϊκά: corrected from ρωμαικι? a long descender through kappa of ἐκ τῆϲ below　　κο^λ　　19–20 A diagonal stroke from εκ in 20 through μα in 19 and into the lacuna above　　21 l. βιβλιδίων　　22 l. ἐγκτήϲεων　　23 l. ἀρκεϲθείϲηϲ　　25 l. προικί

26 l. ἀϲυγγράφων   28 l. πολιτευόμεθα   52 l. Ἀϲκληπιάδου   74 tau of ἀποθέτοιϲ
a correction   86, 88 εϲφρϛ

'19. In the third year of Imperator Caesar Marcus Aurelius Severus Alexander Pius Felix Augustus, month of [Hathyr 17. Aurelia Diogenis also called . . . bore witness that she] has made an extract and collation from the roll(?) of conjoined [petitions submitted] to the prefect Aedinius Iulianus, [*vir clarissimus*], and posted in the treasury building on the current day, of which this is a copy.

'[Imperator Caesar Lucius Septimius Severus Pius Pertinax Augustus Arabicus Adiabenicus] Parthicus Maximus and Imperator Caesar Marcus Aurelius Antoninus Pius Augustus to Eudaemon son of . . . of Hermopolis the great: If as you say(?) . . . your opponent lied in his petition, there will be no *praeiudicium* from the *subscriptio*/answer given . . .

'. . . in a petition presented to the former prefect Maecius Laetus by Sarapias also called Cyrilla and she got(?) a *subscriptio* as follows: . . . having hidden the truth in their petitions(?) and thereby having got answers in accordance with what they requested . . . and such persons are subject to the charge of impiety.

'And from an imperial edict of the same gods Severus and Antoninus posted in the most glorious city of Alexandria, year 8 Pharmuthi 18, in part as follows: Much . . . to our laws . . . as the laws have permitted children and parents if they think that they have been wronged . . . to take counsel concerning children and parents and necessarily(?) . . . [as(?)] the laws command and so on.

'To Marcus Aedinius Iulianus prefect of Egypt from Aurelia Diogenis also called . . . [daughter of *X*, mother —]ra from the city of Oxyrhynchi. The divine imperial constitutions declare that those who have lied in their petitions and [failed to disclose(?)] the true facts, that no *praeiudicium* arose from the *subscriptio* given to them . . . to write their wills in a just manner and that it is possible for children and parents, if anyone(?) thinks [that he has been deprived of(?)] what is due, to [seek to annul(?)] the wills. Which [constitutions], being respected by everyone(?), I set out above, relying on . . . I approach you, my lord, requesting to get from you the help arising from these (constitutions). In times now(?) long past . . . the son of Asclepiades of the same city, his/her mother being Diogenis daughter of Apollonius, citizen, by a public deed . . . registered to me through the registry-office as an unrenounceable gift . . . Megistus son of Spoceus, his/her mother being Tsenosiris, of the village of Cercethyris, each . . . and my father in the meantime having married in succession to my mother and having imposed upon me as a stepmother Aurelia Sarapias also called Charitis(?) daughter of Sarapion the son of Plutarchus, citizen, by whom he had issue . . . through the influence of my stepmother my father went so far as to . . . blamelessly by me(?) . . . [for much(?)] time up to the past year 2, in the month of Pachon . . . the house . . . [presented a petition against] me in the course of which he misrepresented everything and lied . . . under the persuasion of my stepmother he included non-existent accusations and [charges(?)] without grounds against me, as a result of which petition he got this *subscriptio*: [. . . if your daughter(?)] did not accord you the filial duty [appropriate to parents(?)], if you petition me *pro tribunali* . . . Latin. From column 41(?).

'. . . and having perceived the filial duty(?) which I continuously offered to him as a father . . . and being constrained by the truth . . . against me arising from the effrontery of my stepmother . . . lies against me and he lost; and desisting from(?) . . . again through another petition . . . to be deposited with the officials of the record-offices . . . shall make the necessary consideration of your request. And my stepmother not being satisfied with this . . . to deposit the will [before (?)] the court which . . . my father having died(?) on the 30th(?) of the past(?) [month of . . .] in my case(?) . . . the property registered to me by him in accordance with the gift(?) . . . in(?) dowry and the property bought(?) for me by my deceased(?) mother, not properly . . . [I know not in what(?)] way since I am not the child of an unwritten marriage and . . . my stepmother Sarapias also called . . . household goods to the highest value and those in store, not only that but also all the slaves . . . happened to be . . . the law of the Romans . . . we are (Roman) citizens, declares that all the slaves . . . His will, therefore, being illegal and pointless the . . . of the property registered and the slaves from the laws . . . illegally done against me . . . Sarapion also called Deme[tr— . . .] and in the meantime . . . For it is of no small concern to me(?) . . . requesting to get help from you so that I may have been benefited. Farewell.

'For the [handing in] of the petition [I have sent Aurelius Agathus Daemon(?) . . .]. I, Aurelius Theon, have written on her behalf since she does not know [letters].'

(2nd hand) 'I, Aurelius Agathus Daemon, who am acting on behalf of [Aurelia Diogenis](?) . . . Year 3, Hathyr 17. If nothing is prejudged(?) . . . petition the epistrategus, *vir egregius*. Column 60+, roll . . .'

Back (3rd hand) 'I, Aurelius Onesimus, have sealed it.'

(4th hand) 'I, Aurelius Triadelphus(?), have sealed it.'

(5th hand) 'I, . . . , have sealed it.'

Line numbers are those of A unless otherwise indicated.

1 $\iota\theta$. $\iota\alpha$ is a possible, though much less likely, reading. It is not possible to say for certain whether this is in the same hand as the main hand of the text. A numeral at this point is unexpected and difficult to explain. The only texts that might be at all helpful are XVII **2131** 5 and PSI XII 1245.14 = SB XIV 11980. **2131** has, immediately after the certification clause and before the start of the copy of the petition, $\kappa o\lambda\lambda\eta\mu(\acute{\alpha}\tau\omega\nu)$ $A\theta$; similarly SB 11980 has at the same point, i.e., immediately before the start of the petition proper, $[\kappa o\lambda\lambda]\acute{\eta}\mu\alpha\tau o c$ $\nu\theta$. This would seem to suggest that the petition and *subscriptio* as posted up had at their head the $\kappa\acute{o}\lambda\lambda\eta\mu\alpha$ number under which they were filed in the archives. Unfortunately the $\kappa\acute{o}\lambda\lambda\eta\mu\alpha$ number given in the *subscriptio* to **4961** in A 34 cannot be made to agree with that in line 1.

2 There is some ink over the line where $E\mathring{v}c\epsilon\beta o\mathring{v}c$ would have been written, no doubt offset.

$\mu\eta\nu\acute{o}c$. The reading after mu is not easy.

$A\theta\mathring{v}\rho$ $\iota\zeta$. See B 84.

$\mathring{\epsilon}\mu\alpha\rho\tau\acute{v}\rho\alpha\tau o$ $\mathring{\epsilon}\alpha\upsilon\tau\mathring{\eta}\nu$ $\kappa\tau\lambda$. This is the formula found in XVII **2131** 2–4, with the addition of $\delta\iota\grave{\alpha}$ $\tau\mathring{\omega}\nu$ $\mathring{v}\pi o\gamma\epsilon\gamma\rho\alpha\mu\mu\acute{\epsilon}\nu\omega\nu$ $\mu\alpha\rho\tau\acute{v}\rho\omega\nu$ before $\mathring{\epsilon}\xi\epsilon\iota\lambda\eta\phi\acute{\epsilon}\nu\alpha\iota$, SB XIV 11980.10 ff., and XVI 13059.15 ff. Since the line is longer than would be expected (see the introd.), one wonders whether the writer omitted $\mathring{\epsilon}\alpha\upsilon\tau\mathring{\eta}\nu$. $\mathring{\epsilon}\alpha\upsilon\tau\acute{o}\nu$ is omitted in LXV **4481** 14–16, but there the participles $\mathring{\epsilon}\kappa[\gamma\epsilon\gamma\rho\alpha\mu\mu\acute{\epsilon}]\nu o\upsilon$ $\kappa\alpha\grave{\iota}$ $\pi\rho o c\alpha\nu\tau\iota\beta\epsilon\beta\lambda[\eta\mu]\acute{\epsilon}\nu o\upsilon$ follow instead of the infinitives; SB X 10537.2–4, which also omits $\mathring{\epsilon}\alpha\upsilon\tau\acute{o}\nu$, may well have had the same construction. It is also omitted in BGU III 970 = M. *Chr.* 242.3–5, where the verb used is $\mathring{\epsilon}\mu\alpha\rho\tau\upsilon\rho o\pi o\iota\acute{\eta}c\alpha\tau o$. BGU XI 2061.17–20 (with BL VI 20–21), P. Stras. IV 235.3 (with the corrected reading reported in P. Horak 13 introd.), and P. Horak 13 are all incomplete. If we assume that the length of the lines was normally that indicated by A 3 and B 36–7 (cf. A 7 = B 42 n. and the introd.), Diogenis' alias must have been very short; cf. 9 n.

(B 36) $\mathring{\epsilon}\kappa$ $\tau\epsilon\acute{v}\chi o\upsilon[c]$. On the uncertain meaning of the word see R. Haensch, *ZPE* 100 (1994) 502 n. 51.

2–3 $\lambda\alpha\mu\pi\rho o\tau\acute{\alpha}]\tau\omega$. $\delta\iota\alpha c\eta\mu o\tau\acute{\alpha}]\tau\omega$ is also possible at this date; see G. Bastianini, *Pap. Congr. XVII* iii 1339, *ANRW* II 10.1, 583 n. 4.

3 The dating of the prefecture of Aedinius Iulianus (and of the prefects who preceded and followed him) given in the lists by Bastianini, *ZPE* 17 (1975) 308–9, and *ANRW* II 10.1, 513, needs some revision. Bastianini accepts the argument of A. Stein, *Die Präfekten von Ägypten* (1950) 127, that he is to be identified with the man who appears in the Album of Canusium (CIL IX 338 I 4). Stein dates this inscription not later than the autumn of 223 and, since Aedinius Iulianus is there a *vir clarissimus*, argues that he must have ceased to be prefect of Egypt by this date. **4961** disproves this argument, since it shows him as still prefect on 14 November 223. I am grateful to Rudolf Haensch for bringing to my attention the article on this inscription by B. Salway in Alison Cooley (ed.), *The Epigraphic*

Landscape of Roman Italy (2000) 115–71, which includes a discussion of the prefects at this period. (This article supersedes the earlier study by J. Modrzejewski in P. L. Bat. XVII pp. 62–3.) Salway accepts the identification and the date of the inscription, but argues that Aedinius Iulianus could still have been serving as prefect of Egypt until the early part of 224 and is therefore likely to have been prefect when this inscription was set up (pp. 155–6). **4961** strongly supports his view. In fact **4961** is the only papyrus mentioning Aedinius Iulianus that has an exact date. P. Flor. III 382.92 is considered to be the equivalent of 3 November 222 by Stein (followed by Bastianini) because he believed that Aedinius Iulianus could not have been prefect a year later. However, the year number is lost, and **4961** proves Salway to be correct in arguing that the year could as well be year 3 as year 2, i.e. that it could date from 3 November 223. I **35** is dated by the consuls to 223, but the month is not preserved. P. Wisc. I 29r and XLVI **3286** are undated. In SB XVIII 13610 = ChLA XXVIII 865 the prefect's name is wholly restored.

ἐν τῷ ταμικῷ. The ταμικόν is listed as occurring elsewhere in P. Flor. III 382.94 and P. Stras. IV 275.13 only. In the latter, which must be roughly contemporary with **4961**, a report of a trial is quoted as follows: ῥήτ]ωρ εἶπεν ἐ[ν τῷ τα]μικῷ ἐτέθην προ[. In the former a *subscriptio* from Aedinius Iulianus is said to be ἐ]τέθη ἐν τῷ ταμικῷ. In BL I 460, P. Flor. 382.94 is corrected to προε]τέθη, a correction that might be supported by **4961** 3, but which P. Stras. 275 suggests is unnecessary. To these two examples we must add BGU XI 2061.19, where ταμικόν occurs of the location of a petition and its *subscriptio*. The editor read προτε]θέντων ἐν τῷ ταμίῳ, but a photograph kindly supplied by Günter Poethke shows the correct reading to be ταμικῷ.

προτεθέντων . . . [τῇ ἐνεστώσῃ] ἡμέρᾳ. So I **35** 12–13 and SB X 10537.3–4. In SB 10537 this is followed immediately by οὗ ἐστιν [, where we should no doubt restore ἀ[ντίγραφον. For ἀντίγραφον cf. also P. Yadin 33.

3–4 This rescript is also reported in P. Stras. IV 254, though even more fragmentarily preserved than in **4961**. The text is a petition that has at the head at least two constitutions of Severus and Caracalla and reads in line 6] βιβλιδίῳ ἐψεύσατο ὁ ἀν[. The editor comments, 'on se plaint d'un inconnu désigné par ἀν[ήρ ou ἄν[θρωπος'; in fact we can now see that the correct supplement is ἀν[τίδικος. The petition proper does not begin until the following line (as the editor remarks, 'la largeur de la ligne était très grande'). Professor Honoré assures me that, to the best of his knowledge, this rescript is not otherwise known, but he adds that 'it could be said to parallel the principle that a legal ruling given in a rescript is not binding if the facts are misstated in the petition'. Worth comparison with the present rescript is one quoted in Dig. 49.1.1.1 (Ulpian), even though the Greek seems to be corrupt: *quid enim, si in consulendo mentitus est? de qua re extat rescriptum diui Pii* . . . ἐὰν ἐπιστείλῃ τις ἡμῖν ἃ διὰ[?] καὶ ἀντιγράφωμεν ἡμεῖς ὁτιοῦν, ὑπάρξει τοῖς βουλομένοις ἐπικαλεῖσθαι πρὸς τὴν ἀπόφασιν. εἰ γὰρ διδάξαιεν ἢ ψευδῶς ἢ οὐχ οὕτως ἔχειν τὰ ἐπισταλμένα, οὐδὲν ὑφ' ἡμῶν εἶναι δόξῃ προδιεγνωσμένον, τῶν[?] ὡς ἑτέρως ἔχουσιν τοῖς γραφεῖσιν ἀντεπεσταλκότων. Note also CJ 1.22.2, which refers to lawsuits where one party has lied or misrepresented the facts.

4 Presumably Εὐδαίμονι is followed by a patronymic (as is usual in rescripts). Εὐδαιμονίδι cannot be read.

ἀπὸ Ἑρ]μ[ο]ῦ πόλεως τῆς μεγάλης. The epithet at this date seems to be confined to Hermopolis, and the slight traces suit this reading.

εἰ καθ|[ὼς φὴς . . . ἐν τῷ] βιβλειδίῳ. The restoration καθὼς φής is *exempli gratia*. For the expression we may compare LXIV **4437** 2 (where it is garbled), with the note ad loc. See Tony Honoré, *Emperors and Lawyers* (²1994) 38, on the frequency in imperial rescripts of the phrases *si, ut proponis / adleges, dicis*, etc. He describes *ut dicis* as a characteristic expression of his imperial secretary no. 4, whom he regards as in office from 211 to 213 (p. 89). Nothing else is needed at this point to complete the sense, but this would make the line very short.

(B 39) πρόκριμα. I am indebted to Matias Buchholz for the information that πρόκριμα is a calque from Latin *praeiudicium*, which had no earlier use in Greek. He reports that it is first attested in I. Knidos I 31. Kn. V.34 (100 BC), a translation of the *Lex de prouinciis praetoriis*. In papyri it usually appears in the phrase χωρὶς προκρίματος, on which see most recently Fabian Reiter, *Die Nomarchen des Arsinoites* (2004) 312. In **4961** it is being used in meaning (1) of the three meanings classified in H. G. Heumann, E. Seckel, *Handlexicon zu den Quellen des römischen Rechts* ([10]1958) s.v.: 'der durch die vorgreifende Entscheidung entstehende Nachteil'. Cf. the use of προδιεγνωσμένον in the rescript of Pius quoted in 3–4 n.

(B 39) οὐδὲν πρόκριμα ἔσται. The same words occur in LIV **3759** 36–7, though in a different context: there the presiding official, the λογιστής, postpones a case, saying that since it is now evening πρόκριμα οὐδὲν ἔσται.

(B 39) ἐκ τῆ[ς δο]θείσης ἀ.[. Either ἀν[τιγραφῆς, supported by A 6, or αὐ[τῷ ὑπογραφῆς, as in B 48, could be read, although nu is slightly preferable to upsilon.

4–5 These lines must give the start of the second legal ruling cited by Diogenis. Although the content seems to be much the same as the first ruling, and although, as indicated in the previous note, we could read αὐ[τῷ ὑπογραφῆς in line 4, it is inconceivable that we should link the two rulings together, which would mean that the emperors quoted a prefectorial *subscriptio*. However, Diogenis would hardly include a prefectorial *subscriptio* in between an imperial rescript and an imperial edict unless the *subscriptio* included an imperial constitution. I suggest, therefore, that in the large lacuna in line 5 the prefect quoted imperial authority for what follows. At the start of line 5 we could have the ending of ἀντεπέμ]φθη or ἀνεπέμ]φθη, although it is not easy to see how either can have construed. Other possibilities are to restore ἀνελήμ]φθη, for which cf. LIV **3741** 57–8 ἔδοξ(εν) τὴν ἐπιστολὴν ἀναλημφθ(ῆναι) τοῖς ὑπομ(νήμασι), 'resolved that the letter be incorporated in the minutes', or (ἐμ)περιελήμ]φθη, for which we may compare BGU I 194 = W. *Chr.* 84.12–14 βιβλιδίῳ . . . ᾧ ἐνπεριείλη᾿μ᾿πται ἀντίγρ(αφα) ἐπιστολῶν δύο, and SB XIV 11343.3–4 βιβλιδίων . . . οἷς περιείληπται τὰ ὑπ᾿ ἐμο[ῦ κελευσθέντα]. Any of these restorations might perhaps have been preceded by ἄλλο τῶν αὐτῶν, 'another [pronouncement] of the same [emperors]', cf. LX **4068** 12, or a longer form of this; or indeed a statement that this same rescript was to be found in the prefectorial *subscriptio* that follows.

For the prefect Maecius Laetus, see Bastianini, *ZPE* 17 (1975) 304, *ANRW* II 10.1, 512. He is attested in office from May 200 to some time in 203.

καὶ . . [. . . .] ὑπογραφ|[ῆς. Neither in A 5 nor in B 40 is the reading clear. Since ὑπογραφῆς is genitive, we might think of supplying some part of τυγχάνω. The letter before ὑπογραφῆς in B can easily be read as nu, which suggests we might read ἔτ[υ]χεν there (and ἔτ[υχεν in A). We have ἔτυχεν ὑπ[ο]γραφῆς in 18, and καὶ ἔτυχεν ὑπογραφῆς can be paralleled exactly in SB XVIII 13747.13; but in the present text it involves an awkward change of subject.

(B 40) We expect the ὑπογραφή to start with a date. The feet of the letters after ἐχούσης would permit ἔτ[ους, but the symbol ∟ is almost invariable in such contexts; cf., however, SB XXVI 16426.11–13, where what is unquestionably a *subscriptio* begins ἔτους ὀγδόου καὶ ἔτους [ἑβδόμου (of Diocletian and Maximian). It is also possible that no date was given (cf. e.g. P. Diog. 17.3, P. Panop. 23.12–13) and the *subscriptio* began with ἐπ[εί, 'since' (cf. below).

(B 41) εὐτυχίαις. I do not see how this can make any sense in the context. It seems essential to correct to ἐντυχίαις; cf. ἐν τα[ῖς ἐντεύξεςι in A 10.

6 τυχόντες. Again, a correction to τυχόντας looks inevitable.

(B 42) ἐστιν. One might think of this being preceded by δῆλον or a similar word, and one might reconstruct the whole ὑπογραφή, very tentatively, along the following lines: 'Since the emperors / imperial constitutions have ruled that those who concealed the truth in their petitions . . . fail to succeed, it is clear that such persons are also liable to a charge of impiety.'

(B 42) θεί[ου. The reading is not easy but can hardly be avoided. The restoration δ]ι[ατ]άγματο[ς τῶν] αὐτῶν θεῶν κτλ. also looks to be beyond question. This would fit with the length of line suggested by в 36–37. Is it possible that this διάταγμα is the one referred to in BGU VII 1578.6–7 (with the correction in BL VI 17), which seems to relate to accusations of ingratitude by parents against their offspring (see above, introd.)? This edict is described as καθολικόν, but this need mean no more than 'of general application'; see R. Katzoff in *Studies in Roman Law in Memory of A. Arthur Schiller* (1986) 119–26.

7 At the right in A there is some ink above] ̣ ̣ρυ[in the line below. This might possibly be the feet of two iotas, i.e. read Φαρμοῦθ]ι ι[η in A 6 (cf. в 43).

(в 43) ἐπὶ μέρουϲ οὕτωϲ. Similarly LXIV **4435** 2, where see the note.

7–8 Certainly read τῶν] νόμων, with or without an adjective. Just to the left of νόμων there is something written that much resembles a fourth-century stigma. Its purpose is unclear.

8 ἂν ἀδικεῖϲθαι νομίζωϲιν. I am indebted to Dr Arjava for suggesting what must surely be the correct articulation of these words. A similar problem occurs in P. Tebt. I 43 = M. *Chr.* 46.35; this was originally articulated ὡϲ οὐθεὶϲ ἂν ἀδικη[, but in BL II 169 ὡϲ οὐθεὶϲ ἀναδική[ϲει is suggested (cf. already BL I 423 n. 3). ἀναδικεῖϲθαι is attested once or twice in papyri, with the meaning 'reopen a case' or 'appeal for rehearing of a case'; cf. Preisigke, *WB* I and IV (see the discussion in P. Heid. VIII 412 introd. and 15 n.). Neither meaning would suit the present context at all well, and this articulation would leave νομίζωϲιν hard to construe. ἂν for ἐάν is rare in papyrological Greek, but a few instances are attested: see Mandilaras, *The Verb* § 599. This articulation admirably suits the sense required. We may compare P. Kron. 50.8, where one son gets only a tiny legacy διὰ τό, ὡϲ ὁ π[ατ]ὴρ Κρονίων π[ρο]φέρεται, ἐν π[ολ]λοῖϲ ἠδικῆϲθαι ὑπ' αὐτ[ο]ῦ ἐν τοῖϲ κατὰ τὸν βίον.

(в 45) καιοιϲ. καὶ οἷϲ is not promising; more probably we have the end of δι]καίοιϲ. Also possible is ἀναγ]καίοιϲ; ἐν τοῖϲ ἀναγ]καίοιϲ does not seem likely, but the word could be used in the sense of close relatives, as in e.g. XXIV **2407** 36–7.

(в 45) δεον[. Most probably δέον alone or δεόν[τωϲ.

8–9 Certainly οἱ νό]μοι, again, as in 7–8, with or without an adjective. Here it may have been preceded by ὥϲπερ. If οἱ νόμοι κελεύουϲι followed its object, one would have expected κελεύουϲι to have preceded οἱ νόμοι; cf. XXXVI **2757** ii 5–6 and LX **4068** 8–9, the latter a rescript of Severus.

9 There is a strange *vacat* in в between ἐπάρχῳ and Αἰγύπτου, whereas A 9 has the *vacat* more logically before the start of the petition proper. It was normal at this date to address the prefect by his three names plus the title ἔπαρχοϲ Αἰγύπτου: see Bastianini, *ANRW* II 10.1, 587–90.

в 46 correctly includes παρά before Αὐρηλίαϲ.

(в 46) τῆϲ καὶ ̣[. The first letter of Diogenis' alias is most like phi; sigma or omicron are less likely. Presumably the name of Diogenis' father, either with an alias or the mention of some office, stood in the lacuna before the name of her mother, ending -ραϲ. If so, there would have been insufficient room for Diogenis to have mentioned her husband, if she had one: see introd.

10 ἐν τα[ῖϲ] ἐντεύξεϲι ̣ ̣[. Not ἐντεύξεϲιν; ἐντεύξεϲι κα[ὶ ἀποκρυψαμέ]νουϲ (cf. 6) is perhaps not impossible.

The construction here is unclear. In the passages quoted from the legal sources in Heumann–Seckel (see 4 n. above), *praeiudicium* several times occurs along with *fieri*, so that μηδὲν πρόκριμα γενέϲθαι suits well; but we should have expected τοὺϲ ψευϲαμένουϲ and the following participle to be in the dative. In all three places the accusative is a certain reading.

(в 48) ὑ[πογραφῆϲ. The upsilon is certain; not ἀ[ντιγραφῆϲ as in A 6.

11 νουϲ δικαίωϲ γράφειν τὰϲ διαθήκαϲ. Possibly supply διατιθεμέ]|νουϲ, with the sense being that the imperial constitutions declare (or prescribe) that the testators (τοὺϲ διατιθεμένουϲ) should write their wills in a just manner. Alternatively the text may have had βουλομέ]νουϲ *vel sim.*

A reads παϲι; в 49 has correctly παιϲί.

γονεῦϲι. в 49 reads γο]νεῦϲιν, but the letter after γονεῦϲι in A is not nu. It might be epsilon, as might the letter after γονεῦϲιν in в (theta and sigma are also possible), which would point to ἐ[άν; but ἀδικεῖϲθαι (cf. 8) does not suit the trace before νομίζῃ, and ἐάν τιϲ ἀδικεῖϲθαι is too long for the space. The trace also rules out ἐ[άν τιϲ αὐτῶ]ν. Sigma is possible, but ἐ[άν τι]ϲ νομίζῃ is too short.

τῶν καθηκο . [. Either καθηκόν[των or καθηκου[ϲῶν could be read. No doubt Diogenis is referring to the passage from the edict quoted in A 8.

(B 50)]θαι τὰϲ διαθήκαϲ. If the infinitive is governed by ἐξεῖναι, ἀναιρεῖϲ]θαι or ἀνελέϲ]θαι 'to overturn the will' is a possibility, although a verb meaning 'to challenge' (the validity of the will) would seem more suitable. After διαθήκαϲ we no doubt have a strong stop.

(B 50) ἅπερ. This must refer back not only to the διατάξειϲ but also to the διάταγμα in 6, hence the neuter plural.

(B 50) πᾶϲι προϲκυν . ντα προέταξα. The meaning is clear, what was written less so. We may compare SB V 7696.86, θαυμαϲτο[ὶ μ]ὲν [οἱ] νόμοι καὶ προϲκυνητοί, SB XVI 12692.27, etc., θείῳ . . . καὶ προϲκυνητῷ νόμῳ, SB X 10537.11–12, where I read (from a photograph) τῆϲ θείαϲ νομοθεϲίαϲ . . . προϲκυνητῆϲ οὔϲηϲ (for προϲκυνητόϲ as a 3-termination adjective see LSJ). In ChLA III 201.8 we have ἐκ τῶν προ]ϲκυνηταίων (l. -τέων) θεϲπ[ιϲμάτω]ν (cf. lines 25–6). P. Tebt. II 286 = M. *Chr.* 83.22–3 reads προϲκυνεῖ[ν] ὀφείλοντεϲ τὰϲ ἀναγνω[ϲ]θείϲαϲ [imperial] ἀποφ[ά]ϲειϲ, and BGU IV 1073.12–13 = P. Frisch, *Zehn agonistische Papyri* 2.12–13, προϲκυνήϲαντεϲ τὰ θεῖα (sc. διατάγματα). προϲκυνηταια cannot be read nor προϲκυνητέα. I have considered προϲκυνη[θ]έντα: for the passive in a very similar context cf. IGLSyr. VII 4028.42–3, τὴν θείαν ἀντιγραφὴν ὑπὸ πάντων προϲκυνουμένην προέταξεν; but there would be no room for both theta and epsilon, and the past tense is not what we should expect. It is not possible to read προϲκυνητὰ ὄντα, though this may have been what was intended.

ἰϲχυριζομέν[η. Of the meanings given in LSJ, 'relying on' seems best suited here, with reference to the validity of imperial pronouncements.

11–12 Restore πρόϲ]ειμι; cf., e.g., P. Cair. Isid. 79.14, P. Stras. I 57.6.

12 ἐκ τούτ[ων βοηθε]ί[αϲ] τυχεῖν. The usual expression would be simply τῆϲ (ϲῆϲ) βοηθείαϲ τυχεῖν. I have restored τούτ[ων on the assumption that the word refers, like ἅπερ, to the imperial decrees.

With τυχεῖν we come to the end of the preamble, before Diogenis starts to recount the long history of the case.

(B 51) ηδ . . ἤδη is possible; otherwise read ηδι[.

12–14 I should like to believe that the person mentioned in 12–13 was Diogenis' mother, now deceased or divorced, who was the citizen of a Greek city (ἀϲτή). Maternal inheritance is discussed in Arjava, *Women and Law* 94–105, *JRS* 88, 151–2. But if this person was the subject of κατέγραψέ μοι and if καταγραφέντα in A 25 refers to the same registration, as it seems to do, then this was done by a man (τά τε ὑπ᾿ αὐτοῦ μοι καταγραφέντα). One possibility is that ἀϲτῆϲ does not refer to the subject of κατέγραψε but to his mother. Another approach is to suppose that Diogenis' mother was indeed the person who gave the property to Diogenis (ἀϲτῆϲ being either part of a genitive absolute or governed by ὑπό, the subject of the verb being Diogenis); this property was then registered in Diogenis' name by her father as a gift, since she was still in his *potestas* (in terms of Roman law the property would presumably have been regarded as her *peculium*). We might even think of restoring in 12 ἤδη [ἐγὼ οὖ]ϲα ἐπ[ὶ πατρικῇ ἐξουϲίᾳ (but there are of course many other possibilities). Jane Rowlandson, *Landowners and Tenants in Roman Egypt* (1996) 194, remarks on 'a surprisingly large number of instances of land being purchased on behalf of unmarried daughters by their parents', no doubt normally to provide them with a dowry, as Rowlandson implies (cf. the mention of a dowry in A 25). Arjava, *JRS* 88, 158, comments on 'the practice of buying or registering certain property in the name of one's children', referring to several instances in the papyri, e.g. XII **1470**, P. Gen. I 44 = M. *Chr.* 215, and especially SB X 10728, the sale of a house (3–5) ἀγοραϲθεῖϲαν [ὑπ᾿ ἐμοῦ καὶ ϲυν]ταχθεῖϲαν ἐπ᾿ ὀνόματοϲ τῆϲ ἡμετέραϲ θυγατρὸϲ Αὐρηλίαϲ Ἀλεξάνδραϲ οὔϲηϲ μου ὑπ[ὸ] τῇ χειρὶ κατὰ τοὺϲ Ῥωμαίων [νόμουϲ, followed (probably) by a reference to the previous owner (for ϲυν]ταχθεῖϲαν instead of the editor's ἐν?]ταχθεῖcαν, see *ZPE* 160 (2007) 208–10). He also refers to FIRA II 661.viii.2 *si domum . . . pater tuus, cum in potestate eius ageres, nomine tuo donandi animo comparauit . . .* , which may be particularly relevant to the circumstances in **4961**.

13]. υνχ. [. We may have a reference to a cυγχώρηcιc that took place διὰ τοῦ καταλογείου; perhaps cf. P. Berl. Leihg. I 10.17, where ἐνεχυραcία is registered κα[τ]ὰ cυνχώρηc[ιν δι]ὰ τοῦ κατ[α]-λογείου. However, omicron or rho are easier readings than omega (πο]λὺν χρ[όνον cannot be read).

(B 53) ἐν[. One possibility among many is ἔν[γαια (l. ἔγγαια); another is ἔν[γραφον.

14 Μεγίcτου. A very rare name. There are several attestations in LGPN, but none from Egypt. However, Μεγίcτη occurs several times: see D. Foraboschi, *Onomasticon* s.v.; add P. Harrauer 33.100. There is also a feminine name Μεγιcτώ in P. Mich. III 190.29, 34. The person referred to here may have been the previous owner of the property; cf. SB 10728 referred to above. Alternatively it could be the name of Diogenis' husband or intended husband; cf. introd.

I can offer no explanation for ἕκαcτ[ο]c/ἑκάcτ[η]c.

(B 55) ἐν τῷ μεταξὺ χρόνῳ. This suggests that some time had elapsed since the original gift had been registered. Possibly the arrangement was that Diogenis was to take ownership of the property when she ceased to be *in potestate*, and before this happened her father had married again. This would fit with the idea that it was Diogenis' mother who intended the property to come into Diogenis' possession.

(B 55) ἐπιγήμαντοc. The verb is new to the papyri. On the aorist of γαμέω, see Mandilaras, *The Verb* § 306(7).

15 μητρυιάν. This is only the third occurrence of the word in documentary papyri. The other instances are SB XX 15096.8 (μητρυ⟨ι⟩ᾷ; see the correction in *ZPE* 90 (1992) 264) and SB X 10537.24, where again the petitioner is in dispute with a stepmother: he says (to the prefect) οὐκ ἀγνοεῖc καὶ τὸ τῶν μητρυιῶν ὄνομα. Problems caused by stepmothers were well known to Roman law; see introd. It is noteworthy that the stepmother in **4961** is a citizen of a Greek city, ἀcτήν B 56.

Χαριτ.. [. One expects Χαρίτην, but it seems impossible to read this. Χαρίτιν is a much easier reading and such a feminine name is attested (see Pape, *Eigennamen*, and LGPN I, IIIA, IV). The form is not attested from Egypt, but Χαρίτιον is not uncommon. The lacuna may have been filled by Αὐρηλίου, an alias of Sarapion, or simply by θυγατέρα.

16 ἐνεργείηc. B 57 has more correctly ἐνεργίαc. For the use of this noun, cf. P. Lond. V 1731.11, where the expression κατὰ διαβο{υ}λικὴν καὶ cατανικὴν ἐνέργειαν occurs with reference to a divorce.

ἐλήλ[υ]θεν. This seems to be perfect in the sense of aorist; for which see Mandilaras, *The Verb* §§ 472, 474.

After μετά either τολε or τοδε; μετὰ τὸ λεί[or μετὰ τόδε τ[ό are possibilities. Later either]ατω[or]ετω[.

16–17 = B 58 Presumably Diogenis is speaking of her own actions towards her father and claiming that she acted ἀμέμπτωc. After this possibly ὑπ᾽ [ἐ]μοῦ.

17 χρόνον. Although the phrase ἀπὸ τῶν ἔμπροcθεν χρόνων μέχρι κτλ. is very common and quite often χρόνων is misspelt χρόνον, there is no need to assume an error here. (ἐπὶ) πολὺν χρόνον, referring to the length of time over which Diogenis had shown due filial respect towards her father, would make good sense; cf. the previous note.

After the deletion of δεν, which is marked by dots over the letters, we seem to have no more than a large cursive beta plus a diagonal stroke, i.e., the writer omitted any indication of ἔτουc. B 59 reads ἔτουc.

What follows Παχών is uncertain and difficult to reconcile with the reading of B 59. Possibly one version (A) had just the figure, whereas the other (B) had the day in full. Before μου it is not difficult to read cταcηc in A, possibly ἀποcτάcηc, though the traces of the first three letters are very slight. If we read this we should need to correct B to ἀπ]οcτάc⟨ηc⟩ μο[υ; in both texts καί or ἀλλ᾽ could have preceded. If this is on the right lines, it suggests Diogenis left her father's house (rather than gave up all claim to a house that had been given to her).

ε̣ ε̣ τ[. Probably ἔπειτ[α, ἐπ(ε)ὶ τ[, or perhaps ἐπ(ε)ὶ π[.

(B 60) No doubt κατ' ἐ]μοῦ, preceded by a statement that her father filed a petition (against her). For a petition of this nature, cf. BGU VII 1578, discussed in the introd.

(B 60) παρελ[ο]γίϲατο. A comparable use of the word occurs in SB XVI 12692.38 and in CPR XVIIA 24. 5.

18 πιθώ. This must be an attempt at the dative of πειθώ in the meaning 'persuasion'; cf. Gignac, *Grammar* ii 87. The word πειθώ is very rare in documentary papyri, attested elsewhere only in III **474** 37 and XLIII **3106** 9, in both cases with the meaning 'obedience'. In P. Sakaon 38.10 = P. Flor. I 36 = M. *Chr.* 64 the editors restore in a similar context [ἐκ πιθανολογί]αϲ τῆϲ ἑαυτοῦ γυναικ[ό]ϲ.

ἰκῇ [*c.*8]. The only possibility that occurs to me is to suppose that this is for εἰκῇ in the meaning 'without good cause", for which see LSJ Rev. Suppl. Papyrological references to this usage are UPZ I 106.15, 107.17. 108.24 (= C. Ord. Ptol. 62–63); Wilcken translates 'ohne Grund' and Lenger 'sans raison'. After it no doubt a synonym of ἐγκλήματα, e.g. αἰτίαϲ; the two words occur together in P. Tebt. I 27 = W. *Chr.* 331.66–7; cf. also ἀγένητον αἰτίαν in P. Polit. Iud. 1.15–16 and CPR XV 15.16.

(B 61) ὑπ[ο]γραφῆϲ τῆ[ϲ]δε. The same wording in P. Stras. IV 196.10–11.

18–19 γονεῦ]ϲι is a likely supplement. The *subscriptio* may have said, 'If your daughter has not shown you the filial piety that is appropriate for parents . . .'.

19 = B 62 τὸ δ[*c.*7]. One expects something like τὸ δ[ίκαιον ἕξειϲ], but there is insufficient room for this. τὸ δ[έον is a possibility, though there is not really room for ποιήϲω to follow. For τὸ δέον, cf. ChLA X 407.15, τὸ δέον δίκηϲ ἐκτὸϲ ἐπιγνῶναι. (ChLA has δέον{ι} but the supposed iota is in fact part of the nu.)

Ῥωμαϊκά. Probably the original *subscriptio* had *legi* or *recognoui*. On the use of Ῥωμαϊκά, see *Tyche* 3 (1988) 117 and *ZPE* 160 (2007) 206.

κολ(λήματοϲ). In E. Van 't Dack et al. (eds.), *Egypt and the Hellenistic World* (1983) 381, I suggested that in such contexts κολ should be expanded κολ(λημάτων), since this was the only example I had noted of an unabbreviated form of the word (P. Harr. I 68.14). R. Haensch, *ZPE* 100 (1994) 504 n. 56, has pointed out that the genitive singular is used in PSI XII 1245.14 = SB XIV 11980, and this would seem to be more logical; see LXIII **4364** 9 n. After κο^λ we have the foot of xi from ἐνέτ[α]ξεν in the line above; then what must be the column number.

19–21 What is happening here is particularly unclear. The whole of this passage, to καὶ ἡττήθη, could be Diogenis' report of a trial that had taken place. For π[ρο]ϲέφερον, cf. BGU VII 1578.10–11, where the father says τῆϲ δηλουμένηϲ μου θυγατρὸϲ τῆϲ εὖ καὶ καλῶϲ κατὰ τὴν [ἀρχήν μοι προϲφ]ερούϲηϲ. At the start of line 20 εὐϲε]βίαϲ is a probable restoration (cf. 19), with the meaning suggested in the translation. αἰϲθόμενοϲ could be used of an official holding a trial, although it is less easy to see how ϲυνελαυνόμενοϲ τῇ ἀληθείᾳ, if it means 'constrained by the truth', could be used of an official. For its likely meaning here, cf. P. Lond. V 1711.59–60: a man has made an agreement μὴ φόβῳ μὴ δόλῳ μὴ βίᾳ καὶ ἀπάτῃ μήτε ἀνάγκῃ ϲυνελαυνόμενοϲ. Immediately before ο κατ' ἐμοῦ ταυ is good in A 20, but the traces do not seem to permit τ]οῦτο or τὸ] αὐτό (what survives in B 64 is not helpful). If we read just τὸ κατ' ἐμοῦ, the noun to follow could be, e.g., κατάγνωϲμα (the traces in B 64 are too slight to confirm or refute this). If this is the right approach, an official must be the subject of the verb following ἀληθείᾳ in A 20 (assuming we have a verb here). We could easily read οὐ[κ ἔδο]ξεν α[ὐτῷ, but this is ungrammatical. A possible restoration is οὐ[κ ἔτα]ξεν, meaning that the official did not prescribe action to be taken against Diogenis because of the accusations, but on the contrary her father was convicted of lying and lost his case.

A quite different approach is to take the father as subject throughout. Then in A 20 οὐ[κ ἔλη]ξεν is attractive, 'my father, although he perceived my filial affection for him, did not cease . . .' (the verb is used in a similar context in II **237** vi 4); but this does not fit well with ϲυνελαυνόμενοϲ τῇ ἀληθείᾳ, if it means 'constrained by the truth'; 'not being constrained' would fit better. Possibly, again with the father as subject, we might have οὐ[κ ἔδει]ξεν ἅ, perhaps with ἐψεύς]ατο to follow, i.e., he could not demonstrate the truth of his (false) accusations against Diogenis.

However that may be, the occurrence of ἡττήθη in 21 seems explicable only if there had been a trial and the subject of the verb had lost his/her case; see Preisigke, *WB* s.v.: (passive) 'unterliegen (im Prozesse)', a meaning that is found several times in P. Hal. 1 (see Index, s.v.); cf. also XLVI **3285** 14, where ὁ ἡςςηθείς means 'the defeated party' (both texts are legal codes). Since the subject is third person, it should mean that Diogenis' father lost ('he was convicted of telling lies against me and lost the case'). The petition as a whole would seem to make more sense if *she* had lost. Presumably it was the response to the second petition, mentioned later in this line, that was unfavourable to Diogenis and that she is seeking to get overturned or ignored.

21 It might seem that в 65 should correspond to τ' ἐμοῦ in this line. κα]τ' ἐμοῦ is indeed just possible in в 65, but what survives later in the line cannot be reconciled with A 21. In any case the amount lost in A 20 is sufficient to cover all of в 65 which survives. At the right in в 65 not part of τέκνον; possibly]ικνυ (from δείκνυμι?).

τῆς διαμε.[. . .].ης ἀφέμ[ε]νος. After με possibilities are N, C, T, and after it δί]κης could be read (kappa is promising), meaning that her father gave up this case; but neither διὰ μέςον nor διὰ μέςου is attractive, even if there were room for the restoration. For the verb we may possibly compare P. Lille I 29 = M. *Chr.* 369 = Meyer, *Jur. Pap.* 71 ii 28–33, ἐξέ[cτω . . . μὲν τῶι ὀ]φλόντι τὴν δίκην . . . ἀφεῖcθα[ι τῆς κατα]δίκης, which Meyer translates 'von dem Kondemnationssumme (iudicatum) befreit werden'.

(в 66).].ν προτερ. . . . .[. . . . .]θ.[.].[.].[.]α.[. I have tried to read τ]ὴν προτέραν τόλ[μην τ]ῆς [μητρυι]ᾶς [. τ]ὴν προτερ is satisfactory, but the next four letters are much more difficult, and it does not seem possible to read τῆς μητρυιᾶς. At the end of the line ἀφ[is possible.

22 ἀκ.[. . .]c. ἀκο[λούθω]c is too long, and there is barely room if it is spelt ἀκλούθωc (as not infrequently). There is room for ἀκρ[ιβῶ]c, but this hardly suits the context. I have also considered ἀκα[ίρω]c, perhaps meaning that the contract was deposited with the registry 'out of time' and so was not valid (could we possibly compare the mysterious reference in P. Turner 34.6 to διαθήκας [ὑπ]ερχρόνους that were invalid?). Another possibility is to restore ἀκο[ύca]c, referring to the official who heard the case arising from the father's petition; cf. the next note.

κατ' ἐρήμου. This would make sense as a reference to Diogenis' weak position, bereft of parental support; see Preisigke, *WB* s.v. ἔρημος (1) 'mittellos, entblößt' and the reference in IV s.v. (3) to P. Bour. 25.10–12, ἀφ' οὗ δ[ὲ] [my mother] ἐτελεύτηcεν, ἔμινα ἔρημος, μ[η]δένα ἔχουca ἐπὶ ξένοιc τόποιc. As such the word would seem to be part of her own description of herself. The alternative is to understand δίκης, a reference to a trial in which one party is absent (see the discussion in P. Heid. VIII 412 introd. and 7 n.). After it, it seems to be κατε[again. κατ' ἐμοῦ could fit with this alternative meaning of ἔρημος; cf. BGU III 1004.ii.21–2, ἐ[ὰ]ν μὴ παραγένηται ἐν ἡμ[έραις ---] γε[νέcθω] ἔρημος κατ' αὐτοῦ (before γενέcθω the editor restored ἡ δίκη but in P. Heid. 412.7 n. ἡ κρίcιc *vel sim.* is proposed). Thus Diogenis could be saying that a judgement that was unfavourable to her was given in her absence. But the preposition κατά before ἐρήμου is a difficulty with this explanation.

22–3 At the start of this line we should restore, almost certainly, ἀξιώ]|cεωc: see SB XVI 12692.21, τῆς ἀξιώcεωc αὐτῶν τὴν δέουcαν πρόνοιαν κατὰ τ[ο]ὺς νόμους ποιήcαcθαι; cf. PSI V 449.15 and SB XVIII 13260.14. There is no doubt that the *subscriptio* to the second petition by the father (or a decision in a court case arising from this petition) occurs in these lines and ends with ποιήcεται. It is likely that this was unfavourable to Diogenis (see introd.), yet even so it did not satisfy her stepmother.

23ff. Much is lost in these lines, and the sense is obscure. It is probable that at this point Diogenis' father died (see below) and that the dispute was henceforth between Diogenis and her stepmother, the latter having sought to acquire property which Diogenis believed should have belonged to her.

24 δικαστήριον διαθήκην θέϲθαι. The use of the middle of τίθημι with διαθήκη is several times attested. It is unclear why a δικαϲτήριον should be mentioned, although we do hear of a ϲυγγραφή being brought ἐπὶ τὸ δικαϲτήριον in P. Tor. Choach. 12 iv 18 (cf. M. *Chr.* 28.26–7).

ἥτιϲ could refer to the stepmother or to the will (we might perhaps read ἥτιϲ δια[θήκ]η), or to neither. Could we have a reference to the will being opened after the father's death? At any rate, what follows seems to be a reference to the death of Diogenis' father. τελευϲαντ[οϲ] would be a good reading, so it is very tempting to correct to τελευ⟨τή⟩ϲαντοϲ (an error that occurs three times in III **493** = M. *Chr.* 307). In β 70 τ]ελευ[τήϲαντοϲ τ]οῦ [would not conflict with the exiguous traces.

τῆ λ΄. Also possible is τῆ δ΄.

τοῦ δι[ελθόν]τοϲ μ[ηνόϲ. The traces are minimal but consistent with this reading.

(β 71)] εναι.]φεναι is a possible reading.

ἐπ' ἐμοῦ ἀνακαλειϲ [. The combination of these words might suggest that we have an official speaking, referring to someone summoned to appear before him. But it is more likely that ἐμοῦ refers to Diogenis, although its meaning here is unclear ('in my case'?). It may be relevant to quote the passage from CJ 1.3.55(57).2, referred to in LSJ Rev. Suppl. s.v. ἀνακαλέω, which concerns the nullifying of an illegal act: the Greek version reads εὐθὺϲ ἀνακαλεῖϲθαι τὸ γενόμενον καὶ οὕτωϲ ἄκυρον ἀποφαίνειν; in the Latin version *reuocare* is used for ἀνακαλεῖϲθαι.

] ελομεν[ ]να πεμ[. πεμ[is a good reading, and there is probably no room for much to have been lost between the lines. This suggests as a possible reading and articulation ἀ]φελομέν[η]ν ἃ ἐπ' ἐμ[οὶ ἦν] τά τε κτλ., i.e., Diogenis is stating that her stepmother was seeking to deprive her of what was under her (Diogenis') control, both what had been registered to her by her father and the rest. However, the letter before πεμ is more like nu than epsilon.

25 This line is likely to be a reference to property that Diogenis claims is rightfully hers and that her stepmother is seeking to deprive her of. No doubt this forms the subject of all the text down to line 31.

τά τε ὑπ' αὐτοῦ μοι καταγραφέντα. See the comment to 12–14. After it not καί. Since the letter before ιν could well be rho (phi is also possible), one thinks of another reference to the χάριϲ mentioned in β 53, e.g. κατ[ὰ] τ[ὴν χά]ριν. Here, however, ἀναφαίρετον is not a possible reading after it (nu cannot be read, and the descender is in the wrong place for phi).

προοικεῖ (l. προῖκί). There is no problem with the spelling, which is commonly found in papyri; cf. P. Yadin 18.15 n. It is not preceded by ϲὺν τῆ or ϲὺν τῆ ἐμῆ; possible is ἐν. The reference to a dowry further complicates the picture; cf. introd. Whether the use of προίξ and not φερνή is an indication that the parties were operating under Roman law is uncertain. R. Katzoff, *IEJ* 37 (1987) 239, remarks, 'In Roman Egypt *proix* reappeared occasionally . . . as a synonym for *pherne* . . . It is said that this happened under the influence of Romans who translated the Latin *dos* with the classical Greek dictionary word *proix*.' See H. J. Wolff, *RE* XXIII.1 135, 169–70, Günther Häge, *Ehegüterrechtliche Verhältnisse* (1968) 209 f. and index s.v. *dos*.

καὶ τα νη[[*c.*?] εντα μοι. It is quite possible that nothing was lost here and that we should read καὶ τὰ ὠνη|θέντα μοι. If there was a small loss, we might have τὰ ὠνη[τά + participle, e.g. δο]θέντα. There is no explicit reference to property having been bought for Diogenis in what survives of the earlier part of the petition, but cf. 13 n. We may perhaps compare P. Lond. III 977.13–14 (p. 231), where a father sells property ὑπάρχοντά μοι καὶ ὠ[ν]ηθέντα ὑπ' [ἐμοῦ . . . . . .] ἐπ' ἐξουϲίαϲ μοι θυγατρόϲ (now deceased); of the editors' suggestions for the lacuna, the most probable is ὑπὲρ τῆϲ.

(β 72) ὑπὸ τῆϲ [. . . . .] . [. . . .]ου μητρόϲ. [μετηλ]λ[αχυίαϲ μ]ου may be considered but is long for the space. Alternatively we might have a reference to a female relative of Diogenis.

26 να τρόπον. One naturally thinks of κατὰ μηδένα/οὐδένα τρόπον, e.g. 'she could in no way succeed because . . .'. An alternative is οὐκ οἶδα τί]|να τρόπον (cf. XLVI **3304** 13 and perhaps SB XIV 11349.6–7); cf. the suggested translation.

ἐξ ἀςυνγράφων γάμων. I have found no other example of this expression nor any papyrological cal example of the adjective. I do not know whether any legal significance is to be seen in the use of ἀςύγγραφος γάμος instead of ἄγραφος γάμος; presumably both expressions mean that there was no written contract between the married couple. ἄγραφος γάμος occurs in II **237** viii 5–6 and CPR I 18.26, 30 = SPP XX 4 = M. *Chr.* 84 = Meyer, *Jur. Pap.* 89 only; but the same idea, it seems, is conveyed by ἀγράφως ςυνεῖναι and similar expressions, for which see Yiftach-Firanko, *Marriage* 90 n. 37.

The construction of the reference to the stepmother that follows is unclear. Perhaps we should take the two instances of καί as 'both . . . and', and suppose that we have another articular infinitive; there is a trace of a horizontal before the lacuna in B 73, which would suit καὶ τ[ῷ. Also possible is καὶ π[, suggesting π[αρά] or π[ρός]. Whatever the reading, the passage is likely to have referred to the fact that the ἐνδομενεία belonged (or did not belong) to the stepmother.

After μητρυιᾷ B 73 inserts μου. It is far from obvious why the stepmother's name was given again here.

(B 73–4) There is a diagonal stroke starting in the lacuna in B 74 and extending upwards to finish under the gamma in ἀςυνγράφων (B 73).

(B 74) There scarcely appears to be room for αν at the end of ἐνδομενίαν, but it seems necessary to read this in view of οὖςαν following.

27 ακ.[*c.*7 δουλ]ικά. The letter before the lacuna is unclear; epsilon or alpha are perhaps the easiest readings. With the former we might think of ἃ κέ[κτημαι, with the latter ἃ κα[τέλ(ε)ιψε (μοι) or ἃ κα[τέςχον.

α.[. Possibly απ[.

(B 75) ἐ]τύγχανεν ὄντα is presumably a reference to the slaves (a compound verb is unlikely). After it possibly ἀλλὰ ὡς.

(B 75) ⟦ονομως⟧. The deletion is indicated by dots over the letters.

ὡς . . . ὁ νόμος τῶν Ῥωμα[ίων. For the construction, cf. P. Michael. 41.40 (539/554?) ὡς οἱ νόμοι δίδουςιν. ὁ νόμος τῶν Ῥωμαίων is very rare expression in papyrus documents; I have found it elsewhere only in M. *Chr.* 328.9, although the plural occurs more often in the phrase κατὰ τοὺς Ῥωμαίων νόμους (IX **1208** 6, X **1268** 9, XLI **2951** 20, SB X 10728.4–5).

28 πολειτευόμεθα. I have come across no papyrological example of the verb πολιτεύεςθαι used in such a connection, although the phrase ἡ Ῥωμαίων πολιτεία is not uncommon. This can refer to the *Constitutio Antoniniana*: in XII **1458** 4–6, for example, a man says of his name before the *Constitutio* πρὶν δ[ὲ] τυχῖν τῆς Ῥωμαίων πολιτίας. I suggest Diogenis is trying to convey the idea that, since all are now Roman citizens (i.e., post 212), it is the law of the Romans by which they are now governed. Perhaps cf. I. Louvre 4 = SB V 8852.15 ο[ἱ] αἱρο[ύμενοι] βέλτιον π[ολιτεύεςθ]αι, translated 'd'être mieux gouvernés'.

After ἅπαντας we should probably supply τούς and assume that ἅπαντας agrees with δούλους. The first letter after the lacuna following has a long descender, presumably rho or phi. Perhaps μὴ ἀφαι]ρεῖςθαι (passive)?

= B 76. The reference must surely be to Diogenis' father's will. We do not know the grounds on which she claimed it to be illegal, but parents were not normally allowed to disinherit their children in Roman law (see introd.).

It is likely that some action by the stepmother is being described by Diogenis as μάταιος.

29 δούλων ςωμάτων. Neither here nor in the previous line does it seem essential to correct to δουλ⟨ικ⟩ῶν.

ἐκ τῶν νόμ[ων. It is hard to read this in B 77. The traces can be made to fit ἐ. τῶν ν[όμων, but kappa is very difficult.

(B 78) At the start we should probably read κ]ατ̣᾽ ἐμοῦ with something written over the line above ατ.

30 = B 78 This line is badly damaged in both versions. Worse still, I have not succeeded in reconciling what survives in the two versions. B suggests two participles joined by καί and both ending -εντα; but the letter before -εντα is not theta. It is most like mu, and it might be possible to read δ[ιὰ] μὲν τάς or δ[ιὰ] μὲν τῆς; but neither can be reconciled with the traces visible in A.

(B 79) It is odd that this Sarapion should suddenly appear. Was he perhaps the son of Diogenis' father by his second wife (cf. ἐπαι[δοπο]ιήςα[το B 56) or her husband (if she had one)?

30–31 In view of the uncertainty as to the number of letters lost, it is possible we should read here τὸν καὶ Δημη[τρια]|νόν or, if the loss has been underestimated, Δημή[τριον τὸν προτεταγμέ]|νον *vel sim.* (he could have been named in 15 or in B 78). Kappa in τὸν καί is oddly made, perhaps a correction.

31 ἐν τοςούτῳ δέ. The phrase occurs also towards the end of a petition in P. Warren 1.35. After it μετὰ τ[is possible.

(B 80)] ̣ α ̣ ου γὰρ περὶ ὀλίγου μοί ἐςτιν. The sense would be well suited by the reading οὐ γὰρ περὶ ὀλίγου; cf. the phrase περὶ ὀλίγου ποιεῖςθαι, for which see LSJ s.v. ποιέω A II v. However, the letter before ου is most like phi, i.e. ἀφ' οὗ.

32 ca τυχεῖν. Certainly ἀξιοῦ]|ca or δέου]|ca.

(B 81) πρὸς δὲ τὴν τοῦ βιβλε[ιδίου ἐπίδοςιν. This is a statement to the effect that Diogenis has appointed someone to go to Alexandria to hand in the petition for her: see P. Flor. I 6.19–20 (210) πρ[ὸ]c δ[ὲ τ]ὴν ἐπίδοςιν τοῦ βιβλιδίου διεπεμψάμην Νικόδημον βουλευτὴν φίλον. **4961** was no doubt similar, and it seems likely that the name to be inserted is that of Aurelius Agathus Daemon; see the next note.

33 Ἀγαθ[ὸς] Δαίμων. It is hard to find room for two letters in the lacuna, and we should perhaps reckon with the less common form of the name Ἀγαθοδαίμων. The change of hand and the further entry is unexpected (there is nothing comparable in P. Flor. 6). Presumably Agathus Daemon was the man appointed by Diogenis to deliver the petition at the prefect's court; in which case he is likely to be recording here that he in due course received the prefect's *subscriptio*, of which he adds a copy. This should be the hand, therefore, that occurs in B 83–5. There, however, the writing is so poorly preserved that I cannot confidently assert that it is the same hand.

ὁ διαδε[. Presumably a participle from διαδέχομαι, whereby Agathus Daemon is stating that he is acting *in loco* Diogenis; cf. LSJ s.v. IIa for the meaning 'represent', with reference to BGU V 1210.193. In ChLA X 407.9 it is said of a son τ[ὸν οἰ]κεῖον πατέρα ἐφ' ἅπαςιν διαδεξάμενος, but in this case the father is deceased; there may be a similar explanation for a son διάδοχον τοῦ πατρὸς γενέcθαι in II **237** ix 9 (see p. 151).

34 ̣ω ̣. There may well be no letter between omega and τῷ.

B 84–5 A *subscriptio* beginning with the date in the short form (see *Egypt and the Hellenistic World*, cited in 19 n., 374–7) followed by μηδενὸς ἐπεχομένου is attested in XVII **2131** 19, P. Stras. I 57.18 with BL I 406, P. Tebt. II 327.37 (= W. *Chr.* 394), III **439** and SB VI 9340 = P. Lund. IV 1.38–9; cf. III **488** 43, XLII **3027** 5. SB 9340 reads μηδενὸς ἐπεχομένου τῷ κρατίςτῳ ἐπιςτρα[τ]ήγῳ ἔντυχε. We may therefore restore ἐπεχομένου with some confidence, although here there was something more than ἐπεχομένου between μηδενός and τῷ κρατίςτῳ. No wholly satisfactory explanation of the meaning of the phrase has yet been proposed; cf. **3027** 5 n.

Back

B 86 Ὠνήςιμος. The reading is probable. Ὀνήςιμος is not uncommon, but the spelling with omega does not seem to have occurred previously in texts from Egypt. It is found elsewhere: see P. Yadin 11.33. LGPN I records Ὠνάςιμος (Crete), II Ὠνηςίμη (Athens) and IIIB Ὠναςίμα (Boeotia).

87 Τριάδελφος. An uncertain reading.

J. DAVID THOMAS

4962. Letter of Ammonius to Diodorus

45 5B.58/G(1–3)a   16 × 14.2 cm   Third century

Ammonius writes to his 'brother' Diodorus, whom he calls a 'friend' in the docket, informing him that Diodorus' 'brother' has been appointed *komogrammateus*. Whether he had any role in the appointment or he transmits the news as an outsider, we cannot tell. He reminds Diodorus of an earlier service offered to him, states that something of the kind will please his (Diodorus') 'brother' now too, and urges Diodorus to 'let him know about this', i.e., whether similar services would be needed. Ammonius clearly saw this appointment as an opportunity for his own gain.

Normally a three-year liturgy would be something one tried to avoid, but as N. Lewis, *CE* 79 (2004) 231, has put it, 'As custodian of all the village records and the source of all official information supplied to higher officials and to local inhabitants and property owners, a *komogrammateus*, were he so minded, could find all sorts of ways of "cooking" the books so as to help himself and friends, to the detriment of others.' P. Lips. II 145.23 ff. shows that the *komogrammateus* was in a position to harm other people (and so, presumably, to benefit them as well) and also that it was not a liturgy that could be given just anyone. A certain experience, such as having been a *praktor*, was required.

The hand would suit a date in the earlier part of the third century. The reference to the *komogrammateus* indicates that the text cannot be later than 245, the latest attested date for the office in the third century.

The text is written along the fibres. The papyrus is fairly well preserved except for some damage along what was the outside fold of the letter. The sheet was folded vertically twice from right to left and once from left to right, and finally once horizontally. The address is on the second panel from the left (as reckoned from the front). There is a *kollesis c.*0.5 cm from the right edge.

Ἀμμῶνις Διοδώρῳ τῶι ἀδελφῷ
     πλεῖϲτα   χαίρειν.
ὁ ἀδελφός ϲου ϗ[α]τεϲτάθη κωμογραμμα-
τεὺϲ τῆϲ ϛ[. . . .]ω. ἐπειδὴ πρώην
5   ϲε ἀνόκνωϲ ὑπηρετήϲαμεν, οἶμαι
καὶ νῦν ἀρέϲειν τῷ ἀδελφῷ· ὥϲτε
οὖν πρὸ τοῦ{ν} περι⟨ϲ⟩παϲθῶ εἰϲ ἄλλην πρα-
γματίαν περὶ τούτου ⟦ουν⟧ μοι δήλωϲον.
        (vac.)
         ἐρρῶϲθ(αι) ϲε εὔχομ(αι). Μεϲορὴ ι̅η̅.

Back, downwards, along the fibres:

10   ἀπό(δος) Διοδώρῳ   ἀπὸ Ἀμμω(νίου) φίλ[ου

7–8 1. πραγματείαν   8 ΤΟΥΤΟΥ   9 ερρωσθ-ςεευχο̄   10 α^{τοτ}   αμμω

'Ammonius to his brother Diodorus, very many greetings. Your brother has been made *komogrammateus* of S—o. Since we earlier served you unhesitatingly, I believe that we will also now please your brother. Consequently, before I am put to another activity, let me know about this. I pray you are well. Mesore 18.'

Back: 'Deliver to Diodorus from Ammonius, friend.'

3 κ[α]τεστάθη. See N. Lewis, *On Government and Law in Roman Egypt* 109: 'The terms καθίστημι and κατάστασις are not in themselves evidence either of liturgy or of action by the epistrategos.'

κωμογραμματεύς was perhaps a three-year liturgy, in all likelihood served away from one's *idia*. See Lewis, *The Compulsory Public Services*² s.v. (p. 35). See above, introd., on possibilities of abuse.

4 Ϲ[....]ω could be a number of villages in the Oxyrhynchite nome, Ϲεναω and Ϲεντω being the best suited to the available space, but it is of course not certain that the office was to be held in an Oxyrhynchite village.

5 ὑπηρετήςαμεν. Given the semi-official context of the letter, it is not inconceivable that the verb is used in a technical sense, 'to serve as *hyperetes*'; cf. the *hyperetes* of a *komogrammateus* in P. Mich. VI 423.20 (197). In that case, one could think that Ammonius asks Diodorus to intercede so that he (Ammonius) can obtain the post of *hyperetes* to Diodorus' brother, the *komogrammateus*-designate. But this is a mere possibility.

7 πρὸ τοῦ{ν}περι⟨ς⟩παςθῶ. πρὸ τοῦ should be followed by an infinitive in classical Greek, but from the second century the subjunctive is used occasionally. The following examples are known to me: III **611** (ii), XVI **1854** 3 (vi/vii), XXXVI **2781** 4 (ii), P. Lond. IV 1346.10 (710); in BGU III 814.14 (iii) the verb is in the optative because of indirect speech. In **611** and **2781**, as here, τουν is written, and the editors of **611** correct into οὗ ἄν, which is unnecessary. See further R. C. Horn, *The Use of the Subjunctive and Optative Moods in the Non-Literary Papyri* (1926) 128, and B. G. Mandilaras, *The Verb* §598(19).

περι⟨ς⟩παςθῶ. περιςπάω 'draw away, divert, distract' (LSJ) here in the same sense as μεταπεριςπάω 'engage in another liturgy', which is not in *WB* nor in LSJ, but see P. Merton III 117.4 n.; further examples in DDBDP. There is a space between περι and παςθω where the sigma should be. Curiously, but it is surely a coincidence, the sigma is inserted above the line in P. Merton 117.

8 τούτου. The first υ has been inserted later and is Y-shaped while all others are V-shaped.

9 Μεςορὴ ιη̄. According to Lewis, *Compulsory Services*² 35, the starting date for the office was 1 Mecheir. The arguments for this are found in his *On Government and Law* 88, where he argues that complaints about nominations to κωμογραμματεία seem to come in Mecheir or Tybi and that it is 'hardly likely that nominations would be made as far back as Tybi (or even Mecheir) for offices to begin the following 1 Thoth. The normal time for such nominations appears, in fact, to have been in the period Pachon–Mesore.' As Lewis himself admits, there is no conclusive proof. I can only offer the present text as contrary evidence, which points to a starting date on 1 Thoth, unless Ammonius was informing his correspondent five months in advance.

A. BÜLOW-JACOBSEN

4963. LETTER OF HERACLAS TO DIOGENES

101/133(c)   10.5 × 9.5 cm   Third/fourth century

Beginning of a letter. Presumably the letter was rolled vertically and folded once horizontally and broke along this horizontal fold, so that half of the text is missing.

Written along the fibres in a good, rather elegant, upright hand with some corrections by the same writer. No *kollesis* is visible. The left margin shows a tendency to creep towards the right, in opposition to Maas's Law.

Heraclas is ill without specifying from what. On top of this there is a visit from someone clearly known to the addressee who is throwing his weight about and seems to have ordered Heraclas' arrest. The letter is basically incomprehensible because we know nothing of the context. The unnamed person must have been an important one, giving orders and having an assistant.

Ἡρακλᾶς Διογένει τῶι ἀδελφῶι χαίρειν.
γράφω ϲοι, ἄδελφε, τὸ μὲν πρῶτον τῇ νόϲῳ χει-
μαζόμενοϲ· δ[[ευτέρα]]ˋιϲϲῄˊ δέ μοι ἐγένετο ʼἡ νόϲοϲˊ καὶ
ἡ αὐτοῦ ἐπιδημία, διότι ἀπρόϊτόϲ εἰμι.
5   π]αραγενομένου δὲ αὐτοῦ ἐνετείλατο
τ]ῷ ἡγουμένῳ ἐν ἀϲφαλεῖ με εἶναι. καὶ
τοῦ] ὑπηρέτου ἐλθόντοϲ πρὸϲ ἐμὲ παρε[-] ʼκαὶ εἰπ[.].ˊ
. . . .]. δι[. . .].ον τον[..]λον μ[
]. ι καὶ χάριϲ τ.[

.   .   .   .   .   .

Back, downwards, along the fibres:

10   Διογένει.[

				καιειπ[
ιϲϲη	ηνοϲοϲ			
3 δευτερα	και	4 απροϊτοϲ	7 ϋπ-	παρε[

'Heraclas to his brother Diogenes, greetings. I write to you, brother, first because I suffer badly from the illness. The illness struck me twofold—and also his visit, because I cannot go out. When he arrived he told the leader that I be kept secure. And when his assistant came to me he ... and said ...'
Back: 'To Diogenes ...'

3 The correction of δευτέρα to διϲϲή and the insertion of ἡ νόϲοϲ seem to spoil the rather elegant point the writer originally wanted to make, i.e., that he was both ill and afflicted with a visit from whoever the person in question was.

4 ἀπρόϊτοϲ. The word has occurred only in one other papyrus, SB IV 7330.9 (ii), but is fairly common in literary texts from the fourth century onwards. LSJ translate '*not proceeding* or *emanating*';

see also Hsch. α 6834 ἀνέξοδος, and *Suda* α 3692 (= Ps.-Zon. α 238.4) ὁ μὴ τῆς οἰκίας ἐξερχόμενος. In view of the mention of the disease, it is possible that Heraclas was bedridden and unable to go out of his house, but the subsequent reference to his having 'to be kept secure' (6) suggests that he was (also) under arrest.

5 παραγενομένου αὐτοῦ and 7 ὑπηρέτου ἐλθόντος both ignore the basic rule of genitive absolute in having the same subject as the main verb. Confronted with this, Heraclas would undoubtedly have referred to Thucydides 3.13 and Smyth, *Greek Grammar* § 2073. The construction is not uncommon in the papyri: see Mandilaras, *The Verb* §§ 909–10. The second case (7) is less clear, and we could give the writer the benefit of the doubt.

6 ἡγουμένῳ. The term is used to refer to a president of a guild or to a *praeses* of the province Aegyptus Herculia, to which Oxyrhynchus belonged from 315 to 324. The possibilities are discussed by J. R. Rea, LV **3792** 25 n. Here we only know that the ἡγούμενος receives orders from 'him', so he must have been of lower status than 'him', which does not help us much.

A. BÜLOW-JACOBSEN

4964. List of Hamlets and Requisitioned Workers

35 4B.101/G(4–6)a   8.2 × 24.7 cm   Fourth century

This document lists *epoikia* and numbers of men requisitioned for work at Alexandria. The names of the *epoikia* are not attested elsewhere, but they are very probably Oxyrhynchite (cf. 7–8 n.). A date in the earlier part of the fourth century is suggested by the hand and tallies with the fact that the bulk of our evidence for such workers in government service dates from this time.

There is no exact parallel to this text among papyri of this period; only XIV **1747** (iii/iv), which contains a list of persons arranged by village and toparchy, possibly 'required by the government for work of some kind', may but need not (cf. XLVI **3307**) be comparable. Several fourth-century papyri refer to provision of workers for the quarries at Alexandria, those near Alabastrine, or at the bakeries of Memphis or Alexandria; in addition to those listed in BGU XII 2134 introd., we now have LIV **3727** (303) and BGU XIII 2252 (330). Other contemporary documents attest contributions to the salaries and maintenance of such workers (CPR VI 5.1–9; P. Sakaon 22–25; SB XX 14297; P. Hib. II 220; P. Horak 12; XLVIII **3397**). For requisitioned workers in the fourth century, the old study of K. Fitzler, *Steinbrüche und Bergwerke im ptolemäischen und römischen Ägypten* (1910) 121–5, remains useful.

> ϕ μερισμοῦ ἐργατῶν
>   Ἀλεξανδρείας
> ἐποικίου Πυξίνου ἄνδρ(ες) γ
> ἐποικ(ίου) Ὀρφανοῦ ἀν(ὴρ) α
> 5 ἐποικ(ίου) Ε.άτης ἀν(ὴρ) α
>   ἐποικ(ίου) Φανβαρους ἀν(ὴρ) α ‾

ἐποικ(ίου) Νεοφύτου
    Cαραπίωνος ἄν(δρες) δ′
ἐποικ(ίου) Cτύλου ἄν(δρες) β
10   (vac.?)] γί(νονται) ὁμοῦ ἄν(δρες) ιβ ἐργάτ̣[αι

1 ✗   3 ανδρ′   4, 5, 6, 7, 9 εποι^κ   4, 5, 6, 8, 9, 10 αν⁻   10 γʃ

'. . . assessment of workers for Alexandria:
'Of the hamlet of Pyxinus, 3 men.
'Of the hamlet of Orphanus, 1 man.
'Of the hamlet of E–ate, 1 man.
'Of the hamlet of Phanbarous, 1 man.
'Of the hamlet of Neophytou Sarapionos, 4 men.
'Of the hamlet of Stylus, 2 men.
'Total 12 men, workers.'

1 ₰ μερισμοῦ. One may be tempted to resolve (πρώτου); cf. P. Cair. Isid. 71.2 (314) πρῶτος μερισμός (of tax payments), SPP XX 96.2 (c.338) α′ μερισμοῦ. The abbreviation itself, however, with alpha intersected by an oblique stroke, suggests reading ἀ(ντίγραφον), but to this there seems to be no parallel. A similar term is used of workers in P. Hib. II 220.5 (335) ὑπὲρ μερου (μέρου⟨ς⟩) BL IV 40; μερ⟨ιсμ⟩οῦ ed. pr., but cf. P. Sakaon 25.i.7) ἐργατῶν. For the meaning of μερισμός, a levy divided among the contributors, see C. Salvaterra, *Aegyptus* 66 (1986) 57–62.

1–2 ἐργατῶν Ἀλεξανδρείας. The collocation recurs in P. Sakaon 75.2 (316/17 or 331/2 or 346/7), CPR VI 5.2, 11 (336) and SB XX 14297.2 (iv); in the latter two cases, the reference is to ἐπιμεληταὶ ἐργατῶν Ἀλεξανδρείας. In none of these texts is the nature of the work in Alexandria indicated.

3 Πυξίνου. Perhaps from the adjective πύξινος, 'made of boxwood', which occurs in several papyri.

4 Ὀρφανοῦ. Cf. the (rare) personal name Ὀρφανός in P. Bad. II 26.7, 15, P. Leit. 10.1, P. Panop. 22.3 and P. Lond. IV 1419.707 (Πορφανός).

5 Ε̣ ά̣της. The unread letter is unlike anything else in this text. It reminds one of a minute U-shaped kappa, but Ἑκάτης is an implausible place name. Alternatively, read Ἐνάτης, though nu is difficult; for place names formed by an ordinal number, cf. the ἄμφοδον Δεκάτης in Oxyrhynchus (Daris, *Dizionario* Suppl. iii 31), the Oxyrhynchite ἐποίκιον Ἐκκαιδεκάτου (P. Lond. III 775.10), or the κλῆρος Πρώτου (SB VIII 9699 *passim*) in the Hermopolite nome; cf. also Ἐνάτου (?) in SPP XX 1 verso.

7–8 Νεοφύτου Cαραπίωνος. Cf. the Oxyrhynchite place names Νεοφύτου, Νεοφύτου Βάνου (P. Select. 20.3), Νεοφύτου Ἀντιόχου (LXVIII **4702** 7), Νεοφύτου τοῦ Χάριτος (*Tyche* 21 (2006) 3, lines 20 with n., 46). Such toponyms seem peculiar to this region, which strengthens the impression that this and the other *epoikia* in this document are Oxyrhynchite.

9 Cτύλου. Perhaps named after a 'pillar' in the area. For Oxyrhynchite *epoikia* named after natural features, see LV **3804** 48 n.

N. LITINAS

4965. MANICHAEAN LETTER

104/118(a)   9 × 24 cm   Fourth century

The letter is written along the fibres in a fluent documentary hand (cf. e.g. XXXI **2571** of 338). Of the 33 lines, 21 are lacking line beginnings and the first 8–10 letters; the last two lines seem to have been squeezed more narrowly before the end of the sheet.

Ammonius and his brethren write to Philadelphus asking him to receive their brother Nilus, who delivers alms (?) to them. Greetings are sent to everybody in the community of Philadelphus.

A Manichaean background of this letter is evident from the references to the παρακλητικὸς λόγος in 10, the ἐκλεκτοί (*eclecti*, the elects) and κατηχούμενοι (*auditores*, catechumens) in 20–21, and the ἀδελφοὶ ἅγιοι and the κατηχούμενοι respectively in 15–16. A teacher mentioned in 30–31 may be a Manichaean church official of the highest rank.

The letter shows the close relationship between the followers of Mani in different places. Close connections between the ἐκλεκτοί and κατηχούμενοι were essential for survival, since the ἐκλεκτοί were not allowed to produce or prepare their own food but depended on the support of the catechumens.

This is the second letter from Oxyrhynchus that attests a Manichaean community for the city in the fourth century, the other being XXXI **2603** (Christian Letter of Commendation; *ed. pr.* J. H. Harrop, *JEA* 48 (1962) 132–40). Manichaeism was quite widespread in Egypt in the fourth century. We know of larger communities in Kellis and Lycopolis at least (see I. Gardner, S. N. C. Lieu, *JRS* 86 (1996) 146–69).

```
       τῷ κυρίῳ μου] ἀδελφῶι
       Φιλαδέλφῳ] Ἀμμώνιος
       καὶ οἱ παρ᾽ ἐμο]ὶ ἀδελφοὶ
          c.10   ]. χαίρειν·
  5    τὸν ἀδελφὸ]ν ἡμῶν Νεῖλο(ν)
          c.10   ]θαι βουληθέν-
       τα .... ἀπέ]λυσα , ἀλλὰ καὶ
       ἵνα c.7  ]α σὺν τοῖς κατὰ
       τόπον σου ἀδ]ελφοῖς πειθόμε-
 10    νος τῷ παρα]κλητικῷ λόγῳ
          c.10   ]τος μετὰ τοῦ πρε-
       σβευτοῦ ὑπο]δέξῃ. οὐδὲν γὰρ
       ἁγιώτερον] ἡμῖν ἔκρινεν .
```

        *c.*9   μ]ενοι cυνόντεc

15   παρ᾽ ἐμοὶ καὶ ο]ἱ ἀδελφοὶ ἅγιοι

       κ[α]ὶ [οἱ κατηχού]μενοι πάνυ

       cε προ[cαγορ]εύουcιν καὶ

       αὐτόc, κ[ύριέ] μου ἄδελφε,

       προcαγόρευε ἡμῖν τοὺc

20   παρὰ coὶ πάντας ἐκλεκτούc

       τε καὶ κατηχουμένουc

       καθ᾽ ἕκαcτον καὶ μάλιcτα

       τὸν ἀδελφὸν ἡμῶν Θε-

       ό]δωρον, εἰ ἐcτὶν παρὰ coί,

25   καὶ τὸν . . . . . . cιον Θεόγνω-

       cτον καὶ ἐπαφροδιτικῶc

       του . [. .] . δ[. . Ἀ]θαναcίου ὡc

       ι . . [. . . .] . . μ . [.] . δι᾽ ἑτέραc

          *c.*12   ] δήλωcον δὲ

30   ἡμῖν τὰ περ]ὶ τοῦ διδαcκά-

       λου, εἰ . . . . . .] ἐτ[ύ]γχανε

          *c.*12   ]ω . . μιc[.] . . .

          *c.*10 κύ]ριέ μο[υ ἄ]δελφε´

Back, downwards, along the fibres:

       τῷ ἀδελφῷ]   X   Φιλαδέλφωι Ἀμ[μώνιοc

   5 νειλο̄   31 ετ[υ]γ´χανε

'To my lord brother Philadelphus, Ammonius and the brethren with me, . . . greetings. I have sent our brother Nilus . . . who wanted . . . , but also that you may . . . receive together with the ambassador . . . , you and the brethren at your place in faith of the Paracletic Mind; for nothing more holy(?) has he commanded us. All those gathered . . . with me, the holy brethren and the catechumens greet you fully, and you yourself, my master brother, greet for us all the elects and catechumens, one by one, and in particular our brother Theodorus, if he is with you, and the . . . Theognostus, and with a warm heart . . . of Athanasius that . . . through another . . . Tell us about the Teacher, if he was . . . , my lord brother.'

Back: 'To my brother Philadelphus, Ammonius.'

   4 *c.*5 πλεῖcτ]α with *spatium* at line beginning, or [ἐν θ(ε)ῷ πλεῖcτ]α? But the trace on the edge, the right end of a horizontal, is too high for λ, and rather suggests c or ε.

   6 ἐπανέρχεc]θαι or similar.

   7 E.g. εὐθὺc ἀπέ]λυcα or χθὲc ἀπέ]λυcα.

   8 If the general sense of 5–13 is not misunderstood, the object of ὑπο]δέξῃ (13) should be something very valuable for the Manichaean brothers. The *terminus technicus* for the alms is εὐcέβεια or

ἀγάπη, but neither would be possible as object on palaeographical grounds. cπυρίδι]ạ or ἐπιτήδει]ạ are less technical, but could also mean the alimentary support of the elects; cf. P. Kell. I Gr. 63.31–4.

8–9 cὺν τοῖc κατὰ | [τόπον cου ἀδ]ελφοῖc. The τόποc is the place where the Manichaeans meet and live together; cf. the τόποc Μανι in Kellis (P. Kell. IV Gr. 96.320 and 513, and discussion ad loc.), and XXXI **2603** 35. The word can also designate a monastery.

9–10 πειθόμε|[νοc τῷ παρα]κλητικῷ λόγῳ. The παρακλητικὸc λόγοc can hardly be a consolatory speech: 12–13 make it clear that it must be an authority. Mani is the paraclete, usually not the παρακλητικὸc λόγοc; cf. P. Harris I 107.6–7, where Mani is called the παράκλητον πνεῦμα. (παρακλητικόc is *v. l.* for παράκλητοc in Epiph. *Adv. Haer.* 74.7, p. 324.3 Holl, in the important MS J; cf. here 26.) Manichaeans might have called Mani the λόγοc, for that was also Christ's name. For a putative use of *termini technici* in this letter, see also 8 n.

11 ἀποφράcιc]τοc for ἀποφραcίcτωc?, even though the word may be too legalistic; cf. P. Tor. Choach. 12 ii 7, iii 30.

13 [ἁγιώτερον]. [κυριώτερον] could also be considered here.

14 πάντεc οἱ ἄcμ]ενοι cυνόντεc or some similar locution.

15–16 ο]ἱ ἀδελφοὶ ἅγιοι | κ[α]ὶ [οἱ κατηχού]μενοι. Cf. 19–21 τοὺc | παρὰ coὶ πάνταc ἐκλεκτούc | τε καὶ κατηχουμένουc. Manicheism was a firmly hierachical religion in which only the elect were able to receive the last blessings through observation of strict rules and avoidance of 'hurting' the light-particles that, as they believed, are included in all organic material; they were therefore not allowed to bake their own bread, to harvest or even to 'hurt' the water by washing themselves. The term of ἀδελφοὶ ἅγιοι for the elects is attested in the *Kephalaia of the Teacher* 8.16, p. 37 Schmidt.

25 τὸν . . . . . cιον. After ν negligible traces of two or three letters, of which the second may be τ; after that ρ and η possible. No plausible adjective comes to mind.

26 ἐπαφροδιτικῶc obviously for ἐπαφροδίτωc. The additional ικ can also be observed in παρα]-κλητικῷ λόγῳ (10); cf. Alciphr. 4.16.4 ὑποδέξομαι δή cε ἐπαφροδίτωc; *'feliciter'*: see P. J. Parsons, *JEA* 57 (1971) 166 n. 1.

27 τọυ . [. .] .δ[. . Ἀ]θανạcίου. μẹ[τά does not fit the traces.

29 At the beginning perhaps [ἐπιcτολῆc].

30–31 διδαcκά|[λου. 'Teacher' is the title of the second-highest official in the Manichaean church hierarchy; there were 12 'Teachers', and there can be no doubt that one of them would have been stationed in Egypt. Certain private letters in Coptic from Kellis show that such a 'Teacher' was busy traveling up and down the Nile (for missionary reasons?) in the middle of the fourth century (P. Kell. V 20.24, 24.17, 25.42, 49, 29.14, 52.4); of course, it cannot be ruled out completely that an ordinary teacher is meant here.

31 Perhaps εἰ παρὼν] ẹτ[ύ]γχανε.

32 Possibly a form of κομίcαcθαι.

C. E. RÖMER

4966. SALE OF IRRIGATION IMPLEMENTS

50 4B.24/K(1–2)a   15.2 × 16.3 cm   16 March 371

The object of the sale is unusual: a half part of the irrigation devices attached to a well. The price, 12 artabas of wheat, seems low, but we do not know what these devices were. Irrigation equipment was occasionally included in sales of land (cf.

the list in Rowlandson, *Landowners and Tenants* 320), but I am not aware of any other instance of its being sold separately.

The buyer is someone described as a senator, probably a member of the new aristocracy recruited in increasing numbers for the Constantinopolitan senate in the 350s and 360s. His name, Isidorus, as well as the fact that he is described as a landowner in Oxyrhynchus, may suggest that he was an Egyptian, which would make him one of the very few Egyptian senators of the fourth century. He would also be the first Egyptian landowner of senatorial standing to be attested in papyri of this period.

The back is blank.

μετὰ τὴν ὑπατ]είαν τῶν δεσποτῶν ἡμῶν Οὐαλεντι(νιανοῦ)
καὶ Οὐάλεντο]ς αἰωνίων Αὐγούστων τὸ γ, Φαμενὼθ κ.
Φλαουΐῳ] Ἰσιδώρῳ τῷ λαμπροτάτῳ συνκλη-
τικῷ γεο]υχοῦντι ἐν τῇ λαμ(πρᾷ) καὶ λαμ(προτάτῃ) Ὀξυρυγχιτῶν πό(λει)

5   Αὐρήλιος.].χόλιος υἱὸς Ἰουλιανοῦ ἀπὸ λογιστῶν
ἀπὸ τῆς αὐτῆς π]όλεως χαίρειν. ὁμολογῶ πεπρακέ-
ν]αι καὶ παρακεχωρηκέναι σοι ἐντεῦθεν
τ]ὸ κατ᾽ ἐμὲ καὶ ἐπιβάλλον ὁλόκληρον ἥμισυ
μέρος μηχανικῶν ὀργάνων ἐπικιμένων

10 ὑδρεύμασι ἐδάφους Λύκωνος περὶ κώμην
Π]άειμιν δ ϛ πάγου, τιμῆς τῆς συνπεφωνημέ-
νης πρὸς ἀλλήλους τοῦ αὐτοῦ κατ᾽ ἐμὲ ἡμίσους
μέ]ρους σίτου ἀρταβῶν δώδεκα, (ἀρτ.) ιβ″, ἅσπερ αὐτόθι ἔσχον παρὰ σοῦ ἐκ πλήρους διὰ χιρός.

15 περὶ ἧς ἀριθμήσεως ἐπερ(ωτηθεὶς) ὡμολόγησα πρὸς τὸ ἀπὸ τοῦ
ν]ῦν κρατεῖν σε καὶ κυριεύειν σὺν ἐκγόνοις καὶ τοῖς
παρὰ σοῦ μεταλημψομένοις καὶ ἐξουσίαν σε ἔχειν

].[

1 ουαλεντιϛ	3 ϊσιδωρω	l. συγκλη-	4 λαμϛ (*bis*)	ποϛ	5 υϊοϲϊουλιανου
9 l. ἐπικειμένων		11 l. συμπεφωνημέ-	13 ⊤	14 l. χειρός	15 επερ

'After the consulship of our masters Valentinianus and Valens, eternal Augusti, for the 3rd time, Phamenoth 20.

'To Flavius Isidorus, *vir clarissimus*, senator, landowner in the splendid and most splendid city of the Oxyrhynchites, Aurelius —cholius, son of Iulianus, ex-*curator*, from the same city, greetings. I acknowledge having sold and ceded to you henceforth my own and falling to me entire half share of irrigation implements installed in the wells of the ground of Lycon near the village of Paeimis of the 4th *pagus*, the price of my same half-share being agreed between us at twelve artabas of wheat, art. 12, which I received from you on the spot in full from hand to hand, concerning which sum I was asked the formal question and assented, so that from now on you and your descendants and your successors may have possession and ownership and you may have the power . . .'

1–2 On the third consulship of Valentinianus and Valens, see *CLRE* 369–70, and *CSBE*² 188–9. This is the latest occurrence of their postconsulate; the consuls of 371 are first attested on 23 July.

1 Οὐαλεντι(νιανοῦ). It is unusual to find a consul's name abbreviated, though cf. CPR XIX 10.2 (522) Ἰουστ(ινιανοῦ) (see *APF* 51 (2005) 289 for the reading, and *ZPE* 159 (2007) 267 for the date).

3–4 Φλαουΐῳ] Ἰσιδώρῳ τῷ λαμπροτάτῳ συνκλη[τικῷ. See above, introd. Isidorus must have been one of the new Constantinopolitan senators enrolled in increasing numbers since the 350s; see P. Heather, 'New Men for New Constantines? Creating an Imperial Elite in the Eastern Mediterranean', in P. Magdalino (ed.), *New Constantines* (1994) 13–14, 18–20. It is conceivable that Isidorus had a career as a senior imperial functionary, but there is no need to assume that he was the same as the one who served as *praefectus annonae (Africae)* some time in 368–75 (Isidorus 1, *PLRE* I 465).

The term συγκλητικός has not occurred in any other papyrus, but is fairly common in inscriptions, especially of the earlier Roman period, and in literary texts. (Συγκλητικῆς in LIX **4004** 14, a fifth-century letter, seems to be a personal name.)

4 γεο]υχοῦντι ἐν τῇ λαμ(πρᾷ) καὶ λαμ(προτάτῃ) Ὀξυρυγχιτῶν πό(λει). This is the earliest instance of this expression, which becomes common from the fifth century on. The contemporary BGU XIII 2339.5 (378) has γεουχοῦντι ἐν τῷ Ὀξυρυγχίτῃ.

5 .].χόλιος. The only name that could provide a match is Ἀχόλιος, but it is generally very rare; it has occurred only once in papyri, in P. Horak 21.9 (Ant.?; v).

Ἰουλιανοῦ ἀπὸ λογιστῶν. On Iulianus' career, see P. Oxy. LIV pp. 225–6 and LX **4092** introd. The present document does not specify whether Iulianus was alive; his latest previous attestation is in **4092** of 355 (*pace* **4092** introd., Fl. Iulianus, who serves on the staff of the *praeses* of Augustamnica and appears as the lessor in PSI V 467 of 360, a lease of a room in Oxyrhynchus, is in my view not the same man). In **4092** Iulianus and his sister appear as owners of land property κατὰ τὸ ἐπιβάλλον ἑκάστῳ ἥμισυ μέρος (5), which seems to suggest an inheritance divided equally between the two siblings. See further next note.

8–9 τὸ] κατ' ἐμὲ καὶ ἐπιβάλλον ὁλόκληρον ἥμισυ μέρος. This collocation has not been attested otherwise, but is equivalent to τὸ ὑπάρχον (or αἱροῦν) καὶ ἐπιβάλλον μοι μέρος, which is fairly common.

Though these are different properties, this half share could conceivably be related to the half share of Iulianus in **4092** 5. If the latter share goes back to a division of the estate of Iulianus' father, the division would have involved irrigation devices too. The purchase of the half share by Isidorus would be sensible if he had acquired or was about to acquire the other half. A potential difficulty is that the irrigation machinery is not said to lie in a private property (cf. PSI IX 1078.11–12, quoted below), but in an ἔδαφος, a topographical description with no connotations of ownership.

9 μηχανικῶν ὀργάνων. This is the earliest attestation of this collocation.

9–10 ἐπικιμένων ὑδρεύμασι. Cf. LI **3638** 8 (220) ὑδρευμάτων καὶ τῆς ἐπικειμένης αὐτοῖς μηχανῆς; sim. SB XX 14291.5 (iii), XXXIV **2723** 10–11 (469), and (more remotely) PSI IX 1078.11–12 (356) ἀρούρας ὅσας ἐὰ[ν ὦ]σι ἐν αἷς ὑ[δ]ρεύματα καὶ μηχανὴ καὶ ὄργανα.

10 ἐδάφους Λύκωνος. This locality is apparently new. It is unclear whether it is related to the settlement of this name attested in XVI **2000** 2 and XVIII **2197** 27.

11 Π]άειμιν δ´ πάγου. Paeimis belonged in the Western toparchy; its *pagus* location was not known previously. The reading of the figure as δ is preferable to χ, the only other alternative.

12–13 The addition of τοῦ . . . μέρους is not strictly necessary, though cf. PSI VI 705.10 (iii).

13 σίτου ἀρταβῶν δώδεκα. As far as I can see, there is no information for other such prices at

that time; that 10 artabas of wheat were paid as rent of an ὄργανον at Hermonthis in 336 (P. Lond. I 125.16–17 (p. 192), with BL X 97) is the closest to comparative evidence we possess. The only prices of irrigation machinery we have come from the sixth century.

15 περὶ ἧς ἀριθμήϲεωϲ. On this phrase, see LXIX **4751** 10 n.

N. GONIS

4967. Work Contract of Public Herald

65 6B.33/B(1–3)a   13 × 18.5 cm   Sixth/seventh century
Plate V

Only the lower part of this document has survived. The back is blank. Six visible vertical creases suggest that the document was rolled and flattened along its vertical axis from the right to the left side. The rather even damage at the top may have been caused by a horizontal fold, in which case half of the original document in now lost (date, parties and the beginning of the agreement). With the exception of a small margin on the right side, there is virtually no free space on the right and the bottom. The entire document appears to be the product of a single hand, which is practised, but does not offer any particular features for dating the document more precisely than the late sixth or early seventh centuries.

The papyrus records a work contract between an unknown party and Peter son of John for the position of (public) herald to start on 1 Pachon of a fifteenth indiction. Peter acknowledges receipt of the wand and bells (the official 'gear' of the herald) and, as in several other work contracts from this period, agrees to serve for one year. If he withdraws from his position before the end of the year, he will lose his wages; if he is dismissed unreasonably, the hiring party will pay him wages for the entire year.

This is the only contract to provide direct information about town criers, including their gear and the duration of their service in this period. Unfortunately, very little is known about this profession in late antiquity (this is by far the latest reference), but it is unlikely that their duties changed dramatically from the Ptolemaic or Roman times. Town criers were probably the most important means of mass communication on the local level in the ancient world and the Middle Ages, when the rates of literacy were very low. As we might expect, town criers were expected to have the ability to speak well and have a stentorian voice. Ironically, our town crier is illiterate (he cannot sign his own name), so he clearly learned by heart the pronouncements he had to make. Posting announcements in public spaces (especially in the market-place; see P. Mich. XVIII 795.5 n.) was a complementary way of disseminating information, but was intended mostly for those who had at least the ability to read. According to R. Taubenschlag, 'The Herald in the Law of the Papyri', *Opera minora* ii (Warsaw 1959) 151–7, town criers are found in a variety of religious, administrative and public contexts: they make announcements about taxes, emancipation of slaves, sales by auction, leases of land, and summon people in judicial proceedings. More recent studies have shown that town criers in Roman Oxyrhynchus were organized as corporations or colleges for cultic and business activities and were stationed at the temple of Thoeris; see J. R. Rea, *ZPE* 79 (1989) 202; for the Ἐξαγορεῖον of Oxyrhynchus, see LXIV **4441** v 13 n., and for the ἄμφοδον Ἐξαγορίου, see LXVIII **4689** 11. For the early Islamic period, see P. M. Sijpesteijn, *Shaping a Muslim State* (Diss. Princeton 2004) 145 n. 103. On heralds and town criers in classical Greece, see Sian Lewis, *News and Society in the Greek Polis* (1996) 52–6.

4967 presents many similarities with several Oxyrhynchite contracts of the same period, in particular the better-preserved LVIII **3933** (588), a goldsmith's work contract. For a list and discussion of work contracts from Byzantine Egypt, see A. Jördens, *Vertragliche Regelungen von Arbeiten im späten griechischsprachigen Ägypten* = P. Heid. V (1990) 130–84, to which add from Oxyrhynchus LVIII **3933**, **3942**, **3952**, **3958** (perhaps also **3943–6**), and LXXII **4910**.

.   .   .   .   .   .

...[ ].[...].[....]..[*c.*12
τὴν χώραν τοῦ κηρυκτοῦ ἐπὶ ἕνα ἐνιαυτὸν
λογιζόμενον ἀπὸ νεομηνίας τοῦ παρόντος
μηνὸς Παχὼν τῆς παρούσης ιε ἰνδ(ικτίωνος) ἀόκνω[ς
5   καὶ ἀμέμπτων καὶ ἀκαταγνώστως δεχόμενος
τὸ ἐμὸν ὀψώνιον ἤτοι μισθὸν παντὸς τοῦ ἑνὸς
ἐνιαυτοῦ κατὰ μίμησιν τοῦ ἐμοῦ ἑταίρου. ὁμολογῶ δὲ
ἐσχηκέναι παρ' ὑμῶν τὴν ῥάβδον τοῦ κηρυκτοῦ μετὰ τῶν
αὐτοῦ κωδονίων καὶ μὴ δύνασθαί με ἐπαναχωρῆσαι
10   τῆς αὐτῆς λειτουργίας πρὸ τέλους τοῦ ἑνὸς ἐνιαυτοῦ
δίχα ἀρωστείας καὶ πόνου τινός. εἰ δὲ τοῦτο ποιήσω,
ὁμολογῶ ζημιοῦσθαι τοὺς ἐμοὺς μισθούς. εἰ δὲ
κἀγὼ ἐκβληθῶ παρ' ὑμῶν πρὸ τέλους τοῦ ἑνὸς
ἐνιαυτοῦ δίχα εὐλόγου αἰτίας, ἐπὶ τὸ καὶ ὑμᾶς
15   πληρῶσαι τὸν ἐμὸν μισθόν. κύρ(ιον) τὸ συνάλλαγμ(α)
ἁπλ(οῦν) γραφ(ὲν) καὶ ἐπερ(ωτηθεὶς) ὡμολ(όγησα). † Πέτρος κηρυκτὴς υἱὸς
Ἰωάννου ὁ προγεγραμμ(ένος) στοιχεῖ μοι τὸ παρὸν συνάλλαγμ(α)
ὡς πρόκ(ειται). Ἰωάννης ἀξ(ιωθεὶς) ἔγραψ(α) (ὑπὲρ) αὐτοῦ ἀγραμμά(του) ὄντος.
(*m.* 2)   ✠ *di' emu* .... *eteleioth*

4 ινδ⳽   5 l. ἀμέμπτως   8 ϋμων   9 l. κωδωνίων   επαναχωρησαι: παν
crossed out?   11 l. ἀρρωστίας   14 l. τῷ   ϋμας   15 κυρ̅   15, 17 ϲυναλλαγμ⳽

16 απλγραφ   επερωμοઠ   υἱος   17 ιωαννου   προγεγραμઠ   18 προ૬   ιωαννησαξεγραψ૬
αγραμઠα

'. . . the position of herald for one year reckoned from the first of the present month Pachon
of the present 15th indiction, without hesitation and blame and condemnation, receiving my salary,
that is, wages, for the entire one year similarly to my partner. I also acknowledge that I have received
from you the wand of the herald with his bells and I shall not be able to withdraw from this service
before the end of the year, except in cases of illness or pain. And if I do this, I agree to suffer loss of
my wages, but also if I am ejected by you before the end of the year without any reasonable cause,
you will pay my wage. The contract, written in a single copy, is binding and in answer to the formal
question I gave my consent.

'I, Peter, herald, son of John, the aforesaid—the present contract satisfies me as aforesaid.
I, John, having been requested, signed on his behalf since he is illiterate.'

(2nd hand) 'Through me (*name*) it was concluded.'

1 Only a few down-strokes survive in this line; hence it is hard to suggest a secure supplement.
Probably one or two lines of the opening of the agreement are missing. The text might have run,
mutatis mutandis, similarly e.g. to LVIII **3933** 8 ff. ὁμολογῶ [ἑκου]cίᾳ γνώμῃ καὶ αὐθαιρέτῳ προαιρέcει
[c]υ[ντε]θεῖcθαί με πρὸς τὴν cὴν θαυμ(αcιότητα) [ἀπὸ] νεομηνίας τοῦ παρελθόντος μηνὸς Θὼθ τῆς
παρούcης ἕκτης ἰνδ(ικτίωνος) ἐφ' ᾧτέ με τὴν πᾶcαν χώραν τοῦ ἐργάτου τῶν χρυcοχόων παρ' αὐτῇ
ἀποπληρῶcαι κτλ. For the various formulas employed at the beginning of work contracts, see A.
Jördens, P. Heid. V pp. 151–4.

2 For the duration of work contracts, see P. Heid. V pp. 154–5. Year-long contracts, as here,
were common; see Jördens, *ZPE* 64 (1984) 64 n. 3.

3–4 Several contracts begin on the first of a month; see P. Heid. V p. 154 n. 60.

4–5 ἀόκνω[c] καὶ ἀμέμπτων (l. -ωc) καὶ ἀκαταγνώcτωc. For the 'behaviour' clauses (Wohlver-
haltensklauseln) in documents, see P. Heid. V pp. 155–6. These three adverbs, used in combination,
occur only in three other sixth-century Oxyrhynchite contracts in the order ἀμέμπτωc, ἀόκνωc,
ἀκαταγνώcτωc (I **140** 15, XXVIII **2478** 18–19, and LVIII **3933** 15–16).

6 τὸ ἐμὸν ὀψώνιον ἤτοι μιcθόν. No other document in the DDBDP records these two terms
juxtaposed, but cf. LVIII **3952** 35–6 (610), where the latter term appears first and the editor has supplied ὀψώνιον in the lacuna. It has been argued that ὀψώνιον was used to indicate the wages of regular
employees and payments in kind, while μιcθόc was used for occasional employees and payments in
money; see F. Morelli, *Olio e retribuzioni nell'Egitto tardo (V - VIII d.C.)* (1996) 51 n. 24. However, it is possible that in several late documents the two words are used interchangeably.

7 κατὰ μίμηcιν τοῦ ἐμοῦ ἑταίρου. The only other text that records this exact formula is SB
XVI 12717.15 (Heracl.; *c.*640–50) κατὰ μίμηcιν τῶν αὐτ(οῦ) ἑτέρων (l. ἑταίρων); see K. A. Worp, *ZPE*
47 (1982) 289. Our text confirms his reading ἑταίρων. Cf. I **136** 31–2 (583) κατὰ μίμηcιν τοῦ πρὸ ἐμοῦ
προνοητοῦ.

8 ἐcχηκέναι παρ' ὑμῶν. The pronoun is ambiguous, as it can suggest one or two people as the
hiring party. The lack of a title here and elsewhere in the surviving portion may suggest that the hiring party is not of very high rank.

κηρυκτοῦ. *κηρυκτής (*hapax*) = κῆρυξ.

8–9 τὴν ῥάβδον τοῦ κηρυκτοῦ μετὰ τῶν αὐτοῦ κωδονίων. This is the first papyrus to provide
evidence that the wand and the bells are the official 'gear' of town criers in antiquity. The wand is
connected with the κηρύκειον of Hermes (the 'official' messenger of the Greek gods). The use of bells
(not mentioned to my knowledge elsewhere in connection with criers) makes sense, because their
sound would attract the attention of individuals and crowds.

9 ἐπαναχωρῆϲαι. The last three letters are literally squeezed on the right edge of the papyrus. The verb ἐπαναχωρέω, 'to withdraw', is rare in the papyri and appears only in late documents (I **128** 2, P. Erl. 74.5, P. Lond. V 1727.16).

11 δίχα ἀρῳϲτείαϲ καὶ πόνου τινόϲ. Normally this expression appears as part of the 'behaviour' clause (see above, 4–5 n.), but in this case it was probably split because of the reference to the 'gear' of the herald. The two words juxtaposed in work contracts appear to be an Oxyrhynchite feature (I **140** 17, LI **3641** 12).

11–15 The work-related penalty involving the salary is standard; see P. Heid. V pp. 161–2. For similar stipulations in Oxyrhynchite examples, see e.g. **3933** 21–7. In **140** 25–9 (550), a horse-trainer promises to return double the amount of earnest-money in case he withdraws from his duties before the year ends, but he will keep it if he is dismissed without justification.

14–15 ἐπὶ τὸ (l. τῷ) καὶ ὑμᾶϲ πληρῶϲαι. This construction instead of a regular main clause in the *apodosis* is found in several late documents; see e.g. **3933** 23, 26, and especially **140** 28. For another similar construction, see my comments in *BASP* 45 (2008) 67 (18–23 n.).

18 The signatory John and Peter's father must be a case of synonymy, since the name was very common.

19 The name of the scribe is very hard to decipher. Either it must have been short or it was abbreviated. Of the verb only *et* is clearly visible. The rest was written in *Verschleifung*.

T. GAGOS

INDEXES

Letters in raised type refer to fragments, small roman numerals to columns. Square brackets indicate that a word is wholly or substantially restored by conjecture or from other sources, round brackets that it is expanded from an abbreviation or a symbol. An asterisk denotes a word not recorded in LSJ or its Revised Supplement and previously unattested names and places. The article and (in the documentary sections) καί have not been indexed.

I. NEW LITERARY AND SUBLITERARY TEXTS (SECTIONS II–III, V)

Ἀγαμέμνων **4944** 23, 45–6
ἄγγελος **4942** i 14 [**4944** 67]
ἀγορά **4944** 42
ἀγρυπνεῖν **4945** 15
ἀδελφή **4937** B 4
Ἀδρία [**4944** 74]
ἁδύς **4942** ii 8, 11
ἀεικής **4939** 16
ἀέκητι **4939** 26 (bis)
ἀήςυρος **4939** 35
ἀθάνατος **4939** 27
ἀθερίζειν **4939** 28
Αἴας **4944** 43, 47, 53
Αἴγυπτος **4950** 2, 5
αἰετός **4939** 6
Αἰνείας **4944** [34], 62, 72
αἴςη **4939** 31
ἄιcμα **4941** 1 n.
αἰτία **4942** i 4
αἴτιος **4943** 8
ἀκούειν **4937** A 3 [**4944** 109]
ἄλγος **4939** 23
Ἀλεξάνδρεια **4940** ii 8
ἀλείεσθαι **4939** 18
ἀληθής **4940** i 6
ἁλίσκεσθαι **4944** 7
ἀλλά **4936** ii 19, 32 **4939** 26, 31 [**4944** 100] **4945** 20 **4952** ¹5
ἄλλος **4939** 3 **4940** i 10 **4944** 26, [109]
ἅμα **4944** 27
ἄμυδις **4939** 10
ἀμφιδόξως **4941** 11
ἀμφότερος [**4938** 2]
ἄν **4936** ii 17, 33 **4944** 8
ἀνάγειν **4944** [29], 58–9
ἀνάγκη [**4939** 22]
ἀναιρεῖν **4944** 17
ἀναίρεσις **4950** 1

ἀναμφιλόγως **4941** 10
ἄναξ **4939** 16 **4944** ²7
ἀναπείθειν **4944** 33
ἀνάπτυξις [**4941** 14]
ἀνασκευάζειν **4941** 12
ἀναστρέφειν **4945** 3 n., 5
ἀναψύχειν **4942** ii 5
ἁνδάνειν **4939** 27
ἀνήρ **4939** 15, 35 **4941** 13
Ἀντήνωρ **4944** [27], 64, [80–81, 108]
ἀπαγγέλλειν **4945** 20
ἀπάνευθε **4939** 31
ἅπας **4944** 15 **4944** 31 n., 43 n.
ἀπειλητήρ **4939** 18
ἀπέρχεσθαι **4943** 2 **4945** 20
ἀπό **4943** 10 **4944** 67
ἀποθνήσκειν **4945** 9 n., 12
ἀπολείπειν [**4944** 62]
ἀπολλύναι **4950** 9
Ἀπόλλων **4943** 5, 8
ἄπονος **4944** 16
ἀποπλεῖν [**4944** 60–61]
ἀποστρέφειν **4945** 10
ἄρα [**4942** i 13]
Ἀράβιος **4942** i [8], 11, 13
Ἄργιννα **4945** 11
ἄργυρος [**4944** 41]
ἁρμοστός **4941** 2
ἀρτᾶν **4939** 17
ἄρτι **4951** 4
ἀρχε- **4942** i 15
ἄρχεσθαι **4943** 9–10
Ἀρχίλοχος **4952** ¹11, ²3
ἄρχων **4940** i 5
Ἀσκληπιός **4939** 9
ἄστρον **4950** 4
ἀτιμάζειν [**4943** 1–2]
ἀτίμως **4944** 16–17

αὖ **4944** 8
Αὐγέας [**4942** ii 1–2]
αὐλητής [**4942** i 8]
αὐτάρ **4951** 1
αὐτόθι [**4944** 75]
αὐτός **4936** ii 16, 20, 28 **4940** ii 13, 16 **4943** 1(?) **4944** 12, 18, 20, [27], 28, 31, 34, 69, 70, 73, [76, 104, 107] **4945** 13, 23 **4950** 7, 10 **4951** 9
ἀφαιρεῖσθαι **4944** 12
ἄφαρ **4939** 20
ἀφόρητος **4944** 13–14 n.
ἄφυκτος **4939** 32
ἄχος **4939** 20
ἄχρι **4942** ii 2–3

βάλλειν **4939** 22
βάρβαρος **4944** 9, 74, 100, [106]
βαρύς **4940** ii 10–11
βασιλεύς [**4943** 12–13] **4944** 26, [51] **4950** 1, 2–3, 5
βάσκειν **4951** 17
βίος [**4944** 72]
βούλεσθαι **4940** ii 18 n. **4941** 11
Βούπρασις **4942** ii 3
βοῦς **4951** 7 (bis)
*βούςταςις **4951** 5–6

γάρ **4936** ii 24 **4939** 16, 19, 22, 27, 30 **4940** ii 13 **4941** ¹[4], ²4 **4942** i 5–7 n. **4944** 15, 98 **4945** 12, [19] **4950** 9 **4951** 11
γε **4936** ii 17 **4939** 15, 24
γείτων **4936** ii 15
γήθειν **4939** 33
γίγνεσθαι **4936** i 13 **4938** 2 **4939** 33 **4944** 14, [17], 22, 52, [67–8]
Γλαυκέτης **4945** 21, 30 n.

φόνος **4944** 24
φράζειν **4939** 4
φρήν **4936** i 26
Φρύξ **4944** 9
φυγή **4940** ii 5–6
φύειν **4936** ii 8

χαίρειν [**4936** ii 32]

Χαιρέστρατος (**4936** ii 8, 30)
χαρακτήρ **4952** ¹11
Χαρίςιος **4936** i 5 n., 22, 28–9 n.
χειμών **4944** 57–8
χείρ **4944** 46
Χερρόνηςος **4944** 19, [65]
χθών **4939** 10
χόλος [**4939** 18]

χρᾶςθαι **4944** 50, 98, 104
Χρύςης **4943** 1
χρυςός **4944** 40–41
χωρίζειν **4944** 71

ὡς **4936** ii 18 **4939** 5, 7 **4942** ii 4
    4944 96 **4945** 4 **4952** ¹9
ὠχρός **4945** 12

II. RULERS AND CONSULS

Claudius

Τιβερίου Κλαυδίου Καίςαρος Cεβαςτοῦ Γερμανικοῦ Αὐτοκράτορος **4953** 6–8 (year 6)
] Γερμανικοῦ Αὐτοκράτορος **4954** 1 (year not preserved)

Antoninus Pius

Ἀντωνίνου Καίςαρος τοῦ κυρίου **4956** fr. 1.12–13 (year 9) **4957** 8–9 (year 9)
Αὐτοκράτορα Καίςαρα Τίτον Αἴλιον Ἀδριανὸν Ἀντωνῖνον Cεβαςτὸν Εὐςεβῆ **4956** frr. 2–3.2–5 (oath formula)
    4957 23–5 (oath formula)
Αὐτοκράτορος Καίςαρος Τίτου Αἰλίου Ἀδριανοῦ Ἀντωνίνου Cεβαςτοῦ Εὐςεβοῦς **4957** 27–9 (year 10) **4958** 32–5
    (year 11)

Septimius Severus and Caracalla

Αὐτοκράτωρ Καῖςαρ Λούκιος Cεπτίμιος Cεουῆρος Εὐςεβὴς Περτίναξ Cεβαςτὸς Ἀραβικὸς Ἀδιαβηνικὸς Παρθικὸς
    Μέγιςτος καὶ Αὐτοκράτωρ Καῖςαρ Μᾶρκος Αὐρήλιος Ἀντωνῖνος Εὐςεβὴς Cεβαςτός **4961** 3–4, 38
θεῶν Cεουήρου καὶ Ἀντωνίνου **4961** 7

Severus Alexander

Αὐτοκράτορος Καίςαρος Μάρκου Αὐρηλίου Cεουήρου Ἀλεξάνδρου Εὐςεβοῦς Εὐτυχοῦς Cεβαςτοῦ **4961** 2, 35
    (year 3)

Valentinianus I and Valens

μετὰ τὴν ὑπατείαν τῶν δεςποτῶν ἡμῶν Οὐαλεντινιανοῦ καὶ Οὐάλεντος αἰωνίων Αὐγούςτων τὸ γ **4966** 1–2 (AD
    371)

III. MONTHS AND INDICTIONS

Θωθ **4960** 14
Ἀθυρ **4961** [2], 84
Μεχειρ **4957** 29 **4958** 36
Φαμενωθ **4966** 2

Φαρμουθι **4961** [7], 43
Παχων **4961** 17, 59 **4967** 4
Μεςορη **4962** 9
15th indiction **4967** 4 (= vi/vii c.)

IV. DATES

45/6 **4953** 6–8
46/7 **4953** 9
145/6 **4956** 12–13 **4957** 7–9
22 February 147 **4957** 27–9
21 February 148 **4958** 32–6

13 April 200 **4961** [7], 43
26 May – 24 June 223 **4961** 17, 59
14 November 223 **4961** 2, 35, 84
16 March 371 **4966** 1–2

V. PERSONAL NAMES

(*a*) Greek

Ἀγαθὸς Δαίμων, Aur. **4961** 33
Ἀδριανός *see* Index II s.v. Antoninus Pius
Ἀθανάσιος **4965** 27
Αἰδίνιος *see* Μᾶρκος Αἰδίνιος Ἰουλιανός
Αἴλιος *see* Index II s.v. Antoninus Pius
Ἀλέξανδρος *see* Index II s.v. Severus Alexander
Ἀμμώνιος, ex-*praktor* **4953** 5
Ἀμμώνιος, gymnasiarch, s. of Dius and Demetria **4959** 1, 26
Ἀμμώνιος **4965** 2, [34]
Ἀμμῶνις **4962** 1, 10
Ἀντ[, f. of Senpapos **4956** fr. 1.3
Ἀντίοχος, 'br.' of Ammonius **4959** 19
Ἀντωνῖνος *see* s.vv. Antoninus Pius, Septimius Severus and Caracalla
Ἀπολλώνιος, f. of Diogenis **4961** 13, 52
Ἁρμίνϲις, f. of Panechotes **4956** fr. 1.6
Ἄρτεμις, d. of Panetbeus and Sinpmyst( ), w. of Leontas, m. of Pmysthas, Panetbeus and Tanouphis **4957** 16, 20
Ἀϲκληπιάδης, h. of Diogenis **4961** [12], 52
Αὔγουϲτος *see* Index II s.v. Valentinianus I and Valens
Αὐρηλία *see* Διογενίϲ, Ϲαραπιάϲ
Αὐρήλιος *see* Ἀγαθὸς Δαίμων, Θέων,]χόλιος, and Index II s.vv. Septimius Severus and Caracalla, Severus Alexander

Δημητρ-, Sarapion alias **4961** [30], 79
Δημητρία, w. of Dius, m. of Ammonius and Theon **4959** 1
Διογένης **4963** 1, 10
Διογενίϲ, Aurelia, alias N.N., d. of N.N. and —ra **4961** [2], 9, 46
Διογενίϲ, d. of Apollonius, w. of Asclepiades, *aste* **4961** 13, 52
Διόδωρος **4962** 1, 10
Δῖος, s. of Peteuris, weaver **4953** 2
Δῖος, h. of Demetria, f. of Ammonius and Theon **4959** 2

Ἐπιμένης *see* Index VI
Εὐδαίμων **4961** 4

Ἡρακλᾶς **4963** 1

Θεόγνωϲτος **4965** 25–6
Θεόδωρος **4965** 23–4
Θέων, s. of Dius and Demetria **4959** 3, 16, 23

Θέων, Aur. **4961** 33, 82

Ἰουλιανός, f. of Aur. —cholius, ex-*curator* **4966** 5; *see also* Μᾶρκος Αἰδίνιος Ἰουλιανός
Ἰϲίδωρος, Fl., *vir clarissimus*, senator **4966** 3
Ἰϲχυρίων, royal scribe and acting strategus **4958** 1
Ἰωάννης, f. of Petrus **4967** 17
Ἰωάννης **4967** 18

Καῖϲαρ *see* Index II s.vv. Claudius, Antoninus Pius, Septimius Severus and Caracalla, Severus Alexander
Κλαύδιος *see* Τιβέριος Κλαύδιος Παϲίων; *see also* Index II s.v. Claudius
Κυρίλλα, Sarapias alias **4961** 5, 40

Λαῖτος *see* Μαίκιος Λαῖτος
Λεοντᾶς, s. of Tanouphis, h. of Artemis, f. of Pmysthas, Panetbeus and Tanouphis **4957** 1, 14, 30
Λούκιος *see* Index II s.v. Septimius Severus and Caracalla
Λύκων *see* Index VI

Μαίκιος Λαῖτος, prefect of Egypt **4961** 5
Μᾶρκος Αἰδίνιος Ἰουλιανός, prefect of Egypt **4961** 9, 46
Μᾶρκος *see* Index II s.vv. Septimius Severus and Caracalla, Severus Alexander
Μέγιϲτος, s. of Spoceus and Tsenosiris **4961** 14

Νεῖλος **4965** 5

Ὄννωφρις, s. of Sambas and Soeris **4958** 3, 36
Ὄννωφρις, s. of Onnophris, f. of Sambas **4958** 4, 12–13
Ὄννωφρις, f. of Onnophris **4958** 13
Οὐάλενς *see* Index II s.v. Valentinianus I and Valens
Οὐαλεντινιανός *see* Index II s.v. Valentinianus I and Valens
Οὐαλέριος Πρόκλος, ex-prefect of Egypt **4956** fr. 1.9–10 **4957** 5

Πανετβεῦς, s. of Leontas and Artemis **4957** 18
Πανετβεῦς, h. of Sinpmyst( ), f. of Artemis **4957** 20
Πανεχώτης, s. of Harmiysis, h. of Tnepheros **4956** fr. 1.5
Παϲίων *see* Τιβέριος Κλαύδιος Παϲίων
Περτίναξ *see* Index II s.v. Septimius Severus and Caracalla

Πετεῦρις, f. of Dius **4953** 2

Πετοσόραπις, former master of Sarapion **4958** 7–8

Πέτρος, herald, s. of Ioannes **4967** 16

Πετϲεῖϲ **4960** 6

Πλούταρχος, f. of Sarapion **4961** [15], 56

*Πμυϲθᾶϲ, s. of Leontas and Artemis **4957** 16

Πρόκλοϲ *see* Οὐαλέριοϲ Πρόκλοϲ

Πτολεμαῖοϲ, 'br.' of Ammonius **4959** 18–19

Ϲαμβᾶϲ, s. of Onnophris, h. of Soeries, f. of Onnophris **4958** 3, 12, 37

Ϲαραπιάϲ, alias Cyrilla **4961** 5, 40

Ϲαραπιάϲ, Aurelia, alias Charitis(?), d. of Sarapion, aste **4961** 15, 26, 73

Ϲαραπίων, freedman of Petosorapis **4958** 6–7

Ϲαραπίων, s. of Plutarchus, f. of Aurelia Sarapias alias Charitis(?) **4961** [15], 56

Ϲαραπίων, alias Demetr– **4961** [30], 79

Ϲαραπίων *see* Index VI s.v. Νεοφύτου Ϲαραπίωνοϲ

Ϲενπαπῶϲ, d. of Ant—, m. of Tnepheros **4956** fr. 1.2–3

Ϲεουῆροϲ *see* Index II s.v. Septimius Severus and Caracalla, Severus Alexander

Ϲεπτίμιοϲ *see* Index II s.v. Septimius Severus and Caracalla

*Ϲινπμυϲτ( ), w. of Panetbeus, m. of Artemis **4957** 20

Ϲόηριϲ, w. of Sambas, m. of Onnophris **4958** 5

Ϲποκεύϲ, h. of Tsenosiris, f. of Megistus **4961** 14

Ϲώταϲ, 'br.' of Ammonius **4959** 18

Τ[, s. of Psenamounis, h. of Tn—, f. of Psenamounis **4956** fr. 1.16

Τάνουφιϲ, m. of Leontas **4957** 2

Τάνουφιϲ, d. of Leontas and Artemis **4957** 22

Τιβέριοϲ *see* Index II s.v. Claudius

Τιβέριοϲ Κλαύδιοϲ Παϲίων, strategus **4953** 1

Τίτοϲ *see* Index II s.v. Antoninus Pius

Τν[, w. of Τ—, m. of Psenamounis **4956** fr. 1.18

Τνεφερῶϲ, d. of Senpapos, w. of Panechotes **4956** fr. 1.1

Τριάδελφοϲ, Aur. **4961** 87

Τϲενόϲιριϲ, w. of Spoceus, m. of Megistus **4961** 14, 49

Φιλάδελφοϲ **4965** [2], 34

Φλάουϊοϲ *see* Ἰϲίδωροϲ

Χάριτιϲ, Aurelia Sarapias alias **4961** 15 n.

Ψενάμουνιϲ, s. of Τ— and Τn— **4956** fr. 1.15–16

Ψενάμουνιϲ, f. of Τ— **4956** fr. 1.17

Ὠνήϲιμοϲ, Aur. **4961** 86

]ρα, m. of Aurelia Diogenis **4961** [9], 47

].χόλιοϲ, Aur., s. of Iulianus **4966** 5

(*b*) Latin

Acillius *see* Marcus Acillius T—

Annaeius *see* Gaius Annaeius B—

Antonius *see* Lucius Antonius [, Marcus Antonius Cl—

B— *see* Gaius Annaeius B—

Capito *see* Clodius Capito

Cl— *see* Marcus Antonius Cl—

Clodius Capito **4955** ii 16, 25

Crispus *see* Faianus Crispus, Gaius Iulius Crisp(us?)

D— *see* Publius Vettius D—

Dellius *see* Marcus Dellius Quint—

Faianus Crispus **4955** ii 15, 18, 24

Firmus *see* Gaius Iulius Firmus

Flavius *see* Titus Flavius [, Titus Flavius Maior, Titus Flavius Scaevola, Titus Flavius Va—

Gaius Annaeius B— **4955** ii 16

Gaius Iulius Crisp(us?) **4955** ii 12

Gaius Iulius Firmus **4955** ii 10

Gaius Iulius Long— **4955** ii 27

Iulius *see* Gaius Iulius Crisp(us?), Gaius Iulius Firmus, Gaius Iulius Long—, Tiberius Iulius

Iulius Saturninus **4955** ii 21

Long— *see* Gaius Iulius Long—

Lucius Antonius [**4955** ii 21

Maior *see* Titus Flavius Maior

Marcus Acillius T— **4955** ii 19

Marcus Antonius Cl— **4955** ii 2

Marcus Dellius Quint— **4955** ii 8

Marcus Tullius [**4955** ii 4

Publius Ac— **4955** ii 28

Publius Vettius D— **4955** ii 18

Pude(ns?) *see* Quintus Vettius Pude(ns?)

Quint— *see* Marcus Dellius Quint—

VI. GEOGRAPHICAL

VII. RELIGION

VIII. OFFICIAL AND MILITARY TERMS AND TITLES

βαςιλικὸς γραμματεύς **4958** 1
βιβλιοφύλακες ἐγκτήςεων **4961** 22, 67

γυμναςιαρχ( ) (**4959** 27)

διαςημότατος **4961** 2–3 n.

ἔπαρχος **4961** 9, 46
ἐπιςτράτηγος **4961** 34, 85

ἡγεμονεύειν [**4956** fr. 1.10] **4957** 6 **4961** 5, 39–40
ἡγεμών **4961** 3

centuria (**4955** ii 15, 16, 18, 19, 21, 22, 24, 25, 27)

κράτιςτος **4961** 34, 85
κωμογραμματεύς **4962** 3–4

λαμπρότατος [**4961** 2–3] **4966** 3
λογιςτής **4966** 5

πράκτωρ **4953** 6

ςτρατηγία (**4958** 2)
ςτρατηγός (**4953** 1)
ςυγκλητικός **4966** 3–4

ταμικόν **4961** 3, 37

IX. PROFESSIONS AND OCCUPATIONS

γέρδιος **4953** 3
ἐργάτης **4964** 1, 10
*κηρυκτής **4967** 2, 8, 16

προγεωργός **4958** 18
ὑπηρέτης **4963** 7

X. MEASURES

(*a*) Weights and Measures

ἄρουρα (**4958** 16)
ἀρτάβη **4966** 13 (bis)

(*b*) Money

δραχμή (**4953** 8, 9) (**4954** 2, 4, 5)

XI. TAXES

χειρωνάξιον **4953** 11

XII. GENERAL INDEX OF WORDS

ἄβροχος **4958** 30
ἄγειν **4960** 11
ἀγένητος **4961** 18
ἅγιος *see* Index VII
ἀγράμματος **4967** 18
ἀγωνία **4959** 5
ἀδελφός **4957** 18 **4959** 3, 16, 18, 19, 23 **4962** 1, 3, 6 **4963** 1, 2; *see also* Index VII
ἀδικεῖν **4961** 8, 44
αἰςθάνεςθαι **4961** [19], 63
αἰτία **4967** 14
αἰώνιος *see* Index II s.v. Valentinianus I and Valens

ἀκαταγνώςτως **4967** 5
ἀκολουθία **4961** 6, 41
alabastron **4955** ii 26
ἀλήθεια [**4956** frr. 2–3.6] **4961** [5–6], 10, 20, 41, 48
ἀληθής **4957** 26 **4959** 10, 13
ἀλλά **4961** 27 **4965** 7
ἀλλήλων **4966** 12
ἄλλος **4953** 9 (**4956** frr. 2–3.13) **4959** 12 **4962** 7
ἀμέμπτως **4961** [16], 58 **4967** 5
amphitheatrum **4955** ii 20 n.
ἀμφότερος [**4956** fr. 1.6] **4957** 22
ἄν **4959** 12

ἄν (= ἐάν) **4961** 8, 44
ἀναγκαῖος **4959** 13
ἀναγράφειν **4957** 10–11 **4958** 10–11
ἀναδέχεςθαι **4958** 20
ἀνακαλεῖν **4961** 24 n.
ἀνακτᾶςθαι **4959** 7–8
ἀναλαμβάνειν **4957** 12–13 **4959** 7
ἀναπέμπειν **4961** 4–5 n.
ἀναφαίρετος **4961** [13], 53
ἀνήρ **4956** fr. 1.5 **4964** 2–6, 8–10
ἀνόκνως **4962** 5
ἀνόμως **4961** 30, 78
ἀντιγραφή **4961** 4 (B39) n., 6, [41]

XIII. CORRECTIONS TO PUBLISHED TEXTS

PLATE I

4936

4938

4943

PLATE II

4934 →

4937 Side A

PLATE III

4934 ↓

4937 Side B

PLATE IV

4939

Fr. 1

Fr. 2

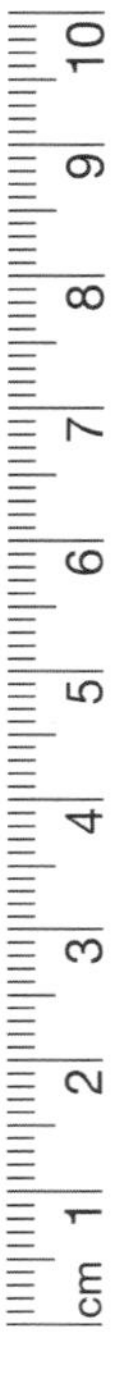

Fr. 3

Fr. 4

Fr. 5

PLATE V

4940

PLATE VI

4941

4942

PLATE VII

4944 (reduced)

PLATE VIII

4945

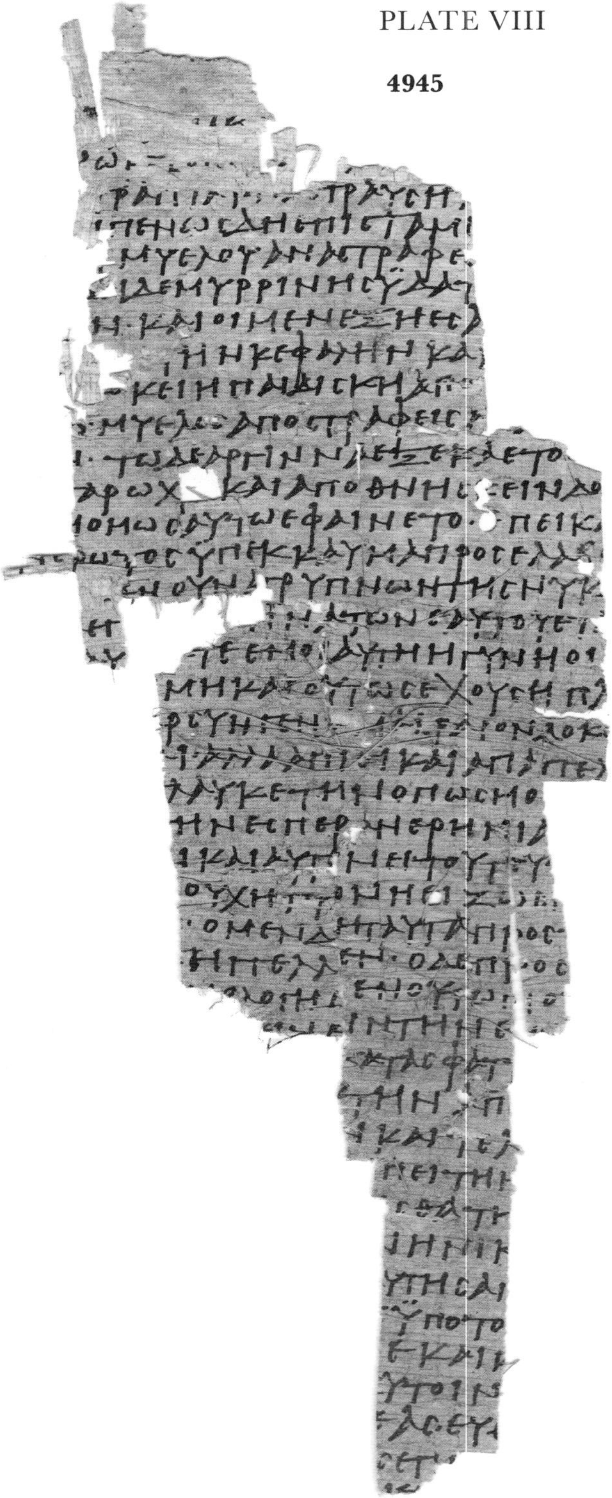

4951

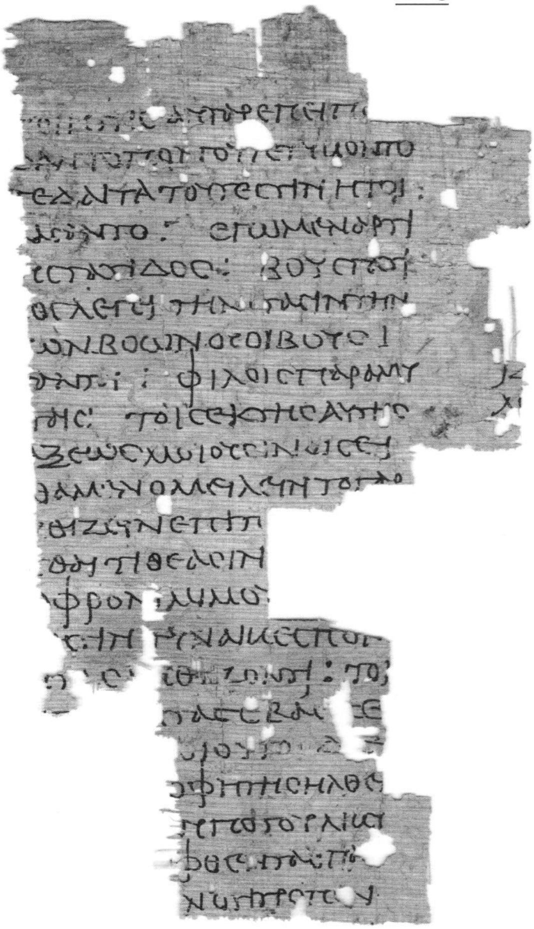

PLATE IX

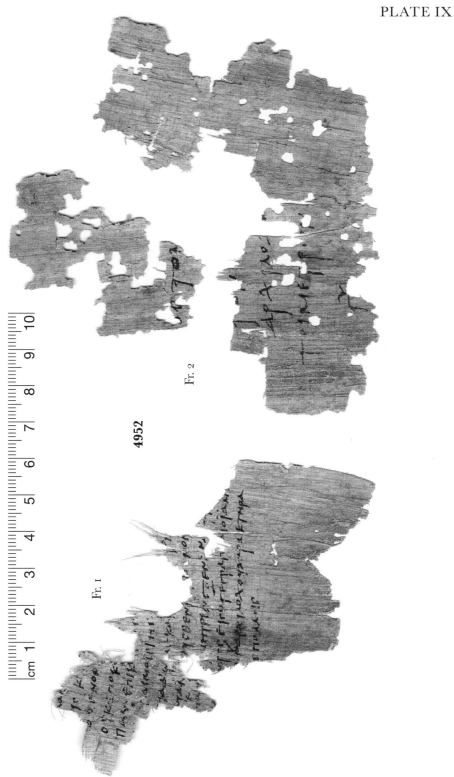

Fr. 2

4952

Fr. 1

PLATE X

4955 (reduced)

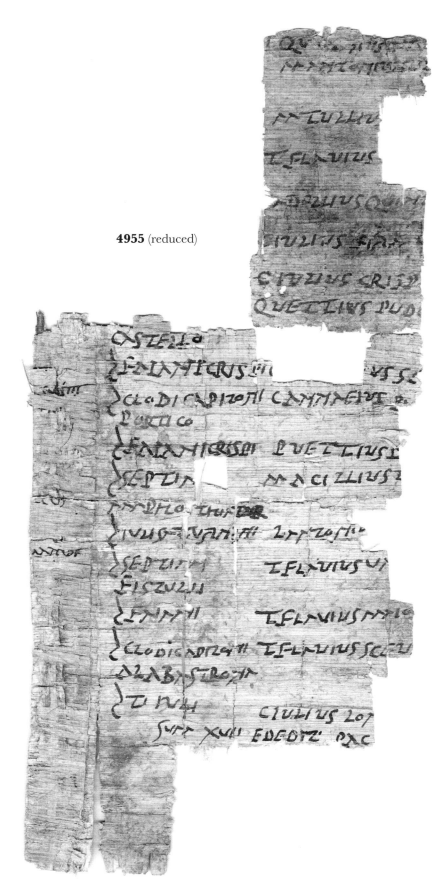

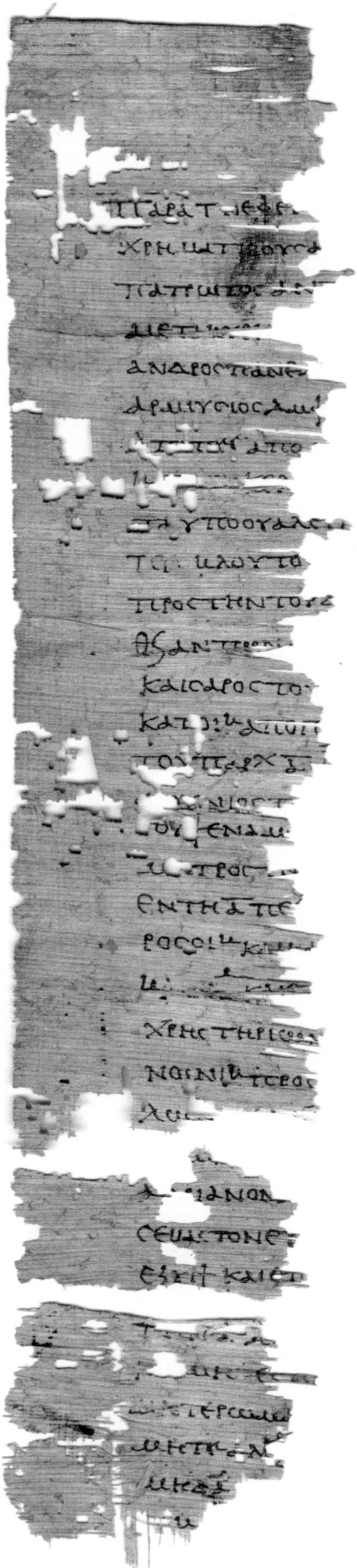

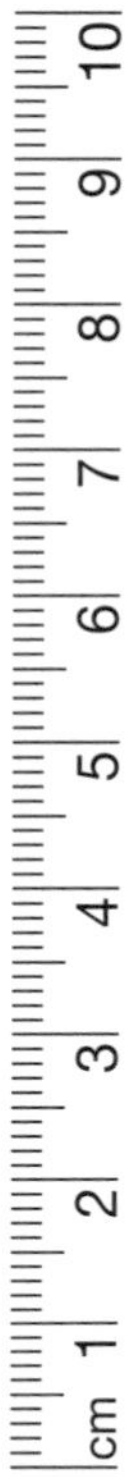

PLATE XI

4956
Fr. 1

Fr. 2

Fr. 3

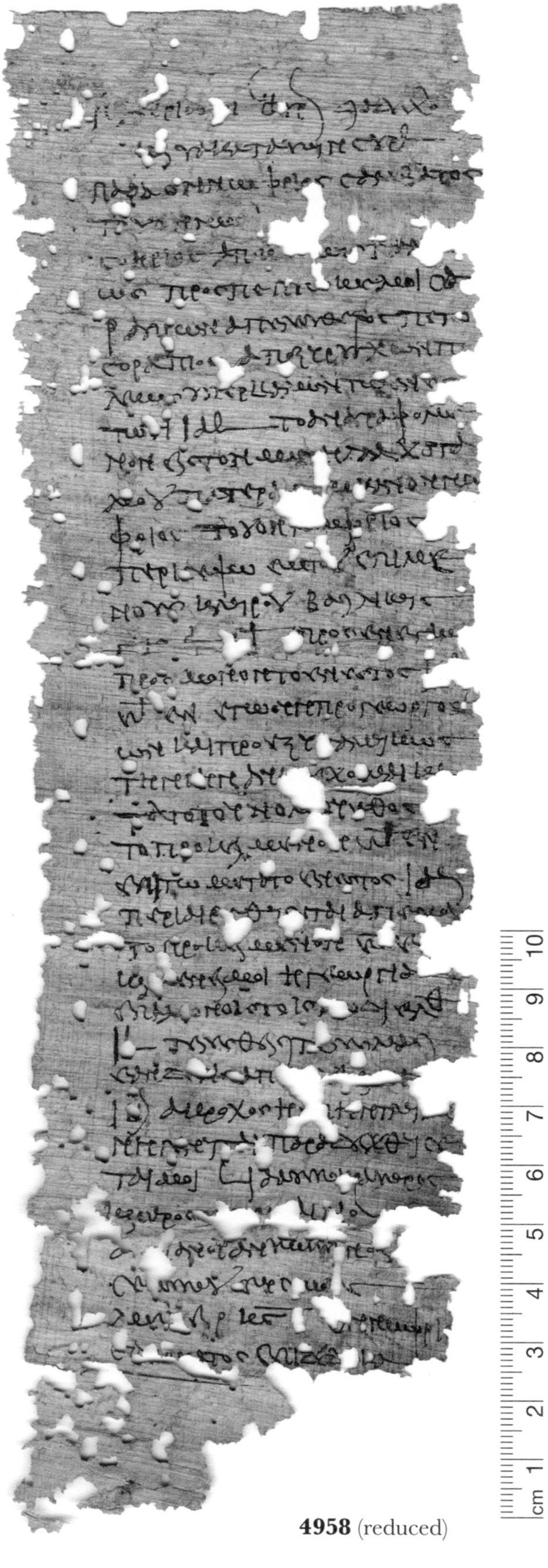

PLATE XII

4958 (reduced)